# SERIALS:
# PAST, PRESENT AND FUTURE

# SERIALS:
# PAST, PRESENT AND FUTURE

## 2ND (REVISED) EDITION

By
CLARA D. BROWN
and
LYNN S. SMITH

## 1980

EBSCO
Industries.
Inc.

BIRMINGHAM,
ALABAMA
1980

ISBN 0-913956-05-8
Library of Congress Catalog Card Number: 80-81267

**SERIALS: PAST, PRESENT AND FUTURE** IS A
REVISED AND ENLARGED EDITION OF
**SERIALS: ACQUISITION & MAINTENANCE**

Printed and Bound in the United States of America

# Preface To The Second Edition

The first edition of this book was written with the idea of helping beginning, bewildered serials librarians unravel some of the mysteries of serials. However, because it was also used as a textbook in some library schools it was thought that a broadening of information to include some of what did happen in the past, what is happening at present and even visualize a bit of what might happen in the future would be advantageous. It is hoped that this overall view will bring to light the facets of the serial world and will help those interested librarians to locate books that have already covered each individual facet in greater depth.

The dilemma of the serials librarian before the 1970's was that so few books had been written on serials, and so few tools gave up-to-date information that librarians had to spend many hours searching in depth about the titles. Now the dilemma is that so much is coming out that it is difficult to cover the vast amount of information. Also, technology is changing the point of view so rapidly that it behooves a person to get a knowledge of the new techniques, but also to keep one's feet on the ground by having some knowledge of what has happened in the past.

Because the routines and Serials Record at the Louisiana State University Library have proven themselves equal to almost every new development in the past twenty years for a manual serials department, it has been decided to leave these original sections intact. Around this core has been built the old and then as many of the new techniques as feasible were included.

Thanks must be expressed for the wonderful response given to bring this book to a conclusion. From the Louisiana State University Library the following people are acknowledged. Above all, appreciation must be expressed to Mildred Hoskins, head of Preparations Department for her response and enthusiasm on the chapter of binding; Eulava S. Dupree and Ethelyn Stott of the Serials Department for their continued patience and interest in all phases of serials as well as Millicent Hennigan in the Catalog Division. Jimmie H. Hoover, head of

v

Government Documents Department gave much support and information on documents. Don Morrison of the Photoduplication Department gave help on reprography. Also of reprography much information has been given by Ron Curtis, Carol Barry, John Purdy, and Andrew Peters, all of Central State University Library, Edmond, Oklahoma. For information about purchasing material in foreign countries thanks must go to Chi Wang, Head of Chinese and Korean section and Robert V. Allen, U.S.S.R. Area Specialist, both in the Library of Congress, and William Lee, Curator of Latin American Collection at Yale University Library.

Lester Brannon of the main Post Office in Baton Rouge gave inestimable help in bringing the mail information up-to-date.

Others who gave help and encouragement were: Mary Ellen Soper of the University of Washington Library School at Seattle; Esther Greenberg, Western Reserve University Library, Ohio; Marcia Tuttle, University of North Carolina Library; Patricia Pratchett, University of Houston Library. As usual, my husband Clair A. Brown gave much encouragement and advice.

From the University of California at Riverside, Beverly Cox, and Margaret Ellis are acknowledged; as well as Neal Edgar, Kent State and Judith Cannan, Library of Congress.

Clara D. Brown worked as Head of Serials at the Louisiana State University library, Baton Rouge. She is now retired.

Lynn S. Smith is working as Head of Serials at the University of California at Riverside.

# Preface To The First Edition

This book is for those new Serials Librarians who are expected to already know all the mysteries of serials and who therefore hesitate to ask questions of their peers for fear of being considered neophytes. Several of the items included are ones which have required considerable personal research because they have been puzzling to other Serials Librarians as well as myself. The book is not for those, the already experienced, and those who are living in a realm of automation.

I wish to acknowledge the library staff of the Louisiana State University Library for the encouragement and help freely given to make this book possible. Special thanks must go to Ethelyn R. Stott, Mildred B. Hoskins, Elizabeth Tarver, Jimmie H. Hoover, Eulava S. Dupree, Eloisa F. Martinez and Marguerite M. Hanchey.

A special thanks must go to my husband Clair A. Brown whose patience and helpful suggestions improved the book immeasurably.

Also, I wish to acknowledge Peter Gellatly and Huibert Paul for the very helpful and constructive criticism given in their review of the book.

# CONTENTS

                                                               **Page**
Prefaces .................................................. v-vii
Chapter I       History of Serials ............................  3
Chapter II      Fundamentals .................................. 17
Chapter III     Equipment and Checking-in Procedures .......... 27
Chapter IV      Selection and Deselection ..................... 79
Chapter V       Finances ...................................... 89
Chapter VI      Ordering .....................................117
Chapter VII     Cataloging ...................................185
Chapter VIII    Serials Processing and Control at the
                Library of Congress ..........................225
Chapter IX      Library Tools For A Serials Department ........237
Chapter X       Mail .........................................253
Chapter XI      Claims and Duplicates ........................265
Chapter XII     Binding ......................................277
Chapter XIII    Gifts and Exchanges and Special Programs ......305
Chapter XIV     Reprography ..................................321
Chapter XV      Copyright ....................................343
Chapter XVI     Miscellaneous Topics
                Circulation of Journals ......................349
                Reading Rooms ................................351

# CHAPTER I
# HISTORY OF SERIALS

# CHAPTER I
# HISTORY OF SERIALS

## JOURNALS

The history of serials could start as Osborn's discussion did in his book, *Serial Publications; Their Place and Treatment in Libraries*, with the very earliest of records, but because he has so adequately covered these early periods, all that remains here is to give a short review. He mentions the annals inscribed on the tombs in Egypt some 4,000 years ago. All through the centuries different types of records and news items have been available, such as almanacs, calendars, newsletters, book catalogs, courants, manuscripts, and bulletins. It has been surmised that if the warnings of the chronicles had been read in Sodom and Gomorrah, a year in advance, fire and brimstone would never have destroyed the city.

Gradually as travel widened the scope of business with far-flung ships of merchandise, more and more records were needed at the central offices. In the thirteenth century in Europe the mercantile houses issued letters telling of pertinent news and business items to their companies. They were handwritten at first; later they were printed.

However, it was many years before journals were published in any abundance. Although movable type was invented by the Chinese about 1040 A.D. it was little used by them because of their complicated typography. As early as 1456 it was known in Europe when the Gutenberg Bible was printed with movable type in Mainz, Germany. From here it slowly spread though the rest of Europe. Then more and more books and journals began to be printed. The first 50 years of such books are called "incunabula." These include all such books through 1501. Books done by block printing or xylographic methods of the same period are not included.

## Scientific Journals

The first scientific journal was a weekly and was published in France in 1665. It was called *Journal des Scavans* (from 1816 *Journal des Savants*). It is still being published and has had only one break in publication, from December 1792 to August 1816. At first it was just a list of principal books published in Europe, then was added a statement of the scope and findings of each book. Later obituaries of notable people with their achievements were added. Next were cited decisions handed down in civil and ecclesiastical courts. Later it informed the readers of current events.

Also in 1665 in England was published the *Philosophical Transactions; Giving Some Accounts of the Present Undertakings, Studies, and Labours of the Ingenious in Many Parts of the World*. Later the subtitle was dropped. It was more scientific than the French one. The Royal Society adopted it as their official organ in 1753. It has continued with only one break, 1676-1683.

A third journal that also started in 1665 was the *Oxford Gazette*, later called the *London Gazette*.

Between 1700 and 1825 there was an increase of learned societies, which led to an escalation of proceedings and transactions. Also, scientific journals began to increase as disciplines advanced and specialized into more and more sections of physics, chemistry, biology, agriculture, medicine, even law reports, and parliamentary debates and statues increased.

Through the last three centuries the people of each century have been impressed with the frightening number of serials, and librarians have had to re-assess the relative importance of books and serials. Serials have come to stay, and rightly so. They are admirably suited to publishing current information, giving more depth than the newspaper, but more up-to-date information, more rapidly than books. Since World War I they have taken their rightful place, encouraged by industry, enlightened reader audience, and sophisticated techniques.

As with all wars, so it was with World War II, which played havoc with all publishing and with that of journals in particular. Attention was shifted to matters other than publishing. Presses were blown up and burned, politics shifted to patriotism, money was used to buy munitions, men were inducted into the services, and thus it was that publishing fell by the wayside. The factors were too numerous to mention all of them.

During all this, the stocks of journals that existed in Europe were sometimes buried for safe keeping. In Germany one editor was ousted by the Nazis, and a more favored one took over the journal. When, after the war, the original editor regained possession, he ignored the voluming and numbering that was done in the war years, and continued the publication from where he left off. So! there were duplicate numberings and different years. Many such happenings occurred to frustrate librarians. Some publishers went underground, or changed the name of the publishing house. Some volumes were spirited over the borders, piece by piece. It took many years after the war to discover what was left intact. Sometimes only one or two copies could be located, and prices went up beyond belief. This resulted in a burgeoning project for reprint publishers.

Also, after the war even more scientific disciplines sprang up as did new journals. Old ones splintered into sometimes a dozen or more sections or titles. This expansion is still influencing serials publishing so that no one can predict what to expect next. And now new institutes and organizations are trying to standardize and bring some sense into all this expansion.

**Modern National Popular Magazines**

In 1709 Richard Steele started a periodical called *The Tatler*, in England. This publication could be considered the first popular magazine. Its early prospect announced: "What e'er men do, or say, or dream, our motley paper seizes for its theme."[1]

*The Spectator* followed in 1711. The London offices of these early publications had representatives in the outlying districts who picked up interesting items from conversations in the various coffee houses. Controversies and gossipings came from White's Chocolate House; poetry came from Will's Coffee House; learning from the Grecian; foreign and domestic news came from St. James Coffee House.

By the time American publishers began publishing they had well established English ones to use as models. The first two were published in a competetive spirit. *American Magazine; or a Monthly View of the Political State of the British Colonies*, was started 1741 by Alexander Bradford and three days later the *Gentleman's Magazine* was published by Benjamin Franklin. Neither publication lived long. Forty-five other magazines followed before 1800 and they were mostly short-lived. They all strived for popularity and avoided such controversial issues as politics and religion. Two other interesting points were that the project was of more importance than profit, and authors usually paid to get their articles published. Many famous names may be found in the pages. By the middle of the century a new phase was started with the popular picture magazines: *Gleason's* and *The Ledger*. Also, in 1857, *The Atlantic Monthly* was started.

During the seventeenth, eighteenth, and early part of the nineteenth centuries American magazines were not the best business ventures in the country. There was small circulation, little advertising to help defray expenses, and therefore few of the magazines lived long. No one year or influence brought the national magazine into being, but a series of events did help from 1700-1900. By 1850 the trade was already taking on a brighter outlook, with advances in the technical improvement of printing, new capital, cheaper pulp paper, and, in 1879, Congress stimulated the growth by providing low-cost mailing privileges.

It was in the 1890's that America went through a period of drastic transition. The economy was changing from agrarian to industrial. Many factors combined to bring this about and to create a national outlook. Railroads were now crossing the country and isolated communities grew into larger towns with new industries springing up along the train routes. (Little was it realized that the trains which broadened and unified America, would experience such financial reverses in the 1970's and be replaced by air-taxis, buses, and other means of transporting news and journals.)

The new mechanical techniques were extended into the magazine industry. Printing presses advanced from the slow flat-bed press to the faster rotary one which aided mass production. Art work techniques also advanced from hand-tinted plates to multicolored ones with the rotary press.

Victorian restraints were being broken, people were broadening their education, and they had more leisure time and broader interests. They were ready for changes and thirsting for information and new ideas.

This national, enlightened outlook went hand-in-hand with new techniques and competition to encourage the expansion of magazines. A new reader audience enticed new young publishers into business ventures. Older, more conservative magazines were driven out by the new ones with greater appeal in both interest and low prices. Mass circulation was creating prices from ten and fifteen cents instead of the old twenty-five and thirty cents.

With circulation growing by leaps and bounds and the reader audience expanding, it was not unusual that advertisers saw the possibilities of getting their newly manufactured products before the attention of the new audience. The publisher could now take his profits from the great volume of paid advertising. When it first found its way into the magazines it had been relegated to the back pages, but gradually it nudged its way into even the articles themselves, much to the chagrin of readers.

There was a period in the 1960's when magazines fell on hard times. Costs of postage, paper and labor outstripped any profit to be made, and the popular magazines fell by the wayside. It was thought that television would probably wipe out the industry altogether. However, in the late 1970's these magazines recovered to the point that the trade suddenly started booming. The magazine industry became very healthy in spite of postage increases and inflation. While earlier magazines were pretty much dependent on subscribers, the increase of many newsstands are resulting in smaller lists of subscribers, but individual sales have gone up tremendously for the recently developing popular ones.

The industry is still dependent on paid advertising and those magazines that can become a vehicle for advertising, gossip and sex are thriving. Let us face it, people like magazines. The feel of them and the portability still have appeal. They give more depth than television and for many advertisers, television is too expensive and already too crowded. Those magazines having the least success recently are the more general ones because there is no generic base for the advertisers. Most curious of all is the fact that in this day of specialization and women's liberation, women's magazines are among the least successful.

Every group of magazines, yes, every title, boasts an interesting history. The women's magazines, the sports, the recreational, the crafts, the cookbooks, could be traced through vicissitudes and triumphs.

There is one group of magazines that has sprung up since World War I that has been frowned upon, extolled, questioned, and has infuriated, entertained, astonished, and amused various classes of people. They are the "little" magazines. The movement began "as a voice of avant-guard literary forms."[2]

Every decade has tinged them with a slightly different point of view according to the atmosphere of the times. In the 1930's they represented the idealistic extremists; in the 1940's they rebuked the way of life; in the 1950's they joined the beatniks; the 1960's made them more politically minded with an awareness of "controversial literary expression"; in the 1970's they were no more even-tempered than in the past.

They are "little" in two points of view. They always have a small circulation and each number boasts but few pages. Their format is usually characterized by eccentricities in size, illustrations and printing—all the way from mimeographed to conventional.

They are casual in trying to get subscriptions, and in invoicing, or even in sending out their numbers on time, being more preoccupied in developing the next number. For this reason few bookstores care to stock them, nor agents to take subscriptions for them. They have little advertising, depending usually on subscriptions and donations. This casual financial approach accounts in part for their short expanse of life. Another reason is that they espouse the current point of view, and this changes with the times; therefore they are left without their particular ax to grind.

Even the numbering of their magazine goes off on tangents, being published "every once in a while", to one title using "now" for the first number; "now now" for the second; and "now now now" for the third. The fact that few "little" magazines last for long saved the day for this one. Another journal announced it had had a "long and glorious career with eight numbers."

There is no doubt that they emphasize independent thinking, usually protesting, but they do give a literary outlet for young and unknown authors, who in turn, may become the well-known authors of the future. They are "one of the few institutions in our society that sanction real creativity."[3]

Then there are the "hybrid littles" which are close relatives of the real "little magazines." They are usually literary, or socio-political, and are usually published by the universities and colleges and often have the word "review" in their title. These two types of magazines are well discussed by Katz in his book, *Magazine Selection.*

## RECENT TRENDS IN PUBLISHING

In comparison to the dilatory beginnings of the number of the early magazines, the recent explosion in both numbers and complexities of magazines and micropublishings lead one to wonder what will be in the future. Perhaps automation, library networks, reprography and conglomerates will ultimately answer all the questions of the future for serials librarians.

### Conglomerates

Mergers of publishers started in the 1940's but little attention was paid to them until recently when they suddenly changed from serpents to dragons. Now there are more than 300 mergers of publishers who have either joined together to remain publishers or become entangled with non-publishing conglomerates.

Most alarming are the communications conglomerates that include magazines, books, television, newspapers and movies. These mass media have greater resources for promotion and distribution, and they can easily out-bid even reprint competitors. This seems the only way to achieve the financial stability to survive. What is to happen next? The various facets of the comglomerate phenomon, the economics, the anti-trust problems, the financial disclosures, and tax questions will, undoubtedly, lead in the future to more questions to be answered by the Federal Trade Commission, and the Department of Justice, and will lead to new serials problems. (See p. 11 for a discussion regarding newspaper chains).

**International Aspects of Publishing**

There are now not only national but international aspects of publishers and subscription agents. Some thirty years ago there was an arrangement with the United Kingdom known as the British Trade Market Agreement. The American and British publishers sold each other publishing rights instead of competing in the same book trade markets. This agreement included all English written books of the British Empire on the one hand, and on the other it included all U.S. dependencies as well as the continental United States.

This agreement was terminated by 21 American publishers after the U.S. Justice Department's decision against it. Also the U.K. Open Market agreement has given British publishers control over publishing rights in the Commonwealth countries. Now the two markets have become one, and the results are that English publishers are setting up offices in the U.S. and the American publishers are becoming more active abroad.

There is nothing to stop individual publishers from continuing the long-time agreement, but the industry-wide basis has certainly changed. George Allen & Unwin of London is one who has established offices in this country. Also other foreign companies are buying American firms. Dutton has been bought by Elsevier in Holland, Bantam is now owned by an Italian group and Viking is owned by Penguin.

## NEWSPAPERS

The history of newspapers interweaves and parallels the history of magazines so closely that it is difficult to decide where one leaves off and the other begins. For 3000 years before the invention of the Gutenburg press there was the spoken newspaper in many countries, including China, which also had the first real newspaper called Ti Pao. It was handwritten, then block printed, and then movable type took precedence in all the newspapers. Because of the intricacies of the Chinese characters, even today only some 6000 characters out of 40,000 are being used by the Chinese printing presses.

The newspapers of each country have a long and varied history. The modern newspaper has little in common with the earlier ones. In the first place it is a far cry from the slow arrival of news by pony express and months by ships, to the more recent media of cable, radio, telegraph, and television via satelites. In the second place the appearance of the newspaper has changed for the better with clearer type, more and better pictures and better paper. The one interesting remainder from the old handbills and broadsides to deck our current papers, is the "scare-head" with large type flaunting itself across the top of the front page.

The first newspaper in Germany was printed in 1609 in Augsburg, and was called the *Avisa, Relation oder Zeitung*. It was a weekly and is still in existence.

Rome had the oldest European newspaper. It started with the spreading of news by placards, which continued to the end of the Empire. In fact, they are still used as posters to spread announcements outside news offices. It is from Italy that we get the word "gazette." It comes from the Italian *gazetta*, which was an Italian coin, and was the cost of the *Notizie Scritte* published in 1566 in Venice.

In France the news announcers were called "nouvellistes." The more gifted ones would also draw pictures with paper and chalk, and, of course, would expect the group of onlookers to pay something after the news was given. The verbal announcing advanced to written newssheets, which later became scandal sheets and fell into low repute. The authors were sometimes put in prison or publicly whipped. The first real newspaper in France was published in 1615.

As in the rest of Europe, the forerunners of newspapers in England were the single sheets and broadsides, posted from time to time in prominent places. They were used even later to print political and religious views which were forbidden in newspapers. As with magazines, newspapers were even more the outcome of newssheets printed from the coffee house gatherings in the eighteenth century. Each town boasted several of them and each coffee house attracted its own clientele—doctors, lawyers, gossips, politicians; each gathered to discuss current items of interest. London offices had representatives that visited these coffee shops both locally and in the outlying districts and reported back the opinions and discussions of these gatherings.

The first English newspaper was printed in 1620 in Amsterdam. The news for these early papers came from soldiers on the continent during the Thirty Years' War. These newsletters were called "corantos". The news came to London and was published weekly and sent to all the district presses. These papers were much more reputable than the French ones and emphasized political news. The first daily was published in 1709 and was called *The Courant*.

In America newspapers started at about the same level as the English papers of the same time. The first newspaper in America appeared in Boston in 1690, but it was suppressed after one issue. It was called *Publick Occurences*. Most of the early colonial papers met the same fate, being suppressed after a few issues. Only one survived these early days. It was the *Boston Newsletter* which lasted 72 years. News was very late, coming from Europe by ships, so the papers had to fall back on literature instead of news in order to come out with any regularity. As the revolution grew, publishers became bolder, and politics and patriotism crept into the news, and when freedom of speech was guaranteed in the new constitution, papers began to reflect some of the more general points of view.

In contrast to the early papers that were so severely suppresssed, and parallel to the "little" magazines are the papers put out by underground presses. They began in the 1960's and seem to be hale and hearty. They too dissent on any topic of current interest from politics and race relations to women's liberation.

Here again, these, as well as variations on the underground presses, pornography, satire and the comics are very well covered by Katz, in *Magazine Selection*.

### Newspaper Mergers

The 1970's have brought about the demise of many newspapers, especially evening papers. As with magazines and books, so it is with newspapers, all over the country small independent local papers are proving attractive acquisitions for the large conglomerates. Among the nation's employers, newspapers are the third largest, after automobiles and steel. Advertisers are the largest source of finances for the papers, and they buy space largely on the basis of circulation.

One of the largest newspaper chains is owned by Knight-Ridder, with Alvah H. Chapman as president and chairman of the board. They now own 32 daily newspapers all over the country with a circulation of 3½ million. At present there are 167 chains that control 60% of the nation's dailies, and it is surmised that within 10 to 15 years the whole country will be owned by 6 to 8 conglomerates.

Some of the first newspapers to collapse were *Hartford Times*, *Cleveland News*, *Detroit Times*, *Boston American*, *Chicago Today*, *Newark Evening News*, and the latest was the *Chicago Daily News* which died at the age of 102. This has left Chicago with no evening paper. Once a paper dies it seldom revives.

### REASONS FOR THE DEMISE OF EVENING PAPERS

1. Smaller circulation is one of the main reasons and with circulation down, the mainstay of advertising revenues is lost.
2. Difficulties of delivering the paper in the evening rush of traffic.
3. Television gives the evening news, and favorite star anchor newsmen have packaged the news into capsules that have caught the approval of many people. However, T.V. news gives only the headlines, while papers are able to give it in more depth.
4. The tax law is wiping out the small hometown papers.
5. Strikes turn people to other media when they cannot get their evening paper for any period of time. Many may not return even after the strike is over.

### ADVANTAGES OF CHAIN OWNERSHIP

1. The best editors, writers, professionals and talent are found here.
2. More coverage and specialized interests are possible.
3. Typesetting has changed to the point that great variety is available in the setting up of the paper, and independent papers cannot afford the sophisticated equipment.
4. Chain ownership frees the paper from the idiosyncrasies of local family ownership.

### DISADVANTAGES OF CHAIN OWNERSHIP

1. Monolithic editorship covers the news of the nation, and a few people are sitting in a remote place, controlling the news, and the thinking of the poeple. The freedom and diversity of American thought is being lost.
2. The personal touch is gone. Local sacred cows of the hometown paper are lost, and not all chains are committed to a hands-off local policy.
3. The careful investigative work which brought to light many exposes by the independent journalists is often lost now.
4. The paper could run into sensationalism.

However, too much control is stirring up federal resistance by the Federal Trade Commission (FTC) and the Department of Justice.

### LIMITS ALREADY SET OR BEING CONSIDERED

1. A maximum has been set on the number of television stations or FM radio stations (7 each) which any one company may control.

2. Cross-ownership (owning newspaper and broadcasting facilities in the same area) is now pending in court. Cable T.V. is adding to the confusion.

VARIOUS LIMITS STILL COMING UP FOR CONSIDERATION

1. Limit the number of newspapers owned by any one chain.
2. Include a circulation formula.
3. Consider a variety of tax shuffles.
4. Application of anti-trust laws.
5. Some legal requirements to publicize group connections.

## Future of Newspapers

Of those newspapers that do survive, their future seems almost amazing. They will be printed in cold type by computerized printing presses which control each of 50,000 very tiny ink drops squeezed out every second, making information changed and up-dated instantly. This is gradually taking over the old type printing presses. Computerized editing is also already a reality. Personalized newspapers to suit one's own tastes and interests is possible if proven desirable for the future. Also being considered for the future is computerized delivery.

As paper shortages, strikes, marketing, inflation, plague the newspaper industry, cables, television, airwaves, and satelites are already being used or contemplated to give electronic systems of communication. England and Japan already have devices that can decode information from regular television screens instead of the regular programs.

## PRESS ASSOCIATIONS

It was as early as 1848 that the first association of newspapers and telegraph owners existed, but it was not until 1893 that this association incorporated. It became the Associated Press. By 1900 it took the form that it still has today. It was a cooperative association of newspapers that banded together to exchange news. It was non-profit and used what funds it had to reduce costs. It has representatives all over the world.

As early as 1882 a private news service was organized by Walter Polk Phillips called the United Press. He also organized the Cable News to get foreign dispatches. In the latter part of the 1880's an investigation brought out the fact that a secret agreement had put the same men in control of all the country's news-gathering agencies, both AP and UP. Various legal battles lasted several years and UP lost. In 1907 a new and powerful United Press was formed out of several smaller presses to help those papers that could not or would not pay the franchise to the Associated Press. It has grown rapidly.

Many more press associations have grown up. One of the most powerful and impressive is Reuter's. This is a private corporation that will sell news to any paper that cares to pay for it.

## City Presses

There are also city presses that combine in large cities to cover local news. As in every phase of publishing, they are now expanding into conglomerates, and owning or being owned by radio and television stations, calling themselves newspaper-broadcasting combinations. This has created, and promises to create, years and years of legal appeals to the ruling against such combinations that was set up by the Federal Communications Commission.

## Syndicates

As early as 1883 publishers were realizing that it would be good business to join forces and share the news and stories for a wider spread in an expanding reader audience, and it was about this time that a poor young immigrant named Samuel S. McClure realized these possibilities to the fullest. His first love was literature and with the combined efforts of his wife he started a syndicate business. He bought up news items and stories and sold them for a profit to the various newspapers. He was a voracious reader and a good business person. In 1892 he started the *McClure's Magazine* in which he published the best of his findings.

Soon other syndicates were formed and each one supplied special feature articles and cartoons. *The New York Herald* supplied feature articles for Sunday papers. Later the *World* supplied the comics called the Yellow Kid. Then came Hearst with his Katzenjammer Kids as well as many feature articles.

As the syndicates expanded they tended to create uniformity and standardization of the national news and feature stories. In this way, the production of news and articles could be on a wholesale basis creating a savings for the entire syndicate—something that was not available to the independent publisher.

## NOTES

1. Gladys Campbell, *Magazines and Newspapers of Today.* (New York: Harcort, c1929), p. 21.
2. William Katz, Magazine Selection: *How to Build a Community-oriented Collection.* (New York: R. R. Bowker, 1971), p. 102.
3. Ibid., p. 103.

**Additional References**

American Library Association. "The 'Bulletin' Down Through The Ages." *Bulletin* 25, 1931: 403-404.

Casford Ethel Lenore. "The Magazines of the 1890's; a Chapter in the History of English Periodicals." *Language and Literature Series* no. 1: University of Oregon Publications, 1929.

Kent, Allen, and Lancour, Harold; eds. *Encyclopedia of Library and Information Science* II: 265-284.

Kobre, Sidney. *Development of American Journalism.* Debuque, Iowa: W. C. Brown, c1969.

Osborn, Andrew D. *Serial Publications: Their Place and Treatment in Libraries,* 2d ed., rev; American Library Association, 1973.

Peterson, Theodore B. *Magazines of the Twentieth Century.* Urbana, University of Illinois Press, 1956.

# CHAPTER II
# FUNDAMENTALS

**Definitions**

Magazines, periodicals, serials and continuations have been defined and discussed in all the earlier books on serials. The terms vary so much and so many exceptions to the terms are permitted that an intelligent discussion often is not possible. They contain two ingredients: they are numbered; they intend to continue for an indefinite period, as opposed to sets which start out with a definite decision on how many volumes will be published. "Magazines" seems generally to mean popular titles read by the general public. "Periodicals" on the other hand might be considered somewhat more scholarly but still have a distinctive title and have a regular periodicity. "Continuations" are publications by corporate bodies and are designated as "bulletins," "proceedings," "transactions," etc. "Serials" are most generally considered to include all the above categories, although in England and Europe the word is somewhat frowned upon and in Germany the definition was at one time broken into intricate small parts. This is still the case in the definition of legal publications. Osborn in his book, *Serial Publications*, gives a very complete discussion on all the various definitions.

Herein the term "serials" is used in its broadest sense: the publication is numbered, and has every expectation of continuing, either regularly or irregularly.

**Central Serials Record**

The Central Serials Record gives either a partial or complete record of each serial title in the library. It may be a manual file such as cards of various sizes (there are almost as many types of card records as there are libraries using them), or it may be electronically controlled by some sort of automation. In the early days the titles could be listed on pages and organized into volumes. The record may be only a current record of issues coming in each day, or a complete history of every serial title in the library, including bound and unbound volumes, missing or lost numbers and volumes, a record of claimed items, call number, various copies and locations of each copy, binding information—just any information pertaining to each title.

Eliminated from the Serials Record are those publications which are a complete unit, such as sets, unless they promise to take many years to be completed, and then even such sets may be cared for easily in the Record. It has been proved that the Serials Record is able to handle almost any type of publication that comes out regularly or irregularly as well as supplements to individual books. Anything that is troubling anyone often gets dropped into the Serials Record.

## Monographs

A monograph is a book with author/s and title, written on one subject. Various monographs may be written on the same subject and an overall main series title may collect them into one place in the library, or they may be scattered throughout the library, depending on the way they are cataloged. They may even be given various sub-series titles, creating confusion for librarians, claimers and patrons. This may give a need for several copies, or at least special notes on the records, if all sub-series are supposed to be complete. These monographic series are published irregularly.

The publisher may or may not give each monograph a consecutive number, but in some cases they may come out for several years without numbers, and then be collected under the one main series. In this case, the early issues may have numbers assigned to them by the publisher. This will leave the early issues already in the library with no numbers. Even in current issues the numbers may be listed only on the covers of the monograph, and if this is removed in binding, again the book is without its number. If, for these reasons, the series must be shown as complete in the library, ways must be found to prove each monograph's number. There are several ways of approaching this.

1. Check the inside covers of later numbers.
2. Check recent publisher's announcements.
3. Check the library tools (see the chapter on Tools—Irregular series).

There is another little problem when it comes to university monographs (see p. 294).

## The Philosophy of the Serials Routines

The philosophy of serials routines is to make a complete and continuing record from the initiation to the shelving of a title. Each routine must be scrutinized often to be sure that certain steps do not become just habit. A routine must continue to be needed, and as time proceeds, new approaches become necessary, and old routines must be discarded. Don't continue to do the same thing in the same way just because it has always been done that way. A file as intricate as this necessitates a continual review of the routines employed in its upkeep. The larger the file grows, the more necessary it is to streamline, if and where possible. However, every change must be considered carefully to be sure it does not set up a chain-reaction to a routine further along the way. Also, the larger the file grows, the more difficult it is to change routines. Two thousand titles can be adjusted a lot easier than seventeen thousand. Don't ever underestimate the file. No matter how small it is at present, it is going to grow in size. What seems expedient in a small file may become very cumbersome when the file increases, and it will be a lot more difficult to change a routine in the larger file.

The routines must be so arranged that the title will be reviewed at every point where it may break down. Continual checking throughout the routines is the key to keeping the surface running smoothly. The question at all points is not what routines can be omitted, but what will be needed over a long period of time. The more titles that can be put on an automatic assembly line, the more time there is left to deal with those impossible ones. "Every title is a 'potential criminal'" according to Jacobs.[1]

## Problems and Policies to Consider in
## Setting Up A New Record

In setting up a new record, decisions must be made as to what information the record will have to provide. What questions will have to be answered for the library clientele, who will be requesting information, and how many people will be using the file at one time? Should the public have access to it—by a service window or by coming into the area? Should it be the only place in the library where holdings can be found? Should it be a current file only? What other phases of library procedures should be absorbed at this point? Each library will have to come to terms with these questions individually, but each must be carefully considered. When all this has been resolved, then decide how to proceed. What problems will have to be faced to arrive at the objective, and what equipment will be available to answer the needs?

**Aims**

1. To get every title requested from the most reliable source—involves a continual study of agents and trends in the publishing field.
2. To keep every title coming—involves claiming, payments, following up on announcements.
3. To keep up with ceased titles, mergers, splits—involves work with tools, agents, publishers, and the Catalog Division.
4. To fill in all lacks in both current and back files—involves a continual searching for suitable agents and new methods of reproducing such material.

All these points will be discussed more fully in later chapters.

Get the serials checked in and on the shelves as fast as possible. This seems like a simple statement but it is surprising how often it is neglected. There are various basic reasons for emphasizing this approach.

1. The faculty and public depend on this material for their most up-to-date information on their subjects. That is the one reason for getting serials as opposed to books.
2. Once all the simple, easy titles are checked in, time may be utilized for the more difficult problems.
3. There is no use setting up a claiming project, while there is unchecked material sitting around on the shelves.
4. Payments often can not be made until the material is checked into the record.

**Simplification**

Keep extra files and color codings to a minimum. Think long before setting up extraneous files. Will they help the routines, or are the added files going to create just one more place to check, and one more file to keep up-to-date?

**Basic Questions of Organization**

When setting up a Serials Department there are several basic questions to be settled, and again each library has to settle these according to the needs and relationships interweaving each Department or Division of the library.

1. Organization within the library. Should Serials be a part of another Department or Division? Serials do not fit easily into the other routines of the library. At least acquiring them and keeping them coming, require different approaches. They are very individual. Their eccentricities are more easily kept under control in a freedom

established within their own Department. There is little use of dividing magazines and periodicals because they do fit easily into one set of carefully thought-out routines. Two departments seldom think alike, and to divide magazines and periodicals might create disunity in similar types of publications.

2. Location of a Serials Department. It is most convenient for a Serials Department if it can be located close to the Catalog Division, shelf list, public catalog, Binding Department, and Reference Department for sharing of their tools and indexes. It saves time and steps. Of course the arrangement of the individual library will dictate its location.

3. Location within the Department. If current mail can come into the Department to be opened and sorted, it allows for better supervision. Also, this allows the personnel to be on hand to handle other routines while opening the mail. This is especially helpful if serials staff members need to be on hand to wait on the public. The one disadvantage is that mail-opening usually adds to the confusion of unorganized bulk within the Department.

4. What are the various uses to be made of the Serials Record? If the information is to be available to the public, more notes will have to be included on the cards, so that such information as location of the physical pieces, and perhaps when something went to binding, etc., can be given quickly to the patron. Also access by the public by means of a window or other device, must be considered. It is assumed that all questions will be answered by the serials personnel since open access of the file to the public would make unchecked pieces too available to it. If the file is just for internal use then there is less need for all types of information to be considered. Some special libraries do use their serials records as serial catalogs. Linda Hall did for many years.

5. Is it to be a current file only, or include retrospective holdings? Will ceased titles be included? All of these items depend on the amount of space available for the record. To include all the above will create a very large file. However, if it is a Central Serials Record, it becomes a very convenient file, and a duplication of routines can be eliminated throughout the shelf list and public catalog. One should assume however, the title entry will be in the public catalog. "An axiom of serial checking on permanent holdings cards is that the records should be so compiled currently that they can be relied upon implicitly in later years."[2] This can easily be kept in line in a central record.

## General Comment on Professional Serials Personnel

The general qualifications of a serials librarian are similar to those of an acquisition librarian. The librarian must have much background in the history and current trends of agents and publishers, and must be aware of the collections in the particular library and the trends toward new areas of interest.

Serials librarians must be able to put up with a great amount of detail and a continual variation of titles, business trends, and financial problems. Many librarians have no patience with these detailed routines.

A knowledge of, and aptitude for, foreign languages cannot be emphasized too much as requirements for serials librarians. Foreign correspondence has to be understood. Numbers, dates, and volumes must be interpreted in all the languages. Explanations about titles, invoices and publishers' anouncements must be accurately translated.

## General Comment on All Serials Personnel

Every person starting to work in the Serials Department should be given to understand at the outset that although responsibility is accepted for one particular phase of the work, there are many jobs to be accomplished. Serials are never finished, so no one person is ever finished. If work lightens for one person, and someone else gets overwhelmed or becomes sick, all the work must go on, and there must be a willingness for each person to take on other jobs. This has a two-point advantage.
1. It gives each person a broader point of view of the whole Department, which builds a true serials expert.
2. All the work is more apt to be carried forward.

## Serials Mysteries

Serials, to the uninitiated, is a simple matter of ordering, paying invoices, checking in, and sending to the shelves such general titles as *Life, Newsweek,* and the *Saturday Evening Post.* Simple? Of course, if that were all there was to it. But there are pitfalls—thousands of them.

Serials, by nature, are individual, erratic, and often unpredictable. The publisher, the date of publication, arrival in the mail, numbering, title variations, mergers, splitting of titles, payments, renewals, replacements, and claiming, all take a great deal of time, letter writing, and ferreting out of problems. They are maddening and frustrating, and burdensome at best, but they never allow one to get in a rut. For every magazine that ceases, five spring up like dragon's teeth. Nothing stays the same in any phase of serials, but knowing what is true today or yesterday will give one a basis for judgment on what may happen tommorrow.

It is well to keep alert to what is happening throughout the world because many events can affect the publishing or the receipt of serials. A war, a revolution, or an economic crisis may play havoc with publishing of titles. Dock strikes, printers' strikes, post office problems, airplane accidents, boats sinking, inclement weather, may all slow down the delivery of serials. Such trifling items as labels falling off, mis-addressed packages, and poorly wrapped packages may take their toll. Editors die, publishing companies get into law suits, mailing lists are lost due to moves, fires, breakdowns of printing presses—all of these mere incidents wipe out or slow down publications.

Each year will bring a different emphasis on problems. One year it will be a particular agent; another year it will be Russian titles; another, Latin American titles. Some years the world is full of revolutions, and in another will be strikes and labor troubles; in another year, inflation, and in another, lack of funds. It is very interesting to look back and wonder why that problem did not continue. Only one thing is certain; there will always be another problem. That is just to keep librarians from becoming bored.

## What May Happen to a Title?

1. A subscription may never get started (it takes one month to several years to get started).
2. It may change title.
3. It may merge (two or more titles may combine).
4. It may split (sometimes it may break into many sections).
5. It may be suspended (from one month to fifty years).
6. Supplements:
   a. May be published only once.
   b. May be one or more to every volume.
   c. May be one or more sub-series
   d. May be a distinctive title.
7. It may change format in the middle of a volume.
8. Indexes may start or stop being published (or have to be ordered separately, or even from a source other than that from which the publication itself comes).
9. It may change frequency.
10. It may change series.
11. It may change numbering.

12. It may jump from five dollars to five hundred or more.
13. International congresses.
    a. Each congress may have abstracts or nothing.
    b. One or more volumes for each congress may be published.
    c. Each congress may be published in a different journal or be an independent publication part of the time.
14. It may cease.
15. An issue may belong to two or more series.
16. It may contain parts of a book to be removed.
17. Some issues may be published as monographs.
18. Some issues may be media formats.

## Possible Divisions of a Serials Department

1. Ordering
   a. Subscriptions
      (1) New
      (2) Renewals
   b. Single purchases
      (1) Replacements
      (2) Backfiles
2. Checking in of Material
   a. Opening mail
   b. (1) Current
      (2) Holdings
3. Invoices
   a. New Subscriptions
   b. Renewals
   c. Purchase of single volumes and numbers and back files
4. Binding
   a. decisions
   b. When to write binding notices
   c. Indexes
   d. How many volumes to bind together
   e. Supplements and special numbers
   f. Special directives
   g. Titles for spines of books
5. Claiming
   a. Regulars
   b. Irregulars
6. Maintaining the Records
   a. Entering new titles in the Serials Record
   b. Withdrawals

c. Odd volumes of duplicates
d. Adding cross-references
e. Discards
f. Temporarily suspended
g. Changing from gift to purchase
h. Changing from purchase to gift
i. Changes of titles
j. Reporting to *New Serial Titles*
7. Statistics
a. Monthly
b. Annual
8. Automation
9. Cataloging
10. Reference

## NOTES

1. R. M. Jacobs, "Focal Point," *Journal of Documentation* 6 (Dec. 1950): 213-228.
2. Andrew D. Osborn, *Serial Publications; Their Place and Treatment in Libraries.* (Chicago: American Library Association, 1955), p. 77.

# CHAPTER III
# EQUIPMENT AND
# CHECKING-IN PROCEDURES

The time and effort spent in the planning stages of a Serials Record will pay off in the long run manyfold. "In designing an installation thought must be given first, not to size, layout, and number of forms, but to the more basic consideration of permanent versus expendable records, slow-moving versus fast, static versus fluid. These are opposing elements, and disaster follows if an attempt is made to unite them."[1] This whole article is so well stated that anyone designing a new Serials Record should read it.

It is essential to consider the overall approach on what will be needed in a Serials Record. Different decisions will make different demands on the space needed for the record, and it is essential to find out about the various possibilities available. There are three courses that may be followed.

The first approach is that all information about each title be kept in the record. This includes information regarding the current status and the back holdings, including incomplete volumes. This may mean a duplication of information in the Public Catalog, if one is listing the holdings there also. Perhaps this may not be such a duplication as it seems at first glance because the emphasis in each case is different. Most of the catalog card is devoted to the bibliographical information of a title and the holdings card accompanying this in the card catalog is of secondary importance. The serial cards, on the other hand, emphasize the accuracy of the holdings and do not concentrate so fully on the bibliographical information. This duplication fulfills two separate needs, if the public does not have access to the Serials Record.

On the other hand there are those librarians who are deep in the new systems of automation, and who maintain the above is no longer valid because libraries (in ever-increasing numbers) have serials lists produced by computers or union lists of systems to which they belong for public holding records.

The second alternative to follow would be to put all information, including back files, into the Public Catalog. This would necessitate the Catalog Division keeping all back records of incomplete volumes, and a constant change of information as a volume is made more complete. In this case, then, the Serials Record could serve only for current information and would, therefore, be much slower in expanding. A system of this sort necessitates a very close integration of the Serials Department with the Catalog Division. If back sets of serials are being filled in, some means has to be carefully considered for keeping completely up-to-date on incomplete volumes for purposes of sending orders to agents.

The third alternative would be to make the serials file a complete record of all serials holdings. In this case, the file would have to include all serials of every type. It could be recommended that the Serials Department be called upon for service to the public, the various branch or departmental libraries, and the other departments in the library, to a greater extent with this approach. It might be advantageous to make all numbering schemes available so patrons with different citations may be helped. With this third course, the Serials Record would expand at about the same rate or faster than the first alternative. (See the discussion of the CENTRAL SERIALS RECORD).

Another consideration is whether to keep one person responsible for the whole file, or to break the file into smaller sections and have one person responsible for each section of titles. Fewer titles would allow each person to be able to keep all pertinent information at his fingertips. No one person can do all the work necessary to keep a large file up-to-date in claiming, noting changes of title, and various other points needed for accuracy.

In a very crowded file, one possibility would be to consider doing different procedures at different times of the day, week or month.

## Comparison of How to Post Holdings

There are two schools of thought on how best to place holdings in the Serials Record. There are advantages and disadvantages to each approach, and again each library must decide for itself what to do.

The first approach is to bring forward all holdings under the most current entry, and make cross-references from all back titles. The big advantage is that the whole record of holdings may be seen at a glance. The main disadvantage is that each time a title-change occurs, the file either has to be erased, or a tab pasted over the old one, or liquid paper may be purchased in ledger buff. Cards will not take this sort of treatment too often. If new cards have to be made up each time, much work is involved with re-typing long runs of holdings. If a computerized approach is expected, then these disadvantages are minor.

The other approach is to break up the holdings and list them under each change of title, with the history being brought out in the bibliographical information. So often, requests are made for information under the title where holdings occurred. A "Title varies" note stamped on the holdings card at the particular volume where the break occurs brings the change quickly to one's attention. This makes for ready information on the telephone or information desk or window. The most recent trend regarding the "Title varies" note is made to read as follows:

1. Close the old title.
2. Add a note: "Continued by _____."
3. Some librarians will give the new title the same call number, but give the new beginning date. Other librarians will assign a new call number if the volume numbering starts over.
4. Add a note to the new title: "Continues _____."

No card is free from needing re-typing. Sometimes new information is learned about a title. Sometimes just the different kinds of handwriting of various personnel cause the necessity of a new card.

## Equipment

Comparing the equipment with the needs is a reciprocal situation. Needs will dictate the equipment, and the available equipment will dictate how best the needs can fit into it. There are several types of files available for the manual Serials Record, put out by several different companies. Each company is most willing to cooperate and adjust the available equipment to suit the library's needs. It would be well to contact the various companies to be able to make comparisons.

There is one thing to keep in mind. No matter how carefully you plan on the type of equipment you think best for your library, be assured that in the course of several years, something will be changed by the company in the name of improvement, be it only metal knobs changed to plastic, and changes in the color of the cabinets. That has happened at Louisiana State University library, 20 years and 60 cabinets later.

The descriptions and discussion of the various kinds of equipment given in Osborn's book, *Serial Publications,* is so complete and concise that only a brief mention will be made here.

It would be well to consider closely the size of cabinets versus the size of cards to be used in the record. One thought to keep in mind is that the larger card, i.e. the 5''x 8'' card, allows much more freedom and space for information. This is one of the places where a decision to use the smaller cards, when the file is small, and uncomplicated, will not pay off when the file grows to impossible proportions.

The Kardex files put out by Remington Rand Corporation have been used very extensively by serials librarians.

Most companies have available rotary, drum-like, wheel-type cabinets. It would look at first glance that this was the answer to serials librarians' dreams. They contain thousands of cards in very compact form. Growing files and lack of space would seem to be answered here. But the very compactness precludes their use. The Serials Record needs to be spread out for flexibility, because many people must be able to use the file at all times. Also, most files of this type utilize finger-finding devices which are much slower than the eye-finding device of the visible file.

Another type of file is put out by the Acme Company and this file is discussed more thoroughly in the following pages. This equipment utilizes wire rods with the cards hung on the rods by means of metal tabs attached to the cards. One set of cards is hung on one hanger per title. These cards necessitate a clear plastic protector slipped over the file line of the main card. It should be pointed out that a frosted edge will cut down the glare of the light reflecting on them.

This file allows for a deep buildup of cards of each title, but this must be included in the specifications when ordering the files as "10 point." This buildup of cards, using current "flimsies," strong holdings card, and a financial card keeps most of the history of each title compactly together and tells at a glance the entire story of the title.

It is better to use cabinets with 13-15 trays rather than 18-20, because it spreads the files better so that more people may use them. ". . . . this spread may have advantages, since a checker can operate in close proximity to his records without blocking them from others who need to consult them."[2] Also, the lower files eliminate continual high reaching. The checkers are also able to sit down while working. This is important when a checker does many hours of checking at the records.

To make the Serials Record even more flexible it is very important to allow space at least between every six cabinets—every three cabinets would be even better. More people can work more easily at the files if the cabinets are not banked too solidly. Library trucks placed in these empty spaces allow for the mail to be broken into smaller alphabetical units which helps to create flexibility. The three shelves on the truck may be utilized with the current mail on the top shelf, to be checked in by the least trained personnel, the other shelves utilized for the more difficult titles to be checked by the more trained personnel. In this way the easily checked material may go through rapidly and get the bulk out of the way. Then time may be spent on the fewer, more difficult titles.

Another way to make space between cabinets is to face every other one in the opposite direction. The alphabet continues in one direction, with room between cabinets for the checker to put the items being worked on while the trays are pulled down. This is done at the University of California, Riverside.

## Use of Color Codings

The use of color coding should be kept to a minimum, but is a very useful device to cover the flexible or changeable elements in the file.

Color may be used in the cards. One may use white cards for the bulk of the file, then use buff cards for lesser items of information such as cross-references, discards, and special routings.

Use a white, clear protective plastic covering over the file line for the bulk of the file, i.e., for purchased current titles and ceased titles. Then for Gift and Exchange titles use a colored protective tab. When changes occur a shift of protective edge along with a minimum of erasing of notations may set the record straight again.

Sliding or stationary colored tabs may be slipped into the protective edge, and may be used for frequency, a different color for each frequency. To cut down on the variation of color, the same color may be used for monthly, bi-monthly and semi-monthly, etc. A change of frequency then may be changed with a shift of color. A special tab may be used on the buff "discard" card so that one need not even have to raise the card to know that the piece may be discarded.

Both sides of the card edges may utilize double metal tabs of different colors. Also the upper and lower locations of these side edges may allow for no end of possibilities. As each change occurs, a change of tab, or removal of the tab will send the next issue on with the new approach.

The Direct Renewal file (see p. 149) may utilize a different colored tab for each month to bring up for review those titles that need to be claimed or reviewed for that month.

Colored pencils may be used for checking in bound and unbound volumes or other information. Remember to put in ordinary pencil the most changeable information so that it may be erased without ruining the card. Even colored dots may give information.

All the above uses of color are only suggestions of what may be done. Other items that could be flagged down in the same way are destinations, languages, subjects, addresses, agents, etc. There is no end of bits of information that may be flagged.

## Material That May Be Included in the Serials Record

1. Magazines and periodicals. There is little argument about the fact that these should be included.
2. Yearbooks and other annuals and biennials. These may also be easily included.
3. Documents. Many libraries put these into a completely different department since they take special approaches and different handling. They may, however, be absorbed in the Serials Record, providing there is enough trained personnel and space in the department. Documents may become very intricate, and take up much space.
4. United Nations Documents. The same is true for these as mentioned in article three for other documents.
5. International congresses. The main publications may be easily handled in the record. An approach may even be set up to take care of the guide books and field trips.
6. Handbooks with supplements. These may be handled by noting the Handbook at the top of the holdings card and setting up the card to check in the supplements.
7. Sets. Even these may be handled in the record, especially if they are to continue for an indefinite number of years. The only reason to include them in the file is that they may be claimed more readily. However, a note should be put on the card to withdraw the title after the set is completed.
8. Numbered monographic series. These are the most controversial of all the series. The only reason for putting them into the record is that they may be more easily claimed. It should be kept in mind that those going into the record should be only the ones that are being set up for current subscription, or that have been filled in quite extensively. To put in all incomplete, sketchy monograph series would enlarge the file to monstrous proportions.
9. Special directives such as "Send direct to the Divisions for Vertical file, without checking in" and "Ordered in the Order Depart-

ment," etc., may be included. These may be put into a separate file. However, this makes another place to check, and clutters up the department with extra files (see SIMPLIFICATION). Many unusual orders may be lost and drift into the "zero materials" (see p.312) if not flagged for the people checking the mail. The title may easily be withdrawn from the Serials Record and the space closed at any time.

10. Blanket or Global subscriptions. One gets an avalanche of non-serial material as well as serials on these. An added card may be used with a note to send all extra material to the Division that purchases the main publications. However, if all this extra material is substantial it may go via the Catalog Division to be cataloged first.

11. Newspapers. Many libraries do not check these into the record because later they pick them up in microfilm format. Without a doubt, the physical pieces bring in much bulk and take much time to record. There are serious doubts that the record of their arrival is important. If the newspaper stops coming in, it will soon be brought to the librarian's attention by the avid newspaper patron. However, the financial record may be entered for control in the Serials Record if not taken care of in the Newspaper Room.

12. Microfilm. This may easily be accepted into the Serials Record.

13. Memberships and Services. There is no reason why, with a special approach, these may not be included in the record.

14. "Discard on receipt." Libraries, as well as individuals get on "sucker lists" and cannot get off them, even by writing. It is cheaper for the company to continue sending, than to go through several thousand address labels in order to eliminate one address. By putting a card in the Serials Record, one may eliminate continual handling of the title from person to person in the library. Or, if one does not mind having another file in the department, the Serials Record need not be cluttered with this information. This leaves space in the record for more entries.

## Most Important Points to Remember in the Serials Record

There is a very complicated approach that may be made very simple if the following points are kept in mind. There are two types of materials in the Serials Record:
1. Subscriptions
   a. Purchased
   b. Gift and Exchange
2. Non-subscription
   a. Purchased special orders and odd gifts

b. Ceased titles

There is one absolute way of making a distinction for what should be checked in automatically and what should be questioned before checking into the record. On each Serials Record card there is a series of boxes, showing "Purchase," "Gift or Exchange," and if an x is in one of these boxes it should mean that all steps have been taken and certain arrangements have been made to keep the title coming currently. One may reasonably expect to receive the next issue. If no x is shown in any of these boxes, it means one is not automatically going to receive anything without taking further steps about putting the title through the current subscription routines.

When giving this information in these various squares a point to keep in mind is to give the source for purchased titles. If it is a gift or exchange title give the address from which it is to be claimed on the card.

One should have the official title on each card for identification purposes. This should be true of even the "Rider" cards because cards that get separated are difficult to identify.

Be aware that titles, format, and make-up of publications change. If the records in the Serials Record are not the proper kinds of cards to fit the materials being received, take time to get them corrected at once.

All records should be arranged for uniform placing of the same information on all the cards. In this way, there is no searching from one type of card to another for the same information.

## Saving Space on the Cards

There are ways of saving space on the cards. Utilize economy in writing and checking in each piece. Use checks whenever possible, and date receipt of material on the Serials Record only when titles come very late, or irregularly. Some serials librarians prefer that one should always record the date of receipt, whether a publication comes regularly or not. That way one may predict dates of arrival of future issues more easily. It will also make claiming easier because dates of receipt allow much better judgment as to when to claim. This is good. It is true that a publication may come regularly for ten years and suddenly get off schedule. This problem will not be solved even by entering once on the record that the publication usually comes at a certain time of the month or year.

A special typewriter ratchet of seven lines to the inch, in place of the usual six lines, will give better utilization of the card.

Use symbols to flag information. Asterisks, squares, circles, etc., will give a great amount of information in very little space, and may be easily changed when information changes.

When a back file is complete, the holdings card may be listed in this way: V.1-  , 1950-   , unless one wants the information showing the physical volumes and dates, and what volumes are bound together, and then the holdings card will have to continue to be utilized.

## Procedures of Handling All Materials in the Serials Record

When opening the mail one should:
1. Check the address label to be sure the material belongs to the library.
2. Don't open the wrapper in such a way as to mutilate the pieces.
3. Save the address label and slip inside the pieces.
4. Arrange the material alphabetically on a library truck so that it may be shifted easily to the proper part of the Serials Record. The larger the bulk of material and the sooner it is broken into some sort of arrangement, the better.

It is a good idea to insist that no person's name be included in the library's address label. Journals may continue to come in for years with a personal name of someone who has long since left the library, and the library mail clerks are left in confusion. The name of the library sometimes changes, or maybe a Division in the library becomes a Department. All these variations of addresses should be written about to correct them, as time permits.

Carefully compare the title, dates, volume, number, part, section, place, or any other combination of these against the entry in the Serials Record to be sure they are actually the same. This information, at times, makes a great difference as to which card should be used for checking in the titles. If the journal is checked in on the wrong card it sometimes results in claiming pieces that are already in the library.

All mail should be cleared off the trucks within the week if at all possible. All easily checked in material should be cleared off the trucks each day and sent on its way. Don't let old mail get buried in the shuffle. It would be preferable to clear out all mail every day.

In writing notes and directives on the cards it is best to write them as if they were to be reviewed a year in the future—and sometimes they are—and give explicit details. Explain what the problem is, and write specifically what action to take. This serves two purposes:
1. It refreshes one's memory concerning the problem.
2. If specific enough directives have been given, another person reading them can carry them out and one often does not have to get back into the problem, which saves time for all concerned.

Be neat at all times and use only the space involved for a particular number or volume. Once you have your record in neat working order, do not scribble in permanent directives. Take time to erase the old directive and type in the new. A record will soon collapse, and the more untidy the cards, the more carless everyone becomes.

Use ordinary lead pencil for temporary notes and date them. These are to be removed when cleared. Type in permanent notes.

Be uniform in checking in material. Set up the record accurately and insist on keeping it that way.

Never write heavily on materials, especially with transliterations and zero materials (see p. 312). Some may have to be returned to the publisher who will not accept mutilated material.

Duplicates of purchased titles should not be checked in automatically. Find out why they are coming (see the chapter on CLAIMS VS. DUPLICATES).

If RUSH is indicated, flag the piece with a slip with RUSH written on it and place it on the proper person's desk. One may also use color as a signalling device for Rush—red or pink are the usual colors. If a person is to be notified, write that person's name on the rush slip.

All loose plates and maps that come in pieces should have the call number written on them and a pocket made before sending them to the shelves. One should not become so automatic about checking in journals that one fails to note inserts, attached and special directives, bound in, or loose indexes, destinations, invoices, etc. Look on each piece for volume, number and date. Do not just automatically assign the next number without looking.

Certain devices may be used for ready directives. If material is going on "Display" the call number on the piece may be circled in pencil. The call number usually sends the title to the proper destination. If another destination is needed, it may be written below the call number on the piece and the different destination may be underlined in color on the card. There is no end to building up these devices if one uses ingenuity. Not all libraries shelve by call number. If other approaches are used, the shelving device will have to be noted clearly in the record.

For titles that do not check into the Serials Record check lightly in pencil on the cover every word under which the entry has been attempted. Write a zero lightly in pencil in the upper left corner of the piece and set aside for more professional checking later (see the section on zero material).

For types of binding or special directives regarding binding and indexes, always check for this information on the back of the flimsy (see the description of Back of "Flimsies").

For titles that go to a Division (via cataloging) check to see if analytics are required. If "tracing" or "partial analytics" are required, write "via cat" by the call number on the piece and send to the Catalog Division. All this may be brought out on the card, if one wants to set up the cards for these routines.

Notice to see if previous issue or issues have been received. If not, claim (see section on claiming).

Always be on the lookout for supplements and copy numbers.

## Authority File

This is a separate permanent record of each title that has been considered in the library. A carbon copy of the ordering letter is the first record to go into the file. It shows from whom ordered, the beginning subscription volume, and any other pertinent information needed. The subscription slip is stapled to this at the time the permanent record is typed.

It is almost more important to put into the file the negative decisions: do not purchase, do not bind, etc. This information comes up for review much more often than those titles that are going to continue without problems. This file may be used to keep a record of who made what decisions regarding each title.

The biggest criticism of a file of this sort is that it may grow by leaps and bounds. Very special care must be given that just any little scrap of temporary information cannot be added to the file. This can happen very easily.

Another criticism could be that all this type of information may be entered into the Serials Record cards themselves. However, a great deal of information may be kept in such a file regarding titles that have had a stormy career.

Many libraries do not have such a file. This is only a suggestion for keeping track of the history of a title. The University of California, Riverside library is one such library that uses the order slip as a temporary check-in record, and it is stapled to the check-in record when made permanent. This eliminates one file.

## Some Special Thoughts

Keep in mind that there are as many ways of setting up routines, and keeping records, as there are libraries and serials librarians—with each one feeling that the approach in that particular library is the one and only. It would be a sorry serials librarian who did not feel that way.

It would be impossible to show many of these systems and forms, else this book would contain nothing else; therefore, two libraries have been chosen to give springboards for suggestions. It is hoped that in presenting these two systems, an answer may be found for someone. The two libraries are:

1. Louisiana State University library, at Baton Rouge, Louisiana (LSU) (see below).
2. University of California, Riverside library, at Riverside California (UCR) (see pp. 39, 43-4).

The University of California, Riverside library, "Serial Review Form" for a new subscription is self-explanatory (see p. 39).

## Louisiana State University Library at Baton Rouge (LSU)
## Serials Record

The LSU serials record has proved itself, in the past 20 years, to be able to accept any type of publication and routine possible in a manual record. It includes both regular and irregular publications, as well as monographs, both numbered and unnumbered, and even sets that take years to be completed.

It contains the entire history of each title in one place. This includes current and back file information, bibliographic information along with special notes about supplements, monographs, binding information, claiming, type of format whether regular, or microfilm, fiche, etc. It includes call numbers, number of copies and locations. The financial record is filed directly beneath the other cards. This allows for easy comparison of material received and payments to be made. It is the easiest card to take out and type, which keeps the record neat, and does away with scribbled pencil notes.

The cards are 5" x 8" which allows ample room for entering legibly all needed information. The system has been described as "sophisticated" by qualified outside librarians.

## Louisiana State University (LSU) Library Subscription
## Authority and Work Form

The subscription form serves many purposes. It gathers more and more information as it is worked on and passed along from one person to another. It is a two-part form, color-coded (the first copy is white, the second is blue). The fronts of both slips are exact duplicates and cover all pertinent information available concerning the title (see p. 40). Each slip serves a different purpose, and the backs give different information (see pp. 41-42).

# UCR LIBRARY

SERIAL REVIEW FORM

Date_____

Title_____

_____

Please include all available information: announcements, reviews,
advertisements, publisher's address, price, etc.

Requester(s)_____     Price_____

Priority:  ☐ core    ☐ useful    ☐ do not purchase

Courses it would support:
   Dept. No.                          Course

Faculty it benefits:

Please justify the subscription to this title in the light of our very limited
budget for new serials.

Other departments interested                    Priority

_____                    _____

_____                    _____

_____                    _____

                    Departmental Liaison_____

                    Library Collection Consultant_____

                    Chief Bibliographer_____

                    Collection Development Officer_____

                    Head, Serials Department_____

The white slip is used first as a request for acquiring the title. It shows who requested and who approved the title. This gives authority to set up the subscription. It is then used as a work slip for verification, and gives the various instructions for actually placing the order. It shows the serials catalogers what searching has been done, thus eliminating duplication of work.

When the actual order has been placed, the two copies of the form are filed in the Serials Record to flag down a new subscription and keep track of the new issues until the title has been officially cataloged, at which time the permanent cards are typed with the official entry. All records are brought into alignment at this time, and the report to the *New Serial Titles* is made. If the library belongs to a network, this must be considered.

This slip is finally filed in the Authority File along with the ordering records from the agent or publisher to serve as part of the future history of the title.

## LSU LIBRARY

CALL NO:  OFFICIAL ENTRY

SOURCE:

PUBLISHER:
ADDRESS:

FREQUENCY:

DESTINATION:

VERIFICATION:

CHECKED FOUND

☐ ON REF  ☐ LAST VOL REF  SR

BEGINNING DATE OF PUBL.:  PC

BEGINNING DATE OF SUBS.:  ORD DEPT

INDEXED IN:  L C D

RECOMMENDATION AS TO DISPOSITION  OCLC

☐ BIND ☐  ☐ PAM BIND  IRREG SERIALS

☐ RETAIN CURRENT ISSUE ONLY  ULRICH

☐ RETAIN ONE YEAR ONLY  FAXON

☐ TO BE DECIDED  EBSCO

RECOMMENDATION AS TO TREATMENT  AYERS

☐ CAT AS SERIALS WITHOUT ANALYTICS  ULS

☐ CAT AS SERIALS WITH ANALYTICS  NST  YEAR

☐ CAT AS SERIALS WITH DISTINCTIVE  NUC  YEAR

    TITLE TRACING.  L C No

☐ CAT AS SEPARATE TITLES

☐ TRY GIFT ☐ EXCHANGE
☐ NOT AVAILABLE G AND E
☐ WILLING TO PURCHASE
☐ CROSS REFERENCES
☐ NOTES
☐ DISPLAY
☐ BOOK POCKETS
☐ GIFT
☐ EXCHANGE
☐ PURCHASED
☐ FUND
☐ PRICE
☐ BACK FILE WANTED: Yes  No
    ☐ SERIALS ☐ G & E

REQUESTED BY:  NOTIFY:  APPROVED BY:
DEPT.:  DIV.:

THE FRONT OF THE WORK SLIP

Much information regarding the title may be filled in by the person requesting the title and by the Division Head.

This form may even be set up in such a way that the Gifts and Exchange area may use it as well. If multiple order forms are being considered, much of this work slip might be incorporated into that form.

For description of the front of the blue slip and backs of both slips see pp. 38, 40-2.

Of course, if the library does not catalog serials, this form might be much simpler, but something has to be used to flag the first receipt of a new subscription.

## LSU LIBRARY

HOLDINGS IN LIBRARY:
COPIES IN HAND:
IN S.R. TO BE CHANGED:
CORRESP.:

NOTES:

CROSS REFERENCES:
ADDRESS:

TO BEGIN:

SOURCE:
FREQUENCY:

| YEAR | VOL. | No. | | INDEX |
|------|------|-----|--|-------|
| | | | | |
| | | | | |
| | | | | |
| | | | | |
| | | | | |

THE BACK OF THE FIRST COPY OF THE WORK SLIP

The back of the first copy is placed face up in the Serials Record and is used to check in the new subscription until the permanent record is typed, at which time this copy may be filed in the Authority File, if the library has decided to have such a file.

# LSU LIBRARY

**HOLDINGS IN LIBRARY:**

**L.U. HAS AS SEPARATES:**
☐ S.R.   ☐ PUBLIC CATALOG:
**NOTES:**

**CROSS REFERENCES:**

| TRADE BIBLIOS: | CHECKED | FOUND | VERIFICATION: | CHECKED | FOUND | LIBRARY RECORDS: | CHECKED | FOUND |
|---|---|---|---|---|---|---|---|---|
| ULRICH | ☐ | ☐ | NST | ☐ | ☐ | SR | ☐ | ☑ |
| FAXON | ☐ | ☐ | ULS | ☐ | ☐ | PC | ☐ | ☐ |
| AYERS | ☐ | ☐ | NUC | ☐ | ☐ | DOC. COLL. | ☐ | ☐ |
| PTLA | ☐ | ☐ | L.C. No.: | | | ORD. DEPT. | ☐ | ☐ |
| WILLINGS | ☐ | ☐ | | | | | ☐ | ☐ |
| ANN do 12 PR. | | | | | | | ☐ | ☐ |
| BIBLIO | ☐ | ☐ | L.C.'s ORD.: | ☐ | ☐ | | | |
| LEITFADEN | ☐ | ☐ | BR. MUS. | ☐ | ☐ | | | |
| DEUT. PRESSE | ☐ | ☐ | BUC. | ☐ | ☐ | | | |

## The Back of the Second Copy of the Work Slip

The second copy remains in the Serials Record until the first pieces of the subscription arrive, at which time it is pulled and accompanies the pieces: first to the professional who reviews the subscription (see REVISING NEW SUBSCRIPTIONS), then to the Catalog Division for official cataloging. This slip shows the Catalog Division what searching has already been done on the title. This may save some duplication of work.

| BA | | AUTHOR, TITLE | | | |
| GL | | | | CB | |
| PS | | | | PRIORITY | |
| ORDER # | | | | CALL # | |
| DATE | | | | | |
| VENDOR | | SERIES | | | |

| CAT # | ITEM # | PLACE | PUBLISHER | DATE |
|---|---|---|---|---|
| FUND | | REQUESTOR | | ED. |
| PRICE | | DESTINATION: REF  Z  RESERVE  SPEC. COLL. | | |
| | | 7-DAY  BIO AGR  PHY SCI  STACKS _____ | | |

DATE RECEIVED

DATA BASE

LC #
ISBN
OCLC #

| LC to 56 (Mansell) | UCLA | BIP |
| LC to 1952 | UCB | PTLA |
| 42-62 (GALE) | UC Cat. 63-67 | FOR. BIP |
| 63-67 | Br. Mus. | BR. BIP |
| 68-72 | NY PL | FORTHCOMING |
| 73 | Hisp. Soc. | OP |
| 74 | U. of Texas | GUIDE TO REP |
| 75 | Harvard U | BOOKS ON DEMAND |
| 76 | LC Mon. Ser. | BOOKS IN SERIES |
| 77 | LC Music. Cat. | NATIONAL BIBLIOGRAPHY |
| 78 | | (Give title and date) |
| 79 | | |
| 80 | Series/Serial over | |

UCR library's order card is used for both monographs and serials. The order card travels with the first piece when it is sent to be cataloged. The pre-cataloging search may be built on the pre-order search without fear of duplication.

RECEIVED _____CHECKED BY _____DATE_____ ___

| G.L. KARDEX | G.L. PUB. CAT. | U.L.S. _____ ___ |
| B.A. KARDEX | B.A. PUB. CAT. | N.S.T. _____ |
| P.S. KARDEX | P.S. PUB. CAT. | LC/NUC _____ |
| PRINT OUT | ULRICHS | OCLC # _____ |
| PROBLEM FILE | ULRICHS Q. | ISSN_____ |
| SER. AUTH. FILE | ANN. & IRREG. | OTHER _____ |
| EBSCO | P.T.L.A. | |
| FAXON | SOURCES OF SER. | |

SERIES SEARCH

Auth. file ☐          Print out ☐          Pub. Cat. ☐          s/o file ☐

Catalog as:

MONOGRAPH: series traced:  number ☐          author ☐          date ☐

series not traced ☐

series classed together: with anals ☐          w/out anals ☐

set: with anals ☐          without anals ☐

series: found as traced on copy ☐

SERIAL:  with anals ☐          without anals ☐

☐ needs series decision card

☐ needs x reference

☐ see reference from _____

If necessary, copy series here exactly as found (include Bd., etc.) _____ ____

_____

_____

BACK OF UCR LIBRARY ORDER CARD

## Samples of the Serials Record Cards (LSU library)

MINOR TITLES COMING BECAUSE OF SOME MORE IMPORTANT TITLE

It is expedient to take a very definite approach regarding minor titles received as part of a subscription to another title. Set up these separate titles on their own cards, and note that they are "coming in because of the other title." To call them "gift" is not good because of the approach of claiming. The two titles hinge so closely on each other that one cannot claim the minor titles as one would a gift. Then too, if the main publication ceases, the other one will probably cease, also.

CURRENT "HALF AUXILIARY" SHEETS OR "FLIMSIES"

The current "half auxiliary" sheets, sometimes called "over-riders" or "flimsies" are of lightweight paper and are the length of the front fold of the holdings card located just below. These over-riders are printed for dailies and weeklies (use the same card for both, see the samples), monthlies, quarterlies, or just lined or blank. These variations will take care of every type of publication called a serial. The back of the slip gives information regarding many items and is alike on all flimsies (see the sample).

## CHECKING IN CURRENT ISSUES ON THE FLIMSIES

When checking the current issues check the frequency. It often happens there is a change. Do not take the volume and number for granted. (An absent-minded student once checked in a weekly magazine, proceeding to the weeks 53, 54, 55, etc. until someone caught up with it about April!) Actually verify the numbers on the piece before entering in the Serials Record.

Write the call number on each piece, making the number legible and neat. It is well to choose a particular part of the cover on which to write this number regularly. If the cover is too dark or slick to be easily read, write the call number on the upper left corner of the first page after the front cover.

Reprints of articles from serials are seldom recorded in the Serials Record. This does not apply to "Reprint editions," or some numbered series that may be already set up in the record that are reprints of various other series. Always check against the Serials Record before discarding.

Many libraries frown on keeping the reprints of single articles by authors. They are usually too scattered to fill in volumes of a title. They are often used by faculty members who are interested in compiling articles on a particular subject. True, they are monographs, and some libraries may catalog them, but they clutter up the shelves with thin, difficult-to-shelve material that usually may be found in the journals. It all depends on the importance of the monograph and the particular library.

Be sure to return all gift acknowledgement cards enclosed in the pieces, after filling in the number or volume received. This is the only way to insure receiving the next number.

When a current flimsy is filled, don't continue to squeeze in numbers on the bottom. Type another flimsy immediately.

It is useful to have checkers initial their work so that the librarian may clarify any corrections with the proper person.

## Current Checking in Card or "Flimsy"

Odd duplicate copy.

Current nos. put on display.
(call no. is circled in pencil).

Tab indicates destination is different
from where call no. would send it.

Typed-in boxes show current
subscription either by Purchase or
Gift and Exchange.

Annual indexes.

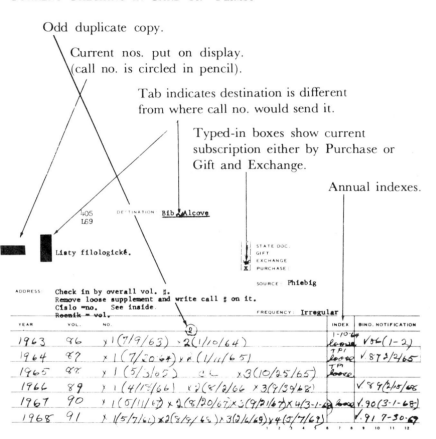

Irregular Flimsy

HG
4501
V26

DESTINATION: Social Science (Last v. Ref)

**Value line investment survey; ratings and reports.**

ADDRESS:

|  | STATE DOC. |
|---|---|
|  | GIFT |
|  | EXCHANGE |
| X | PURCHASE: |

SOURCE: **Faxon**

FREQUENCY: **Weekly**

YEAR *1971*    VOL. *24*    INDEX REC'D.    BIND. NOTIFICATION:

| MONTH | 1 | 2 | 3 | 4 | 5 | 6 | 7 | 8 | 9 | 10 | 11 | 12 | 13 | 14 | 15 | 16 | 17 | 18 | 19 | 20 | 21 | 22 | 23 | 24 | 25 | 26 | 27 | 28 | 29 | 30 | 31 |
|---|---|---|---|---|---|---|---|---|---|---|---|---|---|---|---|---|---|---|---|---|---|---|---|---|---|---|---|---|---|---|---|
| JANUARY | 12 3Pt. (1-5-21) | | | | | | | 133Pt.(1-8-70) | | | | | | 14(1-15-71) | | | | | | | | 15(1-21-71) | | | | | | | | | |
| FEBRUARY | | | | | | | | | | | | | | | | | | | | | | | | | | | | | | | |
| MARCH | | | | | | | | | | | | | | | | | | | | | | | | | | | | | | | |
| APRIL | | | | | | | | | | | | | | | | | | | | | | | | | | | | | | | |
| MAY | | | | | | | | | | | | | | | | | | | | | | | | | | | | | | | |
| JUNE | | | | | | | | | | | | | | | | | | | | | | | | | | | | | | | |
| JULY | | | | | | | | | | | | | | | | | | | | | | | | | | | | | | | |
| AUGUST | | | | | | | | | | | | | | | | | | | | | | | | | | | | | | | |
| SEPTEMBER | | | | | | | | | | | | | | | | | | | | | | | | | | | | | | | |
| OCTOBER | | | | | | | | | | | | | | | | | | | | | | | | | | | | | | | |
| NOVEMBER | | | | | | | | | | | | | | | | | | | | | | | | | | | | | | | |
| DECEMBER | | | | | | | | | | | | | | | | | | | | | | | | | | | | | | | |

1 2 3 4 5 6 7 8 9 10 11 12

## DAILY AND WEEKLY FLIMSY

TS
800
W6

DESTINATION: **Science**

**World wood.**

ADDRESS:

|  | STATE DOC. |
|---|---|
|  | GIFT |
|  | EXCHANGE |
| X | PURCHASE: |

SOURCE: **Popular Subs. Service**

*To begin 1966 —*

FREQUENCY: **Monthly**

| YEAR | SER. | VOL. | JAN | FEB | MAR | APR | MAY | JUN | JUL | AUG | SEP | OCT | NOV | DEC | INDEX | BIND. NOTIFICATION |
|---|---|---|---|---|---|---|---|---|---|---|---|---|---|---|---|---|
| 1966 | | 7 | | | | O.P. | | 3 | | 4 | | 5 | | 6 | | |
| 1967 | | 8 | | 2/16 3-1 | | O.P. | | O.P. | | O.P. | | O.P. | 12-13-67 6 | | | |
| 1968 | | 9 | | 3-1 1 | | 5-13 2 | | 7-16 3 | 7-14 4 | 8-30 5 | | 11-4-68 6 | | cl | V. 9-16 | |
| 1969 | | 10 | 10-37 1 | 10-2 2 | 3 | 12-27 4 | 10-27 5 | 10-37 6 | 7/8 | 11-10 9 | 11-10 10 | 10-27 11 | 11-25 12 | 12-22 13 | 12/22/69 | |
| 197 | | | cl | UTD | | | | | | | | | | | | |

1 2 3 4 5 6 7 8 9 10 11 12

## MONTHLY FLIMSY

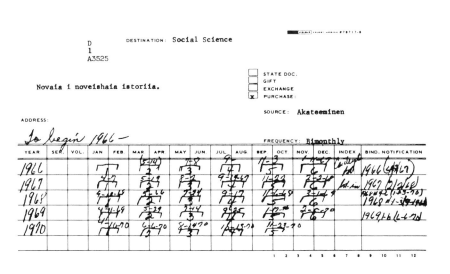

808.85
V83
DESTINATION: Humanities (current vol. Reserve Book Room)

Vital speeches of the day.

☐ STATE DOC.
☐ GIFT
☐ EXCHANGE
☒ PURCHASE:

SOURCE: **Faxon**

ADDRESS:

FREQUENCY: **Semi-monthly**

| YEAR | SER. | VOL. | JAN | FEB | MAR | APR | MAY | JUN | JUL | AUG | SEP | OCT | NOV. | DEC. | INDEX | BIND. NOTIFICATION |
|------|------|------|-----|-----|-----|-----|-----|-----|-----|-----|-----|-----|------|------|-------|--------------------|
| 1970 | 36 37 | | | | | | | | | | | | | | | |
| 1971 | 37 | | | | | | | | | | | | | | | |

## SEMI-MONTHLY FLIMSY

(Use a monthly card with a line drawn diagonally across the month)

D
1
A3525
DESTINATION: Social Science

Novaia i noveishaia istoriia.

☐ STATE DOC.
☐ GIFT
☐ EXCHANGE
☒ PURCHASE:

SOURCE: **Akateeminen**

ADDRESS:

To begin 1966 —

FREQUENCY: **Bimonthly**

| YEAR | SER. | VOL. | JAN | FEB | MAR | APR | MAY | JUN | JUL | AUG | SEP | OCT | NOV. | DEC. | INDEX | BIND. NOTIFICATION |
|------|------|------|-----|-----|-----|-----|-----|-----|-----|-----|-----|-----|------|------|-------|--------------------|
| 1966 | | | | | | | | | | | | | | | | 1966 |
| 1967 | | | | | | | | | | | | | | | | 1967 |
| 1968 | | | | | | | | | | | | | | | | 1968 |
| 1969 | | | | | | | | | | | | | | | | 1969 |
| 1970 | | | | | | | | | | | | | | | | |

## BI-MONTHLY FLIMSY

(Use a monthly card, but bracket two months together)

Always put the address of where
to claim on gift or exchange titles.

382
N2lo

DESTINATION: Social Science

National Foreign Trade Convention.
Proceedings.

☐ STATE DOC.
☒ GIFT
☐ EXCHANGE
☐ PURCHASE:

SOURCE: Publisher

ADDRESS: National Foreign Trade Council, Inc.
10 Rockefeller Plaza
New York, New York    10020

FREQUENCY: Annual

| YEAR | VOL. | NO. | | INDEX | BIND. NOTIFICATION |
|------|------|-----|---|-------|--------------------|
| | | | | | |
| | | Check in on holdings card. | | | |
| | | | | | |
| | | | | | |
| | | | | | |
| | | | | | |

1  2  3  4  5  6  7  8  9  10  11  12

DESTINATION:

☐ STATE DOC.
☐ GIFT
☐ EXCHANGE
☐ PURCHASE:

SOURCE:

ADDRESS:

FREQUENCY:

| YEAR | VOL. | | | | | INDEX | BIND. NOTIFICATION |
|------|------|---|---|---|---|-------|--------------------|
| | | | | | | | |
| | | | | | | | |
| | | | | | | | |
| | | | | | | | |
| | | | | | | | |
| | | | | | | | |

1  2  3  4  5  6  7  8  9  10  11  12

QUARTERLY FLIMSY

BACK OF FLIMSIES

The backs of all "flimsies" are alike. Be sure this side is printed upside-down to the front of the slip to allow ease of reading and noting information, when flipped up in the record. It can be used for noting letters written by different people and to tell who wrote the letter and the action taken. When there are many people in the department, this keeps everyone from writing about the same problem. Claims may be noted and the action taken. Part of the card is reserved for binding information and for any special notes needed regarding supplements.

| MISSING OR DUP. NOS. | WROTE | REPLY | ACTION |
| --- | --- | --- | --- |

| SUPPLEMENTS: | T.P.I. INFORMATION: |
| --- | --- |
| | BINDING: |

THE HOLDING CARDS

The holding cards must be strong enough for hard and continual usage—50% rag content will give this strength.

They are slotted at the center lower edge for frequency signals and protectors. The card is folded with the front measuring 8" x 4-1/4". The upper side of the front part carries the bibliographical information and space at the bottom is left for cumulated index information. When the bibliographical information is too long for one card, another card may be used in the next space below in the tray, and a note put on the second card to check in all holdings on the first card.

The lower part of the card measures 8" x 5". The inside and back of the card has space to designate the holdings, cross references, destination, call number, information regarding analytics, and if the back file is on the Want List. The types of the holdings cards are numbered, either 1-300, or 1-600, while others are yearly, split year, and some are lined or blank. These combinations will cover all frequencies, both regular and irregular.

One may distinguish between bound and unbound volumes by placing a blue check by the volume number on the card, for bound volumes and a light pencil x for unbound volumes. In checking in incomplete back files, if the space on the Serials Record is too small to note all information, use a slip and attach to the record to check in, leaving space for the missing numbers. On the Serials Record card beside that volume write in pencil "See attached slip." When the volume is complete remove the slip.

If any volume should be complete in fewer numbers than were previously issued, note this fact on the Serials Record. For example: v.84, 1956, then for the unusual volume v.86, 1958 (complete in 2 numbers). This often helps in later years to verify the fact that the volume is complete.

If a title on microfilm comes on subscription, it is recorded with a pencilled check x in the proper space of the flimsy. When the year is complete, a blue check is automatically placed by the year on the holdings card. If odd volumes of a title are purchased on microfilm these volumes should have "film" written beside the volume on the Serials Record and be checked in with a blue check. Microfiches are checked in the same way.

Question all back numbers and volumes. Don't check them in automatically. Look for a reason for their arrival. They probably are coming in because of a special order, or a price and availability letter, or a claim having been written. These records will all have to be cleared.

For new subscriptions see the chapter on Ordering.

Bibliographical information.

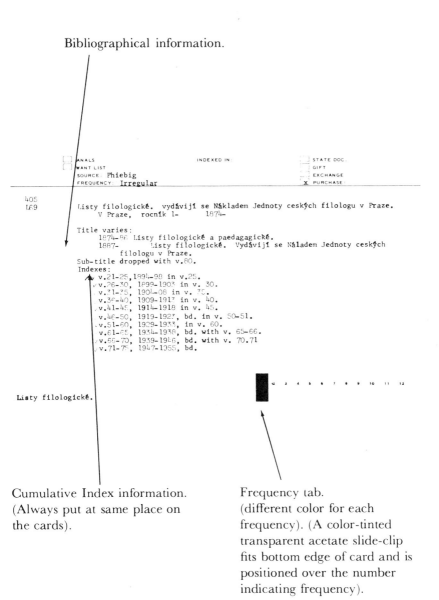

Cumulative Index information.
(Always put at same place on
the cards).

Frequency tab.
(different color for each
frequency). (A color-tinted
transparent acetate slide-clip
fits bottom edge of card and is
positioned over the number
indicating frequency).

FRONT OF IRREGULAR FOLDED HOLDINGS CARD

INVENTORIED:

DESTINATION: **Humanities (v.1-73 in HILL)**

| | | | | | | | | | |
|---|---|---|---|---|---|---|---|---|---|
| 1 | 21 1894 | 41 | 61 1934 | 81 1958 | 101 | 121 | 141 | 161 | 181 |
| 2 TITLE | 22 1895 | 42 1915 | 62 1935 | 82 1959 | 102 | 122 | 142 | 162 | 182 |
| 3 VARIES | 23 1896 | 43 1916 | 63 1936 | 83 1960 | 103 | 123 | 143 | 163 | 183 |
| 4 1877 | 24 1897 | 44 1917 | 64 1937 | 84 1961 | 104 | 124 | 144 | 164 | 184 |
| 5 1878 | 25 1898 | 45 1918 | 65 1938 | 85 1962 | 105 | 125 | 145 | 165 | 185 |
| 6 1879 | 26 1899 | 46 1919 | 66 1939 | 86 1963 | 106 | 126 | 146 | 166 | 186 |
| 7 1880 | 27 1900 | 47 1920 | 67 | 87 1964 | 107 | 127 | 147 | 167 | 187 |
| 8 1881 | 28 1901 | 48 1921 | 68 1941 | 88 | 108 | 128 | 148 | 168 | 188 |
| 9 1882 | 29 1902 | 49 1922 | 69 1942 | 89 1966 | 109 | 129 | 149 | 169 | 189 |
| 10 1883 | 30 1903 | 50 1923 | 70 1946 | 90 1967 | 110 | 130 | 150 | 170 | 190 |
| 11 1884 | 31 1904 | 51 1924 | 71 1947 | 91 1968 | 111 | 131 | 151 | 171 | 191 |
| 12 1885 | 32 1905 | 52 1925 | 72 1948 | 92 | 112 | 132 | 152 | 172 | 192 |
| 13 1886 | 33 1906 | 53 1926 | 73 1949 | 93 | 113 | 133 | 153 | 173 | 193 |
| 14 1887 | 34 1907 | 54 1927 | 74 1950 | 94 | 114 | 134 | 154 | 174 | 194 |
| 15 1898 | 35 1908 | 55 1928 | 75 1951 | 95 | 115 | 135 | 155 | 175 | 195 |
| 16 1889 | 36 1909 | 56 1929 | 76 1953 | 96 | 116 | 136 | 156 | 176 | 196 |
| 17 1890 | 37 1910 | 57 1930 | 77 1954 | 97 | 117 | 137 | 157 | 177 | 197 |
| 18 1891 | 38 1911 | 58 1931 | 78 1955 | 98 | 118 | 138 | 158 | 178 | 198 |
| 19 1892 | 39 1912 | 59 1932 | 79 1956 | 99 | 119 | 139 | 159 | 179 | 199 |
| 20 1893 | 40 1913 | 60 1933 | 80 1957 | 100 | 120 | 140 | 160 | 180 | 200 |

405
L69

| | | | | | | | | | |
|---|---|---|---|---|---|---|---|---|---|
| 201 | 221 | 241 | 261 | 281 | 301 | 321 | 341 | 361 | 381 |
| 202 | 222 | 242 | 262 | 282 | 302 | 322 | 342 | 362 | 382 |
| 203 | 223 | 243 | 263 | 283 | 303 | 323 | 343 | 363 | 383 |
| 204 | 224 | 244 | 264 | 284 | 304 | 324 | 344 | 364 | 384 |
| 205 | 225 | 245 | 265 | 285 | 305 | 325 | 345 | 365 | 385 |
| 206 | 226 | 246 | 266 | 286 | 306 | 326 | 346 | 366 | 386 |
| 207 | 227 | 247 | 267 | 287 | 307 | 327 | 347 | 367 | 387 |
| 208 | 228 | 248 | 268 | 288 | 308 | 328 | 348 | 368 | 388 |
| 209 | 229 | 249 | 269 | 289 | 309 | 329 | 349 | 369 | 389 |
| 210 | 230 | 250 | 270 | 290 | 310 | 330 | 350 | 370 | 390 |
| 211 | 231 | 251 | 271 | 291 | 311 | 331 | 351 | 371 | 391 |
| 212 | 232 | 252 | 272 | 292 | 312 | 332 | 352 | 372 | 392 |
| 213 | 233 | 253 | 273 | 293 | 313 | 333 | 353 | 373 | 393 |
| 214 | 234 | 254 | 274 | 294 | 314 | 334 | 354 | 374 | 394 |
| 215 | 235 | 255 | 275 | 295 | 315 | 335 | 355 | 375 | 395 |
| 216 | 236 | 256 | 276 | 296 | 316 | 336 | 356 | 376 | 396 |
| 217 | 237 | 257 | 277 | 297 | 317 | 337 | 357 | 377 | 397 |
| 218 | 238 | 258 | 278 | 298 | 318 | 338 | 358 | 378 | 398 |
| 219 | 239 | 259 | 279 | 299 | 319 | 339 | 359 | 379 | 399 |
| 220 | 240 | 260 | 280 | 300 | 320 | 340 | 360 | 380 | 400 |

CROSS REFERENCES:

1  2  3  4  5  6  7  8  9  10  11  12

Listy filologické.

## The Inside of a Holdings Card

(showing complete and incomplete holdings, and a "Title Varies" stamp).

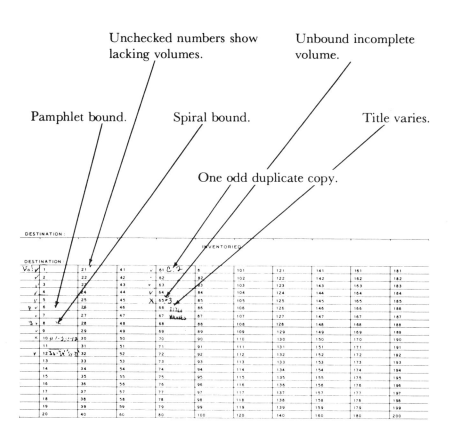

HOLDINGS SHOWING PHYSICAL VOLS.

INVENTORIED :

DESTINATION :

| 1 | 21 | 41 | 61 | 81 |
|---|----|----|----|----|
| 2 | 22 | 42 | 62 | 82 |
| 3 | 23 | 43 | 63 | 83 |
| 4 | 24 | 44 | 64 | 84 |
| 5 | 25 | 45 | 65 | 85 |
| 6 | 26 | 46 | 66 | 86 |
| 7 | 27 | 47 | 67 | 87 |
| 8 | 28 | 48 | 68 | 88 |
| 9 | 29 | 49 | 69 | 89 |
| 10 | 30 | 50 | 70 | 90 |
| 11 | 31 | 51 | 71 | 91 |
| 12 | 32 | 52 | 72 | 92 |
| 13 | 33 | 53 | 73 | 93 |
| 14 | 34 | 54 | 74 | 94 |
| 15 | 35 | 55 | 75 | 95 |
| 16 | 36 | 56 | 76 | 96 |
| 17 | 37 | 57 | 77 | 97 |
| 18 | 38 | 58 | 78 | 98 |
| 19 | 39 | 59 | 79 | 99 |
| 20 | 40 | 60 | 80 | 100 |

#78709-8

| 101 | 121 | 141 | 161 | 181 |
|-----|-----|-----|-----|-----|
| 102 | 122 | 142 | 162 | 182 |
| 103 | 123 | 143 | 163 | 183 |
| 104 | 124 | 144 | 164 | 184 |
| 105 | 125 | 145 | 165 | 185 |
| 106 | 126 | 146 | 166 | 186 |
| 107 | 127 | 147 | 167 | 187 |
| 108 | 128 | 148 | 168 | 188 |
| 109 | 129 | 149 | 169 | 189 |
| 110 | 130 | 150 | 170 | 190 |
| 111 | 131 | 151 | 171 | 191 |
| 112 | 132 | 152 | 172 | 192 |
| 113 | 133 | 153 | 173 | 193 |
| 114 | 134 | 154 | 174 | 194 |
| 115 | 135 | 155 | 175 | 195 |
| 116 | 136 | 156 | 176 | 196 |
| 117 | 137 | 157 | 177 | 197 |
| 118 | 138 | 158 | 178 | 198 |
| 119 | 139 | 159 | 179 | 199 |
| 120 | 140 | 160 | 180 | 200 |

CROSS REFERENCES :

HOLDINGS CARD SHOWING NUMBERS 1-200

DESTINATION:

| 201 | 221 | 241 | 261 | 281 |
|-----|-----|-----|-----|-----|
| 202 | 222 | 242 | 262 | 282 |
| 203 | 223 | 243 | 263 | 283 |
| 204 | 224 | 244 | 264 | 284 |
| 205 | 225 | 245 | 265 | 285 |
| 206 | 226 | 246 | 266 | 286 |
| 207 | 227 | 247 | 267 | 287 |
| 208 | 228 | 248 | 268 | 288 |
| 209 | 229 | 249 | 269 | 289 |
| 210 | 230 | 250 | 270 | 290 |
| 211 | 231 | 251 | 271 | 291 |
| 212 | 232 | 252 | 272 | 292 |
| 213 | 233 | 253 | 273 | 293 |
| 214 | 234 | 254 | 274 | 294 |
| 215 | 235 | 255 | 275 | 295 |
| 216 | 236 | 256 | 276 | 296 |
| 217 | 237 | 257 | 277 | 297 |
| 218 | 238 | 258 | 278 | 298 |
| 219 | 239 | 259 | 279 | 299 |
| 220 | 240 | 260 | 280 | 300 |

☐ ANALS            INDEXED IN:        ☐ STATE DOC.
☐ WANT LIST                           ☐ GIFT
SOURCE:                               ☐ EXCHANGE
FREQUENCY:                            ☐ PURCHASE:

HOLDINGS CARD SHOWING NUMBERS 1-300

INVENTORIED:

DESTINATION:

| 1 | 21 | 41 | 61 | 81 | 101 | 121 | 141 | 161 | 181 |
|---|---|---|---|---|---|---|---|---|---|
| 2 | 22 | 42 | 62 | 82 | 102 | 122 | 142 | 162 | 182 |
| 3 | 23 | 43 | 63 | 83 | 103 | 123 | 143 | 163 | 183 |
| 4 | 24 | 44 | 64 | 84 | 104 | 124 | 144 | 164 | 184 |
| 5 | 25 | 45 | 65 | 85 | 105 | 125 | 145 | 165 | 185 |
| 6 | 26 | 46 | 66 | 86 | 106 | 126 | 146 | 166 | 186 |
| 7 | 27 | 47 | 67 | 87 | 107 | 127 | 147 | 167 | 187 |
| 8 | 28 | 48 | 68 | 88 | 108 | 128 | 148 | 168 | 188 |
| 9 | 29 | 49 | 69 | 89 | 109 | 129 | 149 | 169 | 189 |
| 10 | 30 | 50 | 70 | 90 | 110 | 130 | 150 | 170 | 190 |
| 11 | 31 | 51 | 71 | 91 | 111 | 131 | 151 | 171 | 191 |
| 12 | 32 | 52 | 72 | 92 | 112 | 132 | 152 | 172 | 192 |
| 13 | 33 | 53 | 73 | 93 | 113 | 133 | 153 | 173 | 193 |
| 14 | 34 | 54 | 74 | 94 | 114 | 134 | 154 | 174 | 194 |
| 15 | 35 | 55 | 75 | 95 | 115 | 135 | 155 | 175 | 195 |
| 16 | 36 | 56 | 76 | 96 | 116 | 136 | 156 | 176 | 196 |
| 17 | 37 | 57 | 77 | 97 | 117 | 137 | 157 | 177 | 197 |
| 18 | 38 | 58 | 78 | 98 | 118 | 138 | 158 | 178 | 198 |
| 19 | 39 | 59 | 79 | 99 | 119 | 139 | 159 | 179 | 199 |
| 20 | 40 | 60 | 80 | 100 | 120 | 140 | 160 | 180 | 200 |

#78710-8

| 201 | 221 | 241 | 261 | 281 | 301 | 321 | 341 | 361 | 381 |
|---|---|---|---|---|---|---|---|---|---|
| 202 | 222 | 242 | 262 | 282 | 302 | 322 | 342 | 362 | 382 |
| 203 | 223 | 243 | 263 | 283 | 303 | 323 | 343 | 363 | 383 |
| 204 | 224 | 244 | 264 | 284 | 304 | 324 | 344 | 364 | 384 |
| 205 | 225 | 245 | 265 | 285 | 305 | 325 | 345 | 365 | 385 |
| 206 | 226 | 246 | 266 | 286 | 306 | 326 | 346 | 366 | 386 |
| 207 | 227 | 247 | 267 | 287 | 307 | 327 | 347 | 367 | 387 |
| 208 | 228 | 248 | 268 | 288 | 308 | 328 | 348 | 368 | 388 |
| 209 | 229 | 249 | 269 | 289 | 309 | 329 | 349 | 369 | 389 |
| 210 | 230 | 250 | 270 | 290 | 310 | 330 | 350 | 370 | 390 |
| 211 | 231 | 251 | 271 | 291 | 311 | 331 | 351 | 371 | 391 |
| 212 | 232 | 252 | 272 | 292 | 312 | 332 | 352 | 372 | 392 |
| 213 | 233 | 253 | 273 | 293 | 313 | 333 | 353 | 373 | 393 |
| 214 | 234 | 254 | 274 | 294 | 314 | 334 | 354 | 374 | 394 |
| 215 | 235 | 255 | 275 | 295 | 315 | 335 | 355 | 375 | 395 |
| 216 | 236 | 256 | 276 | 296 | 316 | 336 | 356 | 376 | 396 |
| 217 | 237 | 257 | 277 | 297 | 317 | 337 | 357 | 377 | 397 |
| 218 | 238 | 258 | 278 | 298 | 318 | 338 | 358 | 378 | 398 |
| 219 | 239 | 259 | 279 | 299 | 319 | 339 | 359 | 379 | 399 |
| 220 | 240 | 260 | 280 | 300 | 320 | 340 | 360 | 380 | 400 |

CROSS REFERENCES:

HOLDINGS CARD SHOWING NUMBERS 1-400

DESTINATION:

| 401 | 421 | 441 | 461 | 481 | 501 | 521 | 541 | 561 | 581 |
|-----|-----|-----|-----|-----|-----|-----|-----|-----|-----|
| 402 | 422 | 442 | 462 | 482 | 502 | 522 | 542 | 562 | 582 |
| 403 | 423 | 443 | 463 | 483 | 503 | 523 | 543 | 563 | 583 |
| 404 | 424 | 444 | 464 | 484 | 504 | 524 | 544 | 564 | 584 |
| 405 | 425 | 445 | 465 | 485 | 505 | 525 | 545 | 565 | 585 |
| 406 | 426 | 446 | 466 | 486 | 506 | 526 | 546 | 566 | 586 |
| 407 | 427 | 447 | 467 | 487 | 507 | 527 | 547 | 567 | 587 |
| 408 | 428 | 448 | 468 | 488 | 508 | 528 | 548 | 568 | 588 |
| 409 | 429 | 449 | 469 | 489 | 509 | 529 | 549 | 569 | 589 |
| 410 | 430 | 450 | 470 | 490 | 510 | 530 | 550 | 570 | 590 |
| 411 | 431 | 451 | 471 | 491 | 511 | 531 | 551 | 571 | 591 |
| 412 | 432 | 452 | 472 | 492 | 512 | 532 | 552 | 572 | 592 |
| 413 | 433 | 453 | 473 | 493 | 513 | 533 | 553 | 573 | 593 |
| 414 | 434 | 454 | 474 | 494 | 514 | 534 | 554 | 574 | 594 |
| 415 | 435 | 455 | 475 | 495 | 515 | 535 | 555 | 575 | 595 |
| 416 | 436 | 456 | 476 | 496 | 516 | 536 | 556 | 576 | 596 |
| 417 | 437 | 457 | 477 | 497 | 517 | 537 | 557 | 577 | 597 |
| 418 | 438 | 458 | 478 | 498 | 518 | 538 | 558 | 578 | 598 |
| 419 | 439 | 459 | 479 | 499 | 519 | 539 | 559 | 579 | 599 |
| 420 | 440 | 460 | 480 | 500 | 520 | 540 | 560 | 580 | 600 |

☐ ANALS  
☐ WANT LIST  
SOURCE:  
FREQUENCY:

INDEXED IN:

☐ STATE DOC.  
☐ GIFT  
☐ EXCHANGE  
☐ PURCHASE:

HOLDINGS CARD SHOWING NUMBERS 1-600

INVENTORIED:

DESTINATION:

| | | | | |
|---|---|---|---|---|
| 1800 | 1820 | 1840 | 1860 | 1880 |
| 1801 | 1821 | 1841 | 1861 | 1881 |
| 1802 | 1822 | 1842 | 1862 | 1882 |
| 1803 | 1823 | 1843 | 1863 | 1883 |
| 1804 | 1824 | 1844 | 1864 | 1884 |
| 1805 | 1825 | 1845 | 1865 | 1885 |
| 1806 | 1826 | 1846 | 1866 | 1886 |
| 1807 | 1827 | 1847 | 1867 | 1887 |
| 1808 | 1828 | 1848 | 1868 | 1888 |
| 1809 | 1829 | 1849 | 1869 | 1889 |
| 1810 | 1830 | 1850 | 1870 | 1890 |
| 1811 | 1831 | 1851 | 1871 | 1891 |
| 1812 | 1832 | 1852 | 1872 | 1892 |
| 1813 | 1833 | 1853 | 1873 | 1893 |
| 1814 | 1834 | 1854 | 1874 | 1894 |
| 1815 | 1835 | 1855 | 1875 | 1895 |
| 1816 | 1836 | 1856 | 1876 | 1896 |
| 1817 | 1837 | 1857 | 1877 | 1897 |
| 1818 | 1838 | 1858 | 1878 | 1898 |
| 1819 | 1839 | 1859 | 1879 | 1899 |

| | | | | |
|---|---|---|---|---|
| 1900 | 1920 | 1940 | 1960 | 1980 |
| 1901 | 1921 | 1941 | 1961 | 1981 |
| 1902 | 1922 | 1942 | 1962 | 1982 |
| 1903 | 1923 | 1943 | 1963 | 1983 |
| 1904 | 1924 | 1944 | 1964 | 1984 |
| 1905 | 1925 | 1945 | 1965 | 1985 |
| 1906 | 1926 | 1946 | 1966 | 1986 |
| 1907 | 1927 | 1947 | 1967 | 1987 |
| 1908 | 1928 | 1948 | 1968 | 1988 |
| 1909 | 1929 | 1949 | 1969 | 1989 |
| 1910 | 1930 | 1950 | 1970 | 1990 |
| 1911 | 1931 | 1951 | 1971 | 1991 |
| 1912 | 1932 | 1952 | 1972 | 1992 |
| 1913 | 1933 | 1953 | 1973 | 1993 |
| 1914 | 1934 | 1954 | 1974 | 1994 |
| 1915 | 1935 | 1955 | 1975 | 1995 |
| 1916 | 1936 | 1956 | 1976 | 1996 |
| 1917 | 1937 | 1957 | 1977 | 1997 |
| 1918 | 1938 | 1958 | 1978 | 1998 |
| 1919 | 1939 | 1959 | 1979 | 1999 |

CROSS REFERENCES:

1  2  3  4  5  6  7  8  9  10  11  12

# AN ANNUAL HOLDINGS CARD

INVENTORIED:

DESTINATION:

| 1800/01 | 1820/21 | 1840/41 | 1860/61 | 1880/81 |
|---|---|---|---|---|
| 1801/02 | 1821/22 | 1841/42 | 1861/62 | 1881/82 |
| 1802/03 | 1822/23 | 1842/43 | 1862/63 | 1882/83 |
| 1803/04 | 1823/24 | 1843/44 | 1863/64 | 1883/84 |
| 1804/05 | 1824/25 | 1844/45 | 1864/65 | 1884/85 |
| 1805/06 | 1825/26 | 1845/46 | 1865/66 | 1885/86 |
| 1806/07 | 1826/27 | 1846/47 | 1866/67 | 1886/87 |
| 1807/08 | 1827/28 | 1847/48 | 1867/68 | 1887/88 |
| 1808/09 | 1828/29 | 1848/49 | 1868/69 | 1888/89 |
| 1809/10 | 1829/30 | 1849/50 | 1869/70 | 1889/90 |
| 1810/11 | 1830/31 | 1850/51 | 1870/71 | 1890/91 |
| 1811/12 | 1831/32 | 1851/52 | 1871/72 | 1891/92 |
| 1812/13 | 1832/33 | 1852/53 | 1872/73 | 1892/93 |
| 1813/14 | 1833/34 | 1853/54 | 1873/74 | 1893/94 |
| 1814/15 | 1834/35 | 1854/55 | 1874/75 | 1894/95 |
| 1815/16 | 1835/36 | 1855/56 | 1875/76 | 1895/96 |
| 1816/17 | 1836/37 | 1856/57 | 1876/77 | 1896/97 |
| 1817/18 | 1837/38 | 1857/58 | 1877/78 | 1897/98 |
| 1818/19 | 1838/39 | 1858/59 | 1878/79 | 1898/99 |
| 1819/20 | 1839/40 | 1859/60 | 1879/80 | 1899/1900 |

#*18712.8

| 1900/01 | 1920/21 | 1940/41 | 1960/61 | 1980/81 |
|---|---|---|---|---|
| 1901/02 | 1921/22 | 1941/42 | 1961/62 | 1981/82 |
| 1902/03 | 1922/23 | 1942/43 | 1962/63 | 1982/83 |
| 1903/04 | 1923/24 | 1943/44 | 1963/64 | 1983/84 |
| 1904/05 | 1924/25 | 1944/45 | 1964/65 | 1984/85 |
| 1905/06 | 1925/26 | 1945/46 | 1965/66 | 1985/86 |
| 1906/07 | 1926/27 | 1946/47 | 1966/67 | 1986/87 |
| 1907/08 | 1927/28 | 1947/48 | 1967/68 | 1987/88 |
| 1908/09 | 1928/29 | 1948/49 | 1968/69 | 1988/89 |
| 1909/10 | 1929/30 | 1949/50 | 1969/70 | 1989/90 |
| 1910/11 | 1930/31 | 1950/51 | 1970/71 | 1990/91 |
| 1911/12 | 1931/32 | 1951/52 | 1971/72 | 1991/92 |
| 1912/13 | 1932/33 | 1952/53 | 1972/73 | 1992/93 |
| 1913/14 | 1933/34 | 1953/54 | 1973/74 | 1993/94 |
| 1914/15 | 1934/35 | 1954/55 | 1974/75 | 1994/95 |
| 1915/16 | 1935/36 | 1955/56 | 1975/76 | 1995/96 |
| 1916/17 | 1936/37 | 1956/57 | 1976/77 | 1996/97 |
| 1917/18 | 1937/38 | 1957/58 | 1977/78 | 1997/98 |
| 1918/19 | 1938/39 | 1958/59 | 1978/79 | 1998/99 |
| 1919/20 | 1939/40 | 1959/60 | 1979/80 | 1999/2000 |

CROSS REFERENCES:

1   2   3   4   5   6   7   8   9   10   11   12

# A BIENNIAL HOLDINGS CARD

## FINANCIAL CARD

The financial card is the last card under each title. It is the only one that is easily removed. It gives the title of the publication, the source, the actual volumes and dates included in each payment, if one can pin it down that closely, the number of the invoice, the date approved for payment, and the cost. If indexes have to be requested, note that. If other titles are included in the payment, note that (see also p. 45).

TITLE **Listy filologicke.**

ORDER NO **L.S. 69054**

ADDRESS **Phiebig**

| VOL. AND/OR YEAR | TO BEGIN | SOURCE | INVOICE NO | DATE APPROVED | AMOUNT |
|---|---|---|---|---|---|
| J-D, 1959 | | Phiebig | 38964 | 3/6/59 | 6.40 |
| J-D, 1960 | | Phiebig | 54205 | 3/16/60 | 6.40 |
| v.84  1961 | | Phiebig | 55504 | 8/29/61 | 8.00 |
| v.85  1962 | | Phiebig | 62321 | | 8.00 |
| v.86  1963 | | Phiebig | 70173 | | 9.00 |
| J-D, 1964 | | Phiebig | 76833 | | 9.00 |
| J-D, 1965 | | Phiebig | 86435 | | 19.00 |
| J-D, 1966 | | Phiebig | B-6298 | | 19.00 |
| J-D, 1967 | | Phiebig | B-27741 | | 19.00 |
| J-D, 1968 | | Phiebig | D9874 | | 10.00 |
| v.92  1969 | | Phiebig | D-16136 | | 14.95 |
| J-D, 1970 | | Phiebig | D-18104 | | 15.00 |

PURCHASED:

Aerospace medicine.

Includes: Aerospace Medical Ass'n.
Directory of Members.
List

ADDRESS: Faxon

| | | | | | |
|---|---|---|---|---|---|
| J-D, 1959 | 11/6/58 | Faxon | 9/26/58 | 11/6/58 | 10.00 |
| J-D, 1960 | 10/12/59 | Faxon | 9/22/59 | | 10.00 |
| J-D, 1961 | 11/23/60 | Faxon | #01772 | NOV 29 60 | 10.00 |
| J-D, 1962 | 9/15/61 | Faxon | #10370 | SEP 18 '61 | 10.00 |
| J-D, 1963 | 10/24/62. | Faxon | #26060 | OCT 24 '62 | 12.00 |
| J-D, 1964 | 10/9/63 | Faxon | #40652 | | |
| J-D, 1965 | | Faxon | #07707 | NOV 2 65 | 12.00 |
| J-D, 1966 | | Faxon | #23452 | SEP 10 65 | 12.00 |
| J-D, 1967 | | Faxon | #56010 | DEC 29 66 | 12.00 |
| J-D, 1968 | | Faxon | #79289 | OCT 25 67 | 12.00 |
| J-D, 1969 | | Faxon | 19713 | | 12.00 |
| J-D, 1970 | | Faxon | #55502 | OCT 13 '70 | 12.00 |

MEMBERSHIPS

Since memberships usually involve one payment a year but often include many titles, a device must be set up to keep track of them. See the sample of card that has proved to be quite successful. The same device may be used for "services" and "global subscriptions."

List all the titles that are to come, as well as any special directives or information concerning the membership, on the front of the short flap of a blank holdings card. This information may be checked each year with the new invoice and annual membership card for any changes in the membership. This annual membership card may be clipped to the Serials Record membership card, and changed each year as it comes in. The financial card is filed just below the Serials Record card. These three cards give the up-to-date history of the membership.

American Water Resources Association.  Library Membership.

Includes:

   Hydor.
   American Water Resources Association. Water Resources Newsletter.
   American Water Resources Conferences. Proceedings.
   Hydata.
   Water Resources Bulletin.
   National Symposium on Ground-Water Hydrology. Proceedings.

American Water Resources Association.  Library Membership.

MEMBERSHIP CARD

Certain approaches of which to be aware in memberships:

1. In a very few cases one has to pay each year whether or not anything is being published in that year.
2. A very few societies demand that the member be practicing in the special field.
3. Some societies demand the signature of the head of the library.
4. Some publications may be acquired only by being a member.

5. A.L.A. memberships. One may be (1) an Institutional member, (2) a branch member, (3) an Associate member, (4) or a Standing Order member of the Publishing Department, and still not get everything that they publish. Also there are certain publications that are given only to the officers of the association for that year. One cannot continue to receive them unless a staff member is on that particular committee each year.
6. Some memberships will also bring monographs.
7. Some memberships are unavailable to libraries.

Reasons for becoming members in certain societies:
1. Memberships sometimes reduce cost of either one or several publications.
2. Some publications cannot be subscribed to without being a member.
3. Sometimes one is automatically made a member when subscribing to some publications. (Some societies use the term loosely.)
4. Sometimes it is important that the library be represented in certain societies.

SPECIAL DIRECTIVE CARD

A buff card may be used for cross-references and such special references as "Route to Vertical File without checking in," or "Discard on receipt." In order to keep the discard cards to a minimum, a special project may be set up every few years by dating all receipts in pencil on the cards or on a slip for one year. Those cards that have no dates on the cards at the end of the year may be pulled from the file.

## Sample Copies of Issues

Sample copies should receive a fair amount of attention. First of all, check to see if the title is set up in the record. If so, send as an added copy to wherever the title is going. (If they continue to come, further decisions will have to be made to see if one may depend on the gift copy.) For those titles that are not already set up in the record, further review will have to be made as to whether to take action for purchasing, or on Gift or Exchange, or ignore altogether. However, check them first from the following points:
1. Check stencil (address label) to be sure it belongs to the Library.
2. Check the remainder to see if a change of title is noted in an editorial or elsewhere in the piece, or check any likely tools—*New Serial Titles, Bulletin of Bibligraphy.* Carry through the usual routines for changes of title.

DISCARD.

A-C views.  (Allis-Chalmers publications)

SEE:
    American Documentation Institute.  Short papers. . .

ADI annual meeting.    Short papers ...

Comes on Ass'n. of Classroom
Teachers.  Sub.

Send to Social Science vertical file.

ACT news bulletin.

## SPECIAL DIRECTIVE CARDS

3. Check to see if any other entry comes to mind, i.e., name of city, country, society, association, etc.
4. Check to see if a separate (perhaps ordered though another department).
5. Check to see if it is coming from an agent that sends out only by purchase. (Verify by writing if necessary.)
6. Check invoices to see if it ties in with any unusual title.

7. Check all newsletters, reports, and any other titles that look as if they may be coming on a subscription to some more important title or on membership. Write about them if necessary. Get decisions on how to handle.
8. Check Outstanding Special Orders Slips and Serials Want List to see if an odd volume or number has been ordered or written about.
9. Hold back any title that looks as if it needs further checking or writing about and send the rest to the Divisions for the various decisions needed. (The bulk of material should not be held longer than a week. Get through as much each day as possible.)
10. Once a week go through all problem invoices to keep in mind those very peculiar titles that could be listed under various entries.


## Material That Is Kept for Short Periods of Time Only

In order to establish a more uniform method of discarding issues of a serial title when a permanent file is not kept by the library, and to avoid the situation of discarding a number of issues at one time leaving only one issue (or frequently none) of that title on the shelf, this procedure may be followed:

A record is kept in the Division, such as a notation on shelf labels, showing the discard instructions. For new titles added, the housing area is advised of discard status by a notation on the "New Serials Title" slip sent them by the Serials Department. It is also incumbent on the Serials Department to advise the appropriate area librarian of any new or altered decision made for titles already held in the collection.

As subsequent issues of these titles are received, discarding is done progressively, rather than once or twice each year. In other words, as each month, number, or issue, is shelved, the corresponding issue for the previous year is discarded. Thus, January of 1971 is discarded when January of 1972 is shelved. A full year is thus available at all times, although not a full calendar year. In the case of a decision to "Retain current issue only," the previous issue is discarded on receipt of the latest one.

It is hoped this procedure will eliminate irregular and wholesale discards and eliminate the element of uncertainty as to when and how to discard.

The note "Keep current year only" is entered on the work slip when this goes with the first piece received to the Catalog Division. Such material is checked in on the Serials Record.

## Procedures for Ephemeral Material

There is a fine line to be drawn between what is actually emphemeral and what might be wanted in the library. It is well to keep in mind that one tries to guard against ephemeral material being set up with decisions to catalog the title and check in each piece. This is time consuming and expensive. However, don't be wastebasket happy with decisions. Lean heavily on the decisions of others in the library.

There are certain categories of material that may automatically be discarded without checking to see if they are in the Serials Record. Of course, again, every library will have its own list. Some of these might be:

Fraternity publications (Perhaps the national ones will already be set up in the record and only the local ones will be discarded).

Lists of practitioners in various fields.

Bulletins of state colleges (except those already set up in the record, such as sub-series which may be of great importance).

House organ publications.

Publicity folders.

Propaganda folders.

Compilation of laws.

Newsletters of various societies.

Financial sheets of various societies.

Church publications.

Political flyers.

## Maintaining the Serials Record

ENTERING NEW TITLES IN THE SERIALS RECORD

Temporary records should be used in the Serials Record, the financial record and all else until the official entry is decided upon by the serials cataloger. This usually cannot be done until there are some pieces on hand. When the newly cataloged titles are forwarded from the Catalog Division to the serials record librarian, they should be accompanied by work slips and the material.

The serials record librarian uses these slips to prepare the information for the typist. The librarian underlines the official entry, decides on cross-references, and writes the binding notice if needed. She notes the holdings on the work slip and forwards the pieces to their proper destination.

The typist prepares the permanent record from the work slip, and types the linedex entries if they are being used in  the library. The typist checks in the holdings on the permanent cards.

The serials record librarian then checks to see that the permanent cards are properly made out and the holdings are correct. This is the focal point of making the Serials Record accurate.

The typist makes any necessary corrections in the cards and files them in the record.

The work slips may be utilized for forwarding information and reporting to the *New Serial Titles* if that is being done by the library.

The financial clerk must correct her records to the official title.

## WITHDRAWALS

It is usual to "trace" a lost book for about a year before withdrawing and attempting to replace it. When it is decided to withdraw the book (or discard in the case of worn-out books), the "trace" slip is sent to Serials. The Serials Department notes "withdrawn" or "lost," as the case may be, next to that volume number in the Serials Record and also on the serials shelflist and public catalog if the holdings are listed there. The note is made in pencil if the book is to be replaced; otherwise it is stamped with a permanent stamp. The slip is sent on to the proper person for the statistical count.

Several occasions may arise which necessitate removal of all or part of the holdings of a serial title from the library collection.
1. The pieces may be lost.
2. There may be a change in the curriculum and one or more titles may be removed.

## Procedures

1. A decision form should be signed and filed for future reference.
2. Remove the records from the Serials Record.
3. Remove the record strip from the Division's linedex.
4. Notify the cataloger to clear the rest of the records in the public catalog.
5. Record for statistics if necessary.

## ODD VOLUMES OF DUPLICATES

These may be noted on the Serials Record, just after the volume number. If the destination is different from the main holdings, this may be noted also.

## Adding Cross-references into the File

All personnel using the Serials Record should be on the alert to have cross-references entered as needed. These are more important than those used in the official public catalog. If untrained help is checking the material it saves their time. If agents or publishers use certain casual entries on their invoices (and one cannot change the habits of these people), these should be entered. True, they take up space in the record, but they do save time in many ways.

## "Temporarily Suspended"

It is most important to get this information on the Serials Record immediately and to follow up by claiming occasionally.

## Changing from Purchase to Gift and Exchange and Vice Versa

One should establish as well as anyone can that the gift or exchange arrangement is really going to be permanent. It is much too expensive to get the purchased subscription cancelled and all the records changed only to find the arrangement is going to break down in a year or two. Sometimes, in spite of all one can do, this happens. It is most disconcerting to take the time and effort to establish a title one way, only to find the old arrangement is still in effect. Also, one may have to accept duplicates until the expiration date of the subscription, because enough time must be allowed for the cancellation to take effect. Be very sure to write a letter of cancellation and bring the records in the Serials Record up-to-date immediately.

## Changes of Titles

There are title varies, mergers, and splits in serials. All of these take their toll on a serials librarian's time but they should not be set aside for other routines. The sooner the Serials Record reflects the latest information, the easier it is for everyone. However, there are times when one cannot find out for love or money what is happening to a title. Writing does no good because the publisher sometimes is not sure himself. In these cases put temporary notes on the Serials Record and store the material for a while (sometimes for a few months). Finally the new pattern of publication will emerge. Don't be too hasty to send such titles on their way.

All the above routines have been discussed only to show what items go into maintaining a Serials Record and keeping it from collapsing. Steps of course will vary with each library.

## Checking in All Serials Other Than a New Subscription

TECHNICAL PROCESSING ROOM

(Mail is opened and wrappers are
kept with each item. Mail is sorted
onto trucks about where it will be
placed at the Serials Record file. It is
taken to the Serials Record.)

SERIALS RECORD FILE
(Students take the mail from the top
of the truck and check in all mail
that checks in easily. The bulk of
the mail is processed rapidly. The
call number is put on each piece
and this is circled if it is to go on
display. Write volume, number and
date on the outside of the magazine
if it is located in an obscure place
inside. Once the mail is checked in
it is stamped with library's stamp
[be careful where stamp is
put—should not cover important
information]. Sort according to
destination and send on to the
Division.)

MAIL THAT WON'T CHECK IN EASILY                DIVISION
(Light pencil check marks are made on the item to
indicate where the checker looked and the item is put
on the second shelf of the truck. The serials record
clerk goes through the residue material to see what she
can find, making additional pencil check marks to
indicate where she looked. If unable to find the location
of the item in the Serials Record file, a 0* is put in the
upper left hand corner and it goes on the zero
unchecked-shelf for further decisions. If the location is
found, the item is put in the file tray so that the serials
record clerk can review it for further information. The
professional librarian and serials record clerk discuss
the possibility of making a cross-reference.

*The professional librarian reviews it from all points of view, and if
unable to find its entry in the Serials Record, puts it on the "zero
checked-shelf" to go to Gifts and Exchange, or to the Divisions.

## What May Happen in the Cards

1. Even when the cards are new, neat and clean, careless checkers may soon make them untidy. (This is not so important on the "flimsies," which get changed often, but it takes continual guarding to prevent the holdings card from becoming unreadable.)
2. Wrong titles may get checked onto the card. This may cause no end of confusion.
3. They may get so filled up that, unless closely watched, items get checked in around the edges in spite of strict rules and regulations.
4. The plastic edges may break and get caught and rip the cards. (This does not happen often.)
5. The cards should not get lost if strict rules are made that no cards be removed from the record by anyone except the one person in charge. (Otherwise one will find cards in people's desks, etc. Staff members intend to put them right back, but they do get side-tracked.)
6. Material may get lost from the cards to the shelves. The records are in order but where did the piece go?
7. Small rulers, earrings, pencils may get lost in the trays!

Again—all the steps in this chapter are just suggestions. Use them if they fit the library. Use them as springboards for other routines if they suggest answers to a problem. Use imagination! There is no perfect way to conquer all serials problems, either in a manual file or an automated one. Just when one thinks the file includes all facets of serials procedures, serials themselves find new facets to create more problems!

The following sample forms are of the Serials Record checking-in cards used by the University of California, Riverside library (UCR). In size they are 6" x 4" and are the Kardex cards printed by the Remington Rand Corporation. The first three cards are printed on the back with the same information (see p. 72). The other cards are blank on the back. The fronts of the cards are self-explanatory. The last card in the group (see p. 75) is the payment record card which is mounted above the Kardex so that all the information is together.

**TITLE**

PUBLISHER OR AGENT

ADDRESS

BOUND

PREPARED

FREQUENCY  DAY DUE

SUBSCRIP. DATE

NOS. PER VOL.

VOLS. PER YEAR

IN BINDERY

TITLE PAGE

INDEX

| YEAR | SER. | VOL. | JAN. | FEB. | MAR. | APR. | MAY | JUNE | JULY | AUG. | SEPT. | OCT. | NOV. | DEC. | T.P. | I. |
|------|------|------|------|------|------|------|-----|------|------|------|-------|------|------|------|------|----|
| | | 1 | | | | | | | | | | | | | | |
| | | 2 | | | | | | | | | | | | | | |
| | | 3 | | | | | | | | | | | | | | |
| | | 4 | | | | | | | | | | | | | | |
| | | 5 | | | | | | | | | | | | | | |
| | | 1 | | | | | | | | | | | | | | |
| | | 2 | | | | | | | | | | | | | | |
| | | 3 | | | | | | | | | | | | | | |
| | | 4 | | | | | | | | | | | | | | |
| | | 5 | | | | | | | | | | | | | | |
| | | 1 | | | | | | | | | | | | | | |
| | | 2 | | | | | | | | | | | | | | |
| | | 3 | | | | | | | | | | | | | | |
| | | 4 | | | | | | | | | | | | | | |
| | | 5 | | | | | | | | | | | | | | |

INC.  TITLE

REMINGTON RAND CAT. NO. 1-2007.1 TKP 20041

| JAN | FEB | MAR | APR | MAY | JUN | JUL | AUG | SEP | OCT | NOV | DEC |
|-----|-----|-----|-----|-----|-----|-----|-----|-----|-----|-----|-----|

TYPIST PLEASE NOTE — THIS SCALE CORRESPONDS TO TYPEWRITER (PICA)
KARDEX VISIBLE

CAT. NO. 1-2007.1

✦ SPERRY RAND CORPORATION

SCALE TYPE ON PERFORATED LINE, THEN SEPARATE AT PERFORATION AND REMOVE STUB.

REMINGTON RAND
OFFICE SYSTEMS DIVISION

131

PRINTED IN U. S. A.

---

REMINGTON RAND AP 9013 E

COLOR

STYLE

DATE

VOL.

1. INDEX

2. PLATES

3. SUPPLEMENTS

4. COVERS

5. ADS

---

THE BACKS OF THE FIRST THREE CARDS CONTAIN THE ABOVE INFORMATION

| YEAR | SER. | VOL. | JAN. | FEB. | MAR. | APR. | MAY | JUNE | JULY | AUG. | SEPT. | OCT. | NOV. | DEC. | T. P. | I. |
|------|------|------|------|------|------|------|-----|------|------|------|-------|------|------|------|-------|-----|

TITLE _____ FREQUENCY _____ DATE DUE _____

PUBLISHER OR AGENT _____ SUBSCRIP. DATE _____

TITLE PAGE

ADDRESS _____ NOS. PER VOL. _____

INDEX

BOUND _____ VOLS. PER YEAR _____

PREPARED _____ IN BINDERY

INC. | TITLE | CAT. NO. 1-2006.1 | KP 20040

| JAN | FEB | MAR | APR | MAY | JUN | JUL | AUG | SEP | OCT | NOV | DEC |

TYPIST PLEASE NOTE — THIS SCALE CORRESPONDS TO TYPEWRITER (PICA) SCALE  TYPE ON PERFORATED LINE, THEN SEPARATE AT PERFORATION AND REMOVE STUB
KARDEX VISIBLE
CAT. NO. 1-2006.1

SPERRY RAND CORPORATION    REMINGTON RAND
OFFICE SYSTEMS DIVISION    131
PRINTED IN U. S. A.

---

TITLE _____ FREQUENCY _____

PUBLISHER OR AGENT _____ SUBSCRIP. DATE _____

ADDRESS _____ NOS. PER VOL. _____

BOUND _____ VOLS. PER YEAR _____

PREPARED _____ IN BINDERY

| YEAR | VOL. | MO. | 1 | 2 | 3 | 4 | 5 | 6 | 7 | 8 | 9 | 10 | 11 | 12 | 13 | 14 | 15 | 16 | 17 | 18 | 19 | 20 | 21 | 22 | 23 | 24 | 25 | 26 | 27 | 28 | 29 | 30 | 31 |
|------|------|-----|---|---|---|---|---|---|---|---|---|----|----|----|----|----|----|----|----|----|----|----|----|----|----|----|----|----|----|----|----|----|----|----|
| | | JAN. | | | | | | | | | | | | | | | | | | | | | | | | | | | | | | | | |
| | | FEB. | | | | | | | | | | | | | | | | | | | | | | | | | | | | | | | | |
| | | MAR. | | | | | | | | | | | | | | | | | | | | | | | | | | | | | | | | |
| | | APR. | | | | | | | | | | | | | | | | | | | | | | | | | | | | | | | | |
| | | MAY | | | | | | | | | | | | | | | | | | | | | | | | | | | | | | | | |
| | | JUN. | | | | | | | | | | | | | | | | | | | | | | | | | | | | | | | | |
| | | JUL. | | | | | | | | | | | | | | | | | | | | | | | | | | | | | | | | |
| | | AUG. | | | | | | | | | | | | | | | | | | | | | | | | | | | | | | | | |
| | | SEP. | | | | | | | | | | | | | | | | | | | | | | | | | | | | | | | | |
| | | OCT. | | | | | | | | | | | | | | | | | | | | | | | | | | | | | | | | |
| | | NOV. | | | | | | | | | | | | | | | | | | | | | | | | | | | | | | | | |
| | | DEC. | | | | | | | | | | | | | | | | | | | | | | | | | | | | | | | | |

INC. | TITLE | CAT. NO. 1-2005.1 | KP 20039

| JAN | FEB | MAR | APR | MAY | JUN | JUL | AUG | SEP | OCT | NOV | DEC |

TYPIST PLEASE NOTE— THIS SCALE CORRESPONDS TO (PICA) SCALE—SET PAPER GUIDES SO THAT CARD SCALE WILL REGISTER WITH MACHINE SCALE WHEN CARD IS TURNED INTO WRITING POSITION.   START INDEX 13 POINTS FROM LEFT EDGE OF CARD, USE OTHER POINTS OF SCALE FOR OTHER DIVISIONS OF VISIBLE TITLE, SET TABULATORS TO INSURE PERFECT ALIGNMENT OF EACH DIVISION OF INFORMATION.   FOLD BACK OR REMOVE STUB AFTER TYPING. USE NEW TYPEWRITER RIBBON.
KARDEX VISIBLE DIVISION    REMINGTON RAND —1   DIVISION OF SPERRY RAND CORPORATION    PRINTED IN U. S. A.
CAT. NO. 1-2005.1

74

TYPIST PLEASE NOTE — THIS SCALE CORRESPONDS TO TYPEWRITER (PICA) SCALE.   START ALL TYPING AT SAME POINT ON SCALE.   FOLD BACK OR REMOVE STUB AFTER TYPING

KARDEX VISIBLE
CAT NO. 1-0151

SPERRY REMINGTON

PRINTED IN U. S. A.

| Title | | | | | | | Frequency | | |
|---|---|---|---|---|---|---|---|---|---|
| Call Number | | Publisher | | | | | Source | | |
| | | Address | | | | | Order No. | | |
| | | Bound | | | | | Date | | |
| | | Bindery | | | | | | | |
| 01 | 11 | 21 | 31 | 41 | 51 | 61 | 71 | 81 | 91 |
| 02 | 12 | 22 | 32 | 42 | 52 | 62 | 72 | 82 | 92 |
| 03 | 13 | 23 | 33 | 43 | 53 | 63 | 73 | 83 | 93 |
| 04 | 14 | 24 | 34 | 44 | 54 | 64 | 74 | 84 | 94 |
| 05 | 15 | 25 | 35 | 45 | 55 | 65 | 75 | 85 | 95 |
| 06 | 16 | 26 | 36 | 46 | 56 | 66 | 76 | 86 | 96 |
| 07 | 17 | 27 | 37 | 47 | 57 | 67 | 77 | 87 | 97 |
| 08 | 18 | 28 | 38 | 48 | 58 | 68 | 78 | 88 | 98 |
| 09 | 19 | 29 | 39 | 49 | 59 | 69 | 79 | 89 | 99 |
| 10 | 20 | 30 | 40 | 50 | 60 | 70 | 80 | 90 | 00 |

| Inc. | Shelf | | | Jan | Feb | Mar | Apr | May | Jun | Jul | Aug | Sep | Oct | Nov | Dec | Bind |
|---|---|---|---|---|---|---|---|---|---|---|---|---|---|---|---|---|

Bound:

Prepared:

| | | | | | |
|---|---|---|---|---|---|
| | | | | | |
| | | | | | |
| | | | | | |
| | | | | | |
| | | | | | |
| | | | | | |
| | | | | | |
| | | | | | |
| | | | | | |

TYPIST PLEASE NOTE — THIS SCALE CORRESPONDS TO TYPEWRITER (PICA) SCALE.  START ALL TYPING AT SAME POINT ON SCALE    FOLD BACK OR REMOVE STUB
AFTER TYPING
KARDEX VISIBLE          ✦ SPERRY RAND              REMINGTON RAND
CAT. NO. 1-0151              C O R P O R A T I O N         OFFICE SYSTEMS DIVISION                    131
                                                                                    PRINTED IN U. S. A

ENTRY:

| ORDER NO. | BEGIN: | FREQUENCY | Publisher/address: |
|---|---|---|---|

VENDOR:

| Vol. and/or period cov'd | Date Paid | Invoice No. and/or date | Cost | Vol. and/or period cov'd | Date Paid | Invoice No. and/or date | Cost |
|---|---|---|---|---|---|---|---|
| | | | | | | | |
| | | | | | | | |
| | | | | | | | |
| | | | | | | | |
| | | | | | | | |
| | | | | | | | |
| | | | | | | | |

TYPIST PLEASE NOTE — THIS SCALE CORRESPONDS TO TYPEWRITER (PICA) SCALE.  START ALL TYPING AT SAME POINT ON SCALE    FOLD BACK OR REMOVE STUB
AFTER TYPING
KARDEX VISIBLE                    SPERRY✦REMINGTON
CAT. NO. 1-0151-D                                                              131
                                                                                    PRINTED IN U. S. A

# Automated Serials Check-in

This section is contributed by Lynn S. Smith.

Some libraries have found it to their benefit to automate their check-in procedures, a very labor-intensive function in libraries with extensive serials holdings. Automated check-in can be one of two kinds, "batch," in which information is gathered for a set period of time ("batched") and then keypunched, or "on-line," in which the data base in the computer is actually updated by the check-in operation on-the-spot. Most of these systems are home-grown varieties produced by individual libraries for their own needs, although the programming for some of them is available for purchase. The most prominent serials system available now, however, is OCLC, which was primarily designed as a commerical venture.

OCLC's Serial Subsystem is an on-line system. One must have cataloged the title in question for one's own library in the OCLC cataloging mode (see CATALOGING chapter) so that it can be checked-in. (If the library has not cataloged the item, the system will tell the operator to do so before check-in can take place.) The check-in record will appear on the archive tape, the individual inventory in OCLC of that library's holdings. In the future, the Serials Control Subsystem will have three components: check-in, claiming, and binding control. At present only the first is operational.

The check-in record contains two types of data. The first type of information consists of what is necessary to identify the bibliographic entity in question: author and/or title, key title, ISSN, frequency and regularity. This information comes from the fixed fields in the cataloging record. The OCLC number serves as a link between the check-in record and the full bibliographic information. The second type of information in the record is the local information necessary for checking-in the record.

Following is a copy of an OCLC serials check-in record. (P. 77)

The "alphabet soup" at the top of the record are, in order: ISSN, OCLC number, frequency, regularity, holding library, copy, reproduction (i.e., microfilm), subscription status (active or not), and loan period. The check-in fields are as follows:

CLNO      Call number
LOCN      Location (within holding library)
FUND      Fund
RMKS      Remarks (instructions or notes not found elsewhere)
DEFN      Definition (designation of descriptive terms of levels used: volume, number, part, etc., so that following fields may be interpreted)

The Albertan geographer.
ISSN: 0065-6097  OCLC no: 910291  Frequn: a  Regulr: r
▷ Hld lib: TRNH Copy: 1 Repr:  Subsc stat: a Loan: 1 WEEK ¶

▷ 1 CLNO      G1 ‡b .A43 ¶
▷ 2 LOCN      soc sci/hum ¶
▷ 3 FUND      Geography. ¶
▷ 4 RMKS      Vols. 1-7 have been separately pam-bound. ¶
▷ 5 DEFN      ‡v no. ¶
▷ 6 NEXT      ‡v 12 ‡d 761231 ¶

▷ Date recd:  721128  721128  721128  730507  740715  750628 ¶

▷ 7 CRHD      ‡v 8-1₁ ‡y 1972-197₅ ¶
▷ 8 RTHD      ‡v 1-7 ‡y 1964/65-1970/71 ¶
▷ 9 CLMS         ¶
▷10 BNDG        ¶

### SERIALS CHECK-IN RECORD

NEXT       Next issue expected, and date
Date rec'd  Date received last six issues
CRHD       Current holdings, usually unbound and recent
RTHD       Retrospective holdings
CLMS       Claims (not used)
BNDG       Binding (not used)

All dates are given in the configuration "YYMMDD" (Y = year, M = month, D = day), so that "721128" means "November 28, 1972."

Separate check-in records are needed for each copy of a title which an institution owns. Most of the above fields can be filled in according to the given library's priorities and preferences. This is especially true of holdings statements, which can be as detailed or nonspecific as the library wishes. Missing issues can be specified, if desired, for example.

When an issue arrives in the library and is to be recorded in the automatic check-in mode, the operator searches the on-line catalog for the check-in record just as a search is made for a cataloging record. If the issue in-hand is the "NEXT" issue, the operator instructs the system to update "CRHD" and "Date recd" and to advance "NEXT." Then, today's date will appear as the last date in "Date recd" and the issue is checked-in. However, as we all know, serials have problems and it is very possible that the issue the operator has is not the "NEXT." A different set of procedures must be followed.

If the predicted issue is not received, and the one following it is, the operator informs the system of the missing issue by "checking it in" as "missing." The CRHD field will be updated to show a gap, six question marks ("??????") will be entered as the latest date in "Date recd," and the succeeding issue (the one in-hand) will be the "NEXT" predicted issue. This can then be checked-in.

At any time the operator can override the automatic features and check-in "manually," that is, by supplying all of the information himself rather than allowing the system to do it. For highly irregular serials, this is probably a wiser route to take.

This is only a brief overview, covering the salient points of the OCLC serials sub-system as it exists now. There will be changes as time goes by, so the interested reader is cautioned to fill in and update his knowledge by consulting the *Serials Control Subsystem: Users manual* (Columbus, Ohio, Ohio College Library Center, December 6, 1975) and its addenda, as well as other communiques ad bulletins from OCLC.

## NOTES

1. R. M. Jacobs, "Focal Point," *Journal of Documentation* 6 (Dec. 1950): 213-228.
2. Andrew D. Osborn, *Serial Publications; Their Place and Treatment in Libraries.* (Chicago: American Library Association. 1955), p. 104.

### Additional References

Ohio College Library Center. *Serials Control Subsystem: Users Manual.* Columbus Ohio College Library Center, 1975.

# CHAPTER IV
# SERIALS SELECTION
# AND DESELECTION

## SELECTION

A person just starting to work in libraries will usually not be called on to be an expert on serials selection. It takes many years of living, reading, thinking, studying about books and serials to get the feel for them, but it will not be amiss to have a few basics on selection. Well thought-out principles and policies are the keywords to all library procedures. This holds true in books and serials selection as much as in any other policy, and selection is the hard core of all the library routines. It is imperative for all serials librarians, whether the responsibilities for the decisions be on their shoulders or not, to have a nodding acquaintance with serials selection. "Take away the books [and serials] and however fine the building, equipment, and staff, there is nothing. In this sense, books [and serials] selection must be the most vital operation that librarians undertake."[1]

For many years serials were given a minor role in the consideration of selecting library materials. Gradually they took up more and more attention. They possess a quality not belonging to books. They are first to cover the most recent information, which is, in itself, expanding beyond belief. On the other hand, books usually cover the same information two or three years later. Serials include every phase of interest—science, trade and industry, underground and minority groups — and all have something to say to someone. And it is just this extensive coverage that makes selection a life time occupation for those librarians involved in it. There is the need to balance judgment against the immediate and future needs of each library.

It was assumed for years that the criteria used for books would be adequate for serials. To a certain extent this still holds true, but serials also need further decisions. First of all, book selection is a one-time decision, while serials will usually continue year after year, which leads us to the cost of a serial. While a current year of a title may not seem too high, future costs are an unknown quantity. One thing is almost certain; the cost will escalate sometimes to impossible dimensions. The amount of money available presently and in the future is the first and most important factor in serials selection. "Just to 'stand still,' a number of libraries have cancelled so-called peripheral titles and put a virtual halt to the ordering of new titles other than those considered absolutely necessary."[2]

The largest libraries, and especially the university libraries, are those that suffer most. Balancing budgets against needs compel them to reconsider the earlier concept of needing everything to meet everyone's needs. The smaller libraries may well be able to hold their own still, but even here much thought must go into decisions to choose the most vital titles.

Another dilemma added to serials selection is that decisions to purchase new titles should be made immediately. It is not well to procrastinate too long to see if the title is going to become well established. That may be too late. This first year is decisive with the life of a new journal, and the number of subscriptions the first year may make all the difference on its success. Also, it is difficult to pick up these early numbers later, because cautious publishers print very few numbers beyond their subscription list, and those numbers that are found later will undoubtedly cost several times more.

Now that we have such an overwhelming number of journals from which to choose, listed in the myriads of tools—due to so many competent specialists and retrieval programs—the librarian has a broader base for selecting the best basic journals. The new tools are more accurate, include new titles sooner, and give more complete information for each title.

In spite of all this good information, there is still no infallible course to follow for serial selection. No one can defend all the choices of inclusions and exclusions in the collection, as has been said and will be brought out several times in this text. The vagaries of serials will not allow for cut-and-dried rules. It is always expedient to get in writing a firm acquisitions policy. Not that it may remain static. It should be reviewed intermittently to follow the changed point of view as new areas of interest and new circumstances become evident.

## Fundamentals

A library selection policy should have goals and objectives clearly stated. The collection development policy should include serials and should cover special disciplines, cross-disciplines, as well as general areas such as magazines, newspapers and microforms.

The purpose of each library is three-fold: educational, recreational, and environmental. The needs and interests of each community and campus are as individual as people. For each particular library the best criteria are accuracy, objectivity, and documented information in the journals, while the preferences of the local readers must also be considered.

The first and safest point, most obviously, in serial selection is to choose core titles in all departments and interests. Those titles that are indispensable will hardly be disputed by anyone. To judge what are core periodicals one may utilize various sources. These may be based on:

1. Various indexes which list those titles that are considered basic. See, Katz, William, *Magazines for Libraries*.
2. The number of times that the title is listed in abstracting services. See the Chapter on TOOLS.
3. Reviews of serials in the various subject fields.

The second point to consider is to not let your personal interests overshadow the interests of the patrons. Study the environment in which the library is located and judge accordingly.

1. In college or university and school libraries, the collection must meet the demands of the curricula; secondly, titles which cover the recreational interests may be purchased as far as budgets allow. Faculty research must also be considered.
2. Public libraries are, of course, slanted toward the community. Are the patrons business men, people of industry, housewives, youth, senior citizens? Do not slight the minority and special interest groups. Carter, *Building Library Collections*, discusses this topic extensively.

For many years, the need for a balanced collection tried to include a great deal for everyone. However, the concept of the word "everyone" unthinkingly left out several groups of people. It has only been since the collective mind of the country has been jerked into an awareness of the disadvantaged and minority groups, that they are now being considered in a new light in libraries. "What this comes down to and what is reiterated time and time again . . . is the need for the librarian to get the elevator off the middle floors and try both the basement and the top floors. The problem is no longer one of selection as much as of listening and prompting. What does the reader want, particularly the one who never, or rarely used the library?"[3]

The third point is to consider the quality of the journal. This is sometimes difficult to define. It hinges on so many facets, with each librarian giving precedence of one aspect over another.

1. The editorial staff and contributors.

   The selection of good authors and photographers is vital. Are the articles refereed by experts in their fields? Have the editors culled the ideas for the most pertinent to the subject?

2. The continuity of good editors and authors.

   The quality of a journal depends on the continuity of good editors. Some journals have mediocre years. The question often presents itself as to whether it is advisable to fill in complete runs even though some years have a changed point of view. This must be a very individual decision with each title. Let us take for instance *The Smart Set*. When it started it was a very general magazine concerning itself with the fashions of that day. When Henry Louis Mencken took over its editorship it became a literary magazine. Another example is the *American Mercury* which started out as a literary magazine and later became left-wing. Now one must decide what is needed for emphasis and not hesitate to have incomplete runs if funds do not allow "extras" in the collection.

   Another problem is that good articles get into mediocre journals and vice versa, due to the "publish or perish" point of view of the faculty. All this makes it difficult to formulate an acquisitions policy.

3. Visual aspects of the journal.

   The paper, printing, color photographs, lay-outs, are all to be included in quality. This is the single most expensive part of the final effort of a publisher.

## Aids to Check for Serial Selection

1. The innumerable tools—(see the chapter on TOOLS).
2. Abstracting and indexing services—(see the chapter on TOOLS).
3. Reviews.
4. Advertisements in newspapers and special subject periodicals.
5. Catalogs from the various publishers and agents—(see the chapter on TOOLS).
6. New announcements coming through the mails.
7. Compare other serials on the same subject.
8. Sample copies — solicited and unsolicited.
9. Subject indexes — (see the chapter on TOOLS).

0. A comparison of one's particular library against other libraries with similar interests.
1. Combined periodical exhibits at library conferences.
2. News-stands.
3. Recommendations from faculty, students and other patrons.
   All of these aids are thoroughly discussed in Katz's book, *Magazine Selection*. He has other suggestions regarding the aids.

## ources for Acquiring Serials

1. Purchasing by subscription.
2. Gifts and Exchanges, and barter exchanges with various second-hand agents.
3. Cooperative programs and resource sharing — (see. p. 85).
4. Microforms — see the chapter on TOOLS.
5. Depository for document serials.
6. Bulk purchases (long runs).
7. Blanket orders and approval plans.

## ources for Requests

1. Faculty members. It is assumed that faculty members should know their fields best and should have final say on what is needed in their own fields, but not all departments can be definitive. Preference should be given those departments that are emphasized most strongly in each particular university. But watch out for over-eager departments who may monopolize funds.
2. Book committees take some of the burden off the librarian's shoulders. This is sometimes good. More overall views may come to light with a knowledgeable group studying the needs of all interests.
3. Branch librarians and those in all departments of the library have ideas also. Listen to them. However, there should also be control placed on these requests.
4. Personal knowledge. Keep yourself aware of new titles, and their relative merit. This becomes more and more important.
5. Students have good ideas about what is needed in the collection. Listen, but control these also.
6. Groups such as clubs and organizations will bring out their special interests.
7. A suggestion box is another source.

## Duplicate Subscriptions

Give careful consideration to the question of duplicate subscriptions. How many are really needed? How far will a patron have to go for information? So much depends on the make-up of the library.

1. Material needed in more than one area, such as reference work, and different branches and special collections may need copies.
2. Should one get duplicate copies to save for binding, and use one copy for general use, which in the course of the year is apt to be mutilated or lost?
3. Should one get a prebound copy, or microfilm to supersede unbound issues? (see the chapter on REPROGRAPHY).

## Some Recent Developments in Journals and Readers

1. Interdisciplinary journals have become more and more prevalent. It becomes very difficult sometimes to place them in their proper category. They often displace the older journals which should not be forgotten altogether.
2. Most library users (as is true of the public in general) have become more liberal minded. However, censorship still is no small phase of selection. Katz, *Magazine Selection,* covers this point thoroughly.

## Deselection

At this present time, diminishing budgets have made it mandatory that librarians take a new look at selection policies, and deselection has become the order of the day. So! after building up all the criteria and considerations of Serial Selection, let me challenge you with a few comments that have appeared in recent literature. ". . . there is an increasing recognition that librarians and faculty members alike have developed highly exaggerated notions of the size, range, and depth of the library collections that are actually needed by most library users." He continues, "Studies have repeatedly shown that in general, roughly 80 percent of the demands on a library can be satisfied by 20 percent of the collection."[4]

He suggests that the economic crunch of the 1970's has lessened the number of Ph.D. candidates and research professors. That only in the largest universities does a library collection have to meet more than a very small portion of research professors' needs. In all other cases the largest percentage of professors are having to meet the teaching demands rather than delving so deeply into research. This is a very complicated issue. A lot of university administrators would not argue with De Gennero's point of view, however, and large research universities may think differently.

Publishers are the first to admit that they are profit-oriented. And why not? The whole country seems to be scheming to find new ways of getting ahead, what with escalating costs, and money losing its value so rapidly. Many publishers have searched and found what they consider a good field for their publications, and that is libraries, which they consider their "captive market." They have taken it for granted that librarians still have the same old criteria selection point of view of providing everything for everybody. Some publishers have therefore conrived ways of exploiting libraries. For several years many of them have charged libraries much more for their subscriptions than they do individuals. Other means they have used are: varying the number of volumes a year, with varying costs for each; turning many monographs into numbered series; splitting a title into several new journals. All this was done, taking for granted that such tactics would continue to be accepted by librarians.

But now the time has come for soul-searching and deselection. Librarians have finally come to the point of no return in their budgets. They just cannot spend the money they do not have. Other means are having to be explored, such as maintaining only basic journals in many more departments, resorting to more interlibrary loans, photocopying, utilizing gifts and exchanges, and resource-sharing.

However, the more deselection is practiced, the greater the need for wisdom and judgment as well as more time spent by librarians in this phase of library work. "Obviously, librarians will only weaken their collections and deprive their users if they act arbitrarily or capriciously. First, they need to do a good deal of consciousness-raising to call the attention of library decision makers, users, academies, and government officials to the crisis-proportions of the price escalation problem and questionable practice of differential pricing."[5]

## Points To Consider When Cancelling Titles

The previous idea that it costs less to let a subscription continue than to try to cancel is gone. The reviewing of subscriptions, both systematically and continually, was, for so many years, by-passed if possible by many librarians. Now frantic cancelling seems to be the order of the day and more and more the tendency is to borrow, or use other means such as resource-sharing to obtain those items that may appear to be a one-time request.

1. Call on the faculty members who are specialists in their respective fields. It might be well to keep in mind the "publish or perish" plight

of faculty. Each member is loath to see the journals cancelled that include his or her particular articles.

2. Other librarians will usually gladly give advice.
3. Check with other libraries.
4. Check in abstracting and indexing services.
5. Check the dust factor of the volumes on the shelves, or circulation records if the journals circulate.
6. Reserves and reference are other possibilities.

Then use your own judgment. Somewhere there is a twilight zone of opinion and librarians will have to face up to final decisions and review each title as it is questioned. As the years go by and faculty changes occur, or community views change, there will forever be criticism. What one person calls junk, another calls significant material. Stand behind your decisions, but be willing to admit that you can change your mind if good reasons can be presented.

The question of cancellations soon brings us to the problem of filling in gaps and back files, if and when a title comes up for reinstatement. As mentioned over and over, volumes go out-of-print almost immediately, and costs go up beyond belief in no time.

However, new revolutionary ideas are developing. The words — binding, back files, replacements — are almost becoming an anathema to the new breed of serials librarians, and deselection may be carried one step further. Such phrases as — static growth, useless, outdated collections, reprography — must be considered. "Apart from fiscal necessity (which is something we all must accept), the community college must tailor its collection to the constraints of what is generally a restricted physical location and the needs of a clientele that is interested almost exclusively in present-day materials. Such constraints do not sound all that exceptional, but in the community college they assume a special identity. There, the effort, according to a community college serialist of our acquaintance, is to produce what he calls a condition of 'static growth.' In this particular instance, the condition is achieved somewhat arbitrarily by demanding that every order for a new subscription be accompanied by a request for cancellation of one already existing. The difficulty is of course to keep the collection current and usable without at the same time allowing it to grow in size. And while the community college is quicker to discard than most of us would think advisable — it does not have to worry about any but short-term needs, and so back files become expendable quickly — its problems of acquisition and discarding are no less awkward than those of other institutions. And in one respect, that of spatial restraint, it is likely to be more hard-pressed than the rest of us."[6]

## NOTES

. David Spiller, *Book Selection: and Introduction to Principles and Practice*, 2d ed. rev. (Hamdon, Conn.: Linnet Books, 1974), p. 9.

. William Katz and Peter Gellatly, *Guide to Magazine and Serial Agents* (New York: R. R. Bowker, 1975), p. 11.

. William Katz, *Magazine Selection: How to Build a Community-oriented Collection* (New York: R. R. Bowker, 1971), p. 43.

. Richard De Gennaro, "Copyright, Resource Sharing, and Hard Times: A View from the Field," *American Libraries*, 8 (Sept. 1977): 430-35.

. Ibid. "Escalating Journal Prices: Time to Fight Back," *American Libraries*, 8 (Feb. 1977): 69-74.

. Peter Gellatly, "The Community College Copes," *The Serials Librarian* 2 (Summer 1978): 331-332.

### Additional References

Carter, Mary Duncan. *Building Library Collections*. 4th ed., Mary Carter et. al. Metuchen, New Jersey: Scarecrow Press, 1974.

LSU Library. *A Serials Manual*. Baton Rouge, Louisiana State University Press, 1976.

Osborn, Andrew D., *Serials Publications: Their Place and Treatment in Libraries*, 2d ed., rev: American Library Association, 1973.

Scott, Marion H. ed., *Periodicals for School Libraries*, rev. ed.: American Library Association, 1973.

# CHAPTER V
# FINANCES

## BUDGETING AND ACCOUNTING

Serial selection and budgeting are so closely aligned that it is almost impossible to discuss one without the other. The fluctuation of the annual budget influences the collection more than any other factor. As already mentioned, inflation and proliferation of journals are taking the greater portion of the book budget. The only defense for librarians is to approach the budget each year with much careful reviewing from all possible facets. "The complexities of the budget process vary widely among institutions, campuses, and states, of course. Be ever mindful of the multiple audiences who review the budget request, or speak in many tongues . . ."[1] Librarians are more and more being held accountable for the disbursement of their funds, so be informed.

Some libraries have set up a percentage of monies to be spent for serials versus books which corresponds to the needs of the users. It must be pointed out that when one is setting up a book budget for a library one needs to consider continuing commitment monies first, before any new money is parcelled out. This might seem like a superfluous statement, but, in fact, one library found itself with no money for serial renewals because none had been budgeted, and 150,000 worth of invoices had to be paid. This, of course, was the ultimate thoughtlessness!

It is an ideal approach to divide the allotted book budget so that serials has its own funds and system of accounting.

### Payments of New Subscriptions and Renewals

Of course every library has individual approaches and needs, in the division of funds. There are many ways of organizing the funds for serials:

1. Charge from the book fund each year for each individual title.
2. Charge one, two or three years to Departmental Book funds, then shift into a Serial Fund. This puts brakes on the attitude of the faculty regarding what is taken from their book budget, as does the number 1 above.
3. Set up a portion of the annual book budget and simply call it a Serials fund. This is the easiest from the Serials Department point of view but it puts no brakes on the ordering by the faculty. The thought is that it is not coming out of their budget.

## ADVANTAGES OF THE 3RD POSSIBILITY

a. It takes much less bookkeeping to charge accounts to just one fund rather than keeping track of dozens of departmental funds. However there is one reservation (see below in "disadvantages").
b. It is much easier to envision at a glance the entire budget encompassing serials.
c. Those in charge of an overall book budget resist the continual eating away of funds for serials.

## DISADVANTAGES OF THE 3RD POSSIBILITY

a. The faculty may feel it is not their responsibility to hold the line on new subscriptions, if their book budget is not affected. One way to alleviate this is to charge one or more years to their book funds, until they are certain they want to continue receiving the journal. Then it may be switched to the serial fund. It has been proven that this approach does deter thoughtless spending.
b. As the serial budget grows it becomes more difficult to ascertain just how much each department is spending on serials. Is the fund covering an equitable portion for each department? This is one place where automation will very well take care of the situation.

Another ideal approach is that a board of faculty members, and library representatives be appointed to discuss, and make decisions on all requests dealing with the book budget. They will be able to review and compare requests from all departments, study the need for duplicate subscriptions, and consider long runs of back files and research requests. It should be equally difficult to either add or cancel titles. Both procedures are expensive to promulgate.

Items pertaining to serials, but outside the current subscriptions, should also have their own funds. Some of these items usually account for large sums of money, which should have immediately available funds, to take advantage of bargains when they appear on the market.

These are back files, research items and reprints. Other items needing separate funds are binding and replacements.

## Formula for the Annual Serial Budget

1. Last year's renewal payments.
2. Plus total expenditures for new subscriptions actually received and paid.
3. Check on increases of large items such as abstracting, indexing and loose-leaf services.
4. Be aware of those titles that are apt to publish varying volumes, each at a different price per year.
   This is one of the most unsettling items in the budget.
5. Add 10% for other increases in price. This item grows by such leaps and bounds that it must be considered carefully each year.

## Ways of Reviewing Subscription Costs

1. Use price indexes. They give at a glance the annual increases. *The Library Journal* has annual price indexes that may help.
2. Compare accounting cards, (if the library keeps such).

## A Comparison of Costs, Showing Advances in Prices

*Chemical Abstracts:*

| | | |
|---|---|---|
| 1959 | per year | 80.00 |
| 1960 | per year | 150.00 |
| 1961-1962 | per year | 200.00 |
| 1963-1964 | per year | 500.00 |
| 1965-1967 | per year | 700.00 |
| 1968-1969 | per year | 1050.00 |
| 1970 | per year | 1450.00 |
| 1978 | per year | 3700.00 |

*Chemical Abstracts. Cumulative Indexes* (Now called Collected Indexes, and are 5 year cumulations instead of 10) (not included in subscription costs).

| | |
|---|---|
| 6th, 1957-1961 | 500.00 |
| 7th, 1962-1966 | 1800.00 |
| 8th, 1967-1971 | 2400.00 |
| 10th, 1977-1981 | 7000.00* |
| | 9000.00** |

*If paid in advance
**If not paid until 1982

The above costs are for educational institutions. Copies for industry are somewhat higher.

*Science Abstracts: Electrical and Electronics Abstracts*

| | | |
|---|---|---:|
| 1960 | per year | 15.00 |
| 1961 | per year | 24.00 |
| 1962-1963 | per year | 48.00 |
| 1964-1967 | per year | 60.00 |
| 1968 | per year | 120.00 |
| 1969-1970 | per year | 132.00 |
| 1978 | per year | 510.00 |

*Cumulative Indexes:*

| | |
|---|---:|
| 1960-1964 | 97.50 |

*Science Citation Index* — started out as an expensive project:

| | | |
|---|---|---:|
| 1964, vols. 1-5 | per year | 1500.00 |
| 1965-1970 | per year | 1950.00 |
| 1977-1978 | per year | 3230.00 |

(the permuterm index at 700.00 a year raised the cost of this title)

## Let the Librarian Be Aware of Other Hidden Costs

1. All serials grow in cost each year.
2. Even the current year will cost far beyond the subscription price in handling charges, accounting work and binding.
3. Agents have added charges.
   a. Large agents have considerable overhead, and include more added charges, but they give more services.
   b. Medium and smaller agents, having less overhead, may charge less added charges, unless they aspire to all the profit possible. It may be well to examine closely and question some of these charges. These agents may give less services in spite of large added charges.
   c. The more technical, special and scientific titles may allow for little or no discounts.
   Popular magazines give larger discounts. Large libraries will have to take into account these "mixed" titles in their review of the subscription list.
   d. It is surprising how quickly organizations, associations and a few agents will take advantage of a financial situation such as the sudden devaluation of the dollar to add charges, although the value may have fluctuated and stabilized before the year is out.
4. Items that make up added charges.
   a. The number of workers the publisher or agent needs to carry on the business.

b. The location of the publisher or agent. Is he or she located in an expensive business center, or in a smaller, less expensive area?
c. Postage — domestic publishers and agents pay less (although they are paying plenty) than international agents, sending material from abroad.
d. The number of new subscriptions the library adds each year, also makes extra charges.
e. Cancellation of titles costs something to clear out.
f. Following up on claims is expensive.

When considering other costs, in the areas of accounting and administration, do not set up more annual statistical analysis than is absolutely necessary. Too much precious staff time, too many unneeded files and lists are all time-consuming and vicious. This is a crucial point. Staff time could better be spent in claiming missing numbers — a never ending project. Following are certain statistical forms used at the UCR library:

| Serials Bibliographer | Month_____ |
|---|---|
| Searches: | Book in hand searches: |
| 8000,000 orders: | 9000,000 orders: |

| Replacements | |
| Sent | Received |
| U.S.B.E.: | U.S.B.E.: |
| OTHER: | OTHER: |

SERIALS DEPARTMENT
STATISTICS OF SERIAL HOLDINGS

PHYSICAL PIECES COUNT

A.  BOUND HOLDINGS

1.  Serials newly bound (bindery)
2.  Serials received bound (sub., backfile, bypasses)
3.  Serials received bound (gifts and exchanges)

TOTAL BOUND VOLUMES RECEIVED

B.  BOUND VOLUMES TRANSFERRED OR WITHDRAWN

TOTAL BOUND VOLUMES (reflecting A minus B)

C.  UNBOUND ISSUES COUNT (all unbound serials and newspapers)

D.  MICROFORMS COUNT

1.  Total serial microfilm received as of_____
    a.  New reels received on subscription and backfile
    b.  New reels received as gift or exchange

TOTAL NUMBER RECEIVED AS OF____ _____

2.  Total newspaper microfilm reels received as of_____
    a.  New reels received on subscription and backfile
    b.  New reels received as gift or exchange

TOTAL NUMBER RECEIVED AS OF_____

TOTAL MICROFILM REELS (SERIAL & NEWSPAPER ONLY)

3.  Total number of microcards received as of _____
    a.  New microcards received on subscription or backfile
    b.  New microcards received on gift or exchange

TOTAL NUMBER RECEIVED AS OF_____

4.  Total number of microfiche received as of _____
    a.  New microfiche received on subscription or backfile
    b.  New microfiche received on gift or exchange

TOTAL NUMBER RECEIVED AS OF_____

5.  Total number of microprints received as of _____
    a.  New microprint received on subscription or backfile
    b.  New microprint received on gift or exchange

TOTAL NUMBER RECEIVED AS OF_____

TITLE COUNT

E.  SUBSCRIPTIONS PROCESSED

1.  Total subscriptions processed as of _____     _____
2.  Subscriptions processed
    a.  New paid subscriptions                               _____
    b.  New gift or exchange subscriptions                   _____
    c.  Added paid subscriptions (backfile activated)        _____
    d.  Added gift or exchange subscription (backfile activated) _____

TOTAL SERIAL SUBSCRIPTIONS PROCESSED FOR _____

3.  Subscriptions deleted
    a.  Subscriptions ceased (became added backfiles)        _____
    b.  Subscriptions cancelled (backfile remained)          _____
    c.  Subscriptions withdrawn or transferred               _____

TOTAL SERIAL SUBSCRIPTIONS DELETED FOR _____

4.  NET TOTAL SERIAL SUBSCRIPTIONS PROCESSED AS OF_____


F.  BACKFILES PROCESSED (INACTIVE TITLES)

1.  Total backfile titles processed as of _____     _____
2.  Backfile titles processed
    a.  New paid backfiles                                   _____
    b.  New gift and exchange backfiles                      _____
    c.  Paid, gift, exchange backfiles due to ceased or
        cancelled subscriptions                              _____

TOTAL OF SERIAL BACKFILE TITLES PROCESSED FOR _____

3.  Backfile titles deleted
    a.  Backfiles activated
    b.  Backfiles withdrawn or transferred

TOTAL SERIAL BACKFILE TITLES DELETED FOR _____

4.  NET TOTAL SERIAL BACKFILE TITLES PROCESSED AS OF _____

TOTAL SERIALS (SUBSCRIPTION AND BACKFILE)

NAME _____ MONTH _____ SERIALS CATALOGING

| | STACKS | | OTHER (Reference, SpecColl etc) | |
|---|---|---|---|---|
| | NEW TITLES | ADDED VOL'S & COPIES | NEW TITLES | ADDED VOL'S & COPIES |
| A | | | | |
| B | | | | |
| C | | | | |
| D | | | | |
| E | | | | |
| F | | | | |
| G | | | | |
| H | | | | |
| J | | | | |
| K | | | | |
| L | | | | |
| M | | | | |
| N | | | | |
| P | | | | |
| Q | | | | |
| R | | | | |
| S | | | | |
| T | | | | |
| U | | | | |
| V | | | | |
| Y | | | | |
| Z | | | | |
| Totals | | | | |
| Total original | Total added gov pubs | | | |
| Total | | | | |

ANALYTICS:
  copy:
  variant:
  original:
  title:

CARDS FILED:
  public catalog:
  shelflists:

BYPASSES:

CEASED PUBLICATION:

RUSH CATALOGING:

RUSH ADDED VOLS:

NON-BOOK FORMS CATALOGED:

  microfilm:     microprint:

  microfiche:    cassette:

  microcard:    other:

CARDS TYPED:     OCLC:

  card sets:    in-putting:

  single cards:  editing:

  corrections:

  photos batched:

  masters typed:

  other:

PROCESSING:

  stamping:     added information:

  call no. change:  withdrawals:

  author-title change:  ARC:

  removal:    other:

COMMENTS:

SEARCHING:
  new titles:
  anals:
  other:

AUXILIARY CATALOGING

RECATALOGS:

UNCATALOGS:

TRANSFERS:

WITHDRAWALS:

Name————————————

Month————————————

Searches:
(Requests, catalogs, ads, form selections, proof slips, etc.)

Total:————————————

Book-in-hand Searches:
(Blanket order vols., gifts, by-passes, Abel Approvals, microcards, etc.)

-Replacements-

| Sent | Received |
|------|----------|
| U.S.B.E. (monthly list):———————— | U.S.B.E. (monthly list): ———————— |
| U.S.B.E. (individual cards):———————— | U.S.B.E. (individual cards):———————— |
| Other: (publishers, vendors, want-lists):     ———————— | Other: (publishers, vendors, want-lists):     ———————— |

98

GIFTS RECEIVED

JULY 1, 1977 - JUNE 30, 1978

| titles and/or patron | number of pieces rec. | | no. of pieces used | | number of pieces sent to depts. | |
|---|---|---|---|---|---|---|
| | unbd | bd | unbd | bd | unbd | bd |
| | | | | | | |

## Continuing Subscriptions Versus Temporary Funds

Recently many libraries have managed to acquire funds from the Federal Government and grants from various foundations. These funds are more or less temporary and vary from year to year. It is very unwise to set up subscriptions against these kinds of funds unless there is an absolute guarantee that future funds will be made available from some permanent source.

Subscriptions are a continuing process and are set up to keep coming with as little reviewing as possible. They are usually set up on an "Until Forbidden" basis and computers can accept this. There is no easy way to order on temporary funds and keep the titles coming, or cutting off at a specified date. There will always have to be a closer review of these titles. These outside funds are becoming less and less available.

### DIFFERENT APPROACHES FOR ESTABLISHING SUCH TITLES

1. Does one dare set them up to continue on a "T.F." (see p. 139) basis? Even a promise of more funds may not be fulfilled when the time comes.
2. Should one attempt to order just within the limits of current funds? Then, if further funds become available, continue on such a basis until permanent funds are actually evident?
   No matter how it is done, one must be aware of setting up a whole flock of problems and much correspondence for the future.

## CUTTING COSTS IN BUDGETING

Of course the budget is the guideline on how much may be spent, and if money is not forthcoming, it cannot be spent. However, cutting the budget on serials may be regretted in years to come. In fact, it may prove far more expensive in the long run, if needed titles must be picked up and filled in later.

### Ways of Saving on the Budget

1. Subscribe to only core journals in the least emphasized departments and interests on campuses and in communities.
2. Gifts and exchanges should be carefully considered (see that chapter).
3. Government documents might be more carefully considered. They do cover an infinite number of subjects. Many are free, and there are many ways of getting them (see p. 147).

4. Consider the "T.F." subscription basis with an agent (see p. 139). While most libraries cannot include more than one year in the budget, an agent will usually pass on to the library the advantage of subscribing for more than one year with the publisher.
5. Consider setting up new subscriptions, and cancelling once a year, preferably at renewal time.
6. Control duplicate subscriptions and keep to a minimum.
7. Review the subscription list at least every three years.
8. Consider Resource sharing.
9. Consider interlibrary loan, and other libraries in the vicinity.
10. Microfilming helps (within the boundaries of copyright).
11. Order directories every other year. This may or may not be possible. They often come every year in spite of directives and it costs as much, sometimes more, to return them as to keep them, at least when they come from far distant parts.

### Reasons for Less Funds

ON CAMPUSES

1. Enrollment decline
2. Retrenchments
3. Budget cuts
4. Closing various programs
5. Actual closing of various parts of institutions

"To be sure the acquisitions budget is among the largest, if not the largest single, most flexible pot of money on a campus and is most vulnerable at times of crises."[2]

IN PUBLIC LIBRARIES

1. Same old reasons facing all tax supported institutions. Priorities must be set and libraries are not on the top of the list for funds.
2. Inflation
3. Declining neighborhoods

## WAYS OF RECORDING FINANCIAL RECORDS

Osborn deplores keeping special records for prices. It makes just one more added step in the recordkeeping process. Perhaps it isn't as important as it has been in the past, "Now that price indexes for serials are published annually, there is less reason than ever for posting subscription payments. The same applies for automated systems; there is no gain in cluttering up the computer record for a serial by adding the billing information title by title."[3] However, special financial records may give information in support of collection development, to know what to spend on different types of materials. Also published price indexes do not give adequate breakdowns for academic libraries — although some agents may do this.

The financial record should be placed in such a way as to facilitate a comparison of receipts of issues and volumes, invoices and past payments. It is advisable to arrange these cards so that they may be easily removed from the record to enter the new information in a neat and legible manner. The Louisiana State University library files the financial card directly below all the other records in the Serials Record, and it is the easiest card to remove and type on the new information neatly. For added discussion regarding financial record keeping of LSU library, see pp. 62.

The University of California, Riverside library mounts the payment card above the "Kardex" cards, which also keeps all information together (see pp. 102). UCR has the following approach for keeping track of the costs of serials. There is a "Collection Development Profile" for each active title which gives the entire picture. It is part of the management information file of active titles called TRIP [Titles Requiring Incessant Processing].

A white sheet is used to initiate input to the automated Serials List and TRIP. (Another sheet is used to update.) The white sheet starts with a new title, goes to Cataloging, where it is filled in, and then is completed in Acquisitions before being sent to Automation for inclusion in the Serials List. The bottom third of the sheet is the TRIP and includes profiling for Collection Development, with costs and departments as well as other information of use when looking at the collection such as language, etc.

The Collection Development listings include prices, updated to the Payment Record Card (PRC).

102

UCR SERIALS– **New** <u>Title</u> <u>Input</u>

Initials & Dates:
_____
_____
_____

TRIP [ ] ¥ B G P [ ] [ ] [ ] [ ] [ ] [ ] I.D. Number [ B ] cc 11 TRIP [ ] Copy No.

ENTRY **\*AA**

Corporate entry:

Division between author & title indicated by **,//**

CALL NUMBER **\*AC**                COLOR IF BOUND:

ADDITIONAL DATA

Use field codes in order as follows:

**\*HS** – History Statement

**\*RF** – See Also

**\*RT** – Cross Reference

**\*PS** – Superseded By

**\*RP** – Supersedes

**\*AD** – Holdings

**\*AE** – Holdings

\*DA   *α···*   \*JS   *locatern*   \*JT   \*JU

99's

**CARD 2**   23 [ ]   1– Paid;  2– Gift;  3– Exchange;  4– Reorder;  5– Cancelled;  6– Inactive

DEALER   25–27 [ ]   26–29   ANALS   32–33   BINDERY PRIORITY I/M/S   35–36   53

ORDER NUMBER (start in first box)   55–69   BINDING DESIG.   72–74   FREQUENCY 76–78

**CARD 3**   COST 1   11 12 13  14 15  16 17 18 19   NO. YRS.   21 22 23 24 25  26 27 28 29   NO. YRS.

COST 2   31 32 33 34 35  36 37 38 39   NO. YRS.   COST 4   41 42 43 44 45  46 47 48 49   NO.YRS. 50   YR. PD. 51 52 53

ISSN   55–63 [ ] – [ ] [ ]   COUNTRY   68–71   LANGUAGES   72–74

**CARD 4**   *Coll Dev*   RATINGS   11 12 13   15 16 17   19 20 21   23 24 25   27 28 29

DEPTS.

104

## COSTS ADDED SHEET

| | I.D. Number | Current Fiscal | No.of yrs. | Indices, etc. | No.of yrs. | Year Paid |
|---|---|---|---|---|---|---|

## Miscellaneous Financial Topics

### Sources for Money Symbols of the Various Countries

Ulrich's International Periodicals Directory. 1932-      . New York,
York, R. R. Bowker Co.

Irregular Serials and Annuals; an International Directory. 4th ed., New
York, R. R. Bowker, 1976-1977.

### Payments in Small Amounts Outside the United States

It costs at least $1.50 or more to write a check, therefore, it does
not seem feasible to order, outside the country, insignificant, single
items that cost a small amount of money. Also, it is not legal to send U.S.
currency, and foreign countries cannot use U.S. stamps. One way to get
around all this is to ask an agent that one utilizes for larger orders to
try to locate the items and add them to a larger invoice. This is done only in extreme cases since agents do not think too favorably of this approach.

### UNESCO Coupons

UNESCO coupons may be regarded as international currency for
purchase of books and other printed matter. The coupons are in fixed
amounts, expressed in United States dollars. The following values may
be purchased: $1,000, $100, $30, $1, and blank coupons (which may be
made for amounts from one to ninety-nine U.S. cents).

In each participating country there is a body responsible for their
sale, usually called the National Commission for UNESCO. Publishers
and booksellers dealing with educational, scientific, and cultural
material will usually accept them as payment.

A small brochure of explanation may be obtained from the United
Nations, Sales Section. New York, N.Y. 10017.

### Renewal Notices

One problem with renewal notices is that the publisher will send
out as many as five or six notices regardless of whether or not the
library has already taken steps to renew the title. Each notice will announce in bold type, "Second Notice," "Sixth Notice." Publishers seem
to think that if one is good, six will be that much better. I suspect it is
just another automatic approach and that the renewals cannot be
sifted out from those really expiring subscriptions. But this does
become difficult to explain to an administrator who is very apt to

assume that something must be wrong with the subscription, if a sixth notice comes to attention.

However, the first notice should be reviewed thoroughly with the record. One may be able to pick up collapsed titles because the notices sometimes give new information from which to work. One will get information on those special approaches such as having to pay in advance, or special supplements may be needed, or changes in frequency and price may be announced.

Another problem that faces one very often is whether or not to return the renewal notice on some titles set up directly with the publisher. If one sends them in, duplicates are apt to arrive, and if they are not sent in one may very certainly get lacks. The only recourse is the trial-and-error method. Keep building up on the Serials Record and financial cards information that will help make better decisions when the same thing happens again the following year. In this way, each year the records will become more and more precise.

Another recent tricky approach is that some publishers send out an announcement to look just like an invoice. It may be for some title that isn't really on order for the library. This can get quite sticky if it is from some publisher that has very involved and interweaving titles.

When receiving renewal notices regarding the *National Union Catalog* and the *New Serial Titles*, take time to read the fine print. Here one finds clues as to when new cumulations are to come out and why one will not receive smaller cumulations because larger ones are being produced.

Some agents send a verification list early in the summer giving one a chance to delete or add new titles. Even then sometimes it takes additional letters to keep them coming.

Some agents want a list of renewable titles each year and some do not.

## Philosophy of Reviewing Payments

The philosophy that some librarians take is that it is not necessary to keep accurate financial records and know exactly what is being paid for each year, saying that it all evens out in the long run. The variation of volumes per year in some publications, along with the changes of accountants in agents' and publishers' offices, plus the ceased titles that one can go on paying year after year, to mention only a few of the ramifications of serials, make it seem doubtful that this philosophy is legitimate. It was proved that one library saved over a thousand dollars in one year with one publisher just by having accurate records.

It all depends on whether one wants to save time or money and it has been said that time is money. Each library must decide for itself.

## When to Pay Invoices

NEW SUBSCRIPTIONS AND RENEWALS

1. Pay the first invoice as soon as received because the agent usually has to pay in advance to get the title started. However, don't get so automatic as to go on paying year after year without receiving something. It is amazing how often this may happen. The problem is that one is torn between clearing up all invoices as rapidly as possible and still getting something for the amount already paid. There are a very few agents who will not allow for deletions from their invoices, nor are they too willing to give credit memos. In these cases, I have no compunction about crossing those agents off my list for further business.

2. International Congresses should also be paid as soon as feasible. These publications are published in limited editions with very few copies printed beyond the membership of the organization. The agent often has to pay in advance to get a set, and it is not fair to him to have to carry the cost for two or three years, and the proceedings are sometimes that long in being published. These proceedings soon go out-of-print and are very difficult to locate on the secondhand market.

3. Newspapers must be paid in advance. It is a government regulation that newspapers cannot be sent in the mail if they have not been paid for in advance.

4. Be certain to be on the alert for invoices with discounts if paid within 30 days. Sometimes the savings can be great.

5. Renewal billing — pay if the title is being received with regularity, whether the first piece of the new volume being billed has come or not.

6. Irregular titles — hold the invoice until the piece is received.

7. Memberships (see the section on MEMBERSHIPS).

The above points are only general guidelines. There are many ramifications. When an invoice is obviously wrong, i.e., if it is for a subscription which has been cancelled, or for dates that do not agree with the financial record, or the preceeding numbers have already been paid for and not received, then the invoice must be questioned and the difficulty explained.

Every library has certain rules and regulations to meet, and circumstances with the publishers and agents also have to be considered.

## Items to Keep in Mind When Paying Invoices

1. Has the invoice come from the proper source? It sometimes comes from the publisher when it should have come from an agent. It should not be paid, but forwarded on to the agent with a request that he send his invoice to the library.

2. Sometimes a publisher will have offices in different countries and invoices for the same subscription will come from both offices. Clear this with the proper office and note on the financial record which office is to be paid in the future. (This problem becomes confusing when certain titles have to be paid through one office, and other titles through another.)

3. Some agents use other agents for ordering titles. This really does become confusing if one is using both agents for other titles.

4. Is the invoice for the proper title? Has the title changed, split, or merged? This information often shows up on the invoice, and all records may be brought into alignment.

5. Is the invoice for the proper volumes and year? Publishers often confuse the calendar approach for expiration of titles by saying they will extend a subscription a month or two because missing numbers are out-of-print. Nine times out of ten the next invoice will not reflect this extension, and one is still on the calendar basis. This often makes the library pay twice for two or three issues, because they will probably have to be located on the secondhand market.

6. Some agents invoice for something like "V.3# per compl," or abbreviate this "p.c." or, "cpl." This means that while #1 is the only issue of the volume which has been sent, the invoice includes the remainder of the volume.

7. Note for the future any added information that is on the invoice, such as the need to order and pay separately for annual indexes (some have to be requested each year).

8. Has the cost gone up so much that discontinuance of the title should be considered? However, keep in mind that by the time the invoice is received for the current year, it is usually much too late for immediate cancellation, but the future may be considered.

9. Invoicing may be very vague. One year the invoice will list the year, the next the volume and no year. This may lead to no end of trouble. Volumes and years do not always remain the same, year after year, and if the time comes when one must account for what has actually been paid for and received, it becomes very difficult. Also some publications come out very late and unless claiming and payments are not reviewed together, the gap gets wider between

payments and receipt of publications. It is the casual listing and the too automatic approach that finally become irreconcilable. It is best to try to show both volume and year in the financial record wherever possible. If the book and invoice come together, the information may be jotted on the invoice before book and invoice go two separate ways.

0. Sometimes invoices give as the title only a symbol such as cc4. This is then translated into the real title either at the very bottom of the invoice in small print, or on the back of the invoice.

1. Publishers may also use abbreviations or the tag-end of a title, which leaves one floundering pretty seriously. Sometimes the publisher's catalog will be a help. But often, the volume has just been published and has not been announced yet in their catalog.

2. There has been a rash of new ways of complicating subscriptions — adding new subject matter, setting up different "plans," and in general, becoming so involved and creating such intricate possibilities that if one is not careful one may be buying duplicates without realizing it. All this may send a subscription sky high in price.

3. A librarian may think the entire list of subscriptions is set up with one agent, only to find that the whole list has been sold to another agent; or, certain parts of it have been turned over to someone else, without so much as a "by your leave"; or maybe some agent has become "sole distributor" for a certain title. All of this takes special letters and changing of records. Most of the time one does not know it has happened until an invoice comes in to leave everything in bewilderment.

4. If the invoice is for a new subscription, does the volume begin with the first number? Should the earlier numbers be written about? However, the publisher will often have more concise information as to what is current. It is sometimes best to be flexible and rearrange the library records to fit in line with the publisher.

5. Agents of publishers may credit the wrong account.

6. The wrong publisher or agent may inadvertently be paid by either the library, the business office, or bank.

7. Sometimes an agent or publisher has a habit of applying a check to the oldest invoice in hand against the library. Things may get nicely confused when the library thinks one title is paid and the agent has cleared another. This is especially disconcerting if one is arguing a point of non-receipt, or wrong material against the earlier invoice.

8. Two Departments in the library may be listed on the same invoice. (Hopefully each will be aware of the other.)

19. Agents may repeat charges so that unless the note "added charges" are on the invoice much writing is needed.
20. The proper material may come, but not the proper invoice, and vice versa.
21. The invoice may come months and months ahead of the publications.
22. The journal may come by surface mail and the invoice by airmail.
23. Invoices and magazines may both get lost in transit.
24. Both the journal and/or the invoice may have been sent to the wrong address. (Why the statements always get to the right place is a mystery.)
25. Does the invoice have to be converted into U.S. dollars? (one may pay much too much if someone along the way mistakes foreign money for U.S. money. Notations must be bold and clear.
26. Does the agent send deletion sheets for those titles that may not be paid immediately, but must be written about?
27. "Pro forma" invoices must always be paid in advance.
28. At times invoices are called statements.
29. Watch out for renewal notices, or blurbs that look like invoices.
30. "Hors serie" means outside series and usually means "outside the subscription price." Sometimes one gets unrequested items in this way. Then a decision must be made for the future and one must inform the publisher/agent accordingly.
31. Invoices may remain undiscovered in an issue being checked in and get to binding or even to the shelves.

## Cancellations

It is only fair to the agent or publisher to give enough time to get a cancellation through all processes. Since an agent has to usually pay in advance, the agent must contact the publisher. The agents must renew subscriptions with the publishers about six months in advance. At least two months in advance of the expiration date should be allowed, and as much more time should be allowed as possible. It sometimes costs as much as three dollars to get a cancellation, so it should not be a thoughtless decision. A publisher's system also requires advance processing. Don't be surprised if the cancelled title has not gotten out of the computer after as much as two to three years. It has been known to happen. It might be well to get a statement from each agent being used regarding the cancellation policy because it can vary from agent to agent, but the above guidelines may be a help. One agent states that "All subscriptions are non-cancellable once service has commenced" for that year.

## Credit Memos

One sometimes receives credit memos from the agent or publisher. The easiest way of utilizing them is to put them through along with an invoice of like amount or larger. Seldom may one put them through without another invoice to clear them. Therefore, unless one is using an agent continually, it is better to ask for a check rather than a credit memo. So much depends on the regulations for paying invoices in a particular library that no one else can prescribe the best way to utilize the credit.

Since agents have to pay in advance usually, it isn't fair to ask them to carry the burden of the entire cost of ceased titles when the publication has collapsed. The library has to accept some of this loss. One may sometimes ask an agent if half the cost will be acceptable and the library will pay the other half.

Sometimes one gets credit memos that cannot be used, as when a book is returned and the invoice was not paid. The publisher is simply using it as a means of clearing the books.

Always be able to answer these four points regarding questions about credit memos:

1. Was it previously paid?
2. Date of invoice?
3. Is the order still open?
4. To what fund was it charged?

## Statements

Statements are the most discouraging part of the whole payment problem. They sometimes arrive before a check has had time to get back to the publisher or agent. If payments are received by the agent after the 25th of the month, they will often not be posted until the following month's statement. This looks pretty discouraging, but the first statement need not be taken too seriously. Only when the second or third statement comes in must one begin to make a thorough review of the problem and take it seriously.

Statements often do not have enough information to lead to the proper title. In this case they have to be sent back, requesting the proper identification. One will find that more and more agents will gladly accept fixed numbers (see section on L.S. Numbers as a means of referring to orders because these numbers can be accepted in the computer).

If the checks have gone astray, the statements are sometimes the only clue to this calamity.

## Reading Subscription Dates

With the advent of computers, reading subscription labels has become somewhat of a mystery. Codes and placement of information vary with each title. The placement of information usually appears on the upper or lower right hand corner of the address label. But then it may appear on the left side. Some will code the numbers of the volume, then the month and then the year. Some will code by the number and year only. This may be misleading when number one starts in July. For example 45-70 means the expiration date of May 7, 1970, (or weeks following July 3, 1969); another example is 8-9-70 (expires August 9, 1970). Sometimes the months are listed by letters A for January , B for February, etc. Sometimes the month is just abbreviated, followed by the year so that D-70 means (December 1970). Even in one title there may be variations so that the months 1 to 10 are January to October, then N will be November, and D will be December.

## Drop Shipping

Publishers and agents often have a main office and one or more warehouses, distributed throughout the country. The books are sent from the nearest warehouse to the library, but the invoice is sent from the main office. This is called drop shipping (see Fulfillment Agents, p. 125).

## Special Items

When paying Latin American invoices, do not use window envelopes — they are apt to get removed from the mail and the checks stolen.

For payments regarding payment of invoices to Cuba see p. 136.

# FOREIGN EXCHANGE

In order to convert foreign money invoices into U.S. dollars it is necessary to keep up-to-date with the current conversion rates. These may occur so rapidly that they will often be different from the time the order is placed to the time the invoice is being paid. It is usually understood that the library will use the most current rate at the time of payment. Devaluation and re-evaluation happens every so often in the various countries and this will confuse outstanding orders. It is well to be always on the alert for this information as it appears in the newspapers, T.V., and radio.

It is customary for many institutions in America to pay the invoice to a bank in New York which in turn issues a check to either a correspondent bank in the foreign country or direct to the agent. This results in some additional charges. It is wise not to argue an invoice if it should vary a dollar or so above the original cost of the order. Bank charges are added to the invoice. The amount of the bank charge varies with the amount of payment, and may vary from country to country and bank to bank, as well as year to year.

## Sources For Current Exchange Rates

*Commercial and Financial Chronicle*
*New York Times*
*Wall Street Journal*
American Express
Chase Manhatten Bank and other banks
Foreign Exchange Traders located in the world's major business centers. They may be located in telephone directories of these cities.

## Odds and Ends of Information Regarding Conversion and Dating of Invoices

1. A Canadian dollar is different in value from an American dollar. Sometimes it is worth a few cents more, often it is less.
2. The German Mark is listed D.M. for the West German Mark and D.M.O. for the East German Mark. On the surface one might think that the rate should be different for each, but I quote from one of my German agents ". . . for all practical purposes the exchange rate between East German Mark and West German Mark is 1 for 1, that means that the price for East German publications in West German Marks is the same amount of eastern and western marks. The situation is as follows: "There is no other legal possibility for us to buy from Eastern Germany than through channels where this rate is being charged, and it would be unethical to try for other ways, since Libraries in the East depend for their acquisitions of West German publications on a clearing in the same way.

   East German Marks bought on a free market cannot be used for any acquisitions in Eastern Germany. If someone tried to buy there against cash acquired in this way, he would go to prison in Eastern Germany, and if he did so for business he would be punished in Western Germany too. So the possibility to buy eastern cash on a free market in Berlin is of no practical importance. No bookseller and no library can run such risks, and no one we know even tries it."

3. The Mexicans use the $ symbol as does the U.S. but it equals a peso. M.N. means "monedo nacional" or money of the country.
4. Commas and decimal points are reversed on many foreign invoices. Also, Spanish notation is put like this U.S. 82'78, meaning $82.78 in U.S. dollars.
5. A French franc is different in value from a Swiss franc.
6. Lit. on an Italian invoice means Lira.
7. A Dutch florin on an invoice means a guilder on most foreign exchange lists.
8. Dating is different in Europe. In the United States 1-5-71 means January 5, 1971. In Europe it means May 1, 1971.
9. Some countries have laws whereby everything leaving the country has to be paid in advance. Then once the publishers get their money, they ignore the fact that they have not sent the publications. This is good for several months (sometimes years) of letters and challenges.

India has its problems also, in that pro forma invoices must be approved by a government agency, prior to purchasing foreign publications.

10. "Crossed checks" pertain to British banks and assures extra protection to the person. The way it is done is to make a cross or diagonal parallel lines across the check. Checks drawn on any British bank in accordance with the laws and practice prevailing in Great Britian may be protected by 'crossing'. Such a crossing anticipates that the money will not be paid over the counter to the payee, but that it will be paid to another bank, or if the payee has an account with the bank on which the check is drawn that amount will be credited to that account.

English money is very difficult to discuss at the moment since it has changed from the traditional pound, crown, guinea, shilling and pence to the decimal system. It has however, retained the names pence and pound. There are one hundred new pence to the pound.

It might be well to note that the value of the pound does vary in different segments of the British Commonwealth. It is not known how soon other possessions will change to the decimal system. Australia changed even before England made the change.

The European Common Market is making its influence felt and will probably make further impressions on the book market. It has already added taxes which have raised the price of each publication by about 2%. It is not improbable that in the years to come, uniform coinage will be likely throughout Europe, and the franc, the mark, the crown, the lira will probably become as obsolete as the English shilling.

## NOTES

1. C. James Schmidt, "How to Win the Budget Battle on Campus," *American Libraries.* 8 (Nov. 1977): 569-70.
2. Ibid. p. 570.
3. Andrew D. Osborn, *Serial Publications: Their Place and Treatment in Libraries,* 2d ed., rev. (Chicago: American Library Association, 1973), p. 117.

**Additional Reference**

Katz, William and Peter Gellatly. *Guide to Magazine and Serial Agents.* New York: R. R. Bowker, 1975.

# CHAPTER VI
# ORDERING

If one is setting up very regular run-of-the-mill titles, one may place an order and set aside funds and expect to receive and pay for them in a reasonably short time. If serials were this easy there would seem little need to study about serials. However, there are pit-falls, even with regular titles. They may have ceased and not yet been announced in any of the tools, or one may be pursuing a "ghost" title, which is one that was announced but never published.

Irregular titles present special problems. They may be published very close together, but often, they could be published as much as two or more years apart. This presents problems in ordering as well as in claiming (see p. 265). One may have the most current number in hand, although it is dated five years back. If one orders the "most current number" that is the one you will receive. This causes duplication. On the other hand if one orders the "next number" it may not be received for years. It is therefore expedient to find out by letter what the status is. Otherwise you may be tying up funds that will have to be carried over for a considerable length of time, or have to be cancelled out altogether.

## ORDERING DIRECTLY FROM THE PUBLISHER

No matter how advisable it may seem to purchase all titles from one source, there are many reasons to consider ordering some directly from the publisher. In fact, there are times when that is the only way one may get some titles.

### Advantages of Ordering Directly from the Publisher

1. Some publishers will not deal with agents.
2. If a library is purchasing most of the titles of one publisher, the li-

brary might receive a discount, rather than having to pay a service charge to an agent.

3. The time span for claiming may be less between library and publisher than having to have a middle step with an agent (see Claiming).
4. Most fugitive and irregular titles are best ordered direct. Some agents refuse to accept some of these titles.
5. Memberships are often so involved that only the societies know what they are all about.
   a. Substantial price benefits are given, as well as occasional monographs if ordered direct.
   b. Sometimes one must take a membership out in the name of an individual in the library or faculty.
   c. Sometimes an individual must join and be reimbursed by the library.
   d. Memberships occasionally are automatically thrust upon a library by virtue of subscribing to a journal of a society.
   e. Libraries may become a member of a society for the "prestige value."

   It is wise to keep a list of all memberships. This is sometimes valuable in answering questions coming from faculty and administration. Show the reason why the library is a member.
6. Items that are very expensive, such as *Chemical Abstracts*, *Biological Abstracts*, *Science Citation Index*, and translations should be ordered directly from the publisher. Agents' service charges on a percentage basis can run these items up another $200.00 to $300.00 above the original cost.
7. Services
   Investment and business services are becoming more and more abundant. One cannot get information or a description of "Services" in any of the "library tools," but must write directly to the publisher. (Most of these publishers publish other titles that do get into the tools.) These services usually include loose-leaf updating sheets. Most of the services are renewed by representatives visiting the library, usually a year in advance of expiration. Some examples of "services" are:
   Prentice-Hall which has two representatives:
       (a) for Federal Tax Service.
       (b) for Personnel Management
   Commerce Clearing House
   One must sign up a full year in advance, but the title may be cancelled within a month of delivery without extra charge. After that date there is a small service charge if cancelled. The reason the

representative gives for signing so far in advance is that it saves any price increase that may occur in the meantime.

Polk Directories

These are usually ordered through the representative and are delivered by Western Union and are apt to be handed to the first person in the library that the messenger meets. This leaves everyone bewildered including oneself. These books are so large they don't usually get too lost and whoever has the bulky problem on his desk is only too happy to get rid of it.

8. Societies and Institutions also are very involved.

It is well to order all publications of one society or institution from the same place. This sometimes guards against having to deal with various sources if the titles merge. It is hard enough to have to deal with merging titles put out by various societies and institutions, but ordering all of one society's publications in one way keeps this to a minimum. Some societies will not work with agents, will not take subscriptions directly, and the only way to get the publications is to depend on announcements sent out once a year. These announcements usually come in a mass of second and third class mail, and it is difficult to recall all titles that are in the Serials Record.

9. Little Magazines

Little magazines are a problem all to themselves. These are magazines with a small circulation which must be subsidized. The audience is usually small and well educated. Often they are academic quarterlies, but may be published by any aspirant who has an urge to create a literary journal. They are usually short-lived, and addresses change frequently.

They are significant in that the first articles of many future important authors may appear in them. These journals are the only source for these early articles. These magazines have been changing from the literary approach to the "mod" set. They used to be the avant-garde of the literary world. They are now joining the current "all barriers" down approach.

They are very difficult to locate and should be ordered directly. Also one should not have to try to set them up on just a current subscription approach, but order all one can while they are available. They will not fit into any routine serial approach.

For further discussion see pp. 7-8. Also see Katz, *Magazine Selection*.

10. University Publications

The original reason for the existence of University Presses was that they would publish the more intellectual books with limited appeal.

Now even these presses have to realize a good profit. Libraries are finding it more and more expedient to resort to general over-all orders with the presses in order to get these publications (see blanket orders).

Another category of university publications are those not published by the press. These are sometimes hard to pin down, being published by various departments on the campus and even getting combined with State and United States documents, or different societies. Publication offices are sometimes vague and it is hard to find out who on the campus is responsible. Even the presses are of little help in locating anything outside their own press publications. These university and society publications have another peculiarity, which concerns binding (see p. 293). For certain approaches on how to order university titles, one might consider blanket orders (see p. 141).

11. Microforms (see the chapter on REPROGRAPHY).

### Disadvantages of Ordering Directly from the Publisher

1. To order from many publishers creates much paperwork in correspondence, claiming, and paying hundreds of individual invoices.
2. The publisher does not overprint many numbers of a title, and soon sends on to agents those left over. One reason is that storing such material is costly, and warehouse facilities are usually limited. Therefore the publisher may show little interest in following up on claims.

## SUBSCRIPTION AGENTS

The opposite side of the coin to ordering from publishers is to utilize agents. The need to have a good background on them is as important, if not more so, than any other phase of serials routines. The ramifications are legion and all phases of this topic are very well discussed in Bill Katz's book, *Guide to Magazine and Serial Agents*.

There are large agents, small agents and specialized agents, all accepting various kinds of subscriptions; and there are secondhand and antiquarian agents, specializing in back files and auction material. Few agents care to waste time on small current replacement orders, although some will do such work for some of their larger clients as a favor to them. These small items are nuisances and time-consuming with little returns for all concerned.

The number of agents is considerable although this number has been dwindling recently, which is of concern to librarians.

## Reasons for Reduced Numbers of Agents

1. With reduced budgets librarians are cancelling a great many subscriptions.
2. Scarcity of cash flow has prevented the agents from paying publishers in advance, thus diminishing discounts.

A new trend is appearing among agents. Many are now competing with each other by showing a willingness to accept almost any type of standing order including annuals, monographic serials and some government publications. Even formats are now no barrier. These may include prebound volumes as well as the various microforms. This is a far cry from the past when their interest was in the more regular publications.

It is very necessary that good business relations be maintained between agent and library. Patience, tolerance, and mutual understanding will do wonders in a field where every transaction can easily turn into a nightmare of title changes, wrong payments, and missing numbers. When librarians and agents all attempt to be aware of the limitations and needs of each other, then life will become more tolerable for all concerned.

No agent is legally bound to deliver the titles once he has paid the publisher; he need not refund subscription payment because the publisher may fail to deliver the title due to bankruptcy, or abandons the desired publication, nor does he need to make timely delivery of the title, or search out missing numbers, nor deliver claimed items. "There are too many variables; publisher, mails, too many different areas of responsibility that are beyond the agent's control."[1] Katz has a very good discussion on the legal responsibility of the agent. He also brings out the fact that most agents make concerted efforts to help the librarian wherever possible.

## Advantages of Using an Agent

1. Eliminates ordering, corresponding, paying (all creating much paperwork) to hundreds of publishers.
2. Agents will usually make an effort to satisfy claims.
3. Agents usually offer a variety of purchase plans, one of which should satisfy the needs of the library.
4. The agent orders subscriptions of several libraries from the publisher at one time. This gives advantages to all concerned. The publisher may give discounts to the agent who may in turn pass some on to the library. Because the agent makes these bulk, advance, long-term payments they aid the publisher in judging better

his future business outlook.

5. Automated assistance with collection analysis.

## Disadvantages of Using an Agent

1. Loss of personal contact with the publisher.
2. Area managers vary in different regions and an agent is only as good as service rendered.
3. An Agent, when going out of business, may turn over the entire list to some other agent who may or may not be compatible with a library's needs.
4. Services must be included in almost all costs.
5. Some agents farm out their subscriptions to other agents.

## Selecting an Agent

1. Before deciding on an agent, the librarian must first determine what the needs and types of materials and services are required within the library.
2. Which agent can most easily fulfill those needs?
3. Check carefully the promises, service charges and restrictions made by the agent.
4. Ask colleagues about what they think of an agent. Keep in mind their needs may not be your needs.

## Service Charges

There was a time when service charges were frowned on, and many libraries considered cancelling with an agent who charged service charges instead of giving discounts. That time is past and now it only remains for librarians to be on the alert and weigh the services against the charges. For every service performed by the agent, the library will have to pay. There may be a need to get quotes from different agents. It is quite ethical to request several agents to quote on a particular list of titles in order to make comparisons, providing each agent knows it is a request for quotes and not for bids (see pp. 137-9). Services may vary as much as 4% to 10% between agents on the same list. But in making judgment keep in mind the list should be the same one. Popular titles give more discount, while technical and scientific titles give very little. Take into account "mixed" lists.

Claiming influences service charges. The more claiming, the higher the service charges. Some librarians consider claiming directly with the publisher. It does save time and seems more efficient, and besides, every agent has individual claim forms, which create adjusting to each, and training each library checker. But why take on a task that you are already paying the agent to perform?

## Advantages Provided Through Agent's Service Charges

1. Claiming, as already mentioned (see p. 122).
2. The agent's title catalog is usually available free to subscribers, and is a source of useful and sometimes scarce information.
   a. Indexing information.
   b. Title page and index information.
   c. Often gives new, ceased and delayed title information. This often saves searching through the tools.
   d. Gives prices of titles which aids in decisions when encumbering funds.
3. Some agents send custom-made computerized lists of actual titles for the library, arranged for the choosing by fund, subject, department or any other special fashion.
4. A very few agents will give a "check-in" service whereby the material is checked in, claimed and the issues sent to the library, thus saving on personnel and time at the library.
5. Regarding foreign agents (see p. 128).

## One Agent Versus Many Agents

A further item to consider is whether to stay with one agent or utilize several. So much depends on the response one gets from the agent or agents. Approaches differ according to each library's needs. If one keeps adding titles to one agent's list, year after year, it may be expedient to stay with the agent even though difficulties arise, because the project of changing agents looms large in transferring and making decisions on expiration dates and payments. The trend now, however, is for a library to use more than one domestic agent.

### ADVANTAGES OF USING MORE THAN ONE AGENT

1. Allows for a comparison of costs and services between agents.
2. Agents may vie for all the subscriptions from one library. Competition is a good thing.
3. Different agents may be more successful with one type of material.
4. You do not put all your eggs in one basket.

### DISADVANTAGES OF USING MORE THAN ONE AGENT

1. It is costly to the library. One is apt to order one type of material

from one agent, thus the "mix" of titles is not so likely, which upsets the discounts.

2. Each agent has special forms for claiming, paying and follow-up procedures. This creates a variation of procedures within the serial department.

3. Agents have different ideas on returning duplicates. Some agents say to return them to the agent, or the publisher, and some say to discard. This variation of information must be kept with each title in the record. Much depends on how expensive the duplicate is.

## Changing Agents

Think long and hard before deciding to change agents. "Difficulties in changing agents increase with the number of serials involved. No matter what precautions are taken, no matter how cooperative agents, both old and new problems are unavoidable."[2]

1. Find out what is causing the problems. Perhaps the agent is having temporary set-backs that will clear. Have you taken an inward glance? Perhaps the library records are at fault.

2. Make the change at renewal time.

3. Write both agents and explain the pending change.

4. Be prepared for duplicates and missing numbers for months to come.

## Types of Agents

### LARGE AGENTS

The two largest agents in this country are EBSCO and Faxon. Both are computerized and each has titles listed that the other does not have. Large libraries need both. "As agents grow fewer and as the remaining ones come to depend more and more upon automation, the use of forms poses a real problem. When the agent will not or cannot modify forms (for 'forms' read 'procedures') to suit individual library needs, the librarian had better look for another agent or else modify methods somewhat."[3]

### MEDIUM SIZED AGENTS

Medium sized agents may or may not be computerized, usually not. They cannot handle all types of titles but they do serve all types of libraries. Some of them are international and others are not.

### SMALL AGENTS

Smaller agents can save the library money by having lower

overhead and can have a closer contact with a more personal approach. They usually deal only with popular titles and the library must usually supply much more bibliographical information to the agent.

## SPECIALIST AGENTS

Specialist agents are those that handle one type of serial, or are limited to a special subject. More and more of them are even including government documents and "little" magazines, which were previously by-passed by almost all agents. They are usually used by academic and research libraries. Some of the most used are Harrassowitz, Blackwell, Kraus Reprints and Back Issues.

## FIELD AGENTS

Field agents usually handle semi-popular titles, and the publisher also may serve as the salesperson. Many of them are independent agents, or members of schools, churches or fraternities. Their circulation is small and they usually give 30-50% discount below the publisher's retail price.

## INTERNATIONAL AGENTS

International agents usually have an excellent reputation for good service. They are not plagued with the language barriers, and have the customs regulations and currency exchanges well in hand. Large domestic agencies that have established offices in many foreign countries have the same opportunities for giving good service. However, interest is usually limited only to Europe with most of these agencies. When material is needed in areas of the world that are more out-of-the-way, the problems increase greatly. Then a librarian must turn to agencies within the foreign country and there arises the lack of communication and local information, which will try the patience of even the best of librarians.

## FULFILLMENT AGENTS

Many large publishers lean on a fourth party, the fulfillment agent, to address the mail and look into claims. Because these agents are mostly computerized, the results are not too satisfactory. Their automatic stock answers are less than personal.

## Agent — Librarian — Publisher Relations

There is a library-agent-publisher relationship that must be balanced. This is so well brought out by Katz throughout his whole book, *Guide to Magazine and Serial Agents*. Breakdowns may occur at any of the three points. At one time or another all three are to blame for problems. It is well to remember that the agent is only the middleman and usually cannot make the publisher do more than the librarian could.

For very complicated problems letters are better than forms, representatives are better than letters, and direct calls are best of all because all the information and records may be had at both ends of the line for comparison, and there is give-and-take communication. It is necessary that all three become conversant with all the reasons for breakdowns of subscriptions and that understanding and tolerance be utilized to the utmost. It is only when utter indifference on anyone's part becomes intolerable that drastic measures may be taken. "There are as many reasons for this communication breakdown as there are librarians"[4] — and publishers, one might add.

### FRUSTRATING BREAKDOWNS

#### Breakdowns by librarians

1. Librarian fails to claim on time.
2. Enters needless claims.
3. Fails to keep accurate records.
4. Holds up payments needlessly. This could be the fault of the parent institution and how it processes payments.
5. Blames agent for publisher's vagaries.
6. Fails to give sufficient bibliographical information when placing a new subscription.
7. Fails to order sufficiently far in advance.
8. Fails to check the agent in advance to see if the restrictions of the agent may be reconciled with the library's needs.

#### Breakdowns with agents

1. Agent is indifferent to answering correspondence.
2. Fails to follow up on claims.
3. Fails to explain completely the basis of some problems.

#### Breakdowns with publishers

1. It takes a publisher 20 to 60 to 90 days to process an order.
2. Some publishers will accept subscriptions only from individuals, not from agents.

3. Some organizations will not sell to individuals, or will charge libraries much more than individuals.
4. Many small publishers, usually one-person ventures, are not too business-like, are difficult about adjustments and replacing missing issues, and are slow about claims.
5. Sometimes, no purchase may be made for less than three dollars even though the item may only cost fifty cents. Some societies and publishers often charge institutions and libraries several times more than individuals. The arguments are that libraries often have to have the titles on the shelves for patrons no matter what the cost, and, too, there is multiple use of the volumes in the library which limits the number of copies on which profit may be realized.
6. Other tactics used by publishers are insisting that libraries buy everything they publish (this is true in the case of societies) in order to get the one journal they need. Some societies demand that libraries pay for the membership annually whether or not anything is published.
7. Publishers are unpredictable. One sometimes has to outguess them. They announce one title and change it, even before it is published, or the title may never really get published. This last is called a ghost title.

Their announcements of a new journal seldom give the beginning date. This is unfortunate for librarians, since they try to place their orders with precise information for agents. One never knows how long the announcement has lain on someone's desk before coming to the library as a request for purchase — was it a month, a year? If it has not gotten into the "library tools" one must assume it is fairly new — but how new?

Breakdowns with technical processes of publishers and outside influences

1. Printing problems.
2. Mechanical breakdowns of machines.
3. Paper shortages.
4. Unthinking, irrelevant machine answers by computers, with failure to follow up properly.
5. Strikes, wars, fires, etc.

Breakdowns with postal services

1. Mails are slow.
2. Packages get lost.

3. Have various restrictions.
4. Postage continues to go up, and serials are getting less and less preferential considerations.
5. Some foreign countries may or may not give consideration to libraries.

## Foreign Agents

One of the most difficult tasks a serials librarian has is to acquire foreign material (see pp. 129-37). Should one order all this material from one domestic agent, or utilize an agent in each country? Both approaches have advantages and disadvantages.

### PLACING ALL ORDERS FOR FOREIGN MATERIAL WITH ONE DOMESTIC AGENT

Advantages

1. Language barriers would be eliminated. Large agencies in this country are just as apt to have offices in foreign countries which amounts to a local agent within the country (see below). The same information is available to them and it by-passes the language problem.
2. Claiming is facilitated.
3. The agent is able to inform the library quickly of any changes in the status of titles.
4. Foreign exchange of money is eliminated. Up-to-date conversion rates and money fluctuation are at the agent's fingertips.

Disadvantages

1. Domestic agents seem to express interest in worldwide trade when sometimes they mean only English-speaking countries.
2. No one domestic agent has the answers to all information on all countries. Publishers are sometimes elusive in foreign countries.

### PLACING FOREIGN ORDERS WITH ONE AGENT IN EACH COUNTRY

Due to great distances it would be well to carry on all transactions exclusively by airmail, and insist that the agent receive and send all materials directly from his office.

Advantages

1. The agent most likely is more informed about custom regulations, proper U.S. addresses, and the many vicissitudes of sending materials out of his own country.

2. Local agents have the advantage of knowing the language and a surprising number will at least try to write in English, which has brightened the day for many a serials librarian. Large university libraries in this country who specialize in foreign collections usually have someone who knows the particular foreign language, and this is a great advantage.

Disadvantages

1. Language barriers, as already mentioned.
2. Foreign exhange and fluctuating currency.
3. Local agents sometimes have no more knowledge than the librarian about publisher's addresses, due in many cases to lack of national bibliographies, etc.

## ACQUIRING FOREIGN JOURNALS

There has always been a need for acquiring all kinds of foreign publications, but recently since so many area programs have come into being, the need has multiplied considerably. Acquiring this type of material adds immeasurably to an already busy schedule of the serials librarian. One must utilize imagination and ingenuity and sometimes unorthodox methods in acquiring some materials which are foreign, or elusive and obscure. They require all the unusual methods that come to one's fingertips. Payments in typewriter ribbons, cigars, or stationery can sometimes do wonders to unearth and bring to the library some out-of-the-way item. But how many serials librarians have either the time to spend, or the authority to break over into such unorthodox methods to go down the byways for such materials?

Many factors influence the reasons for publications being difficult to get in various countries. Librarians must be aware of these in order to use judgment and understanding, when dealing with the purchasing of foreign publications.

A very important factor prevalent in some countries is the small number of copies printed over and above the number needed for the already existing subscription list. One reason for this is economic. Lack of funds gives little leeway for expanding programs or encouragement to publishers or agents. Therefore there is a small number of publishing companies and commerical bookstores, and it is not uncommon for many quality publications to be published by banks, governmental departments and semi-public institutions, and many authors are their own publishers and agents in these countries.

Another limiting factor to the small number of copies in their subscription lists is the lack of paper. At any rate, this limited number of a journal can play havoc with getting new subscriptions started. One must wait until the beginning of the new year to be included in the new estimate for publication, or worse still, one must wait until there is a cancellation to get on the subscription list. Back issues go out of print almost immediately and are difficult to locate on the secondhand market.

Another factor that creates difficulty in some countries is the lack of national bibliographies and organized directories of publishers' and agents' addresses. If one has only a vague address there is little use of hoping to depend on an agent within the foreign country because no information is available. About the only way to get around this is to locate some library in this country that is listed as getting the title, and write and ask for information. In this way one may at least get the address and find out how currently it is coming out. This is suggested as a last resort for very difficult titles.

Other factors that create barriers to acquiring publications are tariffs, duty, shipping documents, customs formalities, exchange controls, import and export licensing requirements.

Also aligned with the above problems is the preferential or non-preferential treatment granted to libraries by postal regulations of the various countries. They vary with every country.

Censorship in many countries plays an important role both with the amount and kind of literature published and what can be exported. Wars, local dissensions, national and hemispheric political tensions all create barriers. Buildings and printing presses get blown up or burned, putting a stop to publication. Editorial staffs get included in the strife and have no time to publish, or they are put in prison, or are sent out of the country for their political views. Agents often will be unable or unwilling to deal with neighboring countries. It is curious that no sooner does a country get into the limelight than requests for the country's publications come into the library, and these are the ones that one has the least chance of acquiring. Sometimes our country sets up barriers with other countries such as the embargoes on Cuba and Mainland China. The ban on China has now been lifted, and at times, relations with Cuba seem to be easing. It seems an on-again, off-again affair.

The complicated rules and regulations of tariff, customs, and postal procedures make transactions difficult to clear in any foreign language. Business expressions are often not comparable to literary language, and the results both from the point of English-speaking people, and those in foreign countries can often become confused.

These all combine to create a very discouraging outlook on acquiring publications in foreign countries. For those few fortunate libraries in North America who have qualified personnel who can travel to the various countries, perhaps once a year, and can pluck the books off the publishers' and agents' shelves, buy them, and send them back to their respective libraries, the outlook is not so discouraging.

Some of the possibilities and suggestions for acquiring may be in order. Some libraries are using blanket orders and exchange programs in the various countries. (See the discussion on the various special programs in the section of GIFT AND EXCHANGE.)

Let us consider some specific points of a few of the countries that have difficult problems, and get a little background on the history of publishing in some of these countries.

### Soviet Union

In order to work more understandingly with Russian publications it seems pertinent to give a short resume of the history of Russian publishing, and in order to do this one must realize that the Soviet Union has always been divided into many republics. They are listed below.

1. Azerbaijan, S.S.R., Baku
2. Armenian S.S.R., Erevan
3. Byelorussian S.S.R., Minsk
4. Georgian S.S.R., Tbilisi
5. Kazakh S.S.R., Alma-Ata
6. Kirghiz S.S.R., Frunze
7. Latvian S.S.R., Riga
8. Lithuanian S.S.R., Vilnius
9. Moldavian S.S.R., Kishinev
10. Tajik S.S.R., Stalinabad
11. Turkmen S.S.R., Ashkhabad
12. Uzebk S.S.R., Tashkent
13. Ukrainian S.S.R., Kiev
14. Estonian S.S.R., Tallin
15. Russian Soviet Federated Socialist Republic (RSFSR). It is the largest republic, and the capitol is Moscow, which is also the capitol of the entire USSR.

These local areas have always been very individualistic and independent. Even during the Czarist regimes there was this desire for independence of thought. The small amount of publishing that was done was of very local interest to each small area. At that time publishing was repressed and censored for fear of anti-Christ literature. Then there was a brief period of freedom of thought with the downfall of the Czarists. As the Communists became stronger they attempted to take over the thinking of all literature, but they did not do this without a struggle. The paucity of titles of the early Communists is regretted not only by the Russians but the rest of the world. The small number of books reached an even smaller number of people so that illiteracy was appalling and the Communists were obligated to instigate crash programs. It was necessary that they attempt to curb the nationalistic thinking, and for several years there was a dismal clash of idealogies. The republics did not give up without a struggle.

TYPES OF SERIALS PUBLISHED TODAY

1. Journals — General magazines with regular frequency. Some are centralized in Moscow, but some are intended for more local areas. They consist mostly of political, social and economic journals. Both the national and local ones can be subscribed to through the Soviet export organization v/o (Mezhdunarodnaya Kniga) Moscow G — 200, U.S.S.R.
2. "Agitators" Notebooks — They are designed for party use in preparing speeches. They appear once or twice a month. They are published throughout the country and are available on subscription abroad but their interest is limited.
3. Irregular publications — They usually consist of scholarly papers issued by insitutions. These are important publications but difficult to get abroad either by purchase or on exchange basis. The number of each issue is very limited.
4. Bulletins — They usually consist of informational data to be utilized by specialists in government agencies. The bulletins control the operations of Soviet industry. Most of them cannot be subscribed to through regular channels. Those which are published regularly do not appear in the lists of the Soviet export agency and Soviet insitutions are not allowed to accept foreign subscriptions directly.

Orders for Russian journals must be placed well in advance of publication. This is one of the countries where a small number of copies is published over and above the subscription list. Subscriptions usually have to start at the beginning of the next year, or volume, as the case may be, regardless of when the subscription is placed.

No agent, domestic or foreign, has better luck than another in getting publications. It is all a matter of choosing an agent that best fits the needs of a particular library for ordering and invoicing. Don't keep changing agents for this kind of subscription. Give the agent a chance to get the subscription started. Have patience! Unless the title is listed in the export catalogs it is almost impossible to get it without special approaches for ordering, perhaps by barter exchange.

Since published material is used as an idealogical weapon for the masses, the prices are usually low and the government is willing to pick up the deficit incurred by the publishers, that is, as long as the publishers say what the government wants them to say. The best way to get many publications is on the exchange basis, but this presupposes a knowledge of the language or access to someone who does. One gets long polite letters in Russian in the course of the years and rather involved paragraphs concerning the transaction. If working on the exchange basis, it is necessary to work directly with the local agencies.

When one begins to try to collect in depth beyond what is listed in the catalogs it becomes discouraging indeed. If they are not listed it often means they are not available for export.

"In recent years the number of titles available for export from the Soviet Union has increased considerably. This is particularly true with regard to the bibliographical and abstract serials that are presently offered in a wide variety of titles relating both to science and technology as well as to the social sciences and humanities. These constitute with certain exceptions, all titles issued by organizations at the level of the All-Union government and the fifteen constituent republics of the Soviet Union. Provincial and local publications, however, are not available to foreign subscribers."[5]

## Other Slavic Countries

Everything true of the Soviet Union is also true of other Slavic countries. Subscriptions must be placed well in advance of the publication date, or the beginning of a new volume, to insure getting the first number. Again, only those titles that are listed in annual export catalogs may be gotten easily. These two problems stand out away and above other problems librarians have in acquiring library materials from the satellite countries.

## Japan

On the bright side of the picture is Japan which does give reasonably good service. Japan has a unique position of being able to deal both with the East (the Soviet Union and China especially) and with the West.

**The Peoples Republic of China (PRC)**

The years of the restrictions imposed between the People's Republic of China and the United States brought almost to a close any continuity of getting books and journals. The sources for material were through exchange or what could be found in a few new secondhand book catalogs.

"Many major university libraries in the U.S. were compelled to enter into exchanges to obtain materials not available for subscription in Hong Kong after the severe restrictions on the export of periodicals went into effect in September, 1959. This situation has been carefully exploited by the National Library which has transformed many of these libraries, through their exchange operations, into its acquisition agencies, particularly with respect to materials that are difficult to acquire through the book trade."[6]

It is interesting to note that during the years of the ban, the Peking Library, which contains the largest collection of Chinese books, maintained some connections outside the country. "The most popular room is the periodicals section. The library has 9,000 subscriptions from around the world, and many of these are from the United States, maintained without a break throughout nearly three decades of mutual hostility and distrust."[7]

Recent journals coming out of the Peoples Republic may or may not reflect current happenings from within the country. The necessity of coping with the "gang of four" dissidents has resulted in any references to them being airbrushed out of the journals. This is especially true in the glossy Chinese pictorial magazines. Where these gaps occur there are the letters XXXX noted in the margins.

Now that the ban has been lifted let us see what the picture is and what is available for export. "It may be noted that during the Cultural Revolution (about 1966-1969) many serials in the PRC ceased publication. However, after 1972, a great number of these serials resumed publication; but still, only a small number of serials as well as other publications are allowed to be exported. It is estimated that about 600 serials are published in the PRC, and only about 10% are permitted to be distributed outside of the country, most of these being in the fields of science and technology, and literature.

Since the import ban on printed matter from Mainland China was lifted in 1971, the import of Chinese publications is now considered part of normal trade and may be paid for by check or other monetary instruments through regular U.S. banking procedures. Purchases may be made directly from the official Chinese agency, the Guozi Shudian, P.O. Box No. 399, Peking, China."[8]

The major outlet in the United States for distribution of serials from the PRC is China Books and Periodicals, Inc.

West Coast Center is at 2929 - 24th St., San Francisco, Ca. 94110

East Coast Center is at 125 - 5th Ave., New York, N.Y. 10003

Midwest Center is at 210 W. Madison St., Chicago, Ill. 60606

Purchase of foreign books and serials by the PRC, on the other hand, are made through the China Book Import Corporation.

## Latin America in General

"In Latin America there have been many conferences, discussions, and meetings, both official and non-official, professional and private, to explore ways and means of a mutual understanding, while at the same time taking into due consideration the national character of each Latin American state. However barriers still persist. While many bookstores in Latin America will not bother with billing or shipping, there is at least one book dealer in every Latin American country who is interested in mail orders from American libraries, and who will provide lists of current publications which may be of interest to Latin American collections in libraries of the United States. The larger countries have several such agents whose business is exclusively dedicated to mail-order relationships with North American libraries. Although it is true that the acquisition of Latin American publications requires more than the usual skills expected of acquisition librarians, facilities now exist for any library with a serious interest in creating a Latin American collection to do so."[9]

Librarians with a need or an interest in collecting Latin American materials would do well to acquaint themselves with the organization called SALALM (Seminar on the Acquisition of Latin American Library Materials) which has become a model for other area groups to follow (see under Special Programs p. 314). SALALM has not only concerned itself over the years with the acquisition of Latin American materials but recently has worked out a system for the OCLC group by which cooperating libraries rush catalog books from assigned geographical areas in Latin America for the purpose of providing catalog copy of Latin American imprints promptly for participating libraries in the OCLC system. Yale rush catalogs all Central American and Cuban imprints as its part in this program.

When there is a need for out-of-the-regular type of publications like those published by banks, special organizations and privately printed books, one will find that while they are most willing to send their publications they will forget to keep one on their list for coming issues. For government publications one may write the ministers of the various governments.

## Cuba

The Cuban revolution has created many obstacles for United States libraries to acquire library materials from Cuba. However, these obstacles are not altogether insurmountable. The strained relations of both countries and the resulting sweeping embargoes and restrictions and individual interpretations of people on both sides have discouraged any regular interchange of library materials, but at no time did either country intend this to happen.

Small independent book dealers in Cuba that formerly exported books to the United States were among the first to feel the brunt of the revolution. They were confronted with such obstacles as (1) evidence of advance payment before an export license would allow them to send material to the United States. (2) Due to the vicissitudes of the mails, packages were never received and the transaction had to be repeated with repayment and replacement of material. (3) Communications between the two countries became more and more difficult and even more confused as a change of staff in the Cuban organization created ever accumulating problems.

It is not impossible to obtain library material but it is necessary to get a license from the Treasury Department to authorize the purchase of material. This license must be renewed annually. The source for commercial acquisition of Cuban publications is the Instituto del Libro Cubano, which will not accept U.S. money or checks drawn against U.S. banks, but libraries may deposit Canadian dollars, English pounds or hard cash of any other European country. What will happen next in Cuban relations is anyone's guess.

As far as using book agents outside the country, it is almost impossible, because most of them have ceased to exist throughout other Latin American countries. Only occasionally does one get a list from a stray agent who may be offering some Cuban publications.

Exchanges are still a major source of Cuban publications. Material being sent on exchange to or from Cuba must still be wrapped twice, the first package should be addressed to the book's ultimate destination, and the outer package be addressed as follows:

Sr. Jesus Cruz Gonzalez
Embajada de Cuba
Francisco Marques No. 160
Mexico 11, D.F. Mexico

Most of my information about Latin America and Cuba and Chile in particular was through personal correspondence with Lee Williams, Curator, Latin American Collection, Yale University Library. An enlightening article by him will be found in *Problems of Acquisition of*

*Cuban Library Materials by United States University Research Libraries,* published as Working Paper No. 2 in the book: *Cuban Acquisitions and Bibliography, Proceedings and Working Papers of an International Conference held at the Library of Congress, April 13-15, 1970,* compiled and edited by Earl J. Pariseau, and which was published by the Library of Congress in Washington in 1970.

## Chile

Chile became a difficult area for collecting during the Allende period, 1970-1973. A compilation of a Union List of Chilean imprints 1970-1973 has been published by G. K. Hall Feb. 1977. The title is: *The Allende Years. A Union List of Chilean Imprints, 1970-1973, in Selected North American Libraries, with a Supplemental Holdings List of Books Published Elsewhere for the Same Period by Chileans or about Chile or Chileans.*

## MISCELLANEOUS TOPICS

### Discounts Versus Service Charges

Discounts are a thing of the past and service charges have become inevitable. It is now only a question as to which agent will demand the least service charge in comparison to the kind of service that libraries must demand. Inflation is impartial. It strikes at everyone, even agents, publishers and libraries. There are overhead costs, and look at the cost of postage. The extra routines such as tracing bibliographical information not supplied by the librarian, cost of renewals and adding new titles annually, tracing claims, cancellations, rush service, slowness on the part of the library for payments, all create extra work, and are time consuming and expensive for everyone. To quote one very good agent when I protested a difference in the publisher's charge of $1.50 and his charge of $7.45, "Overhead on any straight transaction, without follow-ups of claims is now in excess of $5.00. . . and we try to make a profit, because we can stay in business only if we make a profit, and we can give our customers service only if we stay in business."

One must, however, be on the alert for unexplained charges by the agent. While it is difficult for an agent to give a flat service charge, especially when considering low versus high discount titles, it is most necessary to continually keep an eye open for unexplained charges.

### Bidding

The practice of bidding for serials subscriptions is a great hindrance. There is no justification, according to Osborn, for submitting a list of renewal subscriptions to various agents each year in order to get the lowest bid. In earlier years this practice was quite common but hopefully is becoming a thing of the past (except in a few states). It is antiquated and cumbersome. Serials are continuing things with idosyncrasies all their own. They do not lend themselves readily to many of the practices applied in purchasing other types of material and services. Some of the factors to be considered are:

The contents and composition of any subscription list is subject to frequent changes — addition of new titles, discontinuance of others for a variety of reasons. It is difficult to fit such material to a contracted amount in any given period, fiscal or calendar. Furthermore, many titles run on a January-December basis, while others are on a July-June basis, and still others on an October-June basis, according to the publishers' arrangement of the issues and volume designations. Many are even more irregular and infrequent, requiring particular handling.

No one agent is able to give complete satisfactory service in all phases of serials acquisition. One may be better for domestic publications while another gives better service on some type of foreign publications. There are always the instances in which an agent will have better access to some area or some field of coverage, although its general service is not strong. Again many titles can only be obtained directly from the publisher or through a membership which is best obtained directly. As a result of these factors, it would be necessary to make contracts with some three or four firms, and still have individual arrangements outside these.

There can be no assurance that the same agent will be awarded a contract on successive years, or that some agent which is unable to give consistently satisfactory service might not bid lower than the preferred and established agent. Experience has shown that in any change of subscription from one agent or source to another there always occur gaps and duplications, both in material and payments, frequently requiring several years of complicated maneuvering to straighten out. This arises from the very nature of publishers' and agents' systems for handling subscription records and mailing operations. Often the establishment of a subscription and the clarification of parts and sections wanted or available is accomplished only after lengthy searching and negotiation on the part of both the library and the agent. Any interruption of a service thus established works a disadvantage.

The overall amount of business done with any one agent does not seem a pertinent factor in deciding if that type of purchase should be subject to competitive bidding. Actually, each title purchased is a separate transaction, as in the purchase of books. Consolidated lists are submitted to the agents as a matter of ordering convenience, rather than making a separate purchase order on each title. From lists, the agents submit *pro forma* invoices covering large sections of those lists, either by alphabetical arrangement or by date of expiration of the current subscription. Again, these are submitted in consolidated form as a matter of billing convenience, rather than handling a flood of separate invoices. These invoices are only an accumulation of separate charges.

Usually the agent who gives the lowest bid is the one who is unaware of the advances in subscription costs and these additional charges will bring the costs higher in the long run. Many agents will not bid against each other.

Also, it is easier and more economical to put subscriptions with an agent on an "until forbidden" basis. This allows the agents more leeway in ordering and can sometimes be a saving for the library. Although most libraries are handicapped in that their funds are appropriated annually, making it difficult to take advantage of the two- and three-year combination of savings offered by publishers, it is sometimes possible to give the agent this leeway on the "T.F." (see above) basis and he may pass some savings on to the library.

## Quotes

Quotes are not the same as bids. When considering which agent to use, it is a good idea to compare them to see which one may work most compatibly with the library's needs. It is not unethical to write to a few agents, perhaps two or three, outlining the needs of the library and requesting information on the services given by the agent and asking for quotes on the library's list of titles. Let each agent know the request is for quotes and information of services, and let each agent know that other agents are also receiving this same request. Most large agencies will be amenable to this procedure, when they would not bid against each other.

## Unusual Arrangements in Purchasing Journals

At times librarians discover that some institution in a foreign country will not sell a publication, nor is it interested in any local journal, on an exchange basis. However, it is interested in a general magazine. An arrangement may be made with a domestic agent to buy this magazine and send it to the foreign institute. The institute will then send its publication to the local library, who in turn pays the agent for the general magazine. This may be done, but it is recommended only in extreme cases. This used to be called "Barter Exchange."

More and more domestic university publications are getting interwoven with publishers in foreign countries — some volumes in this country and some elsewhere. Added to this confusion is a possibility that they also may not be published consecutively. It often happens that they have to be paid in advance. One way to handle such a monstrosity is to set it up as if it were on subscription with the publisher, but also put a note on the serials record cards and a card in the "tickler" file to have it come up in review once a year to write for an announcement for what has recently been published. One really has the control of the subscription under one's own wing.

## Translations

It is difficult to know how to order translations. They come out from a few months to two or three years later than the original title, and are often given a different volume number.

Some translations are announced as "cover to cover." Others are a much abridged account but are longer than an abstract. This is a good reason for carrying both the translation and the original in many cases.

## Periodicals in Reprint

For various reasons, volumes in the original become irreplaceable. With the passing of the years volumes wear out and get lost, and paper disintegrates. The number of volumes published in the early years was smaller so they are less available. Several wars have wiped out volume after volume as did also poor storage of those that were left. The problem of obtaining back files was becoming serious until the demand resulted in a new industry — that of reprinting back files.

Librarians are grateful for these reprints. They make available books that have long been out-of-print and unavailable, and the paper used for reprinting is supposed to last a few hundred years.

However, every library has had a rude awakening. Reprinters have almost "killed the goose that laid the golden egg." They have at times duplicated titles with a great variation of price. Some prices are an exorbitant increase over the original. Think carefully to see if the item is really out-of-print or if by some searching on the "O.P." market one might not find the item for say $27.00 as against $125.00 a volume in reprint.

Reprinters have also announced a title years in advance of reprinting, in order to stake out a claim to it, or as a feeler to see how much demand it might have. This is all well and good, but to put it into their catalog of announcements as if it were presently available (even adding a price) is not playing cricket. So, in placing an order, be sure delivery can be made within the fiscal year before tying up funds that may otherwise have to be carried over five or six years or be cancelled.

Another very recent problem is that the reprinter will announce a title that is to be reprinted in blocks of volumes per year, but to get the reduced cost one must approve the over-all price for the entire run. Then suddenly the whole back file descends on one with no current funds to cover the entire series. Or, worse still, one has ordered only a subseries of a very intricate title, and the whole over-all series arrives. It almost looks as if it is assumed by these reprinters that all institutions are wealthy and want everything that is being reprinted and that if the library gets the volumes in hand it will find a way to pay for them.

## Special Problems Of Ordering
### Blanket Orders

Blanket orders are a type of general ordering that has become more and more prevalent in recent years, and promises to remain and expand whether one likes it or not. These agreements are sometimes with the publisher but often they may be with an agent, and although the plans are numerous they are really dominated by a small proportion of agents and publishers. One area where they are used extensively is university press material.

There are various types of agreements that may be made. The first type is the arrangement that the publisher will send everything he has published, usually in certain fields, but sometimes all his publications are included. In foreign programs, regions and subject matter are a vital concern. Sometimes it is agreed that just separate books will be sent, but again it may include monographic series. Seldom does the agreement include distinctive titles or publications with regular frequencies such as weeklies, monthlies and quarterlies. Another agreement is that materials are sent on approval to be selected and the unwanted books returned.

The advantages to this type of ordering are as follows: It provides a quick way of automatically receiving current material before it goes out of print and without having to place so many separate orders. Fewer invoices are necessary. Bulk ordering from one agent should provide a certain amount of special services. Blanket orders may cover a wide range of subject matter. The physical book in hand may help appreciably in making wise decisions in selection. Librarians are freed from spending so much time on current material and may concentrate on the out-of-print material. When printed slips or lists are sent ahead of the books, there is an added advantage of selecting more precisely what is wanted. Also in countries where adequate bibliographies are lacking, these lists are sometimes the only means for knowing what is being published.

The disadvantages are also numerous. One never can be certain how many books will come in the year, or the cost. This creates budgetary problems, which is an item to consider in years when funds are short. There is always the uncertainty of not receiving a specific title. The publisher may either send too much or too little. Much marginal material will create time-consuming decisions and letters. Blanket orders are costly, one must pay for special services. Many academic and government publications are not included. On arrival of a shipment there is much actual bulk to store until it is processed. It can happen at this point that as much typing and clerical time must be spent to fit the books into the library processes as would have been needed for the original typing of orders. It could happen also, if staff and faculty members must review the books before keeping them, that this becomes a great factor in storage space. Many duplicates may be received due to other programs in the library.

The whole subject of blanket orders is very controversial, but they have proved workable when tempered with discretion and intelligence instead of indifferent acceptance of the agents' decisions. Librarians must not lean exclusively on blanket orders for selection of current material.

What does all this have to do with serials? The fact is, only so far as a Serials Department gets involved with numbered monographic series, because as yet most actual series are not included in blanket orders. However, it never hurts to have a background in closely allied topics. One never knows when a program will broaden into everyone's province.

## International Congresses

International Congresses are some of the most difficult of publications to order. They are usually held every four or five years in a different country each time. They are usually published in the language of the host country so that one has "Proceedings" for English and American; "Verhandlungen" for German; "Comptes Rendus" for French; "Atti" for Italian, etc.

Some Congresses may only publish abstracts of the proceedings. At times they are published independently with from one to twenty or more volumes for each Congress. At other times they may be published in a number of a journal and the next Congress published in another journal. Some Congresses may not publish some particular phase of the Congress, such as nomenclature but will still number it in the volumes. There will always be a gap in the voluming of that particular Congress.

Some Congresses have published pre-conference proceedings and postconference proceedings. They usually publish field trips and separate articles. They are usually published from one to three or four years after the Congress has been held.

Every Congress is published by a different publisher and it seems best to rely on a good agent to follow up on these Congresses rather than try to keep abreast of them as they change their places of publication (see the chapter on FINANCES for payments).

## Newpapers

Newspapers with a very large national circulation like *The New York Times* and *The Christian Science Monitor*, publish a different edition for different parts of the country. Unless otherwise specified, the edition will be sent that includes the library's particular location.

However, the question often arises as to which edition is indexed. This varies with each paper and with the years. I quote from Winchell *The New York Times* "indexes the Late City edition, the edition that is microfilmed and used for bound files, but also serves an an independent index to dates and even as a guide to the reporting of current happenings in other newspapers."[10]

The *Christian Science Monitor* indexed various editions in different years. The Western and New England editions are indexed for the period January 1960-June 1961; beginning with July 1961, the Eastern edition is added. From January 1962 on, the Eastern, Western, and Midwestern editions are indexed.

## Consolidated Orders

Consolidated ordering is a system whereby the agent would hold the numbers as they are published, claim missing numbers, put on call numbers and in short make the volumes ready for the shelves. This would seem to be the librarian's dream to solving all serial problems. However, other problems would be created. The expense would be prohibitive, and the current issues would not be available for a whole year in the library. Many other problems would occur throughout the process. No domestic agent has this sort of plan. Harrassowitz, Nijhoff, and Swets, all are European agents and come as close as any, in that they do collect several numbers of intricate titles and claim the missing issues and send several at one time to the library. See Katz, *Guide to Magazine and Serial Agents* (pp. 54-55). The only other approach that comes close to this is some bookbinders (see pp. 282-3).

## Government Documents

All libraries, regardless of size or type, at one time or another must become conversant with government documents. They are overwhelming in quantity. Osborn estimates that 80% of United States government publications are serial in nature. The United States government is the largest publisher in the world and other governments are not far behind. Government documents are some of the most important source material for research information because they cover a diversity of data extensively and exhaustively. However, a mere perusal of a textbook will not suffice to make their acquaintance, and one must work with them to really know them.

Government agencies of all countries change their agency names from departments to bureaus and vice versa so often that one is at a loss to sort them into their proper entries. This means being continually on the alert for current and past changes, when checking in new material or searching old titles.

Some documents are free for the writing, some may come by depository, and some may be ordered in various ways. Those that must be purchased must be paid in advance, and many are restricted and not intended for the public. Thus, with the many ways of getting them, the only difficulty left is to become conversant with all the possibilities.

### The GPO (Government Printing Office)

"The GPO is the child of Congress."[11] It was created solely for the purpose of printing and binding the material put out by the Congress. The publications are complex, have a variety of sizes and formats — so much so, that as huge as the GPO is, it must still farm out some to be done by commercial industries. These are not to be confused with those publications put out by other agencies of the government.

### The Superintendent of Documents

The Superintendent of Documents is the chief sales agent for government publications. He is centrally located in Washington, D.C. but there are branch book stores in various cities throughout the country that stock about one thousand of the most popular titles. Commercial bookstores have little interest in government documents because of the low discount of 25% allowed by the government regardless of the quantity sold.

## Depositories

Before the printing act of 1895 government docments were disbursed with such generosity that many publications were given small importance in the eyes of the public. This generosity continued so much so that by the mid-nineteenth century public documents were being distributed to incorporated universities, historical societies, public and school libraries, atheneums, literary and scientific societies, and boards of trade. All were being inundated.

### DESIGNATED DEPOSITORY LIBRARIES

Designated depository libraries are those libraries in the United States in which certain Government publications are deposited for the use of the public. Distribution of this material is done by the office of the Superintendent of Documents. The 90th Congress enacted and codified Title 44, which gives authority for the operation of the depository program. Title 44 has been revised, the language simplified and superseded, and obsolete statutes have since been eliminated.

The list of designates is formidable. Two libraries for each congressional district may be designated by the Representative from that district (or at large in the case of undistricted states). Redistricting changes the picture. Also two libraries may be designated in any part of the state by each Senator. The list also includes Puerto Rico and the District of Columbia, Guam, American Samoa, Saint Thomas and Saint Croix, the libraries of land-grant colleges and various others including executive departments in Washington and independent agencies. It is impossible to list all of them here. There is an estimated theoretical total number of authorized depository libraries of 1,390. Before any more depositories may be added, justification must be made by the head of the library desiring it, with similar justification signed by the head of every existing depository within the district. Once a library has been designated as a depository it cannot be removed by the election of a new congressman. It remains a depository until it ceases to exist, or vacates the privilege at its own request. The Superintendent of Docments may terminate the depository only when violations exist.

### REGIONAL DEPOSITORIES

To become a regional depository a library must already be a designated depository. Regional depositories must keep permanently at least one copy of all Government publications made available to depositories, either in printed or microcopy. The only exceptions allowed by the present law are superseded publications and those issued later in bound form, which may be discarded as authorized by the Superintendent of Documents. Regional depositories must provide interlibrary loan and reference service within the area that they serve, and they must assist regular depository libraries, in the disposal of unwanted Government publications which have been retained for at least five years by the regular depositories. These publications are offered first to other depository libraries within the area, then to libraries, and if the documents are still not wanted they may be discarded.

## TYPES OF MATERIAL FURNISHED

Depository libraries may receive one copy of all publications of the United States Government, except those that are judged to be for official use only, or for strictly administrative purposes which have no public or educational value, and those that are classified for reasons of security. Also excluded are those publications that must be self-sustaining and therefore must be sold. These include certain publications of the Library of Congress and the National Technical Information Service.

## SELECTIVE PLAN

Formerly the depositories were compelled to receive the whole output of available publications of the Government Printing Office. This was an overwhelming amount of material to sort and store. At present the designated depository libraries have been granted the privilege of selecting those public documents most suitable for their libraries. The selection is made from a list furnished all depositories for their use in making selections. The list is revised in card form as new series are begun or new agencies are established. These cards are furnished in duplicate and selection is made by returning one copy of the card to the Superintendent of Documents. The request for this material must be made in advance of printing. This selection privilege makes a saving for the libraries in time and storage space, and the necessary advance request saves the government in the cost that would be needed in over-printing copies. The only drawback is that since only sufficient copies are provided, there is no retroactive distribution available for libraries needing back issues.

## Non-GPO Publications

Publications printed and processed by executive and independent agencies in Washington and field offices have their own printing or mimeographing equipment or may send them out on contract. If the

Public Documents library received a copy it is indexed in the *Monthly Catalog*. Also those not listed here may be found in the publication: *Non-GPO Imprints Received in the Library of Congress in [year]: A Selective Checklist*.

There is a "twilight zone" between what depositories may get of non-GPO and even GPO publications. "Every publication listed in the *Monthly Catalog* which is not indicated by the 'dot' or 'bullet' symbol (•) must be procured by other than depository means."[12]

Many of the non-depository publications may be obtained free from the issuing agencies, or from one's elected representatives. Although this is a good source, one should be careful not to over-work this privilege.

Then there is still a group that remains elusive and difficult to locate. A few commercial firms have tried to fill the gap, but their prices are usually exorbitant. Two sources are available, and neither one offers what the other does.

The first is the National Technical Information Service (NTIS) formerly known as the Clearinghouse for Federal Scientific & Technical Information. These publications are listed in the *Monthly Catalog* and are indicated by an "at" sign (@).

The second is the Documents Expediting Project, familiarly known as "Doc Ex." This is now managed by the Federal Documents section of the Library of Congress Exchange & Gift Division. There are four principal services available.

1. Current — for elusive material.
2. Special requests which deal with out-of-print material.
3. Agency mailing lists. Subscribers may be placed on a mailing list to receive specific serial publications and committee calendars.
4. Special offers of older congressional publications. These are distributed on a first-come-first-serve basis.

Membership is on an annual basis and fees are computed on a sliding scale depending on the quantity of materials distributed.

## Other Methods of Acquiring Material

Smaller libraries also have certain means of acquiring non-depository publications. Larger libraries may also use these means to a certain extent.

### COUPONS

These may be purchased in the value of five-cent denomination per coupon from the Superintendent of Documents. These are used for the less expensive pamphlets.

## Deposit Account

Most libraries use this convenient manner of non-depository material. The library may open an account for a minimum of $25.00. The library is sent a supply of Deposit Order Blanks. Periodicals must be ordered by themselves. When the amount runs low, the library simply builds up the account by sending in a new money order.

# Various Files Connected With Ordering

At this point it usually seems necessary to build up special files. At no other place in all the serials routines does one have so many possibilities to consider that will not fit into the Serials Record. All one can do is to make special notations showing in the file that work is being done to acquire the various kinds of purchases.

### Publishers' and Agents' Lists

It is often a great convenience to have every purchased title anchored in such a way as to know the source of one's purchase. So many agents and publishers are very prone to be casual with their entries on invoices and letters and statements, and therefore it is at times almost impossible to pull the correct entry out of a very large file. To simplify the problem somewhat, one may resort to agents' and publishers' lists filed in loose-leaf binders. If each entry is separated by about six lines, one will be able to enter new titles without having to re-type the list too often. A card file would serve the same purpose. These lists may be set up when a great many titles are purchased from one agent or publisher.

Here again, some librarians question the validity of such an approach, saying it is just another file to maintain. If the agent or the publisher does not give the full title of a publication, why not just send it back to him with a short note? However, there will be many notes passing back and forth between the library and publishers, or agents, because abbreviated or garbled titles are continually being sent. Perhaps, if every library in the country continued to hand back such titles, it might result in eliminating the problem.

There are other uses for such a file as mentioned above. Some agents request these lists for checking purposes each year for renewals. The larger agents do not require this sort of check-up because their computers (hopefully?) give the same information.

It is at times very convenient to have at one's fingertips the titles that are listed with each agent. Sometimes in very dire circumstances, one decides to change from one agent to another. This decision should be made only in very rare cases. Also, it has been known to happen that an agent will turn over all, or a partial, subscription list to another agent. It becomes most necessary to follow up on missing volumes and numbers with each agent. Often, neither agent will consider himself responsible for the gaps resulting from such a change. It may also be necessary to change the "source" on the Serials Record cards. If one has ever spent hours upon hours tracing this information through a Serials Record of some 50,000 cards, one will never again let this information slip out of one's fingers. This is the sort of list that could be put into a computer with great success.

## Direct Renewal File

If only one or two titles are being purchased from one source one may put these on 3" x 5" cards and refer to them as the Direct Renewal file. These cards are a help in claiming (see the section on claiming).

This file may also be used as a "tickler" file. More and more publishers will not work with agents and will not accept subscriptions, and insist on payment in advance, and a way must be devised to bring these titles to mind at least once a year. A card may be filed in this file to come up for such a review.

One way of keeping up with these cards is to flag with a colored tab, one color for each month. Each title is reviewed at about a month after it is due. If all is well, it is dated and "okayed." If it must be written about, this is noted on the card and re-flagged with the color that will bring it up for another review the next month.

ORDER ANNUALLY

AMERICAN ANTIQUARIAN SOCIETY, WORCESTER MASSACHUSETTS. PROCEEDINGS.

American Antiquarian Society
Worcester, Massachusetts  01609

*ok 5-8-68*
*ok 5-19-69*
*wrote 5-3-70*

Semiannual

"Over 60 percent of the libraries follow through themselves by using first-of-the-month renewal files, notations on calendars, flags, tickler systems, looseleaf books, notations on cards and a variety of other home remedies."[13]

## New Serial Title Slips File

One way of keeping track of subscriptions that have not yet started to come to the library is to utilize a separate file. So many subscriptions need to be followed up for three or four years, or even longer, before they actually start coming. To lean exclusively on routine claiming through the Serials Record is to sometimes lose track of the title altogether. These titles need to be reviewed often through more current tools, or special letters need to be written, or they may even need to be changed to a different agent. There are those librarians who say that when a library pays for service, it should get service, no ands, buts, or ifs about it. I would like to know how to get action sometimes — take a plane? Sometimes I wish I could!

There are those librarians who say that if you have a copy of the order slip in the Serials Record, you don't need such a file and claiming can be maintained in the normal way. However, it all depends on how well-trained the claimers are to handle the different approaches needed to stir up the title because it often becomes more than automatic claiming. Perhaps checking in more recent tools is needed for additional information — the title may have ceased, or the title or publisher may have changed and the computers and agents have not yet caught up with it.

A file of this sort seldom builds up to more than 400 to 500 titles and it is much easier to check a small file two or three times a year than to wade through 17,000 titles in the Serials Record.

The slips in this file may include: the date the subscription was ordered; the beginning date of the publication; the beginning date of the subscription; fund; person requesting the subscription; the L.S. number (see p. 154), and the agent or publisher.

```
New Serial Title              April 1, 1970

Industrial Minerals.
1967-


                   To begin:  1970-
                   Fund:  8802
                   Dixon, L.


                   IS 700074

Stevens & Brown
```

One may go a step further with this slip. When the first piece of the subscription is received, this may be noted on the slip, and the count of received titles, minus the number of cancelled subscriptions for the year, may be added to the count of total previous titles and this will keep the statistical count of current titles in balance.

Different copies of this same slip may be utilized for other purposes. The second copy of the new serial slip may go to the financial clerk to add the title to the agent's list or make a direct renewal card and a financial card.

The third slip may be sent to the division in the library to let librarians know when action has been taken on the subscription request.

The fourth slip may be given to the Search Department with a stamp on it to show that the back file is requested (if this is the case).

Here again is a lot of detail that one may question, as to whether all these steps are really needed in each library. Keep in mind that the more anchored a title is when it is first put into the record, the less likely it is to collapse and leave loose ends throughout the years.

If one's routines are simple enough, and the rest of the library will depend on the fact that the Serials Department is on its toes (I find they sometimes need convincing when their pet title is not forthcoming immediately); if claiming new subscriptions has been conquered, then the above routines may be superfluous. An alternative would be to lean on the new title subscription slip which has, of course, been put into the record in either routine. Titles may be counted when the permanent cards are typed, and an extra file may be eliminated in the Department.

## Agents' Cards

One may keep a small card file of agents most used for lacks. If responses are noted and dated, it gives a clue to the kind of material for which each agent has an interest. Also, one may get a very enthusiastic response, or on the other hand, nothing but indifference. Agents change their viewpoint from decade to decade, so keep it up-to-date.

## Outstanding Special Orders File

All special orders (which are those for anything except current subscriptions) may be noted on the library's own special order forms or on 3" x 5" slips and filed in the Outstanding Order file. Items that are not of enough importance to check into the Serials Record or be cataloged, but must be ordered, must have a slip that is anchored in some way so that the piece will not slip through into the "zero" material (see p. 312). Usually this type of material is for a title that is not in the record. This slip may be filed in this file.

## Want List File

The Want List file is the catch-all file for all information regarding lacks. The titles may be entered on 3" x 5" cards. The file may be set up on a priority basis, for those "Titles most desired," "Less needed," and "To be considered." Then as funds become available, one has already made decisions regarding the titles.

Also, this file may include items that might be located on Exchange lists that are received from other libraries. Flag these slips so they will not become confused with the titles that must be purchased. These lists must be checked within two or three days. If they cannot be checked in that time, throw them in the wastebasket. Some other library will have requested the items. Another source for gift and exchange items is to write the main libraries within the state of publication. They may have duplicates but do not send out lists.

Now, one is ready to consider the best methods for acquiring the titles that must be purchased. Often the first source is to write the publisher. If he does not have the number/s available then it sometimes becomes a long-time project to locate the material.

Secondhand catalogs are always a good source. Check the slips in the file against the secondhand catalogs immediately as these come into the library. This holds as true with these as with the Gift and Exchange lists. If the catalog remains in the library more than a week one may be fairly certain that some other library has already placed the order. It is sometimes necessary to send a night letter asking the agent to hold the material until an order can follow, or one may actually place a firm order by telegram.

The next best source is to send out lists to interested agents. Whenever one sends these lists, it is well to remember that long, tightly typed lists will probably go right into the agent's wastebasket on arrival. This sort of list is almost impossible. Instead, break the list into short parts and at least double space between each title. This gives the agent space to make notations and the list is much easier on the eye.

Various agents or booksellers may specialize according to language, subject, location, or type of publication. Know the agents and keep track of their responses.

Make at least six copies of the list in addition to the original. Number the list so that it can be distinguished from other lists previously sent. Send out one copy at a time. Use one copy as a master list and note on it the date and name of agent. As orders are filled, cross those titles off the master list and remaining copies.

Record on the back of the Want card that it is on Want List #____ and the date. All action taken may be noted to show what efforts have been made to obtain the material.

Also, a notation of costs of already received volumes will give a clue on what might be a reasonable cost for other volumes. Or, compare the cost with a current price, i.e., by consulting the financial record card in the Serials Record. A mark-up of 100% is sometimes not unusual. One of the greatest difficulties is to know if the price is right. So much depends on the need in the library, the space available for back files, the difficulty of locating, and the availability of the material. Can it be gotten cheaper in reprint? Can it be used on microfilm? As in all commodities, prices change rapidly in the book market. Can the material be borrowed and microfilmed in one's own library, or is it impossible to be sent through mails? Some libraries will not send journals through the mail. Is it a rarity for the library? Rarity for rarity's sake sometimes must be considered carefully for libraries with restricted funds.

To keep the Want List files current, flag down the cards with colored tabs and review as often throughout the year as possible.

If the quote is for only part of what is on the Want card, request an order for those parts available and make another request card for those parts which are still lacking. Note on the back of the original card those volumes or pieces which are unavailable from the publisher or agent as the case may be.

## Exclusive List

An exclusive list includes the needed lacking titles or volumes that are given to one agent to search for a given length of time such as three to six months. The library and the agent must come to a financial understanding ahead of time. The library does not usually agree to accept titles at any price, as might a private collector, but much depends on how badly the volumes are needed by the library. Depending on this point of view, the agent may then send the volumes as located on to the library without further questioning, or he may notify the library of the cost for approval to send the volumes. It is understood that during the stipulated time for searching, the library will not place these titles on any other Want List.

## L. S. Numbers

Neither publishers nor agents like to follow "official" entries when referring to titles in letters and invoices. One device is a numerical list for subscriptions, and computers, being mathematical, seem to take to it very well. Call it an L.S. number list. The "L" refers to "library." The "S" refers to "serials." Use five digits in the number. The number looks like this LS 71001. The "71" refers to the year. The "1" is the first subscription set up in that calendar year. These numbers are listed in a loose-leaf binder and give the number, the title, agent, fund, and cost of the first payment. It is put on the order letter and financial card.

Here is a place where detail and streamlining should be considered closely. Is one building up details that are really needed or should one be streamlining and cutting out detail? It all depends on how easily one can locate the titles on all the records. The agents and computers and library have all been in accord that the L.S. numbers are of inestimable value in saving time.

(Below is a sample sheet of an LS book).

| L.S. No. | Title | Dealer | Fund | Cost |
|---|---|---|---|---|
| 69769 | Quaderni di sociologia. | Ebsco | | |
| 69770 | La Ricerca. | Ebsco | | |
| 69771 | Richerche di matematica. | Ebsco | | |
| 69772 | Rivista di filologia e d'istruzione classica. | Ebsco | SP 30 '69 SERIALS | 11.25 |
| 69773 | Rivista di psicologia. | Ebsco | | |
| 69774 | Rivista di Sociologia. | Ebsco | ✓SEP 30 '69 Sociology | 6.00 |
| 69775 | Rivista italiana di paleontologia e stratigrafia. | Ebsco | | |
| 69776 | Genetics Abstracts. | Inf. Retrieval Ltd. | rr nn '69 Agriculture | $142.50 |
| 69777 | (Agon) —Journal of Classical Studies. | Univ. of Calif. | JAN 23 '70 HUMENITIES | 10.00 |
| 69778 | American Educational Research Journal. | Am. Ed. Res. Journ. | 7-1-69 Serials | $8.00 |
| 69779 | Review of Educational Research | Am. Ed. Res. Assn. | | |
| 69780 | Soviet anthropology and archeology. "Selected articles from Soviet scholarly journals. | Ebsco | SEP 30 '69 SERIALS | 5.00 |
| 69781 | Soviet studies in literature. | Ebsco | | |

Some librarians consider this a lot of extra work. They say the LS numbers do not help pinpoint a title that is garbled, unless the publisher or agent is kind enough to give the LS reference number. They say the whole affair is ironic. In order to save time, both publishers and librarians write something less than the full title and then they have to spend time setting up a reference number and refer to it in correspondence. Would that all librarians, publishers and agents could devise a perfect solution! "You pays your money and you takes your choice."

Now that the International Standard Serial Number (ISSN) — a unique, numerical identifier for each serial — is being depended on more and more by publishers, agents and librarians, this L.S. numbering system may be of less value than previously. Even the Postal Service is now requiring ISSN for privilege to qualify for reduced mailing rates (see also pp. 190, 256).

### Distinctive Address Label

A distinctive address label should be set up to route all material belonging to the Serials Department as it is sorted in the mail room. "In the past neglect of the single factor of a distinctive address for serials has made the handling of second class mail burdensome and inefficient. The neglect will no longer be tolerated in the days ahead as the need for a coding in the mailing address becomes more and more apparent."[14]

## PHILOSOPHY OF SETTING UP SERIALS ORDERS

The following outline may be of help to anyone ordering serials. At least one should set up some sort of an outline to suit the particular needs of the library and follow it until it becomes second nature. In that way steps will not be overlooked. All types of orders should be checked immediately to see if they have originated from the proper sources. Orders may drift in from elsewhere than authorized.

Official Entries: It is necessary to set up each title as officially correct as possible. This will often obviate duplication of titles being set up two or three ways in the file. This accuracy will be greatly facilitated if there is good communication between those ordering serials and the serials cataloger. This precise entry helps locate titles from Public Catalog to Serials Files to Periodical Room in the long run. It also makes revision of files unnecessary.

There are times in searching the Bibliographies and "library tools" for the particular title that one will find a springboard for its entry even though one never finds the exact entry. This is one reason for not assigning all searching to a beginning helper.

Because there are many times when all the information is very vague about a title, it seems best to set up the subscription by letter rather than encumbering funds immediately (see the FORM LETTER FOR A NEW SUBSCRIPTION).

Use forms as far as possible. They save much typing, and the same information will always be found in the same place.

Make certain a title is available before placing a firm order. Otherwise you may tie up funds for too long a time that might better be used for a title that is known to be currently available.

Is the title indexed in the "library tools"? If this information is brought out on the Serials Record it often helps in making decisions as to whether or not individual indexes are needed for binding (see the chapter on BINDING).

## How to Order

1. Give the exact date (and volume if known) with which the subscription is to begin. (In cases where the date is very uncertain, it is better to ask for the most currently available volume. Sometimes, being too specific on the date may result in slowing down the order a year or two or more if the publication is that far behind).
2. If one is ordering from an agent, give the accurate address of the publisher.
3. Give the agent any other pertinent information that will help him to know what action to take.
4. If indexes have to be paid separately, be sure to mention this in the order.
5. Newspapers with a very large national circulation like the *New York Times* and the *Christian Science Monitor* publish a different edition for different parts of the country. Unless otherwise specified, the edition that includes the library's particular location will be sent.

However, the question often arises as to which edition is indexed. This varies with each paper and the years.

## ORDERING PROCEDURES

**Form Letter For A New Subscription**

L.S._____

Gentlemen:

Please enter our subscription order on an "Until-Forbidden" basis for the serial publication listed below beginning with _____ _____. It is understood that should it be inconvenient or impossible to. bill annually for this title, it may be supplied on a send-and-bill basis.

The material sent under this subscription must be sent to the address shown above. All mailing labels, invoices, correspondence, etc., should include our order number.

Re:

Publisher:

Very truly yours,

Serials Librarian

This is the regular "T.F." (Until Forbidden) order letter.

## MULTIPLE ORDER FORMS

Multiple order forms are composed of several slips and are color-coded to suit certain purposes. They may be adapted to aid in various routines such as:
1. Placing the actual order
2. Claiming new subscriptions
3. Keeping the temporary or even the permanent financial record.
4. Notifying the Division that action has been taken on the subscription
5. Utilized in the back file approach
6. Put into the public catalog until the title is actually received or cataloged.

It would be well to decide what similar information is needed on all slips, then arrange it on the face of each slip in the same place. The back of each slip then could cover one procedure.

The forms may be of various sizes, but of course, once a decision is made, all slips will have to be the same size. They may be computer-form size; or, 3" x 5" so that certain copies may be filed in file cabinets; or, they might be the size of the Serials Record cards; or, any size that will fit the particular library.

If the same forms may be used as an all-purpose form for the Serials Department, the Order Department, and the Gift and Exchange Department, this is good and will be a saving to the library. If all three departments cannot be so closely coordinated, then a special form may be made for the Serials Department. If multiple forms are used, then some of the other slips and letters noted in this book may be eliminated, or combined into the form.

Examples from three libraries are given here:
1. Louisiana State University library at Baton Rouge (LSU).
2. University of Washington libraries at Seattle (U of W).
3. University of California, Riverside (UCR).

## Louisiana State University Library — Multiple Form

One set of multiple forms has been developed by The Louisiana State University library. Because an order form letter is used to place subscriptions with the agent, this form is used for internal purposes only. The size is 5'' x 5½'' and may be folded into the size that will fit into most library cabinet files. Nothing is printed on the backs of these slips, and the information on the front is repeated in the same place on each slip, except for a description to suit its particular use, which is placed outside the box located at the center right on the slip.

HOW THE MULTIPLE FORM MAY BE USED INTERNALLY

**No. .**

**PERMANENT RECORD**
**SERIALS DEPT.**
**LOUISIANA STATE UNIVERSITY LIBRARY**
**BATON ROUGE, LA. 70803**

CARD STATUS

CALL NO.
FUND & LOC.

AUTHOR:

TITLE:

PRICE:
DEALER

TO BEGIN:
PLACE:

PUB.:

CAT. NO.

DATE:

ITEM NO.

EDITION:

QUOTED

VOLS.:

ORDER
DATE

NOTIFY:

REC'D.

FREQUENCY:

1. Goldenrod (color) is filed in the New Serials Title file to signify that the subscription has been placed. It is left there until the first piece of the subscription is received, then transferred to the Received file for yearly statistical count.

**SERIALS DEPT.**

# LOUISIANA STATE UNIVERSITY LIBRARY

BATON ROUGE, LA. 70803

| | | |
|---|---|---|
| | **PURCHASE ORDER** FOR VENDOR'S FILE | CARD STATUS |
| | **No.** | |
| | AUTHOR: | |
| CALL NO. | | |
| FUND & LOC. | TITLE: | |
| PRICE: | TO BEGIN: | |
| DEALER | PLACE: | |
| | PUB.: | |
| CAT. NO. | DATE: | |
| ITEM NO. | EDITION: | |
| QUOTED | VOLS.: | |
| ORDER DATE | NOTIFY: | |
| REC'D. | FREQUENCY: | ☐ |

2. First white slip is attached to the carbon copy of the subscription letter and placed in the Authority file. This has now been changed to be used for the Want List file, and the original seventh slip (yellow) has been eliminated. Due to the cost of changing information when having new slips printed, it is being used as is, until such time as money is available to bring it into line. This is a good example of the evolution of routines.

SERIALS DEPT.

# LOUISIANA STATE UNIVERSITY LIBRARY

BATON ROUGE, LA. 70803

| | PURCHASE ORDER | DEALER'S REPORT | CARD STATUS |
|---|---|---|---|
| | **No.** | | SOLD |
| | AUTHOR: | | OP |
| CALL NO. | | | |
| FUND & LOC. | TITLE: | | NYP |
| PRICE: | TO BEGIN: | | TOS |
| DEALER | PLACE: | | |
| | PUB.: | | OS |
| CAT. NO. | DATE: | | |
| ITEM NO. | EDITION: | | DATE EXPECTED |
| QUOTED | VOLS.: | | |
| ORDER DATE | NOTIFY: | | |
| REC'D. | FREQUENCY: | | |

PLEASE RETURN THIS SLIP WITH BOOK, OR USE FOR REPORT ▢

3. Second white slip is sent to the requesting department to notify that the subscription has been placed.

SERIALS DEPT.
# LOUISIANA STATE UNIVERSITY LIBRARY
BATON ROUGE, LA. 70803

|  | **PURCHASE ORDER** | FINANCIAL RECORD | CARD STATUS |
|---|---|---|---|
|  | **No.** | | |
|  | AUTHOR: | | |
| CALL NO. | | | |
| FUND & LOC. | TITLE: | | |
| PRICE: | TO BEGIN: | | |
| DEALER | PLACE: | | |
|  | PUB.: | | |
| CAT. NO. | DATE: | | |
| ITEM NO. | EDITION: | | |
| QUOTED | VOLS.: | | |
| ORDER DATE | NOTIFY: | | |
| REC'D. | FREQUENCY: | | |

4. Green slip (financial record) notifies the accountant to encumber the sum of money the title will cost.

SERIALS DEPT.
## LOUISIANA STATE UNIVERSITY LIBRARY
BATON ROUGE, LA. 70803

| | | |
|---|---|---|
| **PURCHASE ORDER** | ORDER FILE | CARD STATUS |
| **No.** | | |

AUTHOR:

CALL NO.
FUND & LOC.

TITLE:

PRICE:                TO BEGIN:

DEALER              PLACE:

                        PUB.:

CAT. NO.            DATE:

ITEM NO.            EDITION:

QUOTED             VOLS.:

ORDER
DATE                  NOTIFY:

REC'D.                FREQUENCY:

5. Pink Slip is attached to the Serial Financial card to signal the Serials Financial Assistant that the title must be charged against the appropriate fund.

SERIALS DEPT.
# LOUISIANA STATE UNIVERSITY LIBRARY
BATON ROUGE, LA. 70803

| | | CARD STATUS |
|---|---|---|
| | **PURCHASE ORDER** NPAC REPORT | |
| | **No.** | |
| | AUTHOR: | |

| | |
|---|---|
| CALL NO. | |
| FUND & LOC. | TITLE: |

| | |
|---|---|
| PRICE: | TO BEGIN: |
| DEALER | PLACE: |
| | PUB.: |
| CAT. NO. | DATE: |
| ITEM NO. | EDITION: |
| QUOTED | VOLS.: |
| ORDER DATE | NOTIFY: |
| REC'D. | FREQUENCY: |

LOUISIANA STATE UNIVERSITY – BATON ROUGE   □

6. Blue slip is filed in the New Serial Title box on the Serials Financial Assistant's desk and goes with the initial invoice to notify the Accountant to release funds from the encumbered account into the expended account.

7. Yellow slip has been eliminated, see slip no. 2. It was originally given to the Serials Replacement Assistant to set up the process for obtaining the back file if the subscription form indicated that the back file was desired. Otherwise the slip was discarded.

As you see, there is no end to the uses multiple slips may be utilized for. The advantages are: 1. to keep all information at the same location throughout the department. 2. to save much typing.

It must be noted that Osborn does not approve of multiple order forms for serials. "Regardless of how effective multiple-order forms may be for books, they are not the desirable medium for serials, which require, or should require, more clear space than is available on the typical multiple-order form."[15]

## University of Washington Library Multiple Order Forms

The set of forms at the University of Washington library has seven slips in all, of varying colors: one is yellow, one pink, two green, one blue, two white. The size is 5" x 3". The form currently used was designed for both serial and book orders. For example, some of the options on the back of the order slip noting "order status" refer only to book orders.

The fronts of forms 1-4 are similar. The back of each slip shows the different information for the various routines.

The same information is listed on the backs of slips one and two. Slips 3-5 are blank on the back. Three copies of the form are kept for all currently received purchased serials: the top yellow form as the financial record, the third form (green) in a file by order number, and the fifth form (blue) in a file alphabetically under the name of each agent.

Front of the First Slip.

| AGENT | INV. NO. | INV. DATE | DESCRIPTION | FUND | POSTED | AMOUNT | |
|-------|----------|-----------|-------------|------|--------|--------|---|
| | | | | | | | |
| | | | | | | | |
| | | | | | | | |
| | | | | | | | |
| | | | | | | | |
| | | | | | | | |
| | | | | | | | |
| | | | | | | | |
| | | | | | | | |
| | | | | | | | |
| | | | | | | | |
| | | | | | | | |
| | | | | | | | |

## BACK OF THE FIRST SLIP

This side gives the permanent record of all payments on the order.

Two copies of the order slip (the two bottom white copies of the form) are sent to the agent.

| ORDER DATE | ORDER NUMBER | UNIV. OF WASHINGTON LIBRARY | THIS IS A FIRM ORDER UNLESS OTHERWISE INDICATED BELOW |
|------------|--------------|-----------------------------|------|
| MO.   DAY   YR. | | SEATTLE, WASH. 98105 | |
| | | SEE REVERSE SIDE | |

| COPIES | ESTIMATED PRICE | FORMAT | |
|--------|-----------------|--------|---|
| | | | |
| | | | CATALOG & ITEM NO. |

The backs of each of the two white has different information.

## USE ORDER NUMBER ON ALL CORRESPONDENCE

INVOICING
- SUBMIT ALL INVOICES IN TRIPLICATE. (3RD COPY WITH FIRST SHIPMENT, OTHERS UNDER SEPARATE COVER TO ADDRESS SHOWN ON FRONT OF THIS FORM.)
- SHOW ORDER NUMBER ON ALL INVOICES

SHIPPING
- PLACE ACCOMPANYING REPORT SLIP WITH FIRST ITEM SHIPPED ON THIS ORDER
- SHOW ORDER NUMBER ON ALL PACKAGES
- ADDRESS SHIPMENTS TO ADDRESS SHOWN ON FRONT OF THIS FORM.
- SHIP LOWEST COST PREPAID UNLESS OTHERWISE INSTRUCTED

NOTE
- REPORT BEFORE SENDING ANY ITEM THAT IS PART OF A SERIES OR A SOCIETY PUBLICATION UNLESS IT IS NOTED AS SUCH ON THIS ORDER.

The "note" above is applicable only to orders for monographs placed by the Book Orders Section.

**ORDER STATUS**

IF ITEM CANNOT BE SHIPPED IMMEDIATELY, PLEASE INDICATE THE REASON AND RETURN THIS FORM TO US.

☐ NOT YET PUBLISHED.    AVAILABLE _____
☐ OUT OF STOCK.  HOLDING ITEM OPEN
☐ OUT OF PRINT.  WILL SEARCH
☐ OUT OF PRINT.  CANCELLING
☐ CEASED PUBLICATION WITH VOLUME _____ DATED _____
☐ PUBLISHER'S ADDRESS UNKNOWN
☐ SOLD. CANCELLING
☐ CANNOT SUPPLY.  TRY _____
☐ OTHER _____  _____

This is the back of the actual order slip. Note this side gives the instructions for filling the order.

"If we decide to use the Washington Library Network's Acquisitions Subsystem for placing new orders, we will be using the WLN order form. I enclose a sample of this 2-part form. The fronts of the 2 copies are identical; the back of the first copy is blank; the back of the second copy lists the 'Conditions.' This form was also designed for both monographs and serials, and does not at this point supply some information on the form that we would like to have." (Excerpt from a letter describing forms of the University of Washington library.) WLN is Washington Library Network.

STANDING ORDER

**PURCHASE ORDER** # 78-003587
DATE 12/26/78

Abstracts of Soviet medicine.. sub. vol. 5, 1978+.

INSTRUCTIONS
ENTER STANDING ORDER UNTIL FORBIDDEN
wln76100200

| QTY | LIST PRICE | VEN CAT # | | VENDOR ACCT # |
|-----|-----------|-----------|--|---------------|
| 1 | 50.00 | | | |

BILL TO
University of Washington
Suzzallo Library
SERIALS SECTION
Seattle, Wa. 98195

FAXON, F. W., CO., INC.
15 SOUTHWEST PARK
WESTWOOD, MA 02090

SHIP TO
SAME AS ABOVE

SIGN

STANDING ORDER

**PURCHASE ORDER** # 78-035987
DATE 12/26/78

Time; a weekly news magazine.. sub. v. 145, July 1978-.

INSTRUCTIONS
ENTER STANDING ORDER UNTIL FORBIDDEN
wln76143977

| QTY | LIST PRICE | VEN CAT # | | VENDOR ACCT # |
|-----|-----------|-----------|--|---------------|
| 1 | 27.00 | | | |

BILL TO
University of Washington
Suzzallo Library
SERIALS SECTION
Seattle, Wa. 98195

FAXON, F. W., CO., INC.
15 SOUTHWEST PARK
WESTWOOD, MA 02090

SHIP TO
SAME AS ABOVE

SIGN

STANDING ORDER

**PURCHASE ORDER** # 78-035987
DATE 12/26/78

Abstracts of Soviet medicine.. sub. vol. 3, 1978+.

INSTRUCTIONS
ENTER STANDING ORDER UNTIL FORBIDDEN
wln76100200

| QTY | LIST PRICE | VEN CAT # | | VENDOR ACCT # |
|-----|-----------|-----------|--|---------------|
| 2 | 50.00 | | | |

BILL TO
University of Washington
Suzzallo Library
SERIALS SECTION
Seattle, Wa. 98195

FAXON, F. W., CO., INC.
15 SOUTHWEST PARK
WESTWOOD, MA 02090

SHIP TO
SAME AS ABOVE

WLN

CONDITIONS:

1. Prepay all shipping charges, route cheapest common carrier, and bill purchaser as a separate item on the invoice.

2. Three copies of invoice required.

3. Washington State sales tax applies to this order.

4. Unlimited number of purchase orders may be listed on a single invoice. P.O. number must appear on the invoice with the item.

## University of California, Riverside Library

The multiple order form for the University of California, Riverside is made up of ten parts. There are two yellow slips, one blue, four white, one pink, one salmon, and one green. They are blank on the backs. The size is 3 x 5 inches. The first slip is put in the Public Catalog to indicate that a title is on order. The blue slip goes in the Kardex as a temporary record. It is stapled to the permanent record as a record of the order. Two of the forms go to the publisher or vendor as the order. Note that the main order, "Dealer copy" has the library address on it. Others go to internal files. Their use is more or less self-explanatory. Note that there is a lot of clear space on the slips.

ORDER NO.

**RC**

DATE OF ORDER

DEALER

FUND

REQUESTED BY

DATE RECEIVED

COST

LC CARD NO.

**SERIAL**
ON ORDER/IN PROCESS
FOR INFORMATION SEE
SERIALS    DEPARTMENT

ORDER NO
**RC**

DATE OF ORDER

DEALER

**DEALER COPY**

**SHIP TO:**

OFFICIAL PURCHASE ORDER
INVOICE IN TRIPLICATE

**SERIALS DEPT., LIBRARY**
**UNIVERSITY OF CALIFORNIA**
**P.O. BOX 5900**
**RIVERSIDE, CALIF. 92507 U.S.A.**

---

ORDER NO
**RC**

DATE OF ORDER

DEALER

FUND

REQUESTED BY

DATE RECEIVED

COST

LC CARD NO

**KARDEX**
ON ORDER/IN PROCESS
FOR INFORMATION SEE
SERIALS    DEPARTMENT

---

ORDER NO
**RC**

DATE OF ORDER

DEALER

FUND

REQUESTED BY

DATE RECEIVED

COST

LC CARD NO

**S L  TEMP**
ON ORDER/IN PROCESS
FOR INFORMATION SEE
SERIALS    DEPARTMENT

170

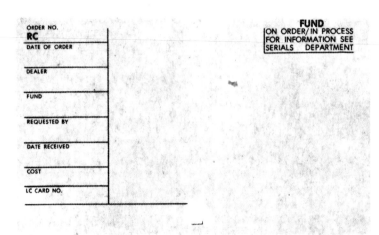

| ORDER NO. | | **FUND** |
|---|---|---|
| **RC** | | ON ORDER/ IN PROCESS |
| DATE OF ORDER | | FOR INFORMATION SEE |
| | | SERIALS DEPARTMENT |
| DEALER | | |
| FUND | | |
| REQUESTED BY | | |
| DATE RECEIVED | | |
| COST | | |
| LC CARD NO. | | |

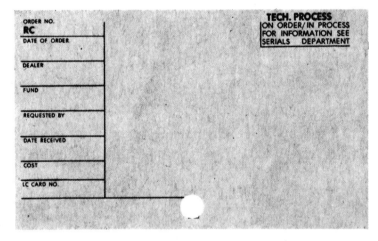

| ORDER NO. | | **TECH. PROCESS** |
|---|---|---|
| **RC** | | ON ORDER/ IN PROCESS |
| DATE OF ORDER | | FOR INFORMATION SEE |
| | | SERIALS DEPARTMENT |
| DEALER | | |
| FUND | | |
| REQUESTED BY | | |
| DATE RECEIVED | | |
| COST | | |
| LC CARD NO. | | |

| ORDER NO. | | **NUMERICAL** |
|---|---|---|
| **RC** | | ON ORDER/ IN PROCESS |
| DATE OF ORDER | | FOR INFORMATION SEE |
| | | SERIALS DEPARTMENT |
| DEALER | | |
| FUND | | |
| REQUESTED BY | | |
| DATE RECEIVED | | |
| COST | | |
| LC CARD NO. | | |

ORDER NO
**RC**

DATE OF ORDER

DEALER

FUND

REQUESTED BY

DATE RECEIVED

COST

LC CARD NO.

**CONTROL COPY**
ON ORDER/ IN PROCESS
FOR INFORMATION SEE
SERIALS     DEPARTMENT

---

ORDER NO
**RC**

DATE OF ORDER

DEALER

FUND

REQUESTED BY

DATE RECEIVED

COST

LC CARD NO

**S S L   TEMP**
ON ORDER/ IN PROCESS
FOR INFORMATION SEE
SERIALS     DEPARTMENT

---

ORDER NO.
**RC**

DATE OF ORDER

DEALER

FUND

REQUESTED BY

DATE RECEIVED

COST

LC CARD NO

PLEASE RETURN THIS COPY
WITH SHIPMENT OR USE TO REPORT.

**DEALER RETURN**

# Final Review And Placing Of A Subscription

A. Subscription (new):
1. Review the actual subscription
   a. Check the Serials Record to see if the title might already be there. True, one may not have the official entry yet, and therefore, may have to recheck the Serials Record a second time after searching, but this first review will sometimes eliminate much searching and verifying if the title is already there.
   b. Is it a duplicate subscription?
      (1) Is the duplication wanted?
      (2) If so, be sure to order from the same source as copy one, and get both copies expiring at the same time. Be sure to notify the agent that it is a second copy.
      (3) It is usually best to make a separate serials card for each copy. In this way, dates of receipt of each copy may be more easily recorded for claiming (see section on claiming). So often one copy will come in before another, or may not come in at all.
   c. Consider the title carefully to see if it might be gotten by gift or on exchange. (This also may come to light in the course of searching the title.)
   d. Read any announcements or blurbs to consider any special approaches.
      (1) Are there separate series, so that each one will need a separate Serials Record card?
      (2) Does it have a loose-leaf format?
      (3) Does it have other minor titles or separates coming with it?
      (4) Does it have special types of frequencies?
      (5) Must it come on a membership?
      (6) Must it be paid in advance?
      (7) Does it have supplements?
         (a) Bound in?
         (b) Separate serial title?
         (c) Is it a numbered monographic series?
   e. Are indexes included in the subscription, or must they be specially requested? This is often not found out until later.
   If indexes have to be paid separately, be sure to mention them in your order. Cumulated indexes are seldom included in subscriptions.

2. Review for treatment in the library
   a. Treatment (if the library catalogs serials). Should it get the complete treatment and/or be treated as more or less ephemeral such as "Keep one year," etc.?
      (1) Serial without analytics?
      (2) Serial with analytics?
      (3) Treat as monographs?
      (4) Should it be put on reference or other locations?
      (5) Should just last volume be put on reference?
   b. Should Library of Congress cards be ordered so as to have them by the time the subscription gets started? (With networks and new L.C. changes, follow any necessary approach.)
      (1) Note beginning date of publication
      (2) Note place of publication
      (3) Note publisher
      (4) Note title
      (5) Note current date
   c. If the library belongs to one of the networks, search and indicate the number and all information to the network.
   d. How should it be bound — regular, cheap binding, or pamphlet covers?
   e. Are back issues desired?
3. Review for information on the cards
   a. Frequency — A title may be anything from daily, weekly, etc.; or irregular, even "every once in a while"; one piece a year, and the next year nothing; or an avalanche of material every month. All this will influence the kinds of cards set up for the record. Also, if this information is noted on the temporary record, it will keep much material from drifting off into the pile of questions.
   b. Destination and routing information (displays, special destination, route before shelving, etc., must all come in for a review).
   c. Book pockets or cards (Will it circulate or not? Of course this depends on the individual library approach).
4. Select the source from which to order.
   a. Determine on the basis of companion titles which are presently supplied — country or language of publication and any other factors.
   b. Direct if the publisher will not supply to an agent.
   c. Note when several services or titles are grouped together under a contract.
5. When to begin the subscription.
   It is getting more and more necessary to place subscriptions in ad-

vance because issues of the first numbers of the current volume are just not available.

    a. Make a decision regarding the beginning date of the subscription. Try to cover a complete year or volume if at all possible. However, many points must be considered.

        (1) Some volumes start in the middle of the year.

        (2) Some volumes cover more than one year.

        (3) Some titles have several volumes a year.

    b. Give the exact date (and volume if known) when the subscription is to begin. In cases where the date is very uncertain, it is better to ask for the most currently available volume. Sometimes, being too specific on the date may result in slowing down the order a year or two or more if the publication is that far behind.

    c. If a paid subscription beginning with other than the first one of the volume — order the first numbers in some way at the time subscription is set up, if at all possible. To delay will make them less available and more expensive.

6. Final Placing of the Order.

    a. Give the agent any other pertinent information that will help him to know what action to take, or what to expect from the publisher.

    b. If ordering from an agent, give the address of the publisher.

    c. Assign the LS number (see p. 154).

    d. Type the "Until Forbidden" letter (see p. 156).

B. Subscriptions (renewals):

    1. Methods used to bring titles to mind for renewal

        a. The agent sends pro forma invoices, or lists (usually annually).

        b. The agent sends actual invoices.

        c. Claiming often brings titles to mind.

        d. Many titles have to be paid in advance, and the agent usually notifies the library with an announcement.

        e. Periodic checking of Direct Renewal File.

    2. Review for source.

        a. Has the invoice come from the proper source?
(If not, send it to the proper source and request an invoice from them).

        b. Is the address of the source the same as previously?
(If not, correct the records in the library).

    3. Review to see if the title is up-to-date, do not continue to pay automatically.

4. Review for a sharp rise in price.
5. Review for drastic changes in format, contents, etc.
C. Special slip orders.
   1. Replacements for lost and mutilated numbers
     a. Searching
     b. Ordering
     c. Payment
   2. Back file orders (see pp. 152-3).
     a. Searching
     b. Ordering
     c. Payment
   3. Added copies

# RECEIVING THE FIRST ISSUE

### Reviewing New Subscriptions

Several points should be considered and reviewed when the first piece of a subscription is received. This careful review at this point will guard against slip-ups that may occur later.

Is the title the one requested? Sometimes it isn't.

Is the title important enough to be paying what the publisher is charging? Once in a while the material is so ephemeral that one will have a right to cancel the order immediately. Usually it is best to wait until the expiration date and cancel at that time. The title should really be considered as thoroughly as available information will allow before ever ordering.

Another point to consider is to check to see if it has started close to the volume and number requested. This is especially important if some of the title is already in the library. One may be duplicating volumes. However, be flexible at this point. The publisher will usually use his judgment on what to send. Go along with him, all things being considered. Sometimes a volume or two, or the beginning numbers of the current volume may be picked up through the back file approach.

### Reviewing Back File Orders When Received

1. Save the labels on all the packages. This will enable one to note the agent and how many packages are supposed to be coming. The package number may prove important. Numbered packages should be held until consecutive numbers are received. Packages to one order may drift in, in several mails.

2. Note the condition of the journals. Pages that are too brittle to bind may not be acceptable. On the other hand, poor paper at the time of publication may mean that no other volume will be found in better condition. In this case, lamination by a binder is the only answer, or consider a copy in reprint.
3. Completeness of each volume must be proved. There are various ways of proving this.

   a. Indexes. (If only annual indexes are missing one may as well accept the volumes because one will seldom find just indexes to volumes available on the second hand market). If they are included, one may lean on them for information regarding completeness.

   b. Contents notes often give a clue to completeness.

   c. Publisher's lists of publications will help.

   d. Covers of later numbers sometimes list what has been published before.

DON'TS:

1. Do not purchase individual numbers unless they fill in an incomplete volume already in the library.
2. Do not purchase a volume in the middle of a long run of lacks. One may find a complete run available later.
3. Do not purchase if the decision has been not to fill in the back file. This should already be noted on the Serials Record.

   Be fair with agents. Do not be too casual about returning ordered copies. Make a final check on the shelves before ordering to be sure the number is still needed. Lost copies may turn up in the meantime. Agents will give more attention and consideration to future orders if contracts are honored as they should be.

   Foreign titles create different problems to those of domestic origin. The domestic titles may be requested from the publisher first and then, if they are not available, be put on lists to try secondhand agents. If the cost is below $1.00 the numbers may be ordered by letter and paid for by stamps or coins. This makes a saving since it costs from $1.50 to $5.00 to write a check, if it has to be paid in this way.

   Stamps and coins will be of no help to foreign agents, because one is not supposed to send coins out of the country, and local stamps may not be used for postage in foreign countries. It would be well to determine the cost of the publication before ordering abroad.

**Possible Routing for a New Subscription**

FACULTY AND LIBRARIANS
(Suggests new subscriptions to
Division Head.)

DIVISION
(Approves suggestion, makes as
many decisions as possible with
information at hand, and sends
subscription form to Serials
Department.)

SERIALS DEPARTMENT
(Verifies information on subscription forms and sets up temporary
file in Serials Record file with
subscription on form letter.
Orders L.C. cards for the publication.) Fewer libraries are doing
this.

**Receipt of the First Piece of New Subscriptions — Unbound**

TECHNICAL PROCESSING
ROOM
(Mail Room)
(Mail is sorted and new subscrip-
tions are sent to the Serials
Record.)

SERIALS RECORD
(First piece is charged to
cataloger and work slip is pulled
and given to cataloger along with
the item.)

CATALOGING
(When cataloger receives L.C.
cards she checks shelf to see if additional pieces have come in.

178

Establishes official entry and call number. Sends all pieces of the publication and cataloging information to Serials Records.)

SERIALS RECORD
(Serials record librarian gets all the information and sets up the permanent record for the serials record file. The publication is stamped with library's stamp and sent to its destination along with any necessary records.)

## Receipt of the First Piece of New Subscriptions — Bound

(Piece is checked in on its temporary record and sent to catalogers.)

— volume and necessary records

CATALOGING
(Establishes official entry and call number. Sends bound volume for marking and appropriate records to the Serials Record.)

records

volume

SERIALS RECORD
(Sets up permanent record in Serials Record file.)

MARKING ROOM
(Marks bound volume and prepares it for its use in the Division. Sends bound volume to Division.)

—volume

(shelving)

One final comment about ordering. No matter what one has gone through to get those items into the library that one has, they will be taken for granted. Any criticism that is made will be for those requests that have resisted all efforts. This is not being cynical, it is just being realistic.

## FILLING IN MISSING MATERIAL

While one person should be responsible for setting up special routines and working on lacks, it should be the responsibility for everyone in the library to bring to the serial librarian's attention the fact that something is missing. In turn such information should be locked into the proper procedure immediately by noting the information on the Serials Record and any other necessary files. Much depends on the approach one takes for claiming of missing numbers not suplied by the publisher or agent, and getting replacements that have been lost or mutilated in the library.

### Sources for Locating Missing and Mutilated Pages

1. Write the publisher. It must be remembered that large publishers seldom keep their numbers longer than 30 to 60 to 90 days, then turn them over to o.p. agents. Lack of storage space is the main reason for getting rid of them. Small publishers are more apt to keep them longer. Once in a while "tear sheets" just may be available free.

   In the first form letter to the publisher try to cover as many points as possible to cut down on future correspondence. Even include a clause to cover the copyright laws of duplicating, since permission is usually given when it is known that the pages are needed to complete a volume for binding. Following are two form letters:

Gentlemen:

RE:

We are interested in learning the price and availability of "tear sheets," of the above pages, or, if unable to supply "tear sheets," the price of the whole number. If these are not available, have you the facilities to photocopy the pages? If so, what would be the price of the service?

These pages are needed to complete our volume for binding. We would like permission to get these reproduced for this purpose.

Very truly yours,

Serials Librarian

Date_____

Requesting Library:

       Serials Department_____

       University Library_____

       University of California_____

       P.O. Box 5900_____

       Riverside, California  92507____

This photocopy request is for library replacement purposes only, and we have made reasonable attempts to acquire an original copy on the open market.

For use of:  Replacement of missing pages.

Author (or periodical title, volume and year)

Title (with author & pages for periodical articles, incl. edition, place & date)

Authorized by:  Lynn S. Smith

Title:          Head, Serials Department - UCR

7172

2. The next source is to purchase the whole number, if available, and use what is needed. This is always the best approach in cases where photographs or colored plates are needed.
3. Reprints of articles are sometimes available.
4. Secondhand catalogs are possibilities. However, another problem here is that secondhand agents do not want to be bothered with odd numbers unless they have them on hand. Odd numbers are not worth the time and expense of searching for the agent to have much interest in them. If a library has been buying long runs of back files from a particular agent, searching for these small items may be done as a favor.
5. Photocopying is often the only way to get the missing material. It might be necessary to borrow on Interlibrary Loan, or from a local library or faculty members.

A serious problem encountered with publishers is the extension of a subscription instead of locating the missing issues. As noted by Katz the most unacceptable approach is the extension of a subscription, with no effort to locate the missing issues. It is better to get a refund, and try to locate the missing issues elsewhere. It is a big problem and almost a losing battle. It costs only 15 cents to extend a subscription, while it costs $1.15 or more per issue to overprint a few thousand copies, store them in a warehouse, process claims, retrieve the issue from the warehouse, wrap it and mail it to the claimant.

### Filling in Long Runs of Lacks

Long runs of lacks is another problem, usually taking much time and searching. It is well to consider whether or not to fill in the back file, when setting up a subscription. At the time it may not be available, or funds may not be forthcoming, or one may not be certain it is actually wanted, but all decisions that can be made as soon as possible will anchor the title that much better. Whatever the decision is, it should be noted on the proper copy of the New Serials slip, and the Serials Record, then this information will be available for all time. If the decision cannot be made until later, make this notation, so the title may be reviewed when the first pieces of the subscription are received.

Want List (see p. 152).

### Sources for Locating Long Runs of Lacks

There are several approaches for locating lacks. Some are often overlooked. It must be remembered that when they have to be purchased they will be apt to run double or treble the original cost.

1. U.S.B.E. (see under special agencies).
   This is one of the very good sources, and has become even better as the years have gone by.
2. O.P. agents (see under Library Tools).
   They usually send out catalogs at different intervals. If it is necessary to send lists it is best to keep them short, and leave much space between the lines for the publishers to make notes. Long lists are cumbersome, hard to read, and agents do not like them. These lists may be handled in several ways: circularize among various agents (do not send to more than one agent at a time), or leave a list with one agent for a specified length of time.

3. Contact local people, scientists and faculty members, departments on campuses; engineers, industry or special libraries. Use your ingenuity.
4. The most current approach is to buy long runs in microforms.

UCR library's Replacement order form. It includes four copies, each copy of a different color. All are blank on the back.

SERIAL REPLACEMENT                    ORDER NO. RC 828853-
                                                        DATE:

ENTRY:


VOLUME/NUMBER/DATE:


PLEASE SEND TO: ———▶ **SERIALS DEPARTMENT**     *If unavailable please return slip.*
                        **UNIVERSITY LIBRARY**          Remarks:
*INVOICE IN TRIPLICATE*  **UNIVERSITY OF CALIFORNIA**
                        **P. O. BOX 5900**
                        **RIVERSIDE, CALIF. 92507**
Ⓤ 250840

## NOTES

1. William Katz and Peter Gellatly, *Guide to Magazine and Serial Agents* (New York: R.R. Bowker, 1973), p. 35.
2. Ibid., p. 66.
3. Ibid., p. 57
4. Ibid., p. 43.
5. Robert V. Allen, U.S.S.R. Area Specialist, Slavic & Central European Division, Library of Congress. Personal Correspondence.
6. G. Raymond Nunn, *Publishing in Mainland China,* Massachusetts Institute of Technology Report no. 4 (Cambridge, England: The M.I.T. Press, 1966), p. 5.
7. John Fraser, "Peking Library Reopens for Foreigners," *Christian Science Monitor,* 6 February 1978.
8. Chi Wang, Head, Chinese and Korean Section, Orientalia Division, Library of Congress. Personal Correspondence, 24 June 1977.
9. Lee Williams, Curator, Latin American Collections. Yale University Library. Personal Correspondence. 3 November 1976.
10. Constance Mabel Winchell, *Guide to Reference Books,* 8th ed. (Chicago: American Library Association, 1967), p. 153.

11. Joe Morehead, *Introduction to United States Public Documents* (Littleton, Colorado: Libraries Unlimited, 1975), p. 4.
12. Ibid., p. 42.
13. William Huff, "The Acquisition of Serial Publications," *Library Trends,* 18 (January 1970): 294-317.
14. Andrew D. Osborn, *Serial Publications: Their Place and Treatment in Libraries,* 2d ed., rev. (Chicago: American Library Association, 1973), p. 93.
15. Ibid., p. 92.

## Additional References

Allen, Walter C. ed., Serial Publications in Large Libraries. 16th Allerton Park Institute, 1969. Champaign, Illinois: University of Illinois Graduate School of Library Science, c1979.

Dudley, Norman, "The Blanket Order." *Library Trends,* 18 (January 1970): 318-327.

Gorokhoff, Boris Ivanovitch. *Publishing in the U.S.S.R.* Bloomington, Indiana: Indiana University Publications. Slavic and East European Series 19, 1959.

Jennison, Peter S. *Books in the Americas: a Study of the Principal Barriers to the Booktrade in the Americas.* Prepared for the American Book Publishers' Council by Peter S. Jennison and William H. Kurth. (Estudios bibliotecarios, no. 2). Washington: Pan American Union, 1960.

Katz, William, *Magazine Selection; How to Build a Community-oriented Collection.* New York: R. R. Bowker, 1971.

Louisiana State University Library. *A Manual on Serials.* 1976.

*Mergers and Acquisition: the Journal of Corporate Venture.* Washington: Merger and Acquisition, Inc. 1, 1965.

Paulson, Peter J., "Government Documents and Other Non-Trade Publishers." *Library Trends,* 18 (January 1970): 363-372.

Rebulda, Harriet K.: "Some Administrative Aspects of Blanket Ordering: A Response." *Library Resources and Technical Services.* 13 (Summer 1969): 342-345.

Thom, Ian Walter, "Some Administrative Aspects of Blanket Ordering." *Library Resources and Technical Services* 13 (Summer 1969): 338-342.

United Nations. *Standing Order Service: a Guide for Librarians and Booksellers.* New York: United Nations Publications, 1977.

# CHAPTER VII
# CATALOGING

**Contributed by**
**Lynn S. Smith**

## Why Catalog Serials?

Many librarians question why serials need to be cataloged since there are so many guides and aids available. After all, bibliographies list the titles and indexes analyze their contents. What more can be desired? Besides, they are the proverbial pain-in-the-neck to control because they are so unstable. Who wants all of this agony—wouldn't it be better just to forget the whole thing?

Absolutely not! Serials are much too important to treat in such a cavalier fashion. Adequate bibliographic control for serials is essential to effective working with them and, amazingly enough, good basic control seems to breed ease in handling these pesky publications.

The basis of this bibliographic control is cataloging. Cataloging has many functions: description, subject headings, etc., but the most important is the choice of entry (and the concomitant added entries, references, etc.). The question is one of identification which is adequate for accurate and prompt processing and ease of access in all records which deal with serials.

Patrons searching for titles which they have found cited in bibliographies should be able to find the same title in the catalogs of the libraries they are using, providing the titles are one-and-the-same. Standardization of entry is important with serials. It is also important to have all records which deal with the same serial in any given library reflect the same entry so that the records become complementary rather than duplicative and confusing.

It is important, then, to remember that "cataloging," when referring to serials, does not only refer to representation of entries in a card catalog, which cataloging for monographs generally does. "Cataloging" for serials refers to the establishing of a canon of bibliographic information about a title (which includes entry, call number, and other data) which is to be used for a myriad of files concerning that given serial. Cataloging of serials is at the core of accurate, adequate, and efficient serials processing.

## Importance of the Choice of Main Entry

The main entry for a serial is particularly important because of the functions based on it. It is the basis of reading room (and sometimes bound volume) shelving. It is the basis of binding. It is the common thread running through all of the records attendent upon serials—the concept of complementary records. The entry chosen for order files must be chosen with care so that expensive duplication will not result. Most computer-produced serials lists are single-access tools, sometimes with needed cross-references, requiring the establishing of a main entry for each title listed. In fact, serials are very often involved in single-access files, putting even greater demands upon the serial main entry than upon that for monographs.

## Main Entries in the Past

The concept of entry for serials has changed somewhat through the years. Under British Museum rule 17 C, periodicals were entered under the form "PERIODICAL PUBLICATIONS," subdivided by place of publication. Corporate publications are put under the appropriate form heading for the academy, society, or institution. Directories are under "DIRECTORIES," almanacs under "EPHEMERIDES," and the like. This put a great burden of geographic knowledge and specialized expertise on the shoulders of the user. Fortunately, this system never really caught on in the United States and is pretty much on the way out in Great Britain, although it can still be seen in the British Museum's *Catalogue.*

The American tradition has always been to use the title-page wording, perhaps with addition or modification, if needed.

The *ALA Cataloging Rules for Author and Title Entries* (1949) deemed "seriality" to be all-important. The principal rule for serials was rule 5, but it, unfortunately, did not cover all types of serials, so catalogers flipped pages back-and-forth to find the appropriate rules for each little problem. By implication, serials were considered different from other publications, and special types were considered different one from another. Entries were sometimes not made under the first word on the title-page (such as forename initials for titles named for a person—"A. Merritt's fantasy magazine would be entered under Merritt's"). The rules called for a lot more title entries than subsequent rules, but not always for the right reasons.

## AACR 1: Rule 6

The rule for choice of entry for serials in "AACR 1," the Anglo-American Cataloging Rules (1967) is rule 6. It is perhaps surprising to find a rule stated specifically for serials, since AACR was trying to get away from dependence upon types of publications. However, serials do present special bibliographic problems not adequately covered elsewhere, so this rule appears.

The basic problem with serials, that of changing author or editorship, is covered in the main provision for serials, rule 6 A, which provides for title entry. The next lettered section, B, has two subsections, the first with an exception. This covers serials issued by a corporate body and is the source of considerable dispute; Section C states that serials issued by a personal author should be entered under his name. The rule is straightforward enough and is not hard to follow. There are questions as to whether it is an appropriate rule for serials, and some libraries refuse to use it. However, it still appears in "AACR 2," so its rationale must be fairly sound. The fourth section, 6 D, deals with title changes, and will be covered later. Right now let's discuss title and corporate entry.

## Corporate Entry

Rule 6B in the North American Text of AACR considers serials issued by corporate bodies. Part 1 gives provision for entry under title if the title is distinctive. However, there is an exception to Part 1 which provides for entry under the corporate body if certain criteria about the title are true. If the title has the name or abbreviation of the name of the corporate body in it, the entry is under the body, with an added entry for the title. If the title consists of a generic term, like "Proceedings," "Journal," etc., thus needing the body's name for adequate identification, enter the publication under the corporate body. If in doubt about these provisions, use corporate entry.

Note that the term "corporate entry," rather than "corporate author," has been used. This is an important concept to remember. It may be that titles falling into these categories are only issued by the bodies whose names they carry, which is not an aspect of "authorship." In many cases, the association or whatever disavows any support of the points-of-view presented in the journal which it sponsors. This is clearly not a case of "authorship." It is interesting to note that most serials currently entered under corporate bodies are entered under an exception, which is clearly a problem in rule-writing.

## Corporate Authorship

Corporate authorship is, however, covered in AACR 1. It is particularly badly worded in the rules, but is the underlying concept of Rule 6B2. Publications issued under the authority of a body are entered under the body under this particular rule. However, the concept of corporate authorship is muddied by the problems of distinctiveness of title covered in the rules covered above. AACR 2 has changed this, however.

## Title Entry

Most serials are entered under title if they are distinctive. The concept of diffuse authorship, calling for title entry, is, unfortunately, not made clear in the rules. However, this is really the basis of Rule 6A. Distinctive title serials issued by corporate bodies are entered under title, with added entry under body, according to 6B1. Even here the concepts are muddy, indicating that the underlying provisions of the old rules are probably still prevailing.

## Title Changes

It is a very rare serial indeed which has not changed its title once in its existence (it's probably changed something else, anyway!). Some titles are continually doing so, so it has befallen librarians to learn to cope with this phenomenon.

There are three basic ways of dealing with title changes: cataloging under earliest entry, latest entry or successive titles.

Earliest title was one of Cutters' alternatives in 1876. The British 1908 rules also made this choice. The reason for this was probably the preponderance of printed book catalogs at the time. Problems, of course, resulted because the entries were outdated and to check new issues in on a record with an antiquated entry was, to put it mildly, the proverbial pain-in-the-neck. For library staff and patrons alike, the major approach would be through cross-references, and this caused confusions. The concept was abandoned.

On the other hand, latest entry provided the one 'pro' of the above, that of a stable entry, while answering all of the negative problems by providing the most current entry for record-keeping. This was a major feature of the American 1908 rules and the 1949 ALA rules. In fact, practice of latest entry cataloging even persisted at the Library of Congress and other major research libraries after the AACR supposedly put an end to the concept. The reasons were the stability and the fact that all of the information was in one place, under the latest entry.

This reason, however, proved to be the downfall of the practice as well. Catalogers at LC researched all of their title changes very thoroughly, which was a boon to other libraries across the country. Notes were very, very full and useful to bibliographers. But it took TIME! Pretty soon catalogers at LC were swamped with work. The practice had to be stopped or the machinery at LC for cataloging serials would. LC switched to the AACR as printed.

Even other libraries noticed the problems of serials cataloging and the enormous expense involved. Although you cannot get away from the fact that serials cataloging is an expensive and work-intensive process—for serials will continue to change and you have to keep up with them—you can, at least, get out of making work for yourself. This is what AACR did.

AACR codified what was happening already at some libraries as a reaction to the expenses of latest-entry cataloging: successive entry. Under this concept, each title is given its fair shake in the catalog—under entry, added entries, and subject headings. Patrons can approach records and get immediate satisfaction rather than cross-references. The title-as-published is used all of the time, making access from citations much easier. Cataloging and other record-keeping is so much more speedily and efficiently done, for there is not so much treading and retreading of the same ground, doing, redoing, and doing over. Updates become clerical tasks and there is little muss-and-fuss.

Rule 6D provides for successive entry. In the North American edition it also provides for exception to this if the title lasts for only a short time. If this is so, a title may be cataloged with a "title varies" note to cover the "title of short duration."

The problem of title changes has been more-or-less taken care of, but there is a loophole. Because of the current international activities to register serials, with the limitations for registry imposed by the organizations involved, there has been a need to change the rules. The real "fly in the ointment" was the problem of serial title changes. One of the solutions, unfortunately, was the dismissal of the concept of "titles of short duration."

## International Registry

ISDS, the International Serials Data System, grew out of a plan by

UNESCO to register all serials published in the world. To this end, a network of ISDS centers has been set up with the International Centre in Paris as the hub of the network.

The International Centre is responsible for developing and producing the registry, for registering serials published in countries without centers or by international agencies, and for coordinating the activities of the national centers.

The national centers are responsible for registration of the serials published within their national boundaries, encouraging publishers to use their numbers issued for their journals in publishing them and referring to them, and contributing to the international registry. There are centers in Argentina, Australia, Canada, Finland, France, the Federal Republic of Germany, Italy, Japan, Nigeria, Sweden, Tunisia, the Union of Soviet Socialist Republics, the United Kingdom, the United States, and Yugoslavia. Most of them are centered in the national library or with the national bibliography. The American one is located in the Serial Record Division of the Library of Congress and is called the National Serials Data Program, NSDP.

Although engaged in other projects, the ISDS Centers have two major functions with regards to the registry of serials. These are the ISSN and "key-title."

The ISSN is an eight-digit number, presented in two groups of four, separated by a hyphen. The eighth digit is a check digit, which is effective in detecting transposition errors. (If a reader is interested in knowing how ISSN are created, one authoritative source is the *Guidelines for ISDS*, and another is page XV of the twenty-one year cumulation of *NST*.) The number is accompanied by a country code and is preceded by the letters "ISSN." For example, the ISSN for *American Libraries* is: US ISSN 0002-9769. The number is an "idiot number" in that it cannot be broken down into meaningful digits like the ISBN can. The number is by no means idiotic, however. This number is a standard, unique, and unambiguous code for the identification of a given serial publication, the only one to which it is assigned. It can be used whenever there is interchange of information about serials, either in a manual or automated system. The number is inseparably associated with the key-title it is assigned to, and any change in the key-title demands a new ISSN. (The new number will bear no meaningful relationship to the old one, however.) Any serial can be identified by the number without problems of entry variation, spelling errors, etc., thus providing some standardization of identification.

The largest computerized data base equipped with ISSN was created with the publication of *New Serials Titles, 1950-1970* by the

R.R. Bowker Co. Bowker was given a block of numbers to assign while ISDS was getting on its feet and getting ready to assume the responsibility. The twenty-one year cumulation of *NST* was published with ISSN. Unfortunately, because of duplication between the Ulrich's and *Irregular Serials and Annuals*, also published by Bowker with ISSN, and *NST*, some titles got two ISSN. This will ultimately be cleaned up by NSDP, and one of the ISSN will be retired and not reused. Also, Bowker did not necessarily assign numbers to key-titles. This will also be revised and corrected as time permits. (In the meantime, generally the lower number is invalid.) But even with all of the errors, the *NST* cumulation is a remarkable file of tremendous import. ISSN are identified for the first time in an important and relevant way. (ISSN have also incorporated into the International Standard Bibliographic Description for Serials (see pp. 204-205). Publishers are printing ISSN in their periodicals and NSDP is strongly urging them to do so. ISSN are also being used now as a postal number by the U.S. Postal Service. More importantly, libraries, dealers, and others are using the standard numbers as part of their bibliographic control devices, which further strengthens the system and encourages its wholesale utilization as a method of unique identification of serial titles. This should promote faster and more accurate transmission of information relation to serial publications.

The ISSN is uniquely and inseparably tied to something called "key-title." It is established by the ISDS center responsible for registration of the serial and is derived from the title information appearing on the publication, exclusive of subtitles. Title-page titles receive preference and others are treated as variants. These ISDS concepts will be important to the future of serials cataloging. The reader is referred to pages 22-31 of the *Guidelines for ISDS* for construction of key-titles.

The most important aspect of key-titles however, is that they will not be stable and will change, just as cataloging titles change now. In fact, due to the fact that key-titles are more related to what actually appears on the serial piece in question than cataloging entry (which could call some things variants and put all under an umbrella corporate entry), there will be more changes than in the past. As the key-title changes, so changes the ISSN. But the cataloging title/entry might not change.

This is the crux of the problem as recently experienced in serials cataloging circles. Because the cataloging entry would not change all of the time the ISSN did, there might be several ISDS records for one cataloging record, causing botheration and confusion. It was proposed that all serials be entered under title so that the changes would be more on a one-to-one basis. As the second edition of AACR, AACR2, was being prepared, this was the thinking that was going into its making.

## AACR 2

The second edition of the *Anglo-American Cataloguing Rules* came out in the fall of 1978. There were some substantial changes between it and the 1967 rules. Some of these came as the result of the desire to bring the two 1967 editions, the North American and the British, together and update them with the addenda which had come out since their publication. Some came as a result of machine applications, including the internal registry problems affecting serials, and some as a result of re-evaluations of the basic principles underlying the rules.

There is no special rule for the entry of serial publications. The concept of authorship is to be enforced, which means that serials without authors will be entered under title. This will result in more title entries since the large preponderance of titles entered under 6B1 exception, as mentioned previously, are not entered under a principle of "authorship." So the *Journal of the American Medical Association* will be under "Journal," not the body. Titles with initialisms in them will likewise be put under their titles, not the body (an added entry will be made). Personal authorship will remain as a viable alternative, much to the chagrin of some.

Corporate authorship will remain as a concept, but the concept will be considerably narrowed. Administrative documents, proclamations, and reports of corporate activity of the body will be put under the body as author. Other publications will not. The character of the publication will have to be examined very closely to see whether the rules for corporate authorship will apply.

In fact, catalogers will have to be really on their toes to interpret the rules in the light of what they see in the publication in-hand in order to apply them correctly in any given situation. Gone will be the crutches and helps of the past. Unfortunately, questions will still remain.

## Forms of Names

Not only have names associated with serials changed over the years, but the forms whereby they are recorded in catalogs have also changed. At one time, it was important to know whether a body was a society or an institution, for it made a difference in how the body was recorded. Societies were entered under their names, institutions under the places where they were located.

AACR 1 changed all of that. Basically all names were to be entered under the forms used by the organizations themselves. But at that time a great hue and cry went up from the Library of Congress and other large research libraries—so many cards would have to be changed! So the Library of Congress created a policy called "Superimposition." If a name had already been established for the Library of Congress catalogs, it was not changed and new subdivisions were added to it as they came along. If, however, a new organization or institution was established, its name was set up according to the new rules rather than the old. Thus, the new rules were "superimposed" upon the old ones.

Now, with international projects and the need for standardization, the Library of Congress has reversed its practice and coined a new word: "Desuperimposition." Superimposition will be cancelled and all headings will be established under the new forms authorized by the *Anglo-American Cataloguing Rules*.

Another change is that some geographic names will be specified by country while others will be qualified by state, rather than country. the U.S., Canada, Australia, the United Kingdom, and the U.S.S.R. are examples of the latter countries, with specific examples being "Adelaide, South Australia" rather than "Adelaide, Australia," as formerly. There will be some other changes in name forms, but these are the major ones.

## Added Entries

Added entries provide additional access points to the bibliographic data in the catalog. They should be made for all alternative approaches of a major nature. These would include title, if the entry is under body, personal author and body if under distinctive title. Alternative titles or variant titles, such as parallel foreign titles, catch titles, abbreviations which are common, partial titles, if appropriate, running, caption, or spine titles, "at head-of-title" notes and the like should be given added entries. Sometimes there is an organization's logo next to the title. If this could be construed as part of the title, it should be given added entry status. If the cataloging is latest or earliest entry, or there is a "title of short duration," these should be traced—all bibliographic entries covered by a bibliographic record should be adequately covered.

If a subtitle entry would give useful access to a title, it might be accorded an added entry. However, be careful not to overdo this. Sometimes a subtitle added entry is useful, but not always.

Editors may be given added entries if they are major enough. Added authors should always be given added entries. Also trace the series which a serial appears in. A good rule-of-thumb—if it seems useful, use it!

## Descriptive Cataloging

Descriptive cataloging is extremely important, for it establishes the identity of the serial in terms of its principal access points and physical description.

As far as the description of serials is concerned, it is most peculiar. Monographs generally are described once and for all, with complete and detailed description. Not so for serials. Serials change a great deal, and to try to pin them down at the start would be to ask for an inordinate amount of revision in order to keep up with the dynamic nature of the publications involved. One makes predictions about future issues based on current ones. There is always a question mark just beyond the present. (There can also be a question mark about the past, if the set is not a complete one.) For these reasons, the rules for description of serials are a mere skeleton, which the cataloger can flesh out, if desired, upon the serial's demise. Serials cataloging is not bibliographic cataloging, but the creation of à practical tool.

Many libraries do not follow all of the rules, feeling that too much detail gets in the way of efficient recordkeeping. It is important to remember, however, that shortcuts lead to a lack of standardization, which can promote even more problems.

The concepts of descriptive cataloging of serials have changed considerably over the years, taking into consideration the problems of too much detail. Early cataloging rules called for much more detail and serials catalogers found themselves being "painted into corners." Digging themselves out as the serials changed was very time-consuming and nerve-wracking. so serials people are grateful for the changes in the rules.

The rules had not totally changed by the time AACR came out in 1967, however. Chapter 7 of AACR still seems to consider that serials are variant monographs, a lamentable practice in the minds of most serials librarians, who feel that serials should be treated by their own standards, rather than those for monographs.

The British and North American texts vary from each other in the treatment of serials. The American text calls for description of only the parts which a given library has. The British text calls for description of a complete or "perfect" set, which is done in most American libraries as well as libraries using the British text. Because a complete text is described, the cataloging doesn't have to be changed as the library fills in its set and makes it more "perfect." In the meantime, the serial records chronicle the library's holdings with exactness.

This last is an important thing to note. One of the major differences between monographic and serial cataloging are the complementary records which attach themselves to the serial in question. It was this concept of serial recordkeeping which, fortunately for the cataloger, brought the downfall of the expensive and complicated cataloging operations of the past and ushered in a more rational approach.

## Body of the Entry and Recording of the Title

The source of data for the recording of the title comes from the title-page or one of its substitutes: cover, caption, masthead, editorial pages, or other place, the title or imprint being from the same place, if possible. The latest volume is generally used as the source of information. Since serial titles can vary so much, the most stable part of the title should be picked.

The "body of the entry" consists of title, subtitle, if needed, volume designation and dates, and the imprint. Subtitles are usually not included, unless they explain the title in a more meaningful way, or they differentiate one title from another.

There has always been a considerable amount of confusion and negative reaction brought up by the emphasis on title-pages when discussing serials cataloging, the argument being that, more often than not, serials do not have title-pages. They are usually cataloged from their covers, or perhaps mastheads, and it is felt that the rules perhaps should be reworded to indicate that the source used should be the one with the most complete information, which does not necessarily mean title-page.

The rules provide some guidelines for the recording of the title. Formerly, the title, if it were a generic title linked with a corporate body, could be truncated to provide a briefer and more straightforward title, to be entered under the corporate body without redundancy. This provision was removed by the dropping of Rule 162B, to coincide with ISDS guidelines (see pp. 191). Generic titles linked to corporate bodies were to be so recorded. Generic titles without links were to have them provided, by use of a hyphen, and thus the title would be able to stand on its own two feet, without help from a heading.

Numbering is to be omitted from the recording of the title if it is to be used for the numbering designation. *Report of the first annual meeting* is recorded as *Report of the annual meeting*, with numbering given as "1st-."

If any other word or phrase precedes the title and might be construed or cited as part of the title, an author-title and/or title reference or added entry with this form of the title is to be made on the catalog entry for the serial. This is normally taken care of by "At head of title" or "Added title information" notes.

## Holdings

Just indicating that a library has a certain title is not sufficient where serials are concerned. Very few libraries, except the very oldest and best-endowed, have every issue of every title to which they have ever subscribed. Serials cataloging needs to be augmented with records of holdings, that is, the volumes or parts of the serial possessed by the library.

In the past, libraries recorded holdings in their public catalogs on separate holding cards or pencilled onto the catalog cards. However, this is very costly to keep up and libraries usually depend upon their central serial records or upon a serials list or catalog of holdings. Gone are the elaborate systems for adding to public holding cards and certainly no one is sorry to have seen them go! Now, most libraries indicate "perfect"holdings by simply putting the inclusive dates of the serial's publication in the space after the title and refer to the other records by means of notes or stamps.

Most libraries do not worry that sometimes serial volumes are unbound. Notes or signs can indicate that more recent issues are in a current reading room, if this is the case. (The libraries which shelve unbound issues with bound ones in the stacks don't have any problem, of course.) Some libraries have very elaborate automated lists which specify bound and unbound holdings.

The holdings information should conform to the usage of the publisher and should be as complete as necessary for clarity. Arabic numerals are used and terminology for volume designation and months or other parts of the year should be in the vernacular. Generally brackets are not used in recording of holdings data.

Some serials may have more than one numbering system. The one which seems most prominent should be used and others relegated to notes for the sake of clarity, although some do prefer to use continuous numbering. The one chosen should be the most consistent system, if that can be established, so that volumes can be bound by it. Notes for numbering irregularities or variations can be brief if all information is adequately maintained on the central serial record for detailed reference work.

The statement of holdings should be updated for changes in series and other changes of numbering (possibly with attendant notes, if these seem needed) and should be closed at the time of the serial's demise. It should be remembered that the dates of a serial's publication are very important as a device for identification of the serial.

## Imprint

The imprint, for serials, is usually limited to the place of publication and the name of the publisher. Changes in the place of publication that do not warrant specific description are indicated by the abbreviation "etc." following the place of publication. If the name of the publisher is essentially the same as the title of the publication, as is often the case with periodicals, it is omitted from the imprint. An example of this would be Monthly Review, Inc., which publishes the *Monthly Review.*

One of the innovations of the new rules provides for the Latin abbreviations "[s.l.]" and "[s.n.]", meaning "sine loco" and "sine nomine" ("without place" and "without name" respectively), indicating that either the place or publisher is unnamed in the publication. (If both are unnamed, a printer's statement is used following the abbreviation in brackets.) This is one of the changes to AACR 1 after the adoption of the new chapter 6 (for a description of monographs) and is a harbinger of AACR 2.

## Collation

The collation statement describes the completed set for serials that have ceased publication. If the library does not have a complete set, the collation appears as a blank followed by "v." or "no.," to be filled in upon the serial's demise.

Illustrative matter is described for the set as a whole, and only those types which are important to the set as a whole are mentioned. Formerly, the practice was to describe serials generally as "illus," unless the types were very important to the genus of publication, such as maps for a cartography or geography publication. With the change in terminology, "ill." is now used, preparatory to adoption of AACR 2.

Size is measured just like for monographs. Variations in the width of serial publications are ignored. In fact, size of the whole serial is often ignored by catalogers since the size may vary. Usually location marks suffice to lead the patron in any given library to oversized or tiny publications. Deviations in collation are not generally considered real problems.

## Series Statement

If the serial is published in a series, the series statement appears in parentheses after the collation.

## Notes

Notes qualify and amplify the formal description set forth in the body of the entry. They record variations from the norm already stated—certainly a problem with serials—and they relate all of the parts to the whole.

Of course, each serial varies considerably from its colleagues in terms of the notes needed, so the listing given in the rules only provides guidelines. The order of notes, as given by the North American rules, is as follows:

Frequency
Report year
Duration of publication
Suspension of publication
Numbering
Connection with preceding publications
Publications absorbed
Organ
Minor variations in title
Issues with special titles
Issuing bodies
Editors
Variations in imprint
Connection with later publications
No more published?
Contents

## Frequency and Duration Notes

Frequency is generally given as a brief word or phrase right after the collation. If it is fairly lengthy, however, it is given as a note. (It may even be given in a note as a quoted subtitle.) If there are numerous changes, the note "Frequency varies" will suffice. Frequency is an important feature of a serial and it is sometimes necessary for identification, so it should be retained in the cataloging record even though it is a changeable piece of information and the cataloger may wish to drop it.

If a serial suspends publication and intends to resume at a later date, the entry is left open and a note is used to show date, or the volume designation, of the last issue published. (Generally dates are used in notes.)

## Numbering

Irregularities and peculiarities in the numbering of a serial publication are described (unless they are limited to the numbering of the parts of a single volume) in the next note.

This can be one of the most fun rules to try to follow for this is where the publications we dearly love tend to show their perverse nature, sometimes quite by accident. A lot of publishers, serials people learn, have real problems with counting, especially in Roman numerals. The catalog cannot hope to cope with a lot of long and involved statements of irregularities, so it is best to give up and let the serials records do it. Indications of problems with numbering should be made in the cataloging for these, however.

Notes may be needed to explain the numbering used in the body of the entry, too. For example, a congress was not published for the first sixteen years it was held. The numbering statement should show "17th- ." There is an obvious discrepancy here which needs to be explained and this can simply be done with a note like: "1st-16th congresses not published."

## Connection With Preceding Publications

With the practice of successive entry cataloging, it is necessary for the users of the catalog to know the history of the publication so they can find the missing links in the chain elsewhere in the catalog. Thus, the relationship between a serial and its immediate predecessor(s) is indicated in the cataloging as the next note. A change in corporate body also necessitates such a note.

If the numbering changes, the terminology is "Supersedes [title]." If the numbering does not change, the phraseology is "Continues [title]." The continuation note may include the numbering, particularly if more than one title is involved, indicating which numbering is being continued.

## Publications Absorbed

If a serial has absorbed another one, the publication absorbed is named and the exact date of absorption is indicated, if possible. This is also a fairly straightforward situation. It should be noted, however, that this is only done when the continuing title remains the same. If the title is changed to indicate the presence of the new title, the new title should be cataloged as a separate entity.

## Organ Notes

If a serial is the organ of a corporate body, this fact is noted, generally in the terms used by the publisher. Sometimes this information is from a quoted subtitle, sometimes from elsewhere.

The rules stipulate that the organ note should be made, even if it duplicates the main entry. Most libraries, in an effort to save time and space, will not make the note in that case, however. They will also not usually repeat the society's name if it is listed as publisher, although some will prefer to leave off the publisher statement and amplify the body's connection with the publication further in the notes.

## Minor Variations in Title

If a change of a minor nature occurs in a title, it can be indicated in a note. General statements can be made such as "Title varies slightly" if this covers the bill. Usually this note is made for minor variations of title (or subtitle, if it is being recorded) which do not affect the filing. However, if the rules calling for "Titles of short duration" (see pp. 188-189) are being used, the brief-lived title can also be recorded in this position.

If there are variant forms of the title appearing on the issues themselves, this is the place for them. Sometimes, the title-page and cover vary. These should be noted so they can be traced and an access problem avoided. Notes can also be made here for common titles like *Silliman's Journal* as well as "at head of title notes" and the like.

## Issuing Bodies

If the name or form of the name of an issuing body changes, and the serial is entered under title, there should be a note to this effect. If there are successive issuing bodies for a serial entered under title, this is also made as a note. Slight variations in body names can be noted here, like the provisions for variations in title, noted above.

## Editors

Notes are not usually made for serial editors unless they are very prominent people or people who have been associated with the publication for a long time. However, editors are often important as added "handles" by which publications can be grasped in the catalog. Often their presence in the cataloging will give character to the publication, such as indication of a political or religous slant to a general periodical which might not be noticed since that type of publication rarely gets subject headings.

## Variations in Imprint

Changes in the place of publication, changes in publisher or in the publisher's name, should be noted if they are important. Generally place of publication *and* publisher is considered an important change, especially if the change is of some magnitude, such as across national boundaries. However, if there have been *lots* of changes, a note "Imprint varies" will suffice. This is one of the too-picky rules which serials people deplore and ofttimes it is ignored or not updated. It should not be ignored if it is useful for access, however.

## Connection with Later Publications

The continuing, superseding, absorbing, or merging publication, that is, the one which follows the one being described, is noted. If the subsequent publication does not follow immediately upon the heels of its predecessor, the fact is noted by dates.

One of the criticisms of the order of the North American rules for notes is that the "befores" and "afters" are not put together for easier following of the linkings. Generally catalogers put them together if both are known at the time of cataloging.

## "No More Published?"

A note reading "No more published?" is added as the penultimate note, if there is doubt as to whether or not the number designated as the last issue was in fact the final issue. If the cataloger is sure that the publication has ceased, of course, the question mark is unnecessary. Some libraries use the expression "Ceased publication." If the title is followed by another title, the note is not used.

## Contents

Contents notes may include listings of individual monographs. This is a dead practice which deserved its death well, for access was considerably impeded by the mass of contents cards for monographic series which patrons refused to wade through. Individual analytics are a much more viable (and humane) alternative. Catalog cards are simply made for the contents in the monographic format, with all access points including series. Filed behind the serial card, they provide valuable reference services.

Contents notes may be interpreted to cover accompanying materials such as recordings or other audio-visual materials. (If such a note is called for, mention should also be made of the location of this material, if it is not to be shelved with the bound volumes.)

Contents notes may also contain notes indicating the scope and nature of the work, like: "Minutes of its sessions."

## Other Notes

It is always helpful to indicate to readers if the journal being cataloged includes bibliographic references; review material: book reviews, film or performance reviews, reviews of recordings, etc.; or bibliographies, filmographies, discographies, etc., if this is substantial to the journal or important in the field. The Library of Congress does not usually do this, which is unfortunate, for many libraries, especially academic ones, would find it of value. Often their catalogers will add such notes.

Other notes may be employed, if desired, depending on the situation. The following is a discussion of some of these, although it makes no attempt to be a complete listing. It would depend on the situation being covered, and the policies of the library concerned, where these would come in the outline of notes.

If the library does not use the rule for entry of a serial under personal author, there will need to be a note of this personal author so that he can be traced. Because such a note reflects an alternative form of entry, it would probably be a good idea to make such a note early on in the notes section, perhaps even the first one, depending on the publication. Because this is a deviation from the rules, this note is not considered in the rules at all.

Language notes may be made if the language of the text is not obvious from the title. Summaries in one language for articles in another is often a useful note, especially in academic libraries.

Another note which would be highly desirable would be one indicating that the serial being described is a translation of another serial. Radiophysics, for example, might be described as "Translated from the Russian periodical Radiofizika." A tracing should be made to make this fact an access point as well. Libraries, particularly libraries with both titles, would find this added entry of use.

There might also be notes such as "Also published in French and German editions," especially if the title is misleading as to the language of the text. There may be textual differences in such situations and citations may be misleading unless the patron's attention is drawn to explanations and alternatives.

The title of a publication which is not in the Roman alphabet, and which has a card typed in the appropriate alphabet, should have a note for transliterated or Romanized title, so that the card can be more easily merged with Roman alphabet files. One of the old monographs rules provided for such a note at the lower right-hand corner of the card and many libraries still put in there. In order to facilitate machine processing, however, LC has put the title at the top of the card in curves, in uniform title position.

Notes may also be needed to clarify the conditions surrounding a publication's state of being. Perhaps the publication is a supplement to another publication. This should be noted. Sometimes history statements have to be written explaining that a publication was issued inside something else, but is now a separate publication. (Since the supplements [etc.] rules are separate ones, these will be discussed a little later on in a fuller manner.)

It may be that notes are needed to indicate the extent of a publication in terms of volumes or parts, since it is usually assumed that a publication comes out in one piece per volume, unless the contrary is indicated.

Government publications and special technical reports may be restricted in their circulation. Libraries may wish to make note of this fact so that patrons will understand that some issues may be unavailable to them, or at least unavailable without special clearance.

Sometimes a library may have a title which has lacks which cannot be filled in except by another edition of the publication. If the desire is to keep these together as one set, rather than as two distinct bibliographic entities, a note should be made to explain the situation. This is quite often the case with reprints, which may have elaborate explanations in the introduction about how difficult it was to get a perfect set, how after much perusal of libraries, this was the best they could do, etc., etc., etc. While not specified as a needed note in the rules, such a note is necessary to describe adequately a given situation. (Again, there may be problems with access from indexes, etc. This needs explanation and clarification.)

Reprints of serials are not treated in the 1967 AACR. Most libraries would probably prefer to deviate from LC, which catalogs reprints as such, and catalog the reprint as if it were the original, with the original imprint, etc. This is because it is felt that the patron might miss the identifying imprint information if it appeared in a note and it is better to sacrifice bibliographic niceties and absolute accuracy according to the rules for usefulness. The patron rarely cares that the publication is a reprint and doesn't normally look for either reprint publishers or reprint series. Libraries following this procedure don't usually include the reprint series and those who do very rarely trace it for serial material. Extra introductory matter or criticism and commentary which appear as footnotes or afterpieces are included in the note for the reprint edition. If there is no special material, "Library has reprint edition" should suffice for these libraries.

A serial which has some volumes in reprint editions may demand such a note. If the serial is still continuing, or if the backfile is incomplete, there is no need to try to pin down which volumes are reprints, since these may change. If the serial is ceased or complete to date, the volumes in reprint may be specified if desired, although there is very little real need for such notes. "Library has some volumes in reprint editions" should suffice.

Like notes can be made for microformats. This is especially useful if the set is a mixed one, with some hardcopy and some in a microformat.

Although these last two suggestions are deviations from LC and AACR-authorized practice, this author feels that such a procedure is more in keeping with rules for serials, and with the practical workings of serials departments, and recommends it over the more cumbersome and monograph-like authorized procedure, which relegates more important serials identification factors to notes.

If a serial is published in another format, such as *Blackbox* in audiocassette, notes can be made to indicate this as with the micro-and reprint formats above. "Multimedia" may be an all-encompassing umbrella-term for serials published in various forms, such as *Aspen* with its posters, tapes, put-together box kits, pamphlets, etc. The serial record can work along with the cataloging as the location of specific descriptions, which would be hard to maintain on the public record.

The International Standard Serial Number (ISSN) came out after the 1967 rules so its use does not appear in the printed rules. The ISBD(S) calls for the area which contains this information to be the last one on the bibliographic record. LC has been using this note on all its recent cards.

It is important to remember that, although these rules are altered by AACR2, most of the principles do not change.

## ISBD(S) and AACR 2

It was decided at an international meeting in 1969 that there was a need for the establishment of a standard set of bibliographic items which should be included in the description, in a prescribed order, for all publications. The International Federation of Library Associations and Institutions took on this job and the International Standard Bibliographic Description was born.

After a monographic standard was devised, a serials version was worked on. ISDS (see pp. 189-192) was brought in and the serials standard deviated considerably from the monographic standard. The "key-title" concept was discussed and it was decided that it was better to have a "distinctive title" concept. These two title areas were not constructed in the same way, which resulted in the problems of entry mentioned earlier. The draft came out in 1974.

A North American position paper was written in 1975 to express concern about the draft standard. This document asked for clarification, better examples, and more compatability with the monographic standard, ISBD(M). The paper also asked for more adequate description of serial runs. The paper asked for a new area to cover the numbering of a serial more adequately. The paper was to be presented at an IFLA meeting in late 1975, but something happened instead which changed the direction of the ISBD program, which had been expanded to include maps, early books, and other media. This was the creation of the ISBD(G).

The ISBD(G) is a general standard description which forms the basis for all of the others. The already-existing ISBD's were rewritten to conform to it, and all the incipient ones would also conform when they were finalized.

The ISBD(G) is arranged by "areas," separated by punctuation marks especially used as delimiters between the pieces of information. The list of areas follows, followed by some examples from the first standard edition of the ISD(S) to show what the descriptions will look like.

Area 1   Title and statement of responsibility area
Area 2   Edition or issue area
Area 3   Medium (or type of publication) specific area
Area 4   Publication, distribution, etc., area
Area 5   Physical description area
Area 6   Series area
Area 7   Notes area
Area 8   Standard number (or alternative) and terms of availability area

The Soviet journal of glass physics and chemistry.—Vol. 1, no. 1 (Jan./Feb. 1975)— . —New York : Consultants Bureau, 1975- .—Ill. ; 27cm

Bimonthly

Translation of: Fizika i Khimiya stekla

Description based on vol. 1, no. 3 (May/June 1975).

ISSN 0360-5043 = The Soviet journal of glass physics and chemistry : $95.00 p.a. : $50 (single issue).

European journal of cancer = Journal europeen de cancerologie = Europaische Zeitschrift fur Cancerologie—Vol. 1, no. 1 (June 1965)— . —Oxford [etc.] : Pergamon, 1965- . —29cm

Quarterly

ISSN 0014-2964 = European journal of cancer : £ 5/5/-per issue : £14 per annum.

(The equals signs denote parallel titles)

This standardized transcript and display of bibliographic information will make bibliographic records from different sources interchangeable and mergeable, breaking down language barriers and allowing for easier coding for the automation of these records. Cataloging and the computer are experiencing an interfacing with the ISBD(S).

The ISBD forms the basis of part 1 of the new AACR, which is about description. The general concepts are explained in the introduction, followed by special interpretations of the rules arranged by format. Serials are described according to the provisions of Chapter 12.

## Supplements and Special Numbers

The AACR provides for several types of treatment for the "Special added attractions" which may come in with serials: dash entries, notes, and separate treatment. Decisions must be made based on the supplement itself—would it be best treated separately or as a subsidiary to the parent publication?

If the supplement is a fairly substantial one, with its own numbering system, etc., it is best to award it separate status, cataloging it as a serial or a series of monographs treated individually, depending on the character of the publication itself. Relatively minor supplements can be "tacked on" to the cataloging for the publication being supplemented, by way of notes.

"Dash-ons" should be mentioned briefly. Although still in the rules, it would seem that libraries are moving away from these because of the problems they cause, especially in automated systems. There will be no provisions for these in the new rules, which should cause some rejoicing.

Special numbers, like supplements, can be either cataloged separately or simply noted. If they are extemely minor, they can be disregarded (but one should be careful with this alternative—it may be more trouble in the long run.) As with supplements, each number should be judged on its own merits.

## Indexes

Indexes to single volumes are not recorded. Multiple-year indexes are recorded, either in tabular form, or in an informal note. (Dash-ons were once an option, but this has been discarded.)

Of course, some indexes are serials in themselves, such as the index to *The New York Times*. These are substantial reference tools in their own right, and are generally treated as separate titles.

## Classification and Subject Cataloging

The general attitude of most librarians seems to be that, since serials are approached only through indexes, it is a waste of time to classify them and give them broad and meaningless subject headings. This is an unfortunate attitude, for all serials are not indexed and not everyone consults indexes anyway.

Patrons usually approach the catalog to see what is in the library. Often patrons take a subject approach and it is best to have periodicals listed there, even in a general way, or they might not even think to look in them. Certainly, this approach would be of tremendous benefit in looking for the indexes, which are, of course, also serials.

Classification does not always provide the same functions that subject headings do. Classification may be broader or narrower in scope than the subject headings used so that oftentimes the two provide complementary and supplementary approaches to the materials. Classification integrates the journal materials with the monographic materials on the same general subject matter on the shelves, and subject headings integrate the same materials in the catalog, perhaps on several levels, depending on the schemes used. Both can provide browsing access for patrons.

Classification should be given to the primary scope of a periodical and subject headings can scatter this scope. Thus, patrons can be encouraged to sample in broader areas than they might normally try, and use of materials, which might ordinarily be overlooked, can be encouraged.

The actual assignment of subject headings for serials is not particularly difficult and normal guidelines for subject-heading assignment can be used. The difficulty stems mainly from the fact that a serial is incomplete when it is being cataloged and the cataloger has to keep this in mind and act accordingly. Since most serials issues are comprised of several articles, there is a built-in caution against the use of headings which are too narrow. Caution, however, needs to be employed in the subject cataloging of monographic series or when a special issue of a journal devoted to a narrow subject or aspect of a subject is the issue for cataloging. In these cases, other materials may need to be consulted: publisher's "blurbs" which may give scope notes or list forthcoming articles, catalogs listing other titles published, etc. Sometimes, waiting for later issues is the only solution. However, this is common for all aspects of serials cataloging and should not be considered a real problem of enormous proportions. Serials cataloging should always give enough leeway for variation without restriction and so that the cataloger won't have to make changes in the future.

Libraries have always felt a little unclear about what to do with periodical publications with regard to classification. Should they be classified or not? Some classify them and shelve the bound and unbound issues together in call number order. Some classify all, some classify none of their serials; some class "continuations" only. Some don't classify periodicals which appear more frequently than once a year, but do classify serials appearing once a year or less frequently; classifying or declassifying as the publication changes frequency. Some cover only subscriptions and gifts and some only defunct titles and short runs. Some do not classify ephemeral materials. The whole concept seems to be on fairly shaky ground in a lot of libraries.

Classifying periodicals does have a number of advantages. The principal one of these is that subject matter can be kept together. It can be argued that subject areas for periodicals are very broad but this seems to be changing as more and more fields are springing up and are being developed into whole disciplines. The character of the classification schedules is changing too.

For titles which are accessed through indexes, the call number may become an arbitrary shelving device, but some titles may have no access through indexes. Even a general classification can be a hint as to the contents of the publication. Finding it amongst the monographs on similar topics will guarantee chance use of it by browsers.

A serials shelflist arranged in call number order can be a very valuable aid in serials reference work. A quick consultation of the schedules followed by an excursion through the shelflist can answer many patron requests about serials. Some retrieval can be done through the subject headings, of course, but sometimes these two subject approaches complement each other rather than give duplicate information.

A lot of material can be manipulated via computer if the information is there to input. Printouts can be generated on various subject areas by sorting on class numbers. They can be placed in strategic locations around the library, far from the catalog or the shelflist, or they can be handed out to patrons for reference purposes.

Call number sorts by computer or manually in the shelflist can provide data useful in periodical selection, just as call number arrangements by Dewey numbers in the subject-arranged NST can. (In fact, these can be coordinated somewhat, particularly in a Dewey-arranged library.) A library can analyze its collection in a subject field by such a mechanical means. This is rough analysis, to be sure, but faster and more convenient than any other method and seemingly highly-regarded in the library world as an accurate sampling procedure. A field can be analyzed for periodical support in a way which would be awkward without a convenient means such as this. Automated circulation systems, such as CLSI, can give important circulation statistical information for a classed serial collection, depending on the profiling used. But a classed collection is essential for this.

A by-product of the current economic situation, rampant inflation and tight budgets, is the need to "deselect" titles which are no longer centrally relevant to the library's needs, or which the library cannot support. A method of going about this weeding process might be a list, preferably computer-produced, like the ones just mentioned, sorted by the discipline supported. Then, the selection officers in each area can pare away at their own disciplinary interests. Profiles of various subjects could be coded by class numbers and matched with each other to show overlaps. This can be a great time-saver at budget time or when the serials come up for renewal. Many automated procedures would be facilitated by call numbers.

Serials do not become less accessible in the collection because they are not monographs. They are not given less than first-class coverage. For the best possible reference work with serials, the collection should be given both call numbers and subject headings.

**Communication Channels**

It must be remembered that serials cataloging, to be effective to the utmost, must be intertwined with serials control records and the other records and procedures which involve themselves with serials control. All records should be based upon the cataloging record which the cataloger creates. The cataloger should become the bibliographic authority for all of the records and record changes of a bibliographic nature (as opposed to those involving acquisitions decisions like changes of vendors) should receive the cataloger's seal of approval. For all of this, there needs to be good communication.

In the past, communications often broke down because of the different requirements different ones had for cataloging information. Generally, people involved with serials control want titles cataloged as fast as possible so that complementary records can be made. For title changes, the records should be updated posthaste.

For the cataloger, this was not a good idea. What seemed practical to the recordkeeper did not seem so to the catalogers, who preferred to catalog from bound volumes which had title-pages. After all, this was the most stable presentation of the title—if you were lucky enough to receive the title-page, of course.

Publication patterns for serials have changed fairly radically in recent years. Few periodicals have separate title-pages anymore. Those who do rarely change their titles for the title-page (at least, no more than for anything else!) Catalogers have also recognized that it is easier to catalog once than to redo or wait. Even LC discovered this in 1968, and has been cataloging from first issue, without mishap, ever since.

As soon as titles change, the cataloger should be notified so that an entry can be established and new records made. Catalogers had more leeway in the past than they will in the future when it comes to changes of title, for there was the option of using the "titles-of-short duration" rule. Even with this gone, however, it is best to have the cataloger look with expert eye at title changes and make the necessary decisions. Having such procedures will require some form to be used as a communication device.

Because serials are in a state of continuous change, having a form to route around to insure that the various records get changed is very important. Then, anyone discovering a change in the course of their work can initiate these "change memos." It is always best to have the catalogers look at the bibliographic changes. Then, terminology can be standardized and correct interpretations made.

## Cataloging Routines

When a new title is received, it should immediately be routed to Cataloging, as suggested earlier. If pre-order searching exists, it should be routed with the piece, or at least be available to the cataloging staff. Thus, previous work can be built upon rather than duplicated.

Searching for catalog copy is generally done in *New Serials Titles* or the *Union List of Serials* (depending upon the age of the title) and of the series of catalogs from the Library of Congress. If a catalog copy is found in an LC catalog, it can be photographed, copied, or sent for through the Cataloging Distribution Service. In this day-and-age of computers, databases which have the MARC serials tapes (q.v.) may also be searched and copy obtained. One of these utilities, OCLC, will be discussed later. OCLC also has contributed copy from libraries other than LC, which can be used as the basis of cataloging. ULS and NST do not, of course, provide cataloging *per se*, but the information obtained is often useful in building a cataloging record or amending one. Other sources such as directories of serials, national bibliographies, other library catalogs, union lists and the like, can be searched depending upon the nature of the serial and the type of information desired. Some of these sources are listed in the "TOOLS" section of this book.

If copy is found it can be used as a basis for cataloging, but it should not be a substitute for the cataloger's own observations. The serial may have changed since it was cataloged and the copy in the source was not updated. Other catalogers make mistakes, even at LC, and these should be corrected, not perpetuated. But the cataloger shouldn't just throw copy away, but make use of whatever is appropriate. Do not be slavish to the copy, but also let others save you some work.

If there is no copy available, the cataloger will have to catalog the publication from scratch, using the guidelines for serials cataloging given earlier.

The cataloger must determine the choice and form of entry. This is important for standardizing reference to the title in question. The "norm" has to be established and variations noted.

The cataloger must read the preface or introduction. The title may be cited there, which will help if the title is unclear elsewhere. Scope will be set forth—useful for subject headings and classification, and historical background may be given—useful for notes and, perhaps linking to other titles.

Read the issue carefully. The numbering may be hidden. There may be several numbering schemes. It may be that articles will have to be read and bibliographies studied for proper subject cataloging. "Blurbs" may need to be consulted for intent. These can be especially important for reprints, for they will explain why the serial is important, citing noteworthy editors, etc., which will need to be covered in the cataloging. Publishing history may also be given. The neophyte cataloger must learn to be aware of everything connected with the serial at hand and must learn to sift out the unimportant from the definitely necessary.

This information all needs to be passed back, hopefully with the issues, to the rest of the serials workers. Copies of catalog cards, workforms, input sheets for automated serials lists—all are used by the cataloger as a communication device. The form is not important. What is important is that the directives established by the cataloger and the bibliographic information set forth be clear and precise and concise. It is also important that the method of communication be part of the normal workflow, not an impediment to it.

Bound volumes need to be recorded somewhere. If an inventory is needed, it is probably best to have a shelflist record of volume-by-volume holdings. If this is not important to the library, perhaps it is best to have the central serial record be the record of bound as well as unbound holdings. It is important to consider the use of the records, whether they are public or not, etc. There is a lot of redundancy in serial recordkeeping. Some is useful, some is not. Long-range planning needs to be done in this regard.

## Automated Cataloging Operations

The preceeding paragraphs speak of a manual serial cataloging set-up. But what happens when the procedures become automated?

Basically the in-house procedures do not change much. There will probably be staff time saved in typing and in searching and the configuration of the cataloging section may vary a little, but the general procedures outlined earlier should hold true still. The communication channels are still vitally necessary.

The real differences come in the interface between man and machine, in this case, the cataloger vs. the terminal. Because it is the most advanced and widespread system with regards to serials, let us see how OCLC works for serials cataloging.

But before we can talk about OCLC, we must first talk about MARC-S. MARC-S is a machine-readable cataloging format for serials. It sets forth bibliographic contents in a structured format using special "content designators" (tags, indicators, and subfield codes) for each bibliographic item. The organization of records accords with library practices, for it is a creation of the Library of Congress. The format is basically the MARC II bibliographic data format (for monographs), with slight modification and extension. All programs based on accessing the MARC II type of file would be able to access serial records in MARC-S with only some modification, primarily in tag names, which need to be changed slightly to accommodate serials. The content designators are the same across all formats of material where the data elements are the same.

MARC-S input is made by batch process from the cataloging workflow at LC (see *Serials Processing and Control at the Library of Congress*). After the cataloging worksheet travels with the issue to Shelflisting or Dewey Classification (if such is desired), it goes to the MARC Office for edition and keypunching. In November of 1966 LC began distributing machine-readable cataloging as part of the MARC Pilot Project. In March 1969 this became fully-blown as the MARC Distribution Service. The MARC Development Office was established in the Processing Department in June 1970 to explore, develop, and implement automation in technical processing at LC. The first serials format was issued in 1969. It was revised by addendum in 1971. The second edition came out in July of 1974.

In February 1973 LC began to convert catalog records for newly-cataloged serials to machine-readable form. All Roman alphabet languages have been included. All serials cataloged for printed cards starting in 1973, as well as older serials for which cards are being reprinted, are included. The first MARC-S tapes came out in June 1973. These records on magnetic tapes are available on subscription.

MARC-S has been instrumental in bringing serials cataloging towards an accepted norm. Its availability as part of the databases of cataloging systems like OCLC put it within reach of libraries across the country and its very presence demands its use as a basis for cataloging far beyond that of the often-tardy NUC's or LC cards.

Serials MARC records are made up of "fixed" and "variable" fields. The fixed field contains twenty-four elements, which describe, in coded form, specified features of the serial or its catalog record. Most are one-character codes. Elements are supplied by the system and are mandatory or optional on the part of the library cataloging the publication in question. Mandatory elements include type of record, kind of publication being cataloged, bibliographic level, latest/successive entry designator, language (important for retrieval purposes), publication pattern of the serial, and dates of publication. If not changed, the system generally goes to a "default" symbol (usually for the most common piece of information filled in on the blanks on the workform).

The variable fields contain the bibliographic information about the title being cataloged. These are the "body of the entry", notes, etc.

on conventional catalog card. Each field is identified by the MARC three-number code ("tag"), preceded by a "start of message" symbol (►). The field ends with a "terminator," which is a paragraph mark (¶). Subfield codes, represented by a "delimiter" (‡) and a letter, may also be present in the cataloging, as shown later in the discussion of OCLC.

Since this is not a manual on either OCLC cataloging or MARC format, it is not necessary to delve deeply into variable field coding. It is however important to know what some of the major ones are. A list follows:

| | |
|---|---|
| 101 | Library of Congress Card number |
| 022 | ISSN |
| 040 | Cataloging source |
| 042 | Authentication center (for CONSER Centers of Responsibility only [see pp. 220-22]) |
| 049 | Holding library code |
| 050 | LC call numbers |
| 082 | DDC call numbers |
| 086 | Government Document call number (formerly Su Docs) |
| 090 | Local call number |
| 100 | Personal name main entry |
| 110 | Corporate name main entry |
| 111 | Conference or meeting name main entry |
| 222 | Key title |
| 245 | Title |
| 246 | Varying forms of title |
| 247 | Former titles or title variations |
| 250 | Edition statement |
| 260 | Imprint |
| 300 | Collation |
| 310 | Current frequency [only if it cannot be expressed adequately in the fixed field information, or if it has changed] |
| 362 | Dates of publication and volume designation |
| 400 | Personal name—title series statement |
| 410 | Corporate name—title series statement |
| 411 | Conference or meeting name—title series statement |
| 440 | Title series statement |
| 490 | Series statement not traced or traced differently |
| 500 | General notes |
| 504 | Bibliography note |
| 515 | Numbering peculiarities note |
| 525 | Supplement note |
| 533 | Photo reproduction note |
| 546 | Language reproduction note |

| | |
|---|---|
| 547 | Former title complexity note ["Title varies"] |
| 550 | Issuing bodies note |
| 555 | Cumulative index note |
| 570 | Editor |
| 600 | Personal name subject entry |
| 610 | Corporate name subject entry |
| 611 | Conference or meeting name subject entry |
| 650 | Topical subject headings |
| 651 | Geographic subject headings |
| 700 | Personal name added entry |
| 710 | Corporate name added entry |
| 711 | Conference or meeting name added entry |
| 760 | Main series entry |
| 762 | Subseries entry |
| 770 | Supplement/special issue entry |
| 772 | Parent record entry |
| 777 | "Issued with" entry |
| 780 | Preceding entry |
| 785 | Succeeding entry |
| 800 | Personal name—title series added entry |
| 810 | Corporate name—title series added entry |
| 811 | Conference or meeting name—title series added entry |
| 840 | Title series added entry |

As can easily be seen, the MARC format parallels the AACR. For subfield and scope notes, it is best to consult the MARC format or various OCLC manuals.

## OCLC

OCLC is a system begun in the brain of Fredrick Kilgour and others. It was originally called the "Ohio College Library Center" and served colleges and universities in the state of Ohio. Since then, it has grown and spread across the country, embracing public and academic and special libraries from sea to sea. Thus, it has changed its name to OCLC, Inc.

OCLC had 250,397 serial records in its database at the end of June 1978 according to the Western Service Center. It is currently the vehicle for CONSER and contains all of its records, including the inloaded MULS and other union list databases (see pp. 218-220). In addition, the *Monthly Catalog* appears on OCLC.

The OCLC keyboard is similar to a typewriter keyboard, with an assortment of extra keys. (It is best to consult *On-line Cataloging* or the "PALINET manual" for an explanation of these.) After "logging in" with an authorization number in Social Security number configuration, one can do a search of the database.

There are a number of ways to search on OCLC. The basic search for a title is 3,2,2,1: the first three letters of the first word (not an article), the first two letters of the next two words, and the first letter of the fourth word. The commas must be input to distinugish between the words and to identify that it is a title search. If the title only has three words, the search key is 3,2,2,; if two words: 3,2,,. Name searches are basically on the pattern of 4,3,1 and must have two commas. A name-title search pattern is 4,4 and must have the single comma.

A new feature has been added recently in order to provide a distinction between searching corporate and personal names. To search a corporate name, the search key is to be preceded by an equals sign ( = ); then proceed as usual.

One of the major problems with OCLC's search key mechanism for authors and titles is that there is only a maximum of 256 entries retrievable. If you search on a name or title (especially one-word titles like Geographica or Life) and the search turns up over 256 entries, you cannot use that search key. This is a severe limitation and OCLC promises us they are working on a solution, particularly for one-word serial titles. In cases of extended searches of less than 256 titles, the system will give a series of indexes to narrow down the search until you can find the one you want.

The fastest searches are numerical ones, however. If the OCLC control number (supplied by the system) is known, it can be searched on by using the number shift and keying the number straight in. Search on LC card number by using the number as printed, including the hyphen. ISSN is keyed in as written, including the hyphen between the fourth and fifth digits. CODEN can also be searched, if desired or known. These searches are the only alternative for those "over-256 problems."

The cataloger may wish to use the information found on the screen "as is." If this is so, he may simply push the PRODUCE button. If not, he may delete, insert, correct and transfer information about on the screen until he is satisfied with the results. If he wishes to check information before actually producing cards, he may shuttle his information into the "save" file for future reference. Thus, the terminal is not tied-up while the checking is going on and another may use the terminal. ("Save" lasts for 7 days.) When the PRODUCE and SEND keys are depressed at the end of the operation, catalog cards will be printed and sent to the Library, holdings will be added to the Library's archive tape, and the library's three-letter code will be added to the holding libraries listing. If, instead of using an already-existent record, the cataloger creates his own, he will request a workform, fill it out, and create a new record for the file. With this outline of MARC variable fields already listed, it should be easy to pick out the information shown on the following serials catalog record screen display. Also following is the catalog card which resulted from the screen display. Note that not all of the fields input or printed on the cards. Some fields are non-printing. Libraries requiring cards fill out profiling forms so that OCLC staff can give them cards within certain proscribed formats. For example, there are several different choices of ways to display the call number in addition to the one illustrated here. Profiling can also provide for the automatic appearance of certain information. The red-letter date for OCLC serials catalogers was 17 October 1977. The message on CRT's across the country that morning was that catalog cards for serials were, at long last, available!

### Serials Catalog Record Screen Display

```
OCLC: 1788131        Rec stat: c Entrd: 740226        ' Used: 760224  ℜ
▶Type: a Bib lvl: s Govt pub:    Lang:  eng Source:    S/L ent: 0⊦
 Repr:    Enc lvl:    Conf pub: 0 Ctry:  nyu Ser tp: p Alphabt: a⊦
 Indx:    Mod rec:    Phys med:    Cont: ^    Frequn: e Pub st: c⊦
 Desc:    Cum ind:    Titl pag:    ISDS:   1 Regulr: u Dates: 1973-9999 ℜ
▶ 1 010        73-645517 ℜ
▶ 2 040        DLC ⨍c DLC ⨍d NSD ℜ
▶ 3 012        2 ⨍b 3 ⨍c - ⨍d 7 ⨍e - ⨍f - ⨍g p ⨍h - ⨍i ---- ℜ
▶ 4 022        0091-620X ℜ
▶ 5 042        1c ⨍a nsdp ℜ
▶ 6 050 00     AP2 ⨍b .S273 ℜ
▶ 7 082        051 ℜ
▶ 8 090        ⨍b  ℜ
▶ 9 049 ▮▮     OCLC ℜ
▶10 222 00     Saturday review. World ℜ
▶11 245 00     Saturday review/world. ℜ
▶12 246 17     SR/world ⨍f <Sept. 11, 1973-> ℜ
▶13 260 00     [New York] ℜ
▶14 265        (Subscription Dept.) P.O. Box 2043, Rock Island, Ill., 61206 ℜ
▶15 300        ⨍b illus. ⨍c 28 cm. ℜ
▶16 350        $12.00 ℜ
▶17 362 0      v. 1-   Sept. 11, 1973- ℜ
▶18 580        Formed by the union of Saturday ⊦
review of education, Saturday review of society, ⊦
Saturday review of the arts, Saturday review of ⊦
the sciences, and World. ℜ
▶19 780 14     ⨍t Saturday review of education. ℜ
▶20 780 14     ⨍t Saturday review of society. ℜ
▶21 780 14     ⨍t Saturday review of the arts. ℜ
▶22 780 14     ⨍t Saturday review of the sciences. ℜ
▶23 780 14     ⨍t World. ℜ
▶24 785 00     ⨍t Saturday review ⨍c (New York ⨍d 1975) ⨍x 0361-1655 ℜ
```

```
AP
2        Saturday review/world. v. 1-      Sept.
.S273      11, 1973- 1974. [New York]
            v. illus. 28 cm.
           Running title: SR/world, <Sept. 11,
         1973->
           Formed by the union of: Saturday
         review of education, ISSN 0091-8555;
         Saturday review of society, ISSN 0091-
         8571; Saturday review of the arts, ISSN
         0091-8563; Saturday review of the
         sciences, ISSN 0091-8547 and World (New
         York. 1972) ISSN 0049-8009.
           Continued by: Saturday review (New
         York 1975) ISSN 0361-1655.
           Key title: Saturday review.
         World, ISSN 0091-620X
           1. Title: S   R/world

OCoLC   17 OCT 77      1788101  'OCLPxc      73-645517
```

## Union Lists and Other Automated Projects

When dealing with serials, the issues of standardization are very important. Serials are not easy to standardize, but somehow they generally end up being that which is first automated in a library, usually in the form of automated serials lists. Libraries then join together in systems or consortia and merge their lists into a union list of serials. Without some standardization, these endeavors usually end up as failures.

Automation can do a number of good things with cataloging data. There is great flexibility in manipulating the data, which can facilitate search and retrieval.

Computerization of cataloging data gives an added dimension to bibliographic control. There is complete access to everything in the record from all possible angles. Changes can be made effortlessly and updating is easy.

Searching could be done on a few important words or part of words as in OCLC system, Stanford's RLIN (Research Libraries Information Network), or the Washington Library Network (WLN) system. Order and catalog copy could be printed out, with desired changes (see pp. 217). The computer record can even be accessed by patrons desiring on-order or cataloging information through special programs and terminals in public areas.

Other cataloging by-products could be produced: book cards, packets, spine labels, all preparatory for an automated circulation system. Lists could be generated for bindery preparation forms, and receipt and claim records. Special lists, such as subject lists, location lists, key word lists, could be run on the machine file. The computer could pull out such information as language, country of origin, price, vendor, and other management data, depending on the information contained within the file itself. List possibilities are endless.

Libraries are finding that their serial subscriptions are taking over the major part of their book budgets with the current rampant inflation. In attempts to stop this before it gets too far out-of-hand, many are taking a long hard look at their serial commitments in terms of their real needs. Some academic libraries are finding it easier to distribute printouts of shelflist-ordered serials for the faculties in the various disciplines they support to evaluate. A number of printouts can be produced so that some titles may be duplicated and distributed to several faculties with overlapping interests. Evaluations can be keyed back into the computer and "deselection" lists generated. (This cannot be done easily without a classed collection, however.)

The most obvious use of automation in the individual library for serials cataloging records is the holdings list, mentioned earlier. In some libraries this serves as the only public record of serials in the library. In others, it serves as an addition to the catalog for holdings information; a more efficient updating than the old practice of writing on the catalog cards. Costs can be cut by putting the list on computer-generated microfiche or film, called COM (Computer Output Microform).

The demise of the book catalog was caused by the lack of a rapid method of updating. Cataloging is coming full circle with the advent of the computer-produced catalog or serials list in book form. This book catalog, unlike its predecessor, can be rapidly updated and superseded.

In this age of ever-shrinking budgets, the accent is on the sharing of resources. Libraries are depending more on the holdings of wealthier neighbors as their own funds diminish. Some libraries are becoming more specialized. Libraries are forming systems. Consortia are becoming a fact of library life right now. The era of splendid isolation of each library unto itself is over. With the boom in technology and the explosion in publishing, no library can hope to control under its own roof all of the materials a serious resercher would need. Catalog records input into an automated system would facilitate circulation, reference, and interlibrary loan functions. The world would become our own library, except in physical terms. Perhaps someday thoses can be improved upon too.

Union lists of periodical holdings in the various operating libraries are essential for smooth operation of these sharing plans. *New Serials Titles* is, of course, the biggest one. The twenty-one year cumulation issued by Bowker in 1972 is the largest machine-readable data base, composed of over 220,000 records. The state of California has large union lists, put out by the State Library, the State College and University System, and the University of California System. The Minnesota Union List of Serials (MULS) is a state list of all universities, public libraries, and state agencies. There are union lists in various subject areas too, such as the *Union Catalog of Medical Periodicals* (UCMP) developed at the Medical Library Center of New York. The list could go on and on.

## CONSER

CONSER (CONversion of SERials) is certainly the most monumental automated union listing effort to date. It is international in scope, involving libraries in both Canada and the United States, and vast in its ramifications, having implications for serials cataloging and processing for the present and near future. Some 200,000 records have been involved so far.

CONSER grew out of concern that there was lack of communication and compatibility between serials files being generated in machine-readable form. This was causing confusion and a solution was needed before everything got thoroughly out-of-hand. The Council on Library Resources agree to fund the project, with additional funding coming from elsewhere, and OCLC agreed to be the conversion vehicle.

The *Minnesota Union List of Serials* (MULS) was chosen as the basis for this union listing activity because it is so MARC-like in structure. The plan was to convert it by computer, with manual edit, to upgraded specifications along the guidelines with which ISDS and NSDP were working. ISSN and key titles would be assigned by NSDP and ISDS—Canada, the Canadian national center located in the National Library of Canada.

The conversion of the MULS list would give the participants an opportunity to reconcile the conflicts which exist between MARC-S, NSDP AND ISDS, Canadian MARC-S, AACR and superimposition and ISBD(S) formats and structures. CONSER has been the impetus for the change to desuperimposed Canadian headings. CONSER was partially responsible for the need to recognize and work with the incompatibility of AACR, ISDS, and ISBD(S) in the matter of title recording, which resulted primarily in title main entry. CONSER also required that MARC-S be amplified to include key-title, which was subsequently done. CONSER has also changed the interpretation of rule 6D2, so that very few titles are cataloged under the "short duration" rule, these being only very minor changes. CONSER has also been instrumental as impetus for the development of an American National Standards Institute standard on a summary holdings statement.

The initial CONSER participants were: the Library of Congress, the National Library of Canada, the National Library of Medicine, the National Agricultural Library, the State University of New York the New York State Library, the University of Minnesota, Yale, Cornell, and the University of California. Later, the University of Florida, with the *Florida Union List of Serials*, and Boston Theological Institute, Harvard and the U.S. Department of the Interior joined, too. The National Federation of Abstracting and Indexing Services (NFAIS) has a cooperative agreement with CONSER to supply up to 25,000 scientific and technical serial surrogates (photocopies of covers, title-pages, and mastheads) to NSDP for the project.

All new serials cataloging from the participating libraries was input into OCLC's on-line shared cataloging system. LC authenticated all non-Canadian names in the database and authenticated the complete cataloging record if previously cataloged by LC. LC also maintained an authority file of AACR-based headings and the older ALA ones, already in the LC files, so that someday a button can be pushed and desuperimposition can happen "as if by magic!"(This will happen only when all of LC's current cataloging is in machine-readable form, probably in 1981.) The National Library of Canada provided authentication functions for Canadian publications.

LC was fully operational in CONSER on 22 June, 1976. During the Project, LC input on a CRT to OCLC. OCLC returned these records to LC in LC's internal processing format so that the MARC records could be produced. LC (NSDP) authenticated key-titles, ISSN, and verified forms of names. LC also varified subject headings and other data on complete records. LC built records on a CONSER base and post edited non-CONSER records. ISDS provided ISSN and key-titles for outside publications through the two national centers involved. These centers of responsibility were the only ones who could change elements, such as name authority or ISSN, within their spheres of influence. These parts of the records will be locked to all others. CONSER tapes are converted into the ISDS exchange format at LC and are one of the principal modes of communication between the Canadian and US ISDS centers and ISDS/IC in Paris.

American and international standards were adhered to so that CONSER was pretty much able to accomodate existing and past standards, rather than set new ones, except perhaps when necessary to resolve conflicts. Records were updated by the participants to insure a record which reflected the changes in the publication it represented.

Records were based on a minimum set of MARC-S requirements, but participants were encouraged to make the records as full as possible. Regular users of OCLC were able to use CONSER records, but not change them.

Tapes of CONSER records will probably be distributed as an adjunct to MARC-S tapes, but this has not yet happened. There are plans, however, to use the tapes when they come out to build union lists. Canadian librarians have fantastic schemes for a whole panoply of union listing activities using CONSER.

The first stage of CONSER is over. In support of planning for CONSER II, which started in January of 1978, the MARC-S and CONSER databases were analyzed and programs for search keys were developed. Meanwhile, the project is continuing in a transitional form (for an unspecified period of time), with OCLC in charge, while LC gears up to take it over.

CONSER manuals are being updated for when CONSER goes online. Special authentication centers, like NLM (for MESH AND NLM call numbers) are preparing to incorporate more detailed procedures into their workflow.

One of the problems of the on-line system will be that the location symbols will not be specific enough. The Minnesota Interlibrary Telecommunications Exchange (MINITEX) is working on some specifications to modify and link location symbols, especially based on MULS information (MINITEX publishes MULS). This will result in improved access.

The basic purpose of CONSER II is to improve user access to serials.

The most exciting thing is that, sometime in the future, all input may be on-line to LC, and *NST* will be automatically updated by contributing libraries in an on-line mode, thus flinging *NST* far into the world of the future!

## BIBLIOGRAPHY

*Anglo-American Cataloging Rules*, prepared by the American Library Association, the Library of Congress, the Library Association and the Canadian Library Association, North American text. Chicago, American Library Association, 1967.

Anable, Richard, "CONSER: Bibliographic considerations," *Library Resources & Technical Services*, v. 19: 341-348, Fall 1975.

Cannan, Judith, Proctor, "The impact of international standardization on the rules of entry for serials," *Library Resources & Technical Services*, v. 19: 164-169, Spring 1975.

Carpenter, Michael, "No special rules for entry of serials," *Library Resources & Technical Services,* v. 19: 327-332, Fall 1975.

Cole, Jim. E., "AACR 6: Time for a review," *Library Resources & Technical Services,* v. 19: 314-326, Fall 1975.

Fasana, Paul, "AACR, ISBD(S) and ISSN: A comment," *Library Resources & Technical Services,* v. 19: 333-337, Fall 1975.

Gorman, Michael, "The current state of standardization in the cataloging of serials," *Library Resources & Technical Services,* v. 19: 301-313, Fall 1975.

Daniels, Mary Kay, "Automated serials control: national and international considerations," *Journal of Library Automation,* v. 8: 127-146, June 1975.

Edgar, Neal L., "Some implications of code revision for serials librarians," *The Serials Librarian,* v. 1: 125-134, Winter 1976-77.

Gates, Barbara A., *Serials Cataloging for the Ohio College Library Center System; a manual,* rev. ed., Richardson, Texas, AMIGOS Bibliographic Council, July 1976.

Hamdy, M. Nabil, *The Concept of Main Entry as represented in the Anglo-American Cataloging Rules; a Critical Appraisal with Some Suggestions: Author Main Entry vs. Title Main Entry,* Littleton, Colo., Libraries Unlimited, 1973.

Henderson, Katherine Luther, "Serial cataloging revisited—a long search for a little theory and a lot of cooperation," *Serials Publications in Large Libraries,* edited by Walter C. Allen. London, Clive Bingley, 1971.

Howard, Joseph H., "Main entry for serials," *Library of Congress Information Bulletin,* v. 33: A-232-A-236, November 22, 1974.

International Conference on Cataloguing Principles, Paris, 1961. *Report,* London, Organizing Committee of the International Conference on Cataloguing Principles, 1961.

_____. Statement of principles . . ., Annotated edition with commentary and examples of Eva Verona, assisted by Franz Georg Kaltwasser, P. R. Lewis, Roger Pierrot, London, IFLA Committee on Cataloguing, 1971.

International Federation of Library Associations. *ISBD(M)—International Standard Bibliographic Description for Monographic Publications,* 1st standard edition, London, IFLA Committee on Cataloguing, 1974.

_____. *ISBD(S)—International Standard Bibliographic Description for Serials,* recommended by the Joint Working Group in the International Standard Bibliographic Description for Serials set up by the IFLA Committee on Cataloguing and the IFLA Committee on Serial Publications. London: IFLA Committee on Cataloguing, 1971.

International Federation of Library Associations and Institutions. *ISBD(S)—International Standard Bibliographic Description for Serials,* recommended by the Joint Working Group in the International Standard Bibliographic Description for Serials set up by the IFLA Committee on Cataloguing and the IFLA Committee on Serial Publications. 1st standard ed. London: IFLA Committee on Cataloguing, 1977.

Library of Congress. MARC Development Office. *Serials: a MARC format.* 2nd edition. Washington, D.C.: Library of Congress, 1974.

Library of Congress. Processing Department. *Cataloging Service Bulletin,* 1-June 1945-. Washington, D.C.: Library of Congress.

Muller, Hans, "Why classify periodicals?" *Wilson Library Bulletin,* v. 14: 758-759, July 1940.

Ohio College Library Center. *On-line Cataloging. Addenda.* No. 1- July 1975-.

_____. *Technical Bulletins.* No. 1- 1976-.

Osborn, Andrew D., *Serial Publications; Their Place and Treatment in Libraries,* Chicago: American Library Association, 1955.

_____. *Serial Publications; Their Place and Treatment in Libraries,* 2nd edition, revised. Chicago: American Library Association, 1973.

PALINET, *Manual for Operation of the OCLC 100 Terminal and the OCLC System.* Philadelphia, PALINET and Union Library Catalogue of Pennsylvania, June 1976.

Paul, Huibert, "Serials: chaos and standardization," *Library Resources & Technical Services,* v. 14: 19-30, Winter 1970.

Pulsifer, Josephine S., "Comparison of MARC serials, NSDP and ISBDS," *Journal of Library Automation,* v. 6: 193-200, December 1973.

Schley, Ruth and Davies, J. B., *Serials Notes Compiled from Library of Congress Cards Issued 1947-April 1951.* New York, Columbia University Libraries, 1952.

Simonton, Wesley, "Serials cataloging problems: rules of entry and definition of title," *Library Resources & Technical Services,* v. 19: 294-300, Fall 1975.

Smith, Lynn S., *A Practical Approach to Serials Cataloging* (Foundations in Library and Information Science, v. 2). Greenwich, Conn., J.A.I. Press, 1978.

Spalding, C. Sumner, "I.S.B.D.: its origin, rationale, and implications," *Library Journal,* v. 98: 121-123, January 15, 1973.

_____. "ISBD(S) and title main entry for serials," *International Cataloguing,* v. 3: A-229-A-232, July/September 1974.

_____. "Keeping serials cataloging costs in check," *Library Resources & Technical Services,* v. 1: 13-20, Winter 1957.

# CHAPTER VIII
# SERIALS PROCESSING AND CONTROL AT THE LIBRARY OF CONGRESS

**Contributed by**
**Lynn S. Smith**

### History of Serial Processing

Serials have steadily increased in importance at the Library of Congress. In the early years one could barely find mention of such publications in the Library's writings, but this has changed considerably in recent years with increased emphasis being placed upon these publications.

Like other libraries, LC found it difficult to contribute adequately to the *Union List of Serials*. Different catalogs had to be consulted for holdings and the accuracy of what was reported was seriously in question. Issues were scattered everywhere and communication was a real problem. An advisory committee to the Librarian of Congress proposed that a central serial record be established.

The Central Serial Record was set up in August 1941. Converison of the other records took place and these other records abolished. Steps were taken to standardize processing. The Central Serial Record became the official shelflist of bound serial holdings. Updating holdings in the Official and Public Catalogs was discontinued. Form card cataloging (see pp. 226-7) was discontinued. (Centralized acquisitions was begun and some of the chaos and disorder of the preceding years was made orderly and organized). Procedures were created for smooth communications between the Serial Record and the Serial Division, where issues were to be centrally housed.

In 1951, to increase efficiency further, simplified checking entries were used in the Serial Record base on the title on the piece-in-hand rather than ALA cataloging rules-based headings. However, this procedure was abondoned in 1952, for it had not produced the economies predicted and had resulted in confusion and wasted time. Interestingly enough, the cataloging rules of the future will duplicate this effort— hopefully without the same problems!

## The Serial Record Today

The Serial Record in the Library of Congress records all serials in the Roman, Greek, Hebrew, and Cyrillic alphabets. The following genera of publications are not included: newspapers, trade catalogs,. telephone books, and a few categories of ephemera (such as comic books, which are received in large numbers through copyright deposit). "Serial" is rather broadly interpreted by the Library to include periodicals, documents, annuals, numbered monographic series (including publishers' series), and certain other publications without either a stated or a logical ending.

The file consists of regular visible file trays, with check-in cards and 3"x5" cards on top of them, consolidating permanent information, and a 3"x5" dead file which sits on top of the vertical file. The Record includes some bibliographic information sufficient to identify the title, such as city of publication and beginning date. (For numbered monographic series, cataloging and classification treatment notes also appear on the record. Other selection and acquisition decisions are part of the permanent portion of the record, too.) Interim check cards are the other part of the record, including receipt, location, and binding information. From time to time this record is consolidated with the permanent record.

## "Form Card Cataloging"

The Library of Congress used to do what was called "form card cataloging" for serials. This was a kind of temporary first-issue cataloging done immediately upon receipt for current titles. Check-in files were made using form card entries. Periodicals and collected sets were cataloged for printed cards from first bound volume. Recataloging would be done if the original first-issue cataloging did not correspond with the entry desired when permanent cataloging took place. For this reason, past entries in NST, provided from form card cataloging, might not always agree with final printed cards as they appear in NUC.

Cataloging was done in two places. The Descriptive Cataloging

Division handled serials cataloging for the card and book catalogs and for printed cards for sale. A cataloging section in the Serial Record Division concerned itself with bibliographic authority work for the Serial Record entries and *NST*. The coordination between these two was not very good, nor could it really be improved upon due to the need for speed on the part of the receipt section and the fact that not everything in the Serial Record would be cataloged for printed cards. There was considerable duplication of effort in establishing an entry and describing the physical issues. Considerable effort would be given by each cataloger to added entries, references, and other redundancies. This was clearly a waste, particularly if recataloging were necessary, which would also involve changing the Serial Record. The duplicative procedures were felt necessary because adequate cataloging could not be done from first issue. Form card cataloging would fill in the gap for check-in purposes until the permanent bound volume was cataloged. It would also keep things up-to-date, which the cumbersome final cataloging procedure could not hope to do.

But form card cataloging proved to be too expensive for the Library to maintain. In an attempt to streamline procedures, save staff time, and use staff more effectively, serials cataloging activities were consolidated in May 1968. The Serials Section of the Descriptive Cataloging Division was transferred to the Serials Record Division and merged with its Cataloging Section. In September 1968, in order to simplify the cataloging of serials, LC adopted the policy of cataloging from first issue received. This effectively cancelled form card cataloging and the resultant costly duplication of effort.

### Latest vs. Successive Entry

In 1971 a severe crisis regarding serials processing was making itself felt at LC. Only about a third of the new titles which were pouring into LC were being cataloged by a very small staff. The Library of Congress had followed the suggestions of the Catalog Code Revision Committee and the nation's research libraries, which had convinced it to follow the old ALA rules for entry, that is, using the policy of latest entry. This gave libraries which desired it the benefit of LC's fairly comprehensive bibliographic research. Such practice was reflected in footnotes to the new printed rules. However, the backlog was growing by leaps and bounds while catalogers spent hours doing research and recataloging. LC was being literally buried in new serial titles. Finally it was decided that LC would accept the *Anglo-American Cataloging Rules* as printed and this was announced in April 1971. Changes of title or corporate heading would cause new records to be generated as soon as the change was identified. Footnotes describing the Library's practices in AACR were cancelled. More serials catalogers were added and catalogers were relieved of marginal duties. Serials cataloging at LC is at present quite up-to-date and the catalogers are even dipping into the arrearages as time permits.

## Cataloging Routines

Cataloging is done from first issue. Titles which are discerned to be new titles are sent for review by a selection officer. This person makes decisions on the retention policy of the particular title. If the title is to be routed to one of the other two national libraries, retained briefly, reviewed later, or discarded, the issues and decisions are returned to the searcher who sent them in. This searcher will put a note of the decision into the Serial Record and dispose of the issue as directed. Titles to be cataloged for the collection are given a priority. The title will be sent to a descriptive cataloger along with appropriate slips to be filled in along the way. Catalogers will already have gotten issues with title or author changes, which arrived with the old visible file entry from the searcher.

The cataloger will catalog the issue-in-hand. Searches are generally only to be made in the Official Catalog and the NST files, except if a conflict arises. Searches for headings can be done elsewhere. Other titles are not usually examined. Notes are sent to the Catalog Maintenance Division regarding titles superseded or continued by other titles so that this information may be added to the catalog cards. The cataloger also provides NST with the necessary data by filling in a slip. The previous entry is photocopied to be forwarded with the current cataloging data and issues to the Subject Cataloging Division.

After the descriptive cataloger has performed his work, the cataloging manuscript sheet goes to a typist to have the Serial Record entry typed, including linking notes to and from other titles, other bibliographic notes, and "see references." The typist also types preliminary cards and slips for the Order Division. The typist also checks in the issue or issues-in-hand.

The Duplicating Unit duplicates the information sending one copy to the Process Information File and the others, with the piece(s), to the Subject Cataloging Division.

Partial records are input to CONSER before the subject cataloging procedures start. Descriptive cataloging, ISSN and key-title are put into the system with the eye to upgrading at the end of the cataloging cycle.

The Subject Cataloging Division is divided into two humanities sections (due to the bulk of materials cataloged), and sections for Far Eastern materials, law, social sciences, life sciences, physical sciences, and children's literature.

If the numbering is continued, and there is no major change in subject matter, a title which has been cataloged for a title change will receive the same call number that the earlier title had. If there has been a major change in subject content, or the numbering has not been retained, a new class number will be assigned. Subject headings will be reviewed on entry-change publications and new ones assigned as necessary. Classification and subject headings will be assigned to new titles. New titles, or titles with new class numbers, will be shelflisted. Temporary cards are put in the shelflist until "bucked" by permanent cards. These cards give locations and sources of cuttering. Those destined to have Dewey numbers will go to the Dewey Classification Division.

Titles needing new subject headings or aspects of headings must await authorization of that subject heading. Journal literature must be searched for appropriate terminology. Sometimes this takes considerable time to research. Then this must be approved, which could take up to a month, meaning the semi-cataloged material sits, making its final appearance in NUC or MARC tapes later than usual. It may take several months for the heading to appear in the published subject heading list. Classification proposals also have to await approval, further delaying things.

The cataloging information will be routed, with other information, to other departments as applicable. The custodial division will get a preliminary card (and the piece). Serial Record gets one to update the checking entry with the call number. Other departments will get their necessary slips. Eventually the manuscript sheet will go for card production. (New titles receive similar processing.)

NSDP receives the cataloging data after the complete cataloging process is through. This data is received in the form of a photocopy of the cataloging worksheet and a copy of the cover/title-page/masthead of the piece which was cataloged, providing documentation for NSDP's work as an ISDS center. ISSN and key-titles are assigned. At the present time, ISSN are entered on the Serial Record, but key-titles are not. This data is also added to the worksheet which goes to NST.

NST will receive the cataloging from NSDP. The staff will assign a Dewey number, if the title does not already have one, and files the record for further processing and input into NST and its Dewey-arranged subject edition. It routes a copy of the worksheet, with additions each as bibliographic information from outside sources, to the MARC-S people.

Editing is done in the MARC (MAchine Readable Cataloging) Office for content designators and editorial details. Then the information is keyed on a magnetic tape selectric typewriter using the standard 175-character ALA character set. The typewriter cassette is converted to machine-readable computer tape and processed to create the bibliographic record and a diagnostic listing which is used to verify the record against the worksheet. Twice a week tapes are sent to the Cataloging Distribution Service Division or CDS Division (the Card Division's new name as of 1975), which prepares the MARC-S records for distribution. Generally, MARC-S tapes and proofslips for printed cards will be available about the same time.

The Editing and Inputting Section of the Division concerns itself with the MARC-S input. In is also concerned with LC's input to CONSER (see pp. 220-222). Full LC cataloging, which is the updating of preliminary records, is done at the end of the cataloging procedure. CONSER tapes are also returned to LC from OCLC for post-editing of the input of other participants and verification by NSDP.

The illustration following, shows an organization chart and a simplified flow chart of serials processing at LC.

The Copyright Office depository is a very major source of material for the Library of Congress, including serials. Often this causes major delays for LC in acquiring information. However, LC does get some preliminary cataloging of these items due to COPICS.

COPICS (Copyright Office Publication and Interactive Cataloging System) was begun in 1972, but serials were not added until early 1976. It is an automating of the *Catalog of Copyright Entries* (CCE), which was formerly produced by photographing cards. In the old manual system, periodical titles were kept in file trays and new issues posted as they were received. The automated system uses a 3-1-1 code like OCLC's for access and posting is much faster. The information is stored on disc until the CCE is run. Corrections can be made online. The CCE is sent to the Serial Record Division on a semi-annual basis. It includes ISSN, key-title, and other information useful to Divison personnel.

## NSDP

NSDP, the National Serials Data Program, has already been mentioned in its relationship to the ISDS (see pp. 189-190). NSDP has separate functions in addition to its workings at an ISDS center, however.

In the middle 1960's, there were plans afoot to create, first, a pro-

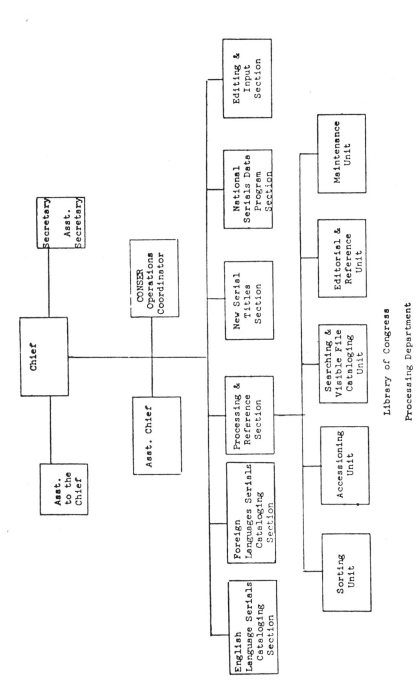

Library of Congress

Processing Department

Serial Record Division Organization Chart: 1977

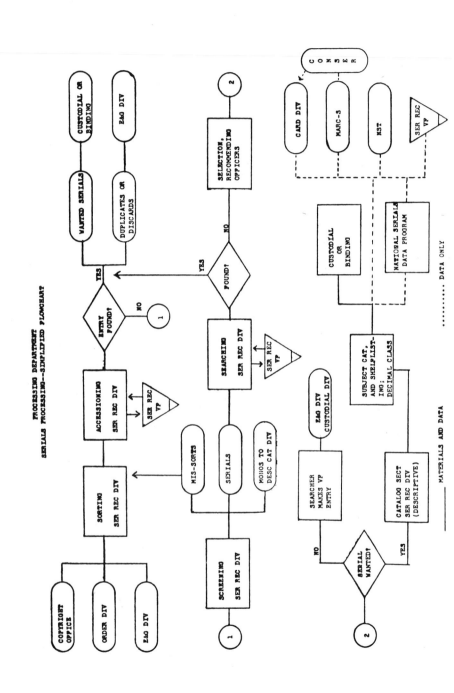

PROCESSING DEPARTMENT
SERIALS PROCESSING—SIMPLIFIED FLOWCHART

gram to cover science and technology serials, and, later, all serials. The plan was to collect bibliographic data on these titles and bring them under some sort of bibliographic control. The MARC serials format (see pp. 212-215) was created and a pilot project was suggested, using the holdings of the three national libraries in this country as the basis.

The National Serials Pilot Project, NSPP, was run in 1969. It was decided that such registry was feasible. Two observations made, that an authority file was a necessity, and that the cataloging rules needed revising, are of particular import to serials catalogers. They resulted in many of the activities currently going on in the library world with respect to cataloging rule changes, desuperimposition, etc. The NSPP also experimented with the American Standard Serial Number, which became the basis of the ISSN. Truly, in many ways NSDP, as it became, was the harbinger of ISDS and today's registry activities.

NSDP became fully operational at the beginning of 1973. It was originally part of the Library of Congress' Processing Department, but in January of 1975 it became part of the Serials Record Division.

NSDP gets input from a variety of sources: magnetic tapes from NLM, NAL, and LC, worksheets from NST, NLM, and NAL, and aperture cards from NLM. These aperture cards are computer tab cards with microfilm of the serial covers and mastheads mounted in them giving the necessary bibliographic data. NSDP also gets MARC serial records, tagged and edited. NSDP may also receive corporate authority information. NSDP also receives requests from publishers requesting ISSN, which may be accompanied by a photo-reproduction of the title-page, cover, masthead, etc., or a mockup or artist's conception of the title-page, cover, etc. NSDP assigns ISSN and key titles to all American serial publications which pass through its hands from one of these sources.

NSDP is maintaining an authority file for corporate entry according to AACR. This authority file shows all forms used by the national libraries, well as the NSDP form.

NSDP is involved currently in national and international networking and registry in both ISDS and as one of the authentication centers for the CONSER Projects (see pp. 220-222).

New Serial Titles, colloquially called NST, is the serials bibliography and union lists published at LC by an office located in the Serials Record Division. It is a list of serials which began publication in 1950 and after. Newspapers, looseleaf publications, books in parts, municipal government serial documents, publishers' series, motion pictures, filmstrips, and phonorecords are excluded. Entries, using either ALA or AACR rules, are sent in by contributing libraries. Brief description is given, including issuing body in parentheses, numbering and dates of the title, frenquency, publisher's address, price, and bibliographic notes. Dewey numbers are given for subject information. (There is also an NST publication arranged by these numbers). Holdings are given briefly, using NUC symbols for reporting libraries.

## Freezing the Library of Congress Catalog

The Library plans to close its card catalogs in 1981, when it will adopt the new AACR. It also plans to make other changes, such as development of new subject headings. LC's current cataloging will be in machine-readable form (or at least most of it will). New AACR 2-based headings will go into effect and superimposition will be no more. Everything will be reasonably "clean." But what of serials in all of this?

CONSER files will be maintained, added to, and updated. CONSER files will contain AACR 2 headings forms so that modification can occur. All live serials processed or reprocessed through CONSER will go into the new catalog, including titles in non-Roman alphabets. Changes will be linked from new to old records (although probably not vice-versa).

The Shelflist will not be closed at the same time as the catalogs, but this may be a future move. The decision will be deferred until after 1980.

There are clearly still questions to be addressed, but these are "in the works" at this time and the outcome is not completely certain. We shall just have to wait.

## LC and AACR 2

One of the features of AACR 2 is that there are choices for options to be followed. LC has made proposals for which of these options it wishes to follow, based on consultation with librarians in this country and agreements made with the national libraries of Australia, Canada, and the United Kingdom.

These options include choices of terminology for the general medium designator and the decision that such terms be stored in the machine-readable files. The full address of the publisher, for all but major trade publishers, will be added to the imprint area, if readily available. (This will have major impact on serials cataloging.) Additional information may be added to the publisher statement if the cataloging agency feels it is of importance.

The number of volumes of a completed work will be filled in. The catalogers at LC will be selective about the description of accompanying material however. If the accompanying material is very extensive, or very different, special notes will be made, but only if they seem warranted.

LC will not make full splitting notes for titles which have resulted from splits, feeling that users would not care. Absorptions will be qualified by dates only if the information is readily available.

Editors will generally be traced, with a designation of function: "ed." Series numbering will be included in series added entries.

These are LC's choices. Because of LC's unique position among American libraries, it is probable that most libraries will follow suit, but this is not yet known. Only time can tell what will happen with AACR 2. (Consult the *LC Cataloging Service Bulletin* for current policy and practice and updates on same.)

## BIBLIOGRAPHY

Library of Congress. Processing Department. *Cataloging Service Bulletin,* 1-June 1945-. Washington, D.C.: Library of Congress.

_____. *Department Memorandum,* No. 111, May 31, 1971.

Spalding, C. Sumner, *The Cataloging of Serials at the Library of Congress; a Report with Recommendations.* Washington, D.C.: Library of Congress. Serial Record Division, February 20, 1956, Retyped August 17, 1956.

# CHAPTER IX
# LIBRARY TOOLS FOR A
# SERIALS DEPARTMENT

Before the 1970's serials librarians were hindered by too few tools, and too little information in those that were published. There was also a great time-lag before the titles got into the tools. Now the titles get in much faster, and the tools are proliferating as fast as the journals themselves.

Those libraries that belong to any of the various types of automated library networks would seem to be the most fortunate. However, much is still needed before these networks become the panacea that they seem to promise. The greatest need is for more standardization of information and entries. Now, the titles are entered just as they are received from the various libraries. The data therefore varies from library to library and is often incomplete. One must search further for the latest information given in tools put out in book form. Not only do the books give more titles, accurate addresses and prices, but they are generous with extraneous information. It is surprising what items of information may be found tucked away between the covers of the tools. It is wise to study each tool carefully from cover to cover. You may be floundering for money symbols, the latest name of a country, abbreviations or acronyms, when all the time this information may be right at hand.

Do not expect to find in the tools every title ever published. Some never get into the tools for various reasons. Sometimes they are too ephemeral, and sometimes they are announced and never published. A word of warning is due about searching titles. Do not spend too much time hunting through all possible sources. It often happens that a title is listed everywhere or nowhere.

New tools are continually being published, and old ones are ceasing just as fast, so it is necessary to be on the alert for these new ones as well as revisions of some of the old ones. Actually the whole library is grist for the mill. Because out of sight is usually out of mind, one may make a small "tickler" file by subjects, for those tools located elsewhere in the library that have proven particularly useful. Announcements of new titles often come out in current numbers of older journals. Even agents, publishers, institutions, associations, societies, and other libraries at times will cooperate in helping run down a particularly elusive title.

In order to keep up-to-date on new tools and editions of older ones it is suggested that publishers' catalogs be checked each year. Four of the most likely catalogs are those of the American Library Association, for general tools; R. R. Bowker, for specific serial tools; the H. W. Wilson list, for specialized subject tools; and Gale Research Company, for various directories.

There has been no attempt to make a definitive list of tools here, nor to analyze them in depth. This has already been done adequately in several recent books about serials.

### Various Types of Tools

Each type of tool fulfills a primary need, although other needs may also be included, as already stated.

1. Union lists tell which libraries own which journals, including which volumes are owned by them. There are large union lists for states and regions and there are local ones. The largest is the *Union List of Serials in Libraries of the United States and Canada,* which covers titles published through 1949. It is continued by *New Serial Titles,* 1950-  and is up-dated by supplements, which are cumulated.

2. Directories show what is currently being published and perhaps where the titles are indexed. Much more information may be gleaned from many of these directories. For a few of the most basic ones see Basic Aids below.

3. Abstracting and Indexing Services have increased many times in numbers in order to cover the flood of recent journals. Many titles overlap in the various services. One may partly utilize this fact as a criteria in serials selection, because it may be assumed that if the titles are listed over and over again they must be the most important and of lasting value, but, here again, the librarian must use personal judgment to choose the most suited to that particular library.

There is a difference between abstracting and indexing services as must be seen at a casual glance. Indexing services list only titles, while abstracting services, of course, give abstracts of the articles and are more specialized. For titles and descriptions of these services, see Katz, *Magazines for Libraries*; Osborn, *Serials Publications*, 2nd ed., rev.; and Sheehy, *Guide to Reference Books*, 9th edition.

All these services are very expensive, and because they do overlap, the librarian must choose wisely. They are also put out in various formats as well as in book form. These formats include; microforms, magnetic tapes; and Selective Dissemination of Information (SDI) on cards, as well as being provided in custom packages.

4. Subject Indexes are also being published by the thousands on every conceivable subject. Some of the oldest are: *Agricultural Index; Art Index; Applied Science and Technology Index; Education Index; Public Affairs Information Service Bulletin.* Each emphasizes a different approach to journals.

5. Computerized-based indexes include many of the above mentioned catagories.
   *Computer Abstracts*, 1957-    . St. Helier, Jersey, British Channel Islands. Technical Information Co.

The abstracts number 4,000 a year, and cover the whole range of computer literature. Also for computer oriented journals see Katz, *Magazines for Libraries*. He gives a good history of these journals.

## Abbreviations

Abbreviations are among the stickiest problems in Serials. Every society and institution thinks it has the only title being published. One has to find out sometimes what subject is being requested to tell what title to search. For example, A.M.A. may refer to the American Medical Association, or the American Management Association, or the American Methodist Association, and goodness knows how many other associations. Multiply this one point many times and one is in confusion worse confounded.

Also each discipline, such as chemistry, botany, etc., has its own way of abbreviating titles. Add to this the computers with their "COBOL" and "FORTRAN" etc., not to mention all the societies and industries that like to turn abbreviations into words, and one has confusion compounded. Librarianship and especially serials libriarianship is turning out abbreviations and acronyms at an alarming rate.

### Abbreviations, Dictionaries, Foreign Trade Terms

Alkire, Leland G., Jr. *Periodical Title Abbreviations.* 2nd ed., Detroit: Gale Research Co., 1977.

Allen, Charles Geoffry, *A Manual of European Languages for Librarians.* New York: R. R. Bowker, 1975.

Buttress, F. A., *World Guide to Abbreviations of Organizations.* 5th ed. London: L. Hill Books, 1974.

Crowley, Ellen T., ed., *Acronyms, Initialisms, and Abbreviations: A Guide to Alphabetic designations, Contractions, Acronyms, Initialisms, Abbreviations, and Similar Condensed Appelations.* 5th ed., 3 vols. Detroit: Gale Research Co., 1976.

Mora, Irmre, ed., *Worterbuch des Verlagswesen in 20 Sprachen. The Publisher's Practical Dictionary in 20 Languages.* Munchen: Verlag Dokumentation, 1974.

Orne, Jerrold, *The Language of the Foreign Book Trade: Abbreviations, Terms, Phrases.* 3rd ed., Chicago: American Library Association, 1976.

Pipics, Zaltan, *Dictionarium Bibliothecarii Practicum in XXII Linguis. The Librarian's Practical Dictionary in 22 Languages.* Munchen: Verlag Dokumentation, 1974.

*Political Handbook of the World, Parliaments, Parties and Press.* 1927- . New York, McGraw-Hill. Lists the latest changes of names of countries and gives the history of each country along with much other information.

Von Ostermann, George Frederick, *Manual of Foreign Languages for the Use of Librarians, Bibliographers, Research Workers, Editors, Translators, and Printers.* 4th ed., rev., and enl. New York: Central Book Co., 1952.

## Addresses — Libraries, Librarians, Publishers, Societies, Institutions

*American Book Trade Directory.* 1915. New York: R. R. Bowker Co.

*American Library Directory . . . A Classified List of Libraries with Names of Librarians.* 1923-. New York: R. R. Bowker Co.

*American Library Directory Updating Service.* 1969-. New York: R. R. Bowker, Co.

*Book Publishers' Directory.* Je. 1977-. Detroit: Gale Research Co.

*College Blue Book.* 1923. Yonkers-on-Hudson, New York [etc.] G. E. Birckel [etc.].

*Encyclopedia of Associations.* 1956-. Detroit: Gale Research Co.

*International Subscription Agents.* 1978. Chicago: American Library Association.

*Patterson's American Educational Directory.* 1904-. North Chicago: [etc.] Educational Directories [etc].

*Publishers' Trade List Annual.* New York: R. R. Bowker Co.

Sources of Serials; A Bowker Serials Bibliography. 1977. New York: R.
R. Bowker Co.
(An international publisher and corporate author directory. To be
up-dated.)
World of Learning. 1947-. London: Europa Publicacations, Ltd.
Yearbook of International Organizations. 1948-. Geneva: Yearbook of
international organization.
Young, Margaret Labash and Harold Chester Young . . . Directory of
Special Libraries and Information Centers. c1977. Detroit: Gale
Research Co.

## Agents' and Publishers' Catalogs

Many agents and publishers send out catalogs of titles that may be
the most valuable source of information for verifying titles, addresses
of publishers, changed and ceased titles. Many of these catalogs come
unsolicited, some come free to those libraries having a list of subscriptions with the agent or publisher, and some must be purchased. To
cover the entire spectrum of agents and their catalogs see Katz, Guide
to Magazines and Serial Agents. The two largest agents in this country,
EBSCO and Faxon, put out the most important of these catalogs.

EBSCO Subscription Services, Librarians' Handbook; a Guide to
Periodicals. Birmingham, Ala., EBSCO Industries, Inc.
EBSCO Bulletin of Serials Changes. bi-monthly. An up-date service.
Faxon's Librarians' Guide to Periodicals. Westwood, Mass. F. W. Faxon
Co. Inc., Library Subscription Agency.
Faxon. Serials Updating Service. A monthly newsletter "containing the
latest known updating information on various serial titles."

They both list very important purchasing information such as the
full title, retail price, frequency and information regarding indexes.
Both are produced by computers and each contains information not included in the other as well as duplicative information.

## Back Issues

This list includes a very few of the longest established agencies
concerned with back issues. Study Katz, Guide to Magazine and Serial
Agencies, and keep alert to the free catalogs of agencies that come to
the library in the mail. Only by trial and error will you find the ones
that will fit into your library's needs. Most international agents have
back-issue departments. Many of the general agents are not interested
in single issue requests and if they condescend to search for them they

will probably add a service charge. Many of these agents are very specialized as to subject matter.

Abrahams Magazine Service, Inc. 56 E. 13th St. New York, N.Y. 10003. A back issue dealer that includes a great many types of library material.

Bliss, P. and H. Middleton, Conn. 06457. Serves all types of libraries and does deal in single issues.

*Directory of Dealers in Secondhand and Antiquarian Books in the British Isles.* 1951-52-   . London, Sheppard Press.

Johnson, Walter J. Inc. 355 Chester St. Norwood, N.J. 07648.

Kraus Periodical Co. Rt. 100, Milwood, N.J. 10546. Deals mostly in reprints.

Zeitlin Periodicals Co., Inc. 817 South La Brea, Los Angeles, Cal. 90036. Deals in back-issues and reprints.

## Basic Aids — Retrospective and Current — Domestic

*Ayer Directory of Publishers, Newspapers and Magazines.* (See under Newspapers).

Katz, William A., *Magazines for Libraries: for the General Reader, and School, Junior College, University and Public Libraries.* William Katz and Berry Gargal Richards. 3d ed., New York, R. R. Bowker. 1978. The Humanities and Social Sciences are being kept up-to-date in the column by Katz in the *Library Journal.*

*National Union Catalog;* A cumulative Author List Representing Library of Congress Printed Cards and Titles Reported by Other American Libraries. 1941-   . Washington Library of Congress.

*New Serials Titles;* a Union List of Serials Commencing Publication after December 31, 1949. Jan. 1950-   . Washington, Library of Congress. Monthly with annual comulations which are self-cumulative through periods of five years. It is a continuation of Union List of Serials. The thought has been expressed that hopefully someday computers will combine the two titles so that searching in both sets for beginning dates would be eliminated.

*Poole's Index to Periodical Literature.* Gloucester, Mass. P. Smith. 1802-1881. Supplements, 1882-1907.

*Publishers' Trade List Annual;* Including Catalogs and Supplements. 1873-   . New York: R. R. Bowker, Co.

Sheehy, Euguene P. *Guide to Reference Books.* 9th ed., Chicago, American Library Association, 1976. This continues Winchell, Constance Mabel. *Guide to Reference Books.* 8th ed.

*Standard Periodical Directory.* 1964-65-   . New York: Oxbridge Publishing Co. Kept up-to-date with supplements.

*Ulrich's International Periodical Directory.* 1932- . New York: R. R. Bowker Co.

*Ulrich's Quarterly.* Has an up-dating service. See under Irregular Titles.

*Union List of Serials in Libraries of United States Canada.* 3rd ed., Edited by Edna Brown Titus . . . New York, H. W. Wilson Co. 5v. 1965. Covers titles through 1949. This continues as *New Serial Titles.*

Winchell, Constance Mabel. *Guide to Reference Books.* 8th ed. Chicago, American Library Association, 1967. See under Sheehy, Eugene P. for a continuation of this title.

*Working Press of the Nation.* 1945- . Burlington, Iowa: National Research Bureau Inc.

    v.1 Newspaper Directory

    v.2 Magazine Directory

    v.3 Radio and Television Directory

    v.4 Feature Writer and Syndicate Directory

    v.5 Gebbie House Directory

1949 edition is just slightly changed

    v.1 Newspaper Directory

        Includes personnel of daily papers, department editors, principal weekly and neighborhood newspapers and principal foreign papers published in the United States.

    v.2 Magazine Directory

        In addition to up-dated listings of all previous publications, many new publications have been added. It provides editorial blueprint of over 4,800 publications in the United States and Canada.

    v.3 TV and Radio Directory

        Gives either a detailed or generalized approach to the radio and television stations of America.

    v.4 Feature Writer, Photographer and Syndicate Directory Gives information of leading free lance feature writers.

    v.5 Internal Publications Directory

        Provides the only complete source of detailed information about internal and external publications of more than 4,000 companies, clubs, government agencies and other groups throughout the United States and Canada.

## Basic aids — Counterparts in Foreign Countries

*Annuaire de la Presse et de la Publicite.* 1- . annee 1880- . Paris: (Title varies several times.)

Annuarie European. European Yearbook. 1955-    . La Haye: Nijhoff.

Anuario Espanol de la Publicidad. 1960-    . Madrid.

British Union-catalogue of Periodicals. New Periodical Titles. Mar. 1964-    . London: Butterworths. Incorporates World List of Scientific Periodicals.

Canadian Serials Directory. 1972-    . Toronto and Buffalo: University of Toronto Press.

Directory of Periodicals Publishing Articles on English and American Literature and Languages. [1960-    . Chicago: [etc.] Swallow Press.

Europa Year Book. 1959-    . London. A survey and directory of European Organizations and countries. Replaces the looseleaf Europa Encyclopedia.

European Yearbook, see, Annuaire Europeen.

Schatoff, Michael, Half a Century of Russian Serials; Cumulative Index of Serials Published Outside the U.S.S.R. Compiled by Michael Schatoff. Edited by N. A. Hale. New York, Russian Book Chamber Abroad. 1970-72.

Willing's Press Guide. 1874-    . London: Willing's Press Service [etc.]

Woodworth, David P. ed., Guide to Current British Journals. 1962-    . London: Library Association. v. 1 Guide to Current British Journals v.2 Directory of Publishers

World List of Scientific Periodicals. See, British Union-catalogue of Periodicals.

## Books and Serials About Serials

Allen, Walter C. ed. "Serials Publications in Large Libraries": [Papers]. (Allerton Park Institute, No. 16). Urbana, University of Illinois, Graduate School of Library Science [c1970].

Brown, Clara D. Serials: Acquisition and Maintenance. Birmingham, Alabama: EBSCO, 1971.

Davinson, Donald Edward. Periodicals; a Manual of Practice for Librarians. Rev. ed. London: A. Deutsch, [1964].

Gable, J. Harris. Manual of Serials Work. Chicago: American Library Association, 1937.

Grenfell, David. Periodicals and Serials: Their Treatment in Special Libraries. 2nd ed. London: Aslip, [Aslip Manuals, v. 3].

Louisiana State University, Baton Rouge, La. Library Serials Manual. 1976. (Negotiating with ERIC for it to be included in their material).

Osborn, Andrew D. Serial Publications: Their Place and Treatment in Libraries. 2d ed., rev. Chicago: American Library Association. 1973.

Serials Librarian. Fall, 1976-    . New York: Haworth Press.

Smith, Lynn S., *A Practical Approach to Serials Cataloging*. Greenwich, Connecticut: J. A. I. Press, 1978.
Stevens, Rolland Elwell, ed. "Problems of Acquisition for Research [Libraries." *Library Trends*, 18 (1970).]

## Ceased Titles

There are never enough lists put out to cover ceased titles and title changes. Undoubtedly there never will be, because such information does not become available sometimes until years later and one needs it right now. Some ceased or changed titles seem to elude all efforts. It often takes writing to the publishers and agents to pin down this information. Some of the most likely places to search are: the library networks, if you are lucky enough to belong to them; for retrospective titles see the *National Union Catalog; Union List of Serials in Libraries of the United States and Canada*. For more current titles see *Bulletin of Bibliography; Ulrich's International Periodical Directory; Ulrich's Quarterly; New Serial Titles; Title Varies; EBSCO Bulletin of Serial Changes*. Also Katz, *Magazines for Libraries*, and the various agents, catalogs are a help. Also must be included:
*Nijhoff Serials*. 1978-     . The Hague: Nijhoff. Gives changes and ceased titles, cumulated index etc. It is free.
*Serials in Transition*. 1977-     . Westwood, Mass.: Faxon. Gives new and ceased titles. "Being a record of the transformation, transmutation, transmigration, and transit of serials as reported in Births, Deaths, and Magazine Notes. . ." It must be purchased.
*Title Varies*. [Chapel Hill, N.C. etc., D. C. Taylor and H. M. Yaple]. Dec. 1973-     . It must be purchased.

## Documents

"Deficiencies in document collecting and servicing represent one of the most serious shortcomings in American libraries. Some of the trouble stems from uncertainty over a wise collecting policy. Libraries could be flooded with documents if they were acquired wholesale; rather than be overwhelmed they have shown a tendency to temporize. . ."[1]
*Annuaire europeen. European Yearbook*. 1955-     . The Hague: Nijhoff. Documents appear in French and English.
*Bibliographie de la France; ou, Journal General de l'imprimie et de la Librairie*. Nov. 1811-     . Paris: Au Cercle de la librairie [etc.] Lists documents in a supplement.
*Europa Yearbook*, 1959-     . 1st ed. London: Europa Publications Ltd.

International Yearbook and Statesmen's Who Who. 1953-    . London: Burke's Peerage.

Palic, Vladimir M., Government Publications; a Guide to Bibliographic Tools, 4th ed. Washington: Library of Congress, 1975.

Political Handbook and Atlas of the World. [1927]-    . New York: Council on foreign relations Inc.

Morehead, Joe. Introduction to United States Public Documents. 2d ed. Littleton, Colorado: Libraries Unlimited, 1978 (a good recent book about documents).

Public Affairs Information Service. Bulletin of the Public Affairs Information Service. Annual Cumulation. [1915]-    . White Plains, N. Y. and New York City: The H. W. Wilson Company, 1915-19; New York, Public Affairs Information Service, 1920-    .

United States Library of Congress. Exchange and Gift Division. Monthly Checklist of State Publications. Jan. 1910-    . Washington: Govt. Print. Off.

United States, Superintendent of Documents. Monthly Catalog of United States Government Publications. 1895-    . Washington: Govt. Print. Off.

United States. Superintendent of Documents. Selected United States Government Publications. 1928-    . Washington: Govt. Print. Off.

United States. Government Printing Office. [Subject Bibliographies] 1974-    . Washington: Govt. Print. Off. (This one takes the place of the former Price Lists, which were issued free on request).

Van Zant, Nancy Patton. Selected U.S. Government Serials; A Guide for Public and Academic Libraries. Chicago, American Library Association. 1978.

World of Learning. 1947-    . London: Europa Publications, Ltd.

## Free Material

The house journals published by commercial and industrial companies and organizations are usually free for the asking. In the earlier days these "free" publications included only local news about employees and happenings within the company. At present they often also give very factual, technical information that may be utilized by libraries. The following tools include some of this "free" material. The tools listing them must be purchased.

Internal Publications Directory. (formerly Gebbie House Directory.

Index to Free Periodicals. Ann Arbor, Mich., Pierian Press. Published twice a year and includes a wide range of topics.

Katz, William A. Magazine for Libraries; for the General Reader, and

*School, Junior College, College, and Public Libraries.* William Katz, and Berry Gargal, 3d ed. New York: R. R. Bowker, 1978.

## Gifts and Exchanges

UNESCO *Bulletin for Libraries.* April 1947-     . United Nations Educational, Scientific and Cultural Organization. Place de Fontenoy, Paris 7e.

USBE (Universal Serials and Book Exchanges, Inc.) (See p. 314 for address).

This is the best approach for exchanges. For further description of this and other agencies see the chapter on Gifts and Exchanges and Special agencies.

DEU (Duplicate Exchange Union) see p. 315.

## Irregulars (Monographic Series) and Annuals

To find this sort of information is one of the most time-consuming problems in verification. Sometimes one can find it on the inside front and back covers of earlier numbers and volumes of the actual publications themselves. Often one has to write to the publishers for a list. At times publishers go back and assign numbers to earlier publications, or stop numbering a series that has been numbered for years. Other times the numbers are found only on the book jackets with no clues on the books themselves. Most libraries usually try to leave publisher's series out of the Serials Record, and the only reason for putting in monographic series is for ease of claiming.

*Books in Series.* 1966-1975-     . New York, R. R. Bowker Co. Kept up-to-date with supplements.

*Irregular Serials and Annuals; an International Directory.* 4th ed., New York, R. R. Bowker, 1976-1977. (This includes abbreviations, abstracting, money symbols, micro-publishers, international organizations, and Proceedings to international congresses).

*The Publishers' Trade List Annual.* 1873-     . New York: R. R. Bowker Co.

*Serials Review.* Ja/Je., 1975-     . Ann Arbor, Michigan: Pierian Press.

*Titles in Series; a Handbook for Librarians and Students.* Jan. 1953-     . New York: Scarecrow Press.

*Ulrich's Quarterly,* 1977-     . New York: R. R. Bowker. Supersedes *Bowker Serials Bibliography. Supplement.*

United States. Library of Congress. *Monographic Series.* Jan/Mr-1974-     . Quarterly with annual cumulations.

## Little Magazines

In the early days it was almost impossible to find out about "little magazines". Now librarians have a much easier time of it. These magazines are being listed in many more tools. Also there is an agency that will be of great help. It is called the Coordinating Council of Literary Magazines (CCLM). 80 Eighth Avenue, New York, 10011. It is a non-profit agency funded by the National Endowment for the Arts; New York State Council on the Arts, and private sources. It will act as liaison between the librarian or subscription agent and small publishers. It will also provide various services.

*International Directory of Little Magazines and Small Presses.* 1965- . Paradise, California: [etc.] Dust Books [etc.].

Katz, William A. *Magazines for Libraries: for the General Reader, and School, Junior College, University and Public Libraries.* William Katz and Berry Gargal Richards. 3d ed., New York: R. R. Bowker. 1978.

Muller, Robert H., *From Radical Left to Extreme Right; a Bibliography of Current Periodicals of Protest, Controversy, Advocacy or Dissent.* 2d ed., revised and enl. [by] Robert H. Muller, Theodore Jurgen Spahn, and Janet Spahn. vol. 1, Ann Arbor: Campus Publishers [c1970- .] Volumes 2, 3. Metuchen, New Jersey: Scarecrow Press.

*The Small Press Review.* Spring 1967- . El Cerrito, California: Dust Books.

## Microfilm, etc., see Reprography

## Newspapers

*Ayer Directory of Publications,* (Newspapers and Magazines), 1880- . Philadelphia: Ayer Press.

*Editor and Publisher. International Yearbook Number . . .* [New York, 1921- . Editor and Publisher.

Der *Leitfaden durch Presse und Werbung.* 1947- . Essen-Stadtwold. Stammverlag G.M.B.H. Changed *from Leitfaden fur Presse und Werbung* with V.29- . 1976- .

*Newspapers in Microform.* 1948- . Cumulated periodically and split into 2 sections; *Newspapers in Microform: United States:* and *Newspapers in Microform; Foreign Countries.* Title varies slightly. *Newspapers on Microfilm,* 1973- . Washington: Library of Congress. Updated annually.

*Willing's Press Guide.* 1874- . London: Willing's Press Service [etc]. It is one of the best guides to newspapers from all over the world.

*Working Press of the Nation.* [1945]-   . Chicago [etc.]: Directory Division, National Research Bureau [etc.]. (V.1, A Directory and Guide to Daily Newspapers and Allied Services Directory.)

## Reprints

*Bulletin of Reprints.* 1964-   . Pullach bei Munchen [etc.] Verlag Dokumentation.

*Catalog of Reprints in Series.* 1940-   . New York: Scarecrow Press. Kept current with supplements.

*Guide to Reprints.* 1967-   . Washington: Microcard Editions. Annual.

*Internationale Bibliographie der Reprints. International Bibliography of Reprints.* 1876-   . Christa, Gnirss, ed. Munchen: Verlag Dokumentation.

Kraus. *Reprints of Selected United Nations Recurrent Publications.* New York: Kraus Reprint, 1977.

Nemeyer, Carol A. *Scholarly Reprint Publishing in the United States.* New York: R. R. Bowker.

Ostwald, Renate. *Nachdruckverzeichnis von Einzelwerken. Serien und Zeitschriften aus allen Wissensgieten (Reprints).* V.1-2, 1965-69.

*Reprint Bulletin.* June, 1955-   . New York: Oceana Publications.

## Reprography — Addresses of Microforms and Reprints

There is an extensive list of companies and addresses in *Guide to Microforms in Print,* see next section.

A.C.R.P.P. (Association pour la conservation et la reproduction photographique de la press) 4, rue Louvois, 75002 Paris, France. This lists an impressive number of French periodicals and newspapers.

AMS Press Inc., 56 East 13th St., New York, N.Y. 10003

J.S. Canner & Co., 49-65 Lansdowne St., Boston, Mass. 02215

Carrolton Press, Inc., 1911 Fort Muer Drive #905, Arlington, Va., 22209.

ERIC Document Reproduction Service. 2020 — 14th St., North Arlington, Va. 22201.

Inter documentation Co., A.G. Postrasse 14, Zug, Switzerland. This originally started in Sweden and is now in Switzerland. It has a strong botanical leaning. Produces both microcards and microfiche.

Readex Microprint Corporation 101 5th Ave., New York, N.Y. 10003. This company supplies:

1. Retrospective series of U.S. documents.
2. U.S. current documents of depository and non-depository publications.

3. Publications of the United Nations for every year since the beginning of the U. N. in 1946.
4. Early American newspapers.
5. British house of Commons sessional papers.
6. Many other series and collections.

University Microfilms International. 300 North Zeeb Road, Ann Arbor, Mich., 48106.

This company supplies:

1. Doctoral dissertations and theses of many American universities. Many of these are no longer available on interlibrary loan from the library having the original copy.
2. Documents — both U.S. foreign, both current and retrospective.
3. Newspapers — both domestic and foreign.
4. Many other types of publications are available.

## Reprography

*Catalog of National Archives; Microfilm Publications.* 1968-    . Washington: National Archives and Record Service, General Services Administration. Annual. Lists many series of records held in the National Archives.

*Directory of Institutional Photocopying Services.* 1969. Distributed by the Photoduplication Department, University of Chicago Library.

*Directory of Library Reprographic Services.* 1959-    . Chicago: American Library Association.

*Guide to Microforms in Print.* 1961-    . Washington: Microcard Editions. Annual. Incorporates International Microforms in Print. 1977-

*MIMC; Microforms Annual.* 1977/78-    . New York: Microforms International Marketing Corp., a subsidiary of Pergamon.

*MTLA; the Micropublishers' Trade List Annual.* 1975-    . Westport, Connecticut: Microform Review.

*Microform Review.* Jan. 1972-    . [Weston, Conn.].

*Newspapers in Microform.* 1948-    . Washington: Library of Congress. Cumulated periodically and split into two sections; *Newspapers in Microform; United States;* and *Newspapers in Microform; Foreign Countries.*

*Reference Guide and Comprehensive Catalog of International Serials,* 1974-1978. Elmsford, New York: Microforms International Marketing Corp., and Maxwell Scientific International, Inc.

*Subject Guide to Microforms in Print.* 1962/63-  . Albert James Diaz, ed., Wash. Microcard Editions. Annual. This is a companion volume to Guide to Microforms in Print.

U.S. Library of Congress. *Library of Congress Catalog; National Register of Microform Masters.* Sept. 1965-  . Washington: Library of Congress.

## Serials Selection — Both Retrospective and Current

At no other point is a greater knowledge of all the tools needed than serials selection. True, there are many tools slanted directly toward selection, but so much is now contained in all the tools that a real knowledge is gained only by being aware of what the entire library and publishers have to offer. Study the various categories of the types of tools: the abstracting and indexing services are very important; the specialized subject indexes of H. W. Wilson are good sources; the union lists, both national and local, tell what other libraries are listing as important. Core lists are being published for many disciplines. Check the various tools listed under Basic Aids. A few not listed there are added below.

*The Booklist.* Jan. 1905-  . Chicago: American Library Association.

*Choice; Books for College Libraries.* Mar. 1964-  . Chicago: American Library Association.

*College and Research Libraries,* 1939/40-  . Chicago: American Library Association.

Farber, Evans Ira. *Classified List of Periodicals for the College Library.* 5th ed., rev., and enl. Westwood, Massachusetts: F. W. Faxon Co. 1972.

*Library Journal.* Sept. 1876-  . New York: R. R. Bowker.

*Publishers' Trade List Annual; Including Catalogs and Supplements.* 1873-  . New York: R. R. Bowker Co.

*Publisher's Weekly.* 1872-  . New York: R. R. Bowker.

*Readers' Guide to Periodical Literature.* New York: H. W. Wilson.

Richardson, Selma K., ed. *Periodicals for School Media Programs.* Chicago: American Library Association. 1978.

*Serials Review.* 1975-  . Ann Arbor, Michigan: Pierian Press.

*Title Varies.* Dec. 1973-  . [Chapel Hill, N.C. etc.].

*Top of the News.* 1943-  . Chicago: American Library Association (For children and young adults).

United States Library of Congress. *Library of Congress Subject Catalog.* Wash. Jan/Mar. 1975-  . Quarterly with annual and quinquennial cumulations.

United States Library of Congress. *Library of Congress Catalog —
Books; Subject.* A Cumulative list of works represented by Library of
Congress printed cards. Wash. Jan/Mar. 1950-1974. Has quarterly
and annual cumulations.

## Translations

In recent years, translations have expanded knowledge for all
countries. Especially in the sciences has the literature been broadened
for the West to include the U.S.S.R., the Far East and the Scandinavian
countries. Each discipline has its special translation tools, and now
various centers have combined to create more general tools. Such
centers as the International Translation centre, Commission of the
European Communities, and the Centre de la Recherche Scientifique
have joined to "advance the literature relating to all fields of sciences
and technology from East European and Asiatic languages into
Western languages. "See, World Transindex below, also see p. 140 for
further discussion about translations.

National Translations Center. *Consolidated Index of Translations into
English.* New York, Special Libraries Association, 1969.

*Translations Register-index.* June 15, 1967-      . New York [etc.]: National Translations Center [etc.]

*World Index of Scientific Translations and List of Translations
Notified to ETC.* 11 vols. Jan/Mar. 1967-1977. Delft, European
Translations Centre. Superseded in part by World Transindex.

*World Transindex.* 1978-      . Delft. The Netherlands. Joint publication
of International Translations Centre, Commission of the European Communities, Centre de la Recherche Scientifique.

### NOTES

Osborn, Andrew D. *Serial Publications; Their Place and Treatment in
Libraries.* 2d ed., rev. Chicago: American Library Association. 1973.

# CHAPTER X
# MAIL INFORMATION

We all take for granted the arrival of our letters and packages through the mail and we so easily become disgusted or even irate if some are late or go astray. Yet how few of us have stopped to think or tried to visualize what it takes to get so much mail to so many destinations in so short a time. Add the Christmas rush and untrained personnel and one begins to wonder how any of it gets anywhere on time, yet most of it does. There were, in 1977, 300 million pieces of mail delivered daily by the Postal Service.

It takes trucks, busses, airplanes, and ships to move the mountain of mail every hour, on the hour, twenty-four hours a day. It takes trained personnel at every point of the way. Sorting of mail has gone through drastic changes in recent years. It is now sorted by ZIP Code. "The five digits in a ZIP Code are in sequence, focusing on successively smaller areas. The first three digits point to one of over 500 key post offices, each of which serves 30 to 200 or more smaller post offices, or to one major city. The two last digits represent the post office or postal installation of destination."[1] This last step is what is called scheme knowledge. Local mail is sorted at the station by ZIP Code then follows the same procedure. Foreign mail first goes to Centralized Sorting Centers, then sent to the proper city and then follows the same procedure.

A recent announcement by the Postmaster General indicates that 90% of the non-local first-class mail now goes by airlift. The jets have been instrumental in bringing this about since they can accept almost any load-weight so that when space is available, all first-class mail is accepted to fill the space. Also many "air-taxis" are utilized to deliver mail. These smaller planes can go into towns where the jets cannot land.

## Size

Mechanization in sorting the mail and the inevitable increases in postage, promises to give "letter size standards" priority attention in the near future. By April 15, 1978 definite regulations were instigated. They "apply only to first-class mail weighing through one ounce and single-piece third-class weighing through two ounces."[2]

Items that are too small or too flimsy to be sorted mechanically will be prohibited. "Other non-standard pieces which exceed any of the maximum dimensional limitations may be subject to a surcharge in addition to the applicable postage and fees."[3]

A template has been drawn up by the post office which gives specific information regarding sizes.

"Envelopes less than one-fourth inch thick which are less than 3.5 inches high or 5 inches long will be prohibited. Also cards and other mail items which are less than seven-thousandths (.007) of an inch thick will be prohibited.

"In addition, all classes of mail (other than keys and identification devices) which are less than the minimum dimensional limitations will be prohibited."[4]

With the advent of electronic devices, sizes of letters and packages are continually coming up for questioning. The 3"x5" size (such as packets of catalog cards) has recently come up for such questioning. It would be well to check with the post office regarding any unusual sizes.

In 1977 the mail was in such a state of flux that it was really difficult to say what was to happen next. There is a proposal being made to renew government control over the U.S. Postal Service, bringing an end to the attempt to making it financially self-sufficient. Another proposal being made is to divide first-class mail into "citizen rate" of one cost for hand-addressed letters, and another cost for "business letters" which are machine-addressed.

First- and second-class mail are sent together with only a difference in cost of postage. Only newspapers and other periodical publications may be mailed at the second-class rates. A periodical must be published at least four times a year or more to qualify. All second-, third-, and fourth-class mail must be paid in advance. That is why newspapers must be paid before expiration.

## Reminder! Letter Size Standards Are Effective In April

With everyone's attention now focused on the new postage rate increase proposed for next year, it is necessary to remind everyone that a separate "Mail Classification" change is scheduled to be implemented in less than nine months.

Size standards for letter-size mail are scheduled to become effective on April 15, 1978. These standards apply only to first class mail weighing through one ounce and single-piece third class mail weighing through two ounces.

The mail classification change prohibits the mailing of pieces which are too small or too flimsy to be mechanically sorted. Other non-standard pieces which exceed any of the maximum dimensional limitations may be subject to a surcharge in addition to the applicable postage and fees.

The template on this page shows the minimum size mailing piece which will be accepted and the dimensions subject to surcharge for first class pieces weighing through one ounce and single-piece third class weighing through two ounces. The typical first class flat, which usually weighs more than one ounce, will not be subject to a surcharge.

It also provides a convenient guide to the proper ratio of height to length. The standard calls for a height to length ratio which falls between 1 to 1.3 and 1 to 2.5. A standard size envelope's upper right corner will fall within the shaded area on the template. Mailing pieces which are outside these ratios will be subject to the surcharge.

Envelopes less than one-fourth inch thick which are less than 3.5 inches high or 5 inches long will be prohibited. Also cards and other mail items which are less than seven-thousandths (.007) of an inch thick will be prohibited.

In addition, all classes of mail (other than keys and identification devices) which are less than the minimum dimensional limitations will be prohibited.

*Continued on Page Eleven.*

Editor's Note: The template used here is reprinted from the January 1977 issue of "Memo to Mailers."

Page 7

## DIMENSIONAL STANDARDS FOR LETTER-SIZE MAIL

(1st-class mail weighing 1 oz. or less, single-piece 3rd 2 ozs. or less, and not more than ¼ inch thick)

Template shows the minimum and maximum sizes and aspect ratios (height in relation to width) to be effective April 15, 1978).

The tip of the upper right corner of the mailing piece must touch the shaded area to be standard. Non-standard sizes are subject to surcharge.

If the mailing piece does not touch or extend past both of these lines, it is nonmailable.

**Place lower left corner at outer edges.**

¼ inch thickness gauge

TOO TALL    TOO WIDE    WITHIN RATIO

Southern Region

## Bits of Information Regarding Mail

For the asking the Postal Service will give one pamphlets, excerpted from the very large Postal Manual which will explain various regulations and information well worth knowing if one is receiving or sending newspapers and periodicals. Also, available free in post offices is a good informational pamphlet put out by the Consumer Advocate Office (see p. 260).

Letters may be put on the outside of packages only within the United States, its territories and possessions. Do not put airmail postage on this letter, or the whole package then of course must go the same way, and the cost for such packages usually becomes prohibitive for libraries. This seems like a small thing to mention, but it is surprising how many library clerks and students do not stop to think about this.

Letters put on the inside of the package must be so noted on the outside because this first-class letter must be included in figuring the postage for the package.

Commercial invoices may be enclosed in the package without so noting on the outside, but here, too, it is a good idea to put this information on the outside of the package.

The mail clerk in the library will undoubtedly have the various important postal books at his fingertips that will aid him and will dictate procedures from his personal experiences with the local post office. It must be noted that the regulations are very detailed and try to cover every contingency, and therefore they are sometimes difficult to interpret; the interpretation by the personnel in each local post office will vary somewhat.

It is not only a good idea to know what the library has to do to meet the regulations of sending out letters and packages but also to know why letters and packages come in as they do from agents and publishers due to regulations imposed on them by the post office. Also knowing these regulations will give a basis for demanding that such regulations be enforced, when packages come to the library mutilated. (See p. 190 regarding ISSN).

## Various Types of Mail

We are all aware of the various classes of mail and have at one time or another run afoul of some regulation. It might be well to just cover the highlights of the various classes.

## First-Class Mail

This includes handwritten or typewritten material and invoices and statements of accounts. It insures privacy. Maximum weight is 70 pounds, and the maximum size is 100 inches in length and girth combined.

## Second-Class Mail

This is used by newspaper and periodical publishers. The material may be sealed. However, if there is third-class or printed matter enclosed, this must be noted on the outside of the envelope and Post Office personnel may open for inspection. This seldom happens but it may.

It is at this point where one begins to get the regulations that publishers and agents have to meet, because it is where bulk mailings begin to be considered. The publisher must consider the kind of serials he is publishing. (1) They may carry general advertising (2) they must have a frequency of not less than four times a year (3) they must be sent from the known business address (4) they must be formed of printed sheets, not stencils, mimeographs, or hectograph process or in imitation of typewriting (5) they must be for the purpose of disseminating information of a public character or devoted to literature, the sciences[4] including labor unions and state departments of agricultural material if they meet the other provisos such as four times a year, printed, etc., art or a special industry (6) they must have a list of paying subscribers. Advertising publications may not qualify for second-class mail. There is no limit of weight to domestic destinations. Each publication must be folded to a size not bigger than nine by twelve inches. Newspapers and light magazines can be folded to a size of about five by twelve inches. Individual copies must have a wrapper, and flimsy material must be put in envelopes.

Newspapers are sent as second-class mail and will be "given expeditious distribution, dispatch, transit handling and delivery" (Postal Service, publication citation 333.242 1 4). They will be dispatched in pouches with first-class mail in surface transportation, and be distributed for the earliest possible delivery.

## Third-Class Mail

Third-class mail consists of mailable matter which is (1) not required to be mailed as first-class mail (2) not entered as second-class (3) it must weigh less than sixteen ounces. There is no maximum limit to size. The following enclosures are allowed (1) single reply envelopes (2) single order form (3) printed circular (4) printed price list (5) an invoice.

## Bulk Mail

Bulk mail comes mostly under third-class, and while librarians do not mail bulk in this way usually, it is well to have some idea about it, because so much comes into the library by this method.

"The bulk rate is applied to mechanically reproduced mailings of identical pieces individually addressed to different addresses in quantities of not less than 50 pounds or of not less than 200 pieces. All the pieces in a bulk mailing must be identical as to size, weight, and number of enclosures but the printed textual matter need not be identical... A fee of $40.00 must be paid each calendar year by any person who mails at the bulk third-class rates. This fee is separate from the $20.00 fee that must be paid to mail under the permit system. Postage must be prepaid."[5]

Some of the material prohibited to be sent in this manner includes first-class material, bills and statements, and bulk mail may not be sent to foreign countries, including Canada and Mexico.

It is sorted by ZIP Code, bundled or sacked and labelled with the proper "permit imprints." It may be deposited at the "Bulk-Permit Office" at the main post office, or at authorized stations or branches designated by the postmaster. It must be a "hand-to-hand" delivery. It may never be deposited in street letter boxes nor given to carriers.

## Fourth-Class Mail (Parcel Post)

Individuals usually send packages fourth-class mail. It includes merchandise and printed matter of 24 pages or more. Parcels mailed within the United States are limited to 40 pounds and must not exceed 84 inches in length and girth combined. Larger packages may be mailed between smaller post offices. For faster delivery over long distances use priority mail (air parcel post) or express mail.

### LIBRARY RATE

It is in the fourth-class mail that the serials librarian should be well aware of the postal regulations since it is here where the "Library Rate" holds true both in receiving and sending material.

"Library Rate" includes books, printed music, bound volumes of academic theses, sound recordings, periodicals, other library materials, museum and herbarium materials, 16-millimeter or narrower width films, filmstrips, transparencies, slides, microfilms and other items.

The identification statement "Library Rate" must show on the address label, and the name of the library or school must show in the return address. The package may not be addressed to an individual but may indicate on the label that it is "to the attention of" an individual.

The post office must be able to easily examine it. If packages are sealed and sent fourth-class it is taken for granted that the post office may open them.

There are many other points to consider and it would be well to consult the postmaster.

## Registered Mail

Registered mail is the safest way to send material. It is controlled throughout the trip and is insured up to $10,000. The full value must be declared. All mailable matter prepaid with postage at first-class or airmail rate may be registered. For an added fee a return receipt may be requested showing to whom, when, and where it was delivered.

## C.O.D. Mail

First, third and fourth-class mail worth up to $200 may be sent C.O.D. The addressee must pay the amount due on the merchandise, plus the money order fee. The material may also be sent by registered mail.

## Express Mail

There is a new service that is being tested. It guarantees overnight delivery for letters and parcels. It lists many other benefits. It is given number one priority on scheduled flights, scheduled pickups, special delivery, money-back guarantee, 365-day, 24-hour service, even on holidays, and nation-wide coverage (405 cities for Programmed Service and Selected Cities for Regular Service).

## Special Delivery

This may be used on all classes of mail. It is given prompt delivery at post office areas within one mile of the destination.

## International Mail

International mail is divided into three categories (1) letters (2) any printed matter sent either way (3) parcel post.

## Postal Union Mail

Postal Union Mail is all mail exchanged between nations in the Postal Union and Spain. It is divided into two groups (1) LC mail which includes letters and cards and (2) AO mail which includes printed matter, samples and merchandise, matter for the blind, and small packets. The weights and requirements for this mail are so detailed that one should consult the postmaster.

## International Money Orders

These may be purchased in amounts up to $100. One must make application to the post office for the international money order. The post office sends the money to Washington, D.C. There it is sent to the country. Some countries request that further forms be filled out. It may take from three to four weeks for the money to get to its destination. The cost for these vary from year to year.

## Insurance

One may insure articles including third- and fourth-class, air parcel post, for loss of, rifling of, or damage up to $200. Material not available for insurance are articles that are so fragile that they may be broken. They are handled as ordinary parcel post. Any article worth more than $200 should be sent by registered mail.

## Money Orders

This is the safest way to send money through the mail. It may be purchased at all post offices, for amounts up to $300.

Many other items of information may be gleaned from the pamphlet put out by the Consumer Advocate Office, U.S. Postal Service, Washington, D.C. 20260. This department is also your advocate and will help with any postal problems.

## General Comment

Packages going abroad should be packed even more carefully than those intended for domestic mails. Sturdy fiberboard should be able to withstand pressures, friction, change of climate.

Customs declaration and other forms must be filled out. They may be obtained from the post office.

Reliable agents abroad are used to filling out the proper entry forms. Inexperienced agents may not be aware of filling out these forms and books may very easily get into the hands of a broker. The cost of getting them will often be outrageous.

Mail will not be delivered to continental China unless addressed to the "People's Republic of China."

## Length of Mailing Time

It takes different lengths of time to get mail from various parts of the world.

Mail from Europe to U.S.A., and Canada..........three to four weeks and sometimes longer

Mail from India........................ten to twelve weeks

Mail from Kenya.............................five months

(We were told it would take two to four months)

Some packages coming from some foreign countries seem poorly wrapped, but it is because of postal regulations within those countries. Some regulations insist the ends of the packages be open for inspection, others won't allow string on the package.

## What May Happen To Mail

1. Christmas mail takes precedence over magazines and ordinary mail, and some publishers are afraid their mail will get lost in the shuffle; therefore expect a delay of magazines during the month of December, and an avalanche in January.

2. Wharf, postal and bus strikes will slow down the mail.

3. When mail has to be stored at wharves or elsewhere, earlier numbers of magazines will get stored to the rear and later numbers will get to the library first.

4. Once in a while a whole package of the same number of a magazine destined for a particular town may arrive in the library just because the library's name happens to be the one on top of the package. Be aware that this can happen. While the Post Office requires that such packages of mail have the individual's address turned inside and a special label on top, showing the package should be opened for re-distribution — still a slip-up may happen.

5. Address labels may come off for various reasons, such as very cold weather, not sufficient adhesives, etc.

6. Mail may meet with such misadventures as getting burned up, falling into the bilge of the boat, getting sunk at sea — all this, and more often than might be supposed.

7. Mechanization has added a new hazard. Packages now fall off conveyor belts and get lost and mutilated.

## SOME THOUGHTS ON THE PAST, PRESENT AND FUTURE OF THE MAILS

Because change is inevitable in everything, so it is with the U.S. mails. Not only did the name change in 1971 from the Post Office Department to the U.S. Postal Service, and it became a quasi-independent office, but it also found itself subjected to a reversal of an historic position. At the time of Benjamin Franklin the mails were meant to help and provide strong impetus to the free press and the new ideas of democracy and self-government. The idea that the postal service should be subsidized persisted until the early 1970's, when suddenly it found that it must pay for itself by at least 1985. To do this it may have to resort to becoming a conglomerate as in Germany with the West German Federal Post Office "which not only delivers mail but operates the phone system, Telex, telegraph, data transmission, and radio and TV transmission, among other things."[6] It not only pays for itself but makes money. However, perhaps other countries are not any better off than we are when it comes to postage rates. In 1976 West Germans had to pay 19 cents for first class mail, the Australians, British and Swedes paid 23 cents, the French paid 18 cents and the Japanese 17 cents. These have undoubtedly increased as has ours in the meantime.

There are three facets of the Postal Service that affect librarians most. The first one is the steep postal rate increase as already mentioned. This, along with other factors, has threatened the existence of some journals, particularly those publications making only marginal profits that are being forced out of existence. These have suffered the most.

The second facet deals with the first-class mail which is threatened by electronic systems. It is thought by experts that by 1985, at least a third of the mail will be siphoned off and that eventually the postal service as we know it today will be replaced by messages printed out and flashed on a screen. Witness today the business done electronically by banks and business houses in paying invoices and sending messages and directives.

The third facet is the bulk mail with its many new aspects. There is less local sorting of the mail and more and more area-wide sorting. These centralized sorting machines demand that as much mail be accumulated into these centers as possible in order that efficiency be realized from the huge, expensive sorting machines. This has resulted in some mail having to travel hundreds of miles on a circuitous route to arrive at a destination only 20 miles from its original starting point.

This is being corrected by what is called a "hold-out" system. If the mail can be moved directly to its destination and still have it profitable for a truck to make the trip, the parcels will be held out of the bulk mail routing and sent with the regular mail. "The magazine industry is a captive customer of our postal system."[7] Some publishers go so far as to hire their own trucks to get their bulk mail as close to the local destination as possible. But in the end it must be delivered the last few miles by the mailman.

## OTHER POSTAL AGENCIES

In the past few years other mail-delivery agencies have sprung up. They are independent, profit-making ventures. One company is the Independent Postal Service of America. It has private mail carriers who deliver advertising circulars and merchandise catalogs from door-to-door. Another company is the American Courier Corporation, that offers overnight delivery.

"Within the past few years, hundreds of private firms, discovering that the mail business is big business have sprouted up to challenge the giant Postal Service, in one way or another. But the greatest success has been scored by an older outfit, the United Parcel Service, which has actually surpassed the Postal goliath in hauling parcel post."[8] It was started in 1961 and in effect is owned by its employees. It started in New York, but soon expanded to 40 states and in 1977 covered all the 48 mainland states. There are certain retail companies in certain states where the service may not deliver. Parcels may weigh from one to 50 pounds. It advertises that it gives better services at better prices, with less damage. Prompt service is guaranteed, and an automatic insurance coverage of $100.00 is given for each package. It offers a regular pick-up service for a small fee, will attempt to deliver the package three times. The packages are more carefully handled with lighter packages put on top in the trucks. Both the U.S. Postal Service and the United Parcel Service utilize mechanized package-sorting machines.

None of these companies may deliver first class mail because the U.S. Postal Service has the legal monopoly for delivering this type of mail. This right has been vigorously guarded by the U.S. Postal Service and perhaps rightly so. The argument is that private enterprise would skim off the cream of delivery to only densely populated areas and would forget the sparsely populated and out-of-the way areas where it would be too unprofitable for them to consider.

## NOTES

1. "A Consumer's Guide to Postal Service." U. S. Postal Service." (Washington, D.C.: Consumer Advocate Office [20260], Mar. 1974), p.16.
2. Memo to Mailers. U. S. Postal Service. (Washington, D.C.: June, 1977).
3. U. S. Postal Service, op. cit., July 21, 1977.
4. Ibid.
5. Ibid., July 18, 1976.
6. David Mutch, "A Post Office that Makes Money." *Christian Science Monitor* Tues. June 15, 1976.
7. Reader's Digest editors. "Will Congress Kill the Magazine Industry?" *Reader's Digest,* 53rd yr., pp. 49-53, Jan. 1974.
8. Timothy D. Schellhardt. "Post Haste: the U. S. Postal System Begins to Take Notice of Speedy Competitors; United Parcel and Others Give Better Service, but U. A. now Fights Back." *Wall Street Journal,* V. 180: Dec. 20, 1972.

# CHAPTER XI
# CLAIMS AND DUPLICATES

## CLAIMING

Continual review of the titles is necessary to be sure that they are coming without interruption. It is this deep, regular, thorough review that keeps the surface running smoothly.

Time limits of notification of lacks vary with different publishers. The variation of time ranges from 30 to 60 to 90 days. Lack of storage space in publishers' warehouses is the reason for the limitation. After the specified time the back files are turned over to secondhand agents and the cost immediately doubles and trebles. It is not long before the numbers go out-of-print.

Some of the main reasons for lacks are that the numbers may go astray in the mail, or they are mis-addressed, or so generally addressed that they never arrive. Another important factor is that the publisher or agent has taken out the old address stencil and has forgotten to put in the renewal. For this reason, February, March, and April are good months to concentrate on claiming, especially if the renewals are on a calendar basis.

Distance of travel must be considered for publications that are coming from foreign countries. They may take many weeks or even months to get to their destination.

If one is using several agents, especially within the United States the librarian becomes loaded with a stock of specialized forms to fill out, since each agent requests that claims be made on a particular form. If these special forms are not used, one may meet with complete resistance and indifference from the agent.

For titles of regular frequencies such as weeklies, monthlies and quarterlies, one can deliberately ask for the next number. For annuals, semi-annuals, biennials and irregular frequencies it is best to ask if one is up-to-date with a particular number.

Where special forms are not requested by the agent and the title is published within the country, a form postcard serves the purpose. For titles published outside the country, letters are best. The simpler the form letter the better. English is no easier for foreigners than foreign languages are for most Americans. A combination form letter combining various questions is difficult at best but sometimes impossible in a different language.

Following are suggested forms for claiming.

LOUISIANA STATE UNIVERSITY LIBRARY
SERIALS DEPARTMENT
BATON ROUGE, LOUISIANA    70803

Gentlemen:

According to our records we have not yet received the item(s) noted below. Will you kindly send this to us and/or answer those questions checked below. Thank you for your cooperation.

Our records show_____.

RE:

REPLY:

____Has this title ceased publication? If so, with which issue did it cease?

____Please list those issues claimed which are out of print.

____Has this been published yet? If not, please give expected date of publication?

____Other.

Very truly yours,

Serials Claims Assistant

## SERIALS CLAIM

PLEASE SEND THE REQUESTED ISSUE(S) ON RECEIPT OF
THIS CLAIM. YOUR COOPERATION IS APPRECIATED.

_ IF THE BELOW MATERIAL HAS BEEN SHIPPED WITHIN
THE PAST THIRTY DAYS. **DO NOT DUPLICATE.**

THANK YOU  _____

**MAIL
TO**
⟶
⟶

PLEASE REPLY TO:   **SERIALS DEPT., LIBRARY**
(ON REVERSE SIDE)   **UNIVERSITY OF CALIFORNIA**
**P.O. BOX 5900**
**RIVERSIDE, CALIFORNIA 92507 U.S.A.**

ENTRY:                                    DATE

ORDER NO._____

PAYMENT INFORMATION_____

WE DID NOT RECEIVE THE FOLLOWING ISSUE(S):
YEAR                    VOLUME                NO.

**PLEASE REPLY TO THIS CLAIM ON REVERSE SIDE AND RETURN**

This form is in triplicate. One slip is folded and put into the Payment Record Card (PRC) slot. One is sent as the claim, and one is kept as a record on the claimer's desk.

# UNIVERSITY OF CALIFORNIA, RIVERSIDE

BERKELEY · DAVIS · IRVINE · LOS ANGELES · RIVERSIDE · SAN DIEGO · SAN FRANCISCO  SANTA BARBARA · SANTA CRUZ

THE UNIVERSITY LIBRARY                                    P.O. BOX 5900, RIVERSIDE, CALIFORNIA 92507


Gentlemen:

Please verify the following information for your publication:


_____ Ceased publication with issue vol./no._____ for _____.

_____ Latest edition or vol./no. published_____, date_____, price_____.

_____ Subscription price _____ per year, for _____ issues.

_____ Title change, new title as of vol./no._____ year_____ is _____

_____.

_____ Earlier editions or issues/volumes still available.
       Are the following still available? If so, please quote price.



_____ Not our publication, published by _____.

_____ Other.

Your cooperation in providing this information will be gratefully appreciated.
Please indicate your answer on this letter and return. THIS IS NOT AN ORDER.
May I request, please, that you direct your reply to my personal attention?
Thank you for your kind consideration of this matter.

                                        Sincerely,


                                        Serials-Acquisitions
                                        University Library
                                        P.O. Box 5900
                                        University of California
                                        Riverside, California 92507

# UNIVERSITY OF CALIFORNIA, RIVERSIDE

BERKELEY · DAVIS · IRVINE · LOS ANGELES · RIVERSIDE · SAN DIEGO · SAN FRANCISCO  SANTA BARBARA · SANTA CRUZ

THE UNIVERSITY LIBRARY     P.O. BOX 5900, RIVERSIDE, CALIFORNIA 92507

Gentlemen:

Our records show that we have not received

ordered on our purchase order number RC_____, dated_____.

_____Paid on_____

_____Please invoice in triplicate.

Please supply the material ordered, or tell us when we may expect shipment. Address invoice and issues to:

    Serials Department, Library
    University of California
    P.O. Box 5900
    Riverside, California 92507
    U.S.A.

Thank you for your kind attention to this matter.

Sincerely,

UNIVERSITY OF CALIFORNIA
UNIVERSITY LIBRARY
SERIALS DEPARTMENT
P.O. BOX 5900
RIVERSIDE, CALIFORNIA   92507

**Change of Address**

TO:


Concerning our order _____

_____.

Purchase order number

Order date

Attached is the mailing label from the current issue.


PLEASE SEND FUTURE ISSUES AND INVOICES TO:

Serials Department
University Library         PLEASE NOTE EXACT, COR
University of California    ADDRESS.
P.O. Box 5900
Riverside, California   92507

Thank you for your kind attention to this matter.

Sincerely,


Notations should be made in the Serials Record that the claim has been made and note the current date. When the answer is received, record not only the date of the answer, but show what number is the up-to-date one. If the actual number is not recorded, and a year goes by, it is puzzling to know whether new numbers have been received. It is surprising how often untrained personnel forget to give all this information. Half the good work and effort is lost in the passing of time, if notations are not detailed and dated. This information is also conclusive proof to the clientele and staff members that claiming has been done. Otherwise, how can one prove that the publication is up-to-date, even though it is ten years behind in publication? Yes, it calls itself an annual, and yes, it intends to continue. The big problem is probably that the society is trying to find funds for further publication.

If several people are doing the claiming, one may flag with a colored tab on the outside of the tray indicating where the next claiming is to start. Also the same color tab that is used for weeklies may be so indicated on the outside of the trays. There are not usually so many weeklies and one won't have to pull out every tray to find them.

All serials librarians in universities are having a particular problem and it is growing each year. This is that branches of the university are building up in various cities all over the state. These conglomerates confuse the publishers and agents especially in other countries. If each branch of the university does its own ordering of books and serials, its own paying and claiming, it leaves all concerned in a state of confusion. The agent insists the order has been sent, or the library insists payment has been made. After much probing and writing it turns out that some other city has gotten into the picture. This happens so often that it cannot be taken lightly, and hopefully there will be an answer to it in the future. Confusion is there and must be met someway, somehow.

One may develop a very sophisticated system of claiming. Long colored tabs may be slipped under the protective edge of the card. A slit in the middle of the card keeps them in place. A series of numbers on the lower right-hand edge of the card combines to show when the last issue was received. As each new issue is received the tab is slipped along to the next number on the edge of the card. Then, in the claiming process one may claim those titles where the tabs are out of line. It is a good system but it has its disadvantages. (1) The tabs slip out of line as many people use the trays. (2) The publication dates vary with each title. (3) The whole system may become just one more detail out of a thousand others in training new personnel. The fixed frequency tabs prove to be a simple, adequate and workable system for most untrained personnel.

Claiming is a never-ending process and anyone running out of work in other phases of serials should always be able to help carry on this project.

THOUGHTS FOR NEW PERSONNEL WORKING WITH CLAIMING

There are several approaches to claiming — all good and all to be utilized. At one time or another every title in the file takes some sort of special attention. However, certain basic rules may be considered.

1. Automatic — Anyone checking in mail should immediately claim any current missing numbers as soon as discovered.
2. Systematic — One person is employed to claim systematically.
   a. The claiming is done according to frequency for domestic titles.
      Claim *Weeklies* about once a month
        *Monthlies* about every other month
        *Quarterlies* about three times a year
        *Annuals, semi-annuals, biennials* about once a year
        *Irregulars* anytime left in the year
   b. Gift and Exchange material is claimed like any other, unless it has broken down altogether. Then the Gift and Exchange librarian will have to write a special letter to bring it back into line.
   c. Material coming in from foreign countries necessitates a different consideration. It sometimes takes several months for some journals to come from distant places.
   d. At infrequent intervals date "Discard on receipt" for a few months and if no longer receiving, the card may be pulled. This helps to clear the record of extra cards.
3. Other approaches to claiming
   a. Utilize inquiries of all library personnel and patrons when volumes or numbers are missing or behind schedule.
   b. When paying invoices, lacks often come to one's attention.
   c. Direct "Renewal Cards" bring a certain number of titles up for a review each month. (See the chapter on Ordering).
   d. New Subscriptions should come up for review about three times a year to see if new information can be sent to the agent to help get difficult titles started. One may bring to light recent information by checking the new tools.
   e. The current correspondence file constitutes a further review when the unanswered letters are gone through once a year.

**Points to Remember in Claiming**

Do:
1. Use complete bibliographical information, giving complete title, and showing volume or numbers, month and year.
2. Claim current lacks only, write special letters about collapsed titles.
3. Show clearly the correct return address.

4. Be on the alert for titles that might be published under two or more series. The volume may have gotten checked in on one or the other series and not noted on the series in question.
5. Some volumes do not get published consecutively. Watch for such notes on the Serials Record.

Don't Claim:
1. Volumes or numbers issued before the subscription began.
2. Volumes from one agent if a change was recently made to another one. Check the financial card to see where the change was made.
3. Lacks that have been turned over to the Search Department as out-of-print.
4. Gift or Exchange titles that have collapsed altogether. Ask the Gift and Exchange librarian to write about them.
5. Special sources such as faculty gifts. Ask the Gift and Exchange librarian to look into these.
6. International Congresses are a law unto themselves. See the explanation in the chapter on ORDERING.

Don't get too automatic about claiming. It is sometimes useless to claim an outdated directory. It is better to forget about it and try getting the current one. The same is true with material that reaccumulates into larger units. If one claims this type of material one probably will be told in no uncertain terms by the publisher that the number being claimed is not needed. But unless the claimers are on their toes, this may be done.

Following is a form that the University of California, Riverside library has which keeps track of claims for statistical purposes (see p. 274).

## DUPLICATES

Duplication of material is the opposite side of the coin to claiming. One may claim too much just as one may claim too little. This seems a shocking statement but claiming may and does bring duplicates.

Another important reason for duplication is that the publisher or agent has not removed the last year's address stencil and has put in a new one for the current year. In this case both labels must be sent back for comparison of expiration dates. Sometimes one has to wait until the next number is received if the address labels have been thrown away too soon.

Don't ever write information on the duplicate piece. The publisher or agent will not accept its return if it is mutilated in any way.

One only worries with purchased duplicates, although gift items

# CLAIMING STATISTICS

**JULY**
Claims Sent_____
Claims Rec'd_____

**MARCH**
Claims Sent_____
Claims Rec'd_____

**AUGUST**
Claims Sent_____
Claims Rec'd_____

**APRIL**
Claims Sent_____
Claims Rec'd_____

**SEPTEMBER**
Claims Sent_____
Claims Rec'd_____

**MAY**
Claims Sent_____
Claims Rec'd_____

**OCTOBER**
Claims Sent_____
Claimd Rec'd_____

**JUNE**
Claims Sent_____
Claims Rec'd_____

**NOVEMBER**
Claims Sent_____
Claims Rec'd_____

**DECEMBER**
Claims Sent_____
Claims Rec'd_____

**JANUARY**
Claims Sent_____
Claims Rec'd_____

**FEBRUARY**
Claims Sent_____
Claims Rec'd_____

**ANNUAL TOTAL**
Total Requested_____
Total Received_____

often become involved. A gift subscription sometimes can put one into bewilderment. Will the gift copy continue to come? Or should one accept the gift copy (creating duplicates) for the space of a year or two, in favor of stopping and starting the purchased title all over again? Some gift subscriptions last only a year or two.

There are libraries that do not bother with investigation of any duplicates. They are simply recorded and shelved. It is a fact that careful checking and reviewing does take time that sometimes seems could be put to better advantage. A fine balance has to be made on clearing the ephemeral duplicates rapidly and checking carefully on the more expensive items.

## Thoughts Given to New Personnel Working with Duplicates

All duplicates are placed on the storage shelves set aside for that purpose. They are kept long enough to see if more copies keep coming. They are reviewed every few weeks.

## Philosophy

1. Try to find a reason for the duplication. Try to bring together all pertinent information so the picture will be made as clear as possible. If one can give the agent any clues as to why the duplicates are coming, he is much more apt to be able to stop them. If they are coming from a source other than the agent, one will have better judgement on what other action to take.
2. Does the material show a pattern of duplication?
3. Does the address label show it was intended for the library, or any person in particular, or is it a very general address? This creates one of the more difficult problems of the Serials Department.
4. Could it be coming as a gift?
5. Has a copy actually been checked into the Serials Record? Even further checking may be needed by going to the shelves.
6. Be on the lookout for supplements, and revised editions and numbers, and extra parts of the same number. Particularly be on the lookout for the French words "bis" and "hors" which mean extra material.
7. Check the current correspondence file to see if a letter might have caused the duplication.
8. Is there information on the serials record cards showing one has already been given directives as to whether to return duplicates or keep them? Once this information is given by the agent one may use it for future duplicates.

9. Could it be coming on a replacement order?

After eliminating all the above categories there is left in the duplicate pile the following:

1. All duplicates received because of claims.
2. All bound volumes.
3. All duplicates that are coninuing to come as unwanted extra subscriptions.

All three categories should be written about and the journals shelved on the duplicate shelves with dated slips, awaiting answers and directives as to whether or not they should be returned or kept and, if the former, to whom they should be sent. Continually compare any invoices to see if the library is being charged for them.

When a duplicate is returned, a letter should accompany it, attesting to the fact that it is being returned and giving the title, volume, number, year, and by what kind of mail (parcel post, insured, etc.) it is being sent. There is no way one can prove that the volume or piece was really returned once the books get out of the library. This is usually not realized or thought necessary until one is faced with such a dilemma and has to spend a morning searching for a book that was returned some months previously.

The way that different agents and publishers view the problem of duplication of materials has to be taken into consideration, and their opinions influence the manner in which duplicates received through their service are handled.

Harrassowitz usually wants duplicates sent to another subscriber in this country. When writing about a duplicate, give the symbol which appears in pencil on the front of the piece, and information will be returned telling where to send it.

Pergamon wants all duplicates returned.

Phiebig usually wants duplicates returned to the publisher or agent that it may use. Write and ask what to do.

### Disposal of Surplus Duplicates

For a discussion of disposing of extra duplicates, see the chapter on Gifts and Exchanges.

# CHAPTER XII
# BINDING

## DECISIONS

### General Comment

The decisions of binding serials involves so many more complexities than those of individual books, that much hard thinking must take place, because whatever decisions are made will probably continue for the lifetime of the title.

The preparation of binding may be located in various departments of the library such as the Catalog Division, Public Services, or set aside in a department of its own. Sometimes binding information is kept in the Serials Record and it becomes the bindery authority. But clearly, no matter where it is located, the very nature of its intricacies will interweave with the Serials Department. Also, responsibility may vary from professional personnel to a binding record clerk.

A decision and history of each title is usually kept in order to insure a reasonable uniformity of the title, and a record is kept of any special idiosyncrasies that might follow the title through its life. Usually a card file will suffice, and this sort of information lends itself beautifully to computer records. Uniformity is the keyword to all decisions — do not do something one way and then another.

Decisions! decisions! They are always with us and no less here than anywhere. The decision of whether or not to bind should be made at the time of setting up the subscription. If the decision cannot be made at the time due to the lack of information, a pencilled note may be made on the Serials Record card to review this decision upon receipt of the first piece, or completion of the first volume. Getting this decision made as soon as possible will guard against leaving the title or volume so long in limbo that missing numbers will not be available at a future date.

If material has already been a long time in the library and action is needed, special decision forms might be used such as the following, to send through the various Divisions to get the title on its way to be bound.

## SERIALS DECISION FORM

CALL NO.                  INITIATED BY _____

                                   SER. _____

                                   DIV. _____

TITLE:

                                 OTHER _____

                                   DATE _____

SHELVED _____ IN CSR _____ CURRENTLY REC. _____

         SOURCE _____ FREQUENCY _____

TITLE ALREADY BEING BOUND? _____ SIG. _____ DATE _____

_____

_____

### HOLDINGS

_____

_____

(SHOW VOL OR NO., & DATE   (PLEASE VERIFY FROM  (USE BACK OF
                                    SHEET IF NECESSARY) SHELF OR CSR)

_____

_____

INDEXED IN_____      DESCRIPTIVE COMMENT_____

                                     (CONDITION, FORMAT,_____

LIBRARIAN'S RECOMMENDATION
(IF TO CANCEL, PLEASE GIVE     ETC.) _____
JUSTIFICATION)

   CANCEL                    _____      _____

   KEEP CURRENT
     ISSUE ONLY            _____

   KEEP ONE YEAR ONLY_____

DISCARD ON RECEIPT    _____

BIND_____        REGULAR_____

               PAM BIND_____

               NORBIND_____

SUGGESTED BINDING SCHEDULE:

_____ SIG. _____ DATE _____

TECH. SERV. DECISION:

All necessary binding information may be noted on the current "flimsy" of the Serials Record at the time of setting up the subscription.

The former binding decision form is used by Louisiana State University library, Baton Rouge. It is a single sheet and is blank on the back.

The following forms are used by University of California, Riverside. There are three copies of the slip: two are similar on the front with detailed information, the third has less information on the front.

Title: (Do not use periods to indicate double spacing. Type line for line — double space when necessary for author or sub titles.)

How Many Vols. of This Title in This Order?_____

| | (one line only) | Call Nos. |
|---|---|---|
| Series, Part, Index or Supp. | | |
| | (one line only) | |
| Vol. Year or Number | | |
| | (one line only) | |
| Series, Part, Index or Number | | |
| | (one line only) | |
| Month | | |
| | (one line only) | Imprint |
| Year | | |

How Many Vols. of This Title in This Order?_____

Variations of the fronts

| Specifications | Material | Cloth Color | |
|---|---|---|---|
| Full Bind | Morocco | Red | 399 |
| | Select Leather | Wine | 340 |
| ¾ Bind | Lib. Buck. | | |
| | | Tan | 396 |
| ½ Bind | Vellum | | |
| ¼ Bind | | Brown | 13 |
| Music | Leather Color | Light Blue | 7 |
| Recase | Red | Blue | 91 |
| | Wine | | |
| Flexible Cover | Brown | Blue-Black | 18 |
| Pocket | Blue | | |
| | Black | Black | 75 |
| Foldouts | Green | | |
| No Trim | Bright Green | Light Green | 68 |
| | Tan | Green | 92 |
| Rush | | | |
| Standardized | Boxes | Orange | |
| Labels | Closed | | |
| Sample Sent | Open End | | |
| | Slip Case | | |
| Rush | Portfolio | | |

| Covers: | Ads: |
|---|---|
| Bind all | Bind all |
| Bind fronts | Last copy only |
| | Remove all |
| Remove all | Bind as attached inst. |
| Bind as indicated | Index: |
| | None wanted |
| | Bind in front |
| Bind "as is" | Bind in back |
| Stubs for:_____ | Bind "as is" |

Ⓟ f    i

All three copies are similar on the back with a great deal of descriptive information to the binder.

## Decisions on What to Bind

It goes without saying that binding is a necessity for most serials. To bind or not to bind usually means to preserve in some sort of manner.

1. Any title that is expected to become a permanent part of the library collection should be bound in one form or another.
2. Heavily used or frequently mutilated titles (Should the library get a second copy and hold in reserve for binding, or make arrangements to purchase a prebound copy?) (see below).

3. Substitute microform for binding, when the materials make binding difficult, or when use is expected to diminish substantially when it becomes non-current? (see also p. 283).
4. If the material is to continue to be heavily used, both the original and microform might be necessary.
5. Where the material merits keeping for one or two years only and then discarding, the solution may be to put it in some sort of substitute binding (see pp. 290-292).
6. For smaller libraries, if space is at a premium, they might consider keeping unbound for a certain length of time and then discarding. Or, at least bind only those titles that will make good reference material. It may be necessary to consider whether this library is close enough to a larger library where binding most everything is a routine matter. Another alternative is to keep a microform collection, if the budget and space again allow for such treatment.

### Decisions to Make for All Titles

1. Should jackets be preserved?
2. How much advertising should be saved?
   a. All numbered pages?
   b. Save all advertising as a potential for historians and artists?

### Decisions on What Not to Bind (Special Collections and special libraries may make a decision).

1. University and college catalogs.
2. Ephemeral titles that have only current interest (see substitute bindings).
3. Newspapers (see p. 292-3).
4. Some annual reports (see also substitute bindings).
5. Some volumes that are sent to storage with a low priority usage (see also substitute bindings).
6. Incomplete volumes with heavy usage. (One possibility is to stub.)

STUBBING (THERE ARE TWO TYPES OF STUBBING UTILIZED IN VOLUMES).
1. When a missing number occurs in a volume (but hopefully will be available later) and the volume is to be bound as it is at present, strips of paper the height of the book and 3/4 inch wide are included where the missing number occurs. If the space is less than ½ inch, stubbing will not be done. Stubbing helps to keep the spine the proper width so that the same cover may be utilized when the number is found and the volume returned to the binder for inclusion.

2. The other type of stubbing is done when numbers are of various heights in the same volume. Stubs 3/4 inch wide are used to extend the shorter issues and make them all the same height. In this way the spine remains firm and keeps the books from slipping around on the shelves. Experiment station bulletins are a good example of this type of binding.

## Decisions on When to Bind

Many items must be considered when making decisions on when to bind. Volumes have a tendency to be completed either annually or semiannually. Should one bind early in the year, or later?

As with all businesses, binders cannot afford to have slack periods throughout the year, so it is necessary to keep a steady flow of volumes going to the binder. This may be done in great part, without inconveniencing either the binder or the patron by choosing different categories at different times of the year. The disrupting effect of recalling volumes after they have been sent should be considered very carefully. Transporting them back and forth causes confusion, costs money and, if possible, never should be done.

1. The needs of the patrons and the librarians must be carefully balanced. (Even different curricula may determine times to bind).
2. The TPI (see p. 294) will usually be the first consideration.
3. Interest and use must be considered. Popular titles may be bound later. If the title is used a great deal currently with less interest later, bind later. If interest in the title continues, this takes much thought even to the point of binding each number separately.
4. Don't postpone binding by storing. Binding becomes more and more expensive each year, as well as resulting in lost numbers if held too long, and means double handling. This also results in increase in expense of replacements.
5. Bind reference materials in slack periods. University and college libraries may bind such material between terms (see also #3 above).

## Duplicate Subscriptions

Some journals get such constant use that it becomes necessary to get a duplicate copy for binding. At times this is really a saving. Replacing many missing and mutilated numbers may result in spending more than actually having a second protected set.

There are a very few binders which will set up an arrangement to purchase and bind a volume at the end of the year. One such binder is the PBS — Prebound Periodicals, formerly called Periodical Binding Service of the American Binder, Inc., 914 Jefferson, Topeka, Kansas 66607.

In their brochure they list a formidable number of reasons for using this type of service, all quite reasonable and worth careful consideration.

1. Eliminates combing through issue after issue looking for mutilation.
2. Eliminates need for seeking to secure replacements of missing issues or mutilations.
3. No need to keep track of loose current numbers.
4. Eliminates storage space.
5. Cuts costly binding preparation tasks.
6. Eliminates "always at the bindery" problems.
7. The volume has mint condition issues.
8. The company does the claiming needed.
9. Eliminates binding incomplete volumes.

They bind the completed volume in class A library bindings and it takes 60 to 90 days to receive the volume after its completion.

Some libraries prefer to order microfilm for the permanent copy. It must always be kept in mind that you must have already subscribed to one original copy of the magazine. Also it must be kept in mind that there is a lag of at least six months in getting the microfilmed copy. In cases of newspapers the lag may be as much as a year or two. Some companies offer microfiche in the same way.

## Ways to Economize

1. There should be only one person as liaison officer between the library and the binder. This saves confusion, misunderstanding, and duplication of effort.
2. Compile a workable set of specifications that will fit your particular library.
3. Choose a reputable binder that will be able to fulfill your needs.
4. Come to a complete understanding with the binder with regard to the contract. Much may be permanently worked out, and not left to chance, or gone over time and time again. In other words, get the standing specifications set up immediately.
   a. Quality of cloth.
   b. Colors of cloth.
   c. Types of boards to be used on the covers.
   d. Keep lettering to a minimum. (Use alternatives to goldleaf, and use abbreviations as much as is reasonable).

e. Make rubbings, or photocopy the spines for the binder to check each time.

f. Decide on the size of type and measurements from the bottom of the volume.

g. Discuss the trimmings of pages.

h. Agree on the handling of supplements, monographs, special numbers, advertisments and covers.

5. Special handling.

a. Sewing — hand or bench sewing.

b. Gluing.

6. Leave some things to the binder's good judgement.

a. The use of lighter weight cloth (vellum) on the more ephemeral titles.

b. Let the binder remove pages that are to be taken out. Untrained personnel may ruin the volume.

## Standards

It is reasonable to say that no binding is cheap. There must always be a compromise between service, economy, and esthetics. As costs continue to rise, decisions become more difficult. Standards that were once taken for granted are one by one shifting to less expensive and simpler ones. The first to go of these early standards was leather bindings, which have been replaced by vellum and buckram. Now the latest innovation is vinyl material which is still somewhat in the experimental stage. The color does not go all the way through as does buckram, but this promises to be remedied. There is at present only one company that makes bookcloth. Some libraries have advocated binding the whole collection in one color, and what a dismally monotonous library that must be!

The next early standard to be left behind was gold lettering. White is now the preference because it is more easily read in the stacks. Next to go were headbands, and finally sewing was replaced by flexible glue for all but the very heavy volumes, or volumes which need to be laid flat, such as music.

For some discussion on standards see Osborn.[1]

Early discussions may be found in *Development of Performance Standards for Binding Used in Libraries, Phase II* (LTP Publications no. 10) Chicago: Library Technology Project, A.L.A. 1966. In 1967 they were approved as standards by A.L.A. and Special Libraries Association.

## Collation

Collation is often intricate and must be done by a trained person who can visualize all the ramifications. It should be done so well at the library that the binder will not have to duplicate the process. This saves trips back and forth between the library and binder, and extra charges for binding, as well as locating lacking numbers before they become out-of-print. Some librarians feel collating is a waste of time. This turns out to be very expensive at times because any volume may turn out to be a troublemaker.

POINTS TO CHECK

1. Are there any changes of publication — changes of title or volume numbering, etc.? What Departments or Divisions in the library should be notified of these changes? (see below for suggestions of forms that may be used to notify anyone needing to know of these changes).
2. Are all issues in the order in which they will be bound? Someone has to do this, be it staff or binder.
3. Are indexes included?
4. Scan the TPIC (see p. 294) to see what is called for in the volume.
   a. Part 2 issues or special issues?
   b. Supplements — should they be included in the volume, or bound separately? Where to bind — with the issue, or at the end of the volume?
   c. Are parts of books included within the volume? So many foreign journals include them, to be deleted, and cumulated to be bound later.
5. Are there missing numbers, pages, or mutilations?
6. Are maps or charts included? If so, should they be put in pockets, bound separately, or sent to the Map Collection? Indicate at the proper place in the volume as to what has been done with them.
7. Some journals have media in them, such as sound-sheets, slides, microfiche.

## Features of Serials That May Require Notification of Changes Throughout the Library

Many times, publications change their approach so much that they need to be reviewed by various Divisions before binding. The following are certain items that make this necessary:
1. Change of entry
2. Change in titles

3. New supplements (bound in or loose)
4. Special issues
5. Change of publisher
6. Change in the system of numbering
7. Change in series
8. Absorption of, or combining with, other titles
9. Special notes about publication, i.e. suspension, cessation, etc.
10. Division of title
11. Reversal of title

It is best that these features be caught before binding and lettering the next volume. (See below for suggestions of forms that may be used to notify anyone needing to know of these changes. The first is an LSU library form, the second is one of UCR library's forms. (This latter form may be initiated by anyone for any reason; binding charges are simply an example of such a reason.)

When it is necessary that the next volume be caught for the changes, the following slip may be hung over the Serials Record card.

```
Call No.          Title:




 




Route this volume with the binding notification slip to
Catalog Division for Catalog revision.  It will be sent
to Preparations Department after revision
```

CHANGE MEMO

TITLE_____

_____

CALL NO.                    LOCATION DIRECTIVE

_____Add/correct information        _____Cross Reference needed

_____Transfer of title              _____Ceased publication
     (attach all records)           _____Added volumes

_____Title withdrawn                _____Replacement of bd. volumes

_____Cancellation                   _____Declare missing, reorder

SOURCE OF INFORMATION_____

_____INITIATOR_____DATE_____

WRITTEN EXPLANATION_____

_____

_____

_____

CIRCLE RECORDS AFFECTED, CROSS OUT WHEN COMPLETE

SERIALS CATALOGING                  SHELVING AREAS

  Pulled_____bd. vols.                _____RR label/issues

  Remark bd. vols.                    _____Backfile label/issues

  Public catalog only                 _____Annual reports/issues

PROCESSING                            _____Outside Serials Dept.

  Kardex                            CLAIMING-ORDER-PAYMENT

  Problem Box                         Payment record card

  Statistics form                     Control slip

  Printout                            Fund slip

  Newspaper list                      On order/in process file

  TRIP_____.                   Cancellation letter sent

  Provenance_____              Public catalog

 Bindery Prep. records                Deselection list

 Annual report file                   Exchange file

Notify Reference                      Reorder with_____

Notify Music                          Claim record

Notify Math                           Replacement file

Notify Circulation

SERIALS DEPARTMENT CHANGE MEMO
9/25/78

## Thickness of Volumes

1. The ideal thickness for a regular volume is 2½ inches.
2. The type of paper must be considered when deciding on the thickness of volumes. Heavy paper will of course make thicker volumes. Some cheap paper will not sew well.
3. Binding too many volumes together creates problems for patrons when more than one person wants to use volumes close together. Also this may mean that two or three years may go by, awaiting time to bind, and indexes are located in several places in one physical piece. If large volumes have to be consulted often they are more apt to go to pieces.
4. Librarians are increasingly binding smaller units, especially if the title circulates. Sometimes the decision is made to bind each number separately. Indexes then may be gathered into five or ten years and bound together.
5. When there is a change of size in the middle of a volume bind the two sizes independently.
6. The same is true of title changes, i.e., bind the different titles independently.
7. If the size of volumes has to be changed, note the new information immediately on all records.
8. Volumes with map pockets in back should not be too thick. (Sometimes there are enough maps to make a separate portfolio and label spines "text" and "maps.")
9. Glued spines should be especially noticed so that they are not too thick and heavy.
10. Do not bind heavily-used volumes too thick. They are hard to use and wear out too quickly.

## Title-pages and Indexes

Each book is more usable with its own index, even though cumulated indexes are published later, or if the title is indexed later in indexing or abstracting services, especially if a circulating volume. The cumulated indexes come out so much later and are not so exhaustive. Publishers are apt to put TPI's (see p. 294) any place they feel like it in different volumes, but try to be consistent when binding.

While a certain pattern of publication of indexes may be ascertained for a title, it is not at all certain that the next year it will be the same. Usually it will continue in the same way for years, but keep in mind that it may change.

CERTAIN POINTS TO KEEP IN MIND REGARDING INDEXES

1. Indexes to single volumes
   Necessity for indexes:
   a. To prove completeness of volumes.
   b. To prove what should be contained in the volume.
      (Sometimes special supplements and extra parts and numbers are to be included in the volume, and the only way one may be sure the volume is complete is to check the index.)
   c. To make the volume more usable.
   d. There are certain publications that are useless without the index. Only the librarians using the material may decide this.
   e. There are certain magazines that are indexed in various tools so that indexes are not so vital to them.
2. When volumes may be bound without indexes:
   Serials are not bound without indexes as a rule. If the index is unusually late and less than 8 pages, an exception may be 'made since it could be tipped in later. If the volume is apt to have to be rebound due to the index being too thick, the volume should be held until it can be bound all at one time. Rebinding is expensive. When the thickness indicates, the first half of a volume may be bound, withholding the last half until the index arrives. These may be string bound or stapled together if use warrants it until the index is received.
3. Where found: This may vary from year to year, although the pattern is usually the same.
   a. Last number of the volume either at the front, back or middle of the piece, either bound in or loose.
   b. First number of the next volume. Locations may be the same as above.
   c. They may come separately, either close to when the volume is finished, or in very unusual cases as much as four years late. Indexes that come in loose may have the call number written on them as on any other piece and sent to the Divisions with a binding notification for the volume/volumes.
4. In a split volume where to put the index?
   a. If in front, then the volume will usually have to wait until the volume is complete.
   b. If in the back, the first parts are already bound and probably shelved elsewhere.
5. Cumulated indexes are usually published and bound separately, but once in a while they are published at the end of the last volume in the cumulation. When this happens this information must be

brought out on the spine of the volume and be noted on the Serials Record.

## Lettering

Get the lettering established with the binder and keep it. Work closely with the binder to make rubbings, photocopies, or computerized records of the spine, so that all volumes will continue to be uniform. If the record is computerized be even more careful because of the permanent aspect. Strike a happy medium of information instead of overloading or leaving too much off.

1. Keep titles short and abbreviated.
2. Use initials of well known associations as UNESCO, ALA, etc., when possible.
3. Omit all items such as the words for volume in the various languages.
4. Use Arabic numbers instead of Roman numerals.
5. Omit words showing possession by the library if they can be found elsewhere in the book.
6. Be consistent for all titles as far as possible.

## SUBSTITUTES FOR COMPLETE BINDING

Through the years various substitutes for full binding have been tried. The availability of new supplies and equipment has encouraged many different approaches. Some have proved successful, others have dropped by the wayside.

### Reasons for Substitute Binding Are:

1. Some paper is too thin or brittle and will not withstand the rigors of all that it takes to do full binding, so other means must be devised. For such fragile volumes some alternatives are:
   a. Tie between cardboards.
   b. Put in boxes or other containers.
   c. Spiral bound envelopes.
2. Some numbers are too thin.
   a. Pamphlet binders may be used.
   b. Spiral binding.
   c. Envelopes.
3. Incomplete volumes.

Many times incomplete volumes have to be held together because missing numbers cannot be readily located for filling in. It is difficult to suggest the length of time a volume should be held when certain numbers cannot be found. Almost every volume is an individual case. So much depends on how much use the volume gets, how current the material is, the quality of paper, how very unavailable the out-of-print numbers are. A special review may bring out the fact that only a few pages are involved and they might be reproduced in some manner. (See comments on reproducing).

    a.   They may be preserved temporarily in inexpensive pamphlet binders.

    b.   Insert stubs in the bound volume so that enough space will be left to add the missing pages later.

    c.   Togic bind (see p. 292).

## Types of Substitute Binding

1. String binding: Journals up to 1½ inches in thickness are placed in table clamps, then notched with a hand hack-saw at the top and bottom of the spine approximately 1/16 - 1/8 inch deep. These notches are tied with strong cord and covered with a plastic adhesive. This method is good for volumes with missing or mutilated issues awaiting replacements and will be commercially bound within one year. This is not a suggested method for old journals which have already become brittle.

2. Norbinding: This method is similar to that of string binding. The difference is that end sheets, which are of a quality of paper comparable to end sheets used by commercial bindings, are put on the front and back of the book, before sawing the spine. These sheets protect the book better for temporary circulation and provide a place to put the call number and the title.

3. Stapling: Stapling machines which accommodate 7/8 inch staples may be used for thin journals (distributed through Demco and Gaylord Library Supply Catalogs). If necessary they may be stapled from top and bottom for a more secure volume. This method is not satisfactory for a wide variety of materials or volumes to be shelved for long periods of time. Some difficulties may be experienced in getting the machines serviced or obtaining parts within a reasonable length of time.

4. Pamphlets: Pamphlet binders are used for single issues of previously bound volumes, thin paper backs, and pamphlets. The materials are glued into the pamphlet binder with a plastic adhesive and then stapled, either from the side or saddle style when possible. This type of binding may be considered permanent

because it has such a long shelf life. Should not be over ½ inch thick.

5. Spiral binders: Spiral binding is not an inexpensive method, in that good quality boards (8-10 ply) are necessary for the front and back, also spirals of various widths must be kept in stock. The main purpose for the spiral binder is for publications to be placed on reserve for hard usage and to reinforce soft covers of books originally purchased in spiral binders; a special machine is needed.

6. Togic binding machine: The togic binding machine is the most versatile. It is made in Japan and distributed in the United States by Bro Dart. It may be used for temporary binding (with or without covers) of journals with missing issues, loose leaf publications, annual reports, experiment station pamphlets, and paperback publications with loose pages. Complete brochures may be obtained from Bro Dart for further information on the operating instructions.

The Togic binding may also take care of numbers one through three above as well. This type of binding does not mutilate the material as much as other methods. However, it is for larger libraries because of the cost of the machine.

7. Permabinding — this is a commercial type binding used for paperbacks (single issues). It is not recommended for slick surface paper or for pieces that have folded pages or important information on the verso of the covers.

## Special Problems

### Newspapers

Newspapers have always been cumbersome and hard to bind and store. Most libraries have in recent years resorted to getting them microfilmed. There has been an evolution in their binding through the years.

1. The earlier bindings of leather back and cloth sides deteriorated.
2. The full canvas or duck binders were real dust catchers.
3. The full buckram bindings were not strong enough.
4. The canvas back and buckram sides have proved most successful.
5. The use of grips attached to the spines have aided in removing them from the shelves more easily.
6. The binding unit was once every month; now the unit is more likely to be ten days to two weeks.

7. The paper becomes brittle sooner than most other publications which now leads to microfilming them as the best answer to the problem.
8. They should be stored in a controlled atmosphere.
9. Single issues for special collections — put in an envelope in a pamphlet binder, or portfolio (newspaper size). This will keep them from cracking at the fold. Lay them flat on the shelves to keep them from warping.

## Monographs

1. If they are called for in the index of the main volume, they should be bound in if the size permits.
2. If not, bind separately and catalog separately.

## Maps

1. They may be sent to the map room with a note in the book stating their whereabouts.
2. If kept in the book a special pocket may be made.
3. They may be spiral bound in an envelope and shelved beside the main volume.

## Advertising

Advertising may be handled in many ways, and many librarians have various points-of-view.
1. Some say to keep only that which is included in the pagination.
2. Some say to ignore the pagination and leave it all out, because this will cut down on the size of the volume.
3. Some say to save all the advertising; it is needed by historians and scholars. This may mean breaking the volume into several sections, which becomes costly.

## Series, Sub-series and Miscellaneous Items

1. Series and sub-series: Many societies, associations, and all universities assign an overall number to all their Bulletins and then assign a different number to those same publications dealing with similar subject matter. It is seldom that the overall numbering is used because many items may be so ephemeral that they are not wanted. On the other hand the sub-series dealing with special subject matter may be very important, and it is cataloged and brought out as such.

2. Numbering and internumbering: Some publishers put the same book into several series and also call it a separate book. It may happen that one copy is being purchased and checked in on several cards. It may then appear that certain volumes are lacking on the shelves in the various series. If all the series must be completed, a copy will have to be purchased for each series.

   (All irregular publications need special handling.)

3. University studies: Often these are not published in order. Each volume may deal with a certain subject and only as some one writes on that subject is a number added to that volume. This means that a volume could often sit on the shelves as an incomplete volume for as much as ten to fifteen years. The only way one can tell that a volume is complete is when one gets an index. Many later volumes may be already completed and bound in the meantime.

4. Experiment station publications: These do not have indexes and the only way one can tell about binding is that enough numbers have come in to make the right size volume. Only the person who has the material in hand can tell when a volume is thick enough to bind. One does have to contend with later revisions of many of these numbers and may spiral bind, or pamphlet bind, or if very thin — insert in a pocket at the back of the bound volume for several revisions.

## ROUTINES

Make certain the Serials Record has space to note the kind of binding needed, i.e. regular, temporary, etc., information regarding T.P.I. (Title-page and index) or T.P.C. (Title-page and contents). Also may be noted special information about supplements or special directives, and how many volumes to bind together.

Also leave space to check in the index and charge the volume to binding by date. The index may accompany the piece and a binding notice form to the Division or actual location of the serial, unless the volume is on "display" when the notice may be written after the second number of the next volume is received. This allows a number of the title to be on the shelves at all times.

"A binding notification slip is the means by which all persons concerned with serials are made aware that unbound issues of a title are ready for binding."[2]

If the Serials Department is at a distance from the actual physical volumes, or several Divisions in the library are gathering the volumes for binding, there are various ways of carrying on a continuity of routines. The person checking in the material at the Serials Record will be the first to know a volume is ready for binding and may write up the basic information (see p. 295 for serials form). The slip may then be sent to the Division where the physical volume will be gathered. It is the person who has the actual volume in hand, along with the index who can tell whether the volume is complete, or what numbers, supplements, extra numbers, etc., are lacking. However, one person in the library should do the final revision of the binding notice to be certain that it is checked against the Serials Record for uniformity of entry, the right number of volumes being bound together, the right abbreviations being used, etc. When all is uniform the person holding the volume in hand may send it and the notification to Preparations. This final revision by one person is more than necessary if several people in the library are gathering binding. If space in the Serials Department is at a premium, it will be easier to do this paper shuffling rather than bring the physical volumes to the record to be checked. Nothing clogs an area so much as physical volumes, and they are heavy to move around, whereas slips are light.

In order to keep the whole process flexible, the Divisions may request binding notifications if the Serials Department has missed writing them. Also irregular numbers will have to be treated this way since only the person working in the stacks and close to the physical pieces can know when enough numbers have accumulated to make a bindable size volume.

The Preparations Department may forward the volumes on to Binding, and hold binding notices in their own department.

It will help everyone concerned if a volume is immediately arranged by the person collecting the volume in the stacks, as it would be read, with number one at the top and all other numbers made consecutive throughout. It may more easily be checked against the index, a step which must be done before sending it on to Preparations since everything called for in the index must be bound together. This routine will bring out irregularities and catch needed supplements and special numbers that must accompany the volume.

When the volumes are returned to the library from Binding, Preparations may collate the volumes note the physical volumes on the back of the binding notice and send the volumes to the Divisions to be shelved and the binding notice to the Serials Department, where the count of physical volumes may be taken from the slips and sent to the

Catalog Division for the annual report, and in the Serials Department a student may check in on the Holdings card of the Serials Record the volumes as noted on the back of the slip. Here again, revision of the student's work has proved a necessity.

Now suppose there are missing numbers or pages when the volume is collected in the Division. A second ordering slip requesting the lacks or replacements is attached to the binding notice and returned to the Serials Department, while the incomplete volume is held in the Division. In Serials a new routine takes place. The information regarding the order for replacement and the current date is noted on the binding notice and it is clipped to the Serials Record card.

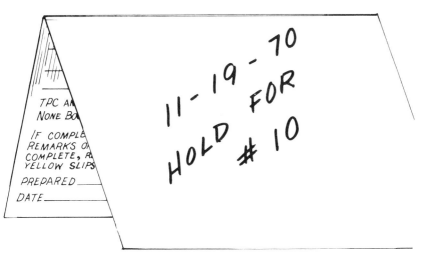

This is a signal to everyone that there is something wrong with the volume, why it is not being bound, but that action is being taken. When the piece is obtained, the binding slip is attached to the newly received piece and both are sent to the Division to start on their regular trip to Preparations.

All these routines for getting a volume bound may sound like a lot of paper shuffling but it really works quite smoothly and it does lead to continuity from one department or division to another. With the complexity of indexes, supplements and all the other ramifications of serials, one cannot toss off the work in simple steps, or by-pass several revisions.

298

POSSIBLE BINDING ROUTINES

SERIALS RECORD

(May initiate binding notification when record shows material to be bound is complete).

DIVISION

(May request binding notification from Serials Record).

—request for binding notification

SERIALS RECORD

(Writes binding notification and charges material to be bound to binding in Serials Record file. Sends binding notification to Division).

— notification

DIVISION

(Takes material to be bound from shelf. Sends material and binding notification to Preparations).

— notification and unbound material

PREPARATIONS
(Sends material to binder).

— unbound material

BINDER

— bound volume

PREPARATIONS

(Sends bound volume to Division, notification of completion of binding process to Serials).

— notification     — bound volume

SRIALS RECORD

(Adds bound volume to holdings card).

DIVISION

(Shelve)

Another possibility is that the Serials Department could send the Binding Notification slip to Preparations, which gathers and prepares the journal for binding in the same step.

## A Quick Review of the Routines — For the Serials Department

1. Disposition of the title.
    a. Keep?
    b. Discard?
    c. Retain one year only, then discard?
    d. Vertical file?
2. When to write the Binding notices.
    a. Are the volumes complete?
    b. T.P.I. and/or Indexes? Annual? Cumulative?
    c. How many volumes bound together?
    d. Supplements and special numbers?
    e. Special directives?
3. Charge to binding on the Serials Record card.
4. Revise the records.
5. Send the Binding notices to the Division (or Preparations) for collecting the pieces.
7. When the Binding notices are returned from Preparations
    a. Check in on the Serials Record noting the proper symbols for physical volumes, dates, etc.
    b. Revise the records once more.

## A Quick Review of the Routines — For the Preparations Department

Check the volumes against the Binding Notification for:
1. Correct call number
2. Title
3. Destination
4. Series
5. Volume number
6. Date
    a. Partial volume, Jan-Mr. 1977
    b. Complete volume, show the year only
    c. Fiscal
        1) Fiscal biennial 1976/77
        2) Calendar year, 1976-77
    d. More than one volume or number, 1976-77
    e. More than one year 1977-78
7. Title pages — loose, or bound in, or none

8. Supplements, maps, resumes, photographs, as well as regular supplements may be called for in the TPIC
9. Stub for missing issues
10. Bind all in the proper sequence for the binder
11. Thickness of one unit should not exceed 2½ inches

## THE NEW COMPUTERIZED BINDING PROCEDURES AT LOUISIANA STATE UNIVERSITY LIBRARY

The Louisiana State University Library was most fortunate in having the opportunity to work with the binder Hertzberg-New Method Company on a pilot program for automating the record-keeping process for binding. Before the new system was installed the department was able to send the binder only 250 titles in a two-week period. After the program was perfected the total jumped to 500 titles in the same period and the library now has no back-log of titles to bind.

It took about a year and a half to plan and work out the system. Now a library of the same size (some 15,000 titles) or larger could set up the same system in about six months. The library took each title and reviewed it completely and brought all information for each title into alignment. It also supplied the binder with the updated information to be housed in the computer bank.

**Current Volume Record**

1st panel gives title no. & consecutive shipment no.

2nd panel gives new title, information, call no. color no. etc.

3rd panel gives sub-title, or series, or supplements etc.

4th panel gives bibliographic variables i.e. Jan-June 1978 etc.

Other panels are self-explanatory

HERTZBERG-NEW METHOD, INC.    KM-3
VANDALIA ROAD, JACKSONVILLE, ILL.
WHEN WRITING USE PRESSURE
THIS IS A NO CARBON REQUIRED 3 PART FORM

| TITLE NUMBER | SHIPMENT NO. |
|---|---|
| NEW TITLE | |

THIRD PANEL

FOURTH PANEL

| CALL NUMBER | | CHANGE CALL NO. |
|---|---|---|
| | | ADD'N. TO CALL NO. |
| | | NO TRIM |
| | | MAP POCKET |
| COLOR NUMBER | | |

1. PACKAGE SEPARATE AND GIVE TO HNM DRIVER

This is a three-part form that is initiated in the library. Each page is a different color.

Copy 1 is sent separately to the binder in an envelope at the time of the shipment.

Copy 2 goes with the volume.

Copy 3 is the library's record which remains with the binding notice.

Hertzberg has all titles of all the libraries he works with in one bank of information — some 40,000 titles.

Hertzberg has a separate bank of information for each library.

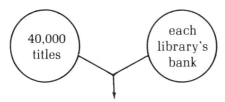

40,000 titles

each library's bank

The above two banks are combined to pull out the information for the current volume.

| TITLE NO. | ACCOUNT NO. | LOT AND TICKET NO. |
|---|---|---|
|  |  |  |

CLOTH COLOR                                                                    HEIGHT

| CHARGING INFORMATION | | | | HEIGHT | PICA | WRAP |
|---|---|---|---|---|---|---|
| STUBBING |  |  |  |  |  |  |
| HINGING |  | EXTRA LETTERING |  |  |  |  |
| EXTRA TIME |  | BINDING CHARGES |  |  |  |  |
| EXTRA THICK |  |  |  |  |  |  |
| HAND SEW |  |  |  |  |  |  |

C 58757

This two-part form is created from the stored banks of the computer records at the binder's plus the current volume slip. The original slip comes back to the library with the invoice. The carbon copy remains with the book and is attached to Binding Notices to be posted by Serials department in the record.

302

| TITLE NUMBER | COLOR | HEIGHT | PREFIX | CALL NUMBER |
|---|---|---|---|---|
| P-0675.3700- | 0057 | *** NO MATCHING TITLE ON DISK *** | | S*590*P63* |
| S-1064.8000- | 0091 | 10 0/0 SOIL*BIOLOGY*AND*BIOCHEMISTRY* | | S*590*S577* |
| | 43-13 | | | |
| S-1067.0000- | 0082 | 10 1/8 SOIL * SCIENCE * | | S*590*S6* |
| | 43-13 | | | |
| S-1069.1100- | 0075 | 11 1/8 SOIL * SCIENCE * SOCIETY * OF AMERICA * 42-12 PROCEEDINGS * | | S*590*S64A13* |
| | 42-6 | | | |
| S-1064.5500- | 0079 | 09 1/8 SOIL*AND CROP*SCIENCE*SOCIETY*OF*FLORIDA*43-18 PROCEEDINGS* | | S*590*S65* |
| | 42-11 | | | |
| S-1070.0000- | 0060 | 09 3/4 SOILS AND * FERTILIZERS * | REF* | S*590*S67* |
| | 42-14 | | | |
| S-1072.0000- | 0075 | 10 1/4 SOILS AND*FERTILIZERS*IN TAIWAN* | | S*590*S68* |
| | 42-13 | | | |
| M-0165.700- | 0073 | 11 1/8 MANITOBA * DEPARTMENT * OF * AGRICULTURE * AND * CONSERVATION * 43-13 SOILS * REPORT | | S*599.1*M3A2* |
| | 42-6 | | | |
| J-0073.0090- | 0080 | 10 1/8 JAPAN*NATIONAL*INSTITUTE UF*AGRICULTURAL*SCIENCES*43-15 BULLETIN* | | S*599*.6*J3A3* |
| | 42-9 | | | |
| C-1790.8500- | 0016 | 09 5/8 CSIRO * DIVISION * OF SOILS * 43-16 TECHNICAL * PAPER * | | S*599*.7*A1A255* |
| | 42-10 | | | |
| I-0102.1200- | 0075 | 10 1/8 ILLINOIS*AGRICULTURAL*EXPERIMENT*STATION*43-15 SOIL*REPORT | | S*599*I5A3* |
| | 42-9 | | | |
| N-1006.0000- | 0073 | 11 1/8 NEW ZEALAND*SOIL*BUREAU*43-12 BULLETIN* | | S*599*N56A3* |
| | 42-14 | | | |
| A-0591.2000- | 0057 | 09 5/8 AGRICULTURAL * METEOROLOGY * | | S*600*A35* |
| | 43-15 | | | |
| O-0397.0000- | 0075 | 9 3/8 ORGANIC * GARDENING * AND * FARMING * | | S*605*.5*O7* |
| | 43-15 | | | |
| G-0611.0000- | 0082 | 09 1/4 GRUNDFOR--BATTRINU* | | S*605*G75* |
| | 43-15 | | | |
| I-1247.5900- | 0016 | 11 1/8 IOWA*AGRICULTURAL*AND HOME*ECONOMICS*EXPERIMENT*STATION*43-13 REPORT* | | S*61*E15* |
| | 42-6 | | | |
| 1-1243.1300- | 0075 | 11 1/8 IOWA * AGRICULTURAL * AND HOME * ECONOMICS * EXPERIMENT * STATION * 43-13 BULLETIN * | | S*61*E22*aNaS* |
| | 42-6 | | | |
| 1-1248.0000- | 0075 | 11 1/8 IOWA*AGRICULTURAL*AND HOME*ECONOMICS*EXPERIMENT*STATION*43-13 RESEARCH*BULLETIN* | | S*61*E3* |
| | 42-6 | | | |
| S-1281.0000- | 0057 | 11 1/8 SOUTHERN WEED * CONFERENCE * 43-12 PROCEEDINGS | | S*610*S08* |
| | 42-6 | | | |
| A-2699.0500- | 0020 | 09 5/8 AUSTRALIA*COMMONWEALTH*SCIENTIFIC*AND RESEARCH*ORGANIZATION*IRRIGATION*RESEARCH*STATION*43-19 TECHNICAL*PAPERS* | | S*613*A88 |
| | 42-10 | | | |
| J-0678.0000- | 0057 | 11 1/8 JOURNAL * OF * SOIL * AND * WATER * CONSERVATION * | LACOLL* | S*622*S55* |
| | 42-11 | | | |
| S-1069.2000- | 0015 | 11 3/8 SOIL*AND WATER*MANAGEMENT*INVESTIGATIONS*43-12 REPORT* | | S*63*E2* |
| | 42-6 | | | |
| K-0043.3000- | 0075 | 09 1/8 KANSAS* AGRICULTURAL * EXPERIMENT * STATION * 43-17 REPORT * | | S*63*E3* |
| | 42-11 | | | |
| K-0068.0000- | 0075 | 09 1/8 KANSAS * AGRICULTURAL * EXPERIMENT * STATION * 43-17 BULLETIN * | | S*631*A5* |
| | 42-11 | | | |
| F-0068.2000- | 0082 | 11 3/8 FARM*CHEMICALS*AND CROPLIFE* | | S*631*A5* |
| | 43-11 | | | |
| | 0082 | 11 3/8 FARM * CHEMICALS * | | |
| | 43-11 | | | |

A print-out is made by the binder for the entire shipment. The library gets two arrangements of print-outs each time. The library may request as many copies of each as is necessary depending on the number of people working with the shipment at the library. Every three or four months the library gets a new print-out, or sooner if needed (depending on the number of new titles added).

## A Description of the Print-out:

1. The upper left-hand corner gives the customer's number.
2. The upper right-hand corner gives the date the print-out was run.
3. The code number or title number gives:
   a. Spine lettering — type, size and spacing.
   b. Color of buckram.
   c. Height of book.
   d. Call number (which includes prefix if necessary).
4. Third panel is for subtitle if it varies.
5. Fourth panel supplies the bibliographical informaiton which is supplied by the library each time for each unit.
6. The call number is the last item of information.
7. Color — if for additional copies the color has varied.

## Items That Need Special Attention:

1. Title changes — both titles continue to be entered indefinitely. There is a different code number, but the call number remains constant.
2. Different location may be indicated by a prefix to the call number.
3. New titles are added every four months. These shipments include only new titles. The library sends complete information the first time a new title is sent. Full information is given with the first volume, then if there is a long run reverts to the usual procedures.

### NOTES

1. Andrew D. Osborn, *Serial Publications; Their Place and Treatment in Libraries.* 2d ed., rev., (Chicago: American Library Association, 1973).
2. Louisiana State University Library. *A Manual on Serials.* 1976.

### Additional Reference

Diaz, Albert James, ed. *Microforms in Libraries, A Reader.* Microform Reviews, Inc.: Weston, Conn. 1975.

# CHAPTER XIII
# GIFTS AND EXCHANGES
# AND SPECIAL PROGRAMS

So often, the quality of a library is measured by the size of the book budget. This tends to minimize the importance of Gifts and Exchanges. Yet, considering it in another light, one may say that this department extends the book budget.

No one can deny that this department is able to get materials which might otherwise be unobtainable to the library. Developing contries both in the East and West, having little in finances, are both willing and able to exchange publications. Governmental and institutional material is part of this type that may be gotten more readily by exchange than by purchase.

However, many librarians feel that domestic exchange is not as free as it looks. Money and personnel are needed to conduct the routines. And what about the immense rise in postage in recent years! This one item alone has discouraged some libraries in carrying on the program, or at least curtailing it drastically. Often the library does not have sufficient publications available of its own and has to purchase them. The value of the material received is uneven and some is very ephemeral. Service with other libraries may become erratic, taking much time in claiming, with small returns.

With ingenuity and imagination one may utilize many sources for acquiring material. One way is to ask outright for it as a gift. Some institutions consider it an honor to have their publications placed in a library. It never hurts to try.

Local material may have to be gotten by means of the telephone, or personal visits to the institutions. These local contacts may sometimes do wonders. However, annual visits may be needed to keep the material coming.

The most usual approach, of course, is to send out form letters (see pp. 308-310), showing an interest in exchange of journals. It is well to list what the library has available to offer, so a comparable basis can be established immediately. Sometimes a second letter has more success than the first.

One thing to keep in mind is that although a title may be available on exchange, some volumes may be so expensive that they must be purchased. Note this information on the Serials Record so claiming will be done by means of a special letter.

Many of the developing countries do not have the means to do a great deal of buying so they must lean on the exchange approach. Keep in mind that this exchange basis is an important factor and that agents in this country are also aware of this and utilize it as well as libraries. Therefore, seriously consider exchange direct before putting such titles into the hands of an agent. One may not have to have a middleman.

## Sources for Getting Exchanges

With budgets becoming tighter and tighter it behooves librarians to cast around for other means of getting library materials. Perhaps the alternatives of purchasing materials may outweigh the rising cost of postage that is now often given as a reason to curtail gifts and exchanges. One may turn to more sources than ever before — sources that have, through the years developed into efficient possiblities.

1. USBE (Universal Serials and Book Exchanges, Inc.) According to Osborn, this "is the major American and international outlet for the exchange of publications." It is the largest resource in the world. For a description, see Special Programs.

2. British Library Lending Division
   According to Osborn it is, "The biggest single development in the circulation of periodicals [which] came with the establishment of the National Lending Library for Science and Technology in Boston Spa, Yorkshire."[1] See Special Programs

3. UNESCO Bulletin for Libraries is another current source for exchange possibilities. It is complemented by the Handbook on the International Exchange of Publications.

4. Duplicate Exchange Union of the Resources and Technical Division of the American Library Association (see p. 315).

5. Special Libraries Association has sponsored exchanges. 235 Park Avenue, So. New York, N.Y. 10003.
6. Science Book and Serial Exchange.
   It is just recently established. The Coordinator is Raymond L. Hough. Ann Arbor, Michigan.
   There are other, perhaps less productive, older, more routine sources.
1. College and university libraries.
   Most of them have been shying away more and more from gift and exchange.
2. Government bodies.
   Much more is available here than has been utilized by many libraries (see p. 147).
3. Learned societies.
   What with costs of production of publications going up by leaps and bounds this source has been becoming less productive.
4. Libraries in general.
   Perhaps, now that deacquisition has set in, more and more broken sets may be available.
5. Non-profit-making organizations.
   See below, Free Magazines.

Free Magazines
   There are several basic facts about free periodicals of which one must be aware.
1. The first objective of organizations giving away their journals is to influence opinion. Some others do include much information. Be aware of the intent of the journal.
2. Free journals often do not have long lives. Others soon cease to be gifts and must be purchased.
3. Some organizations want to put their journals in the hands only of those individuals who will help out the company. They are reluctant to give them to libraries. It is sometimes all in knowing how to ask for them.
4. Few free journals get in the abstract and index services. Pierian Press is now producing an index to these.
   There is a very concise article about Free Magazines by Wall, C. Edward, "A New Look at Free Magazines." See the bibliography.[2] Also see "free materials" in the chapter on TOOLS.

## Philosophy of Gifts and Exchange Department

   Think carefully before accepting a gift that has strings attached and requests for appraisals. One should always keep in mind that material may be politely refused, or accepted with the understanding that it may be discarded, sold, or exchanged if not needed in the library. Collections that cannot be interwoven into the over-all library collection may cause problems.

1. They may need a special room, and special librarians to supervise them.
2. They may have to be set aside in special shelving areas, creating further places to search out books and information.

### Giving a Helping Hand

It has recently been suggested that libraries who are deacquisitioning, and perhaps discarding holdings, could send them to some of the centers, so that other libraries may take advantage of filling in broken sets. "In making these acquisition/deacquisition decisions, all libraries should keep in mind that exchange services can be used to reduce collections as well as to build them."[3]

## Routines

Following are some suggested letters that may be of help in a Gifts and Exchange Department.

**UNIVERSITY OF CALIFORNIA, RIVERSIDE**

BERKELEY · DAVIS · IRVINE · LOS ANGELES · RIVERSIDE · SAN DIEGO · SAN FRANCISCO          SANTA BARBARA · SANTA CRUZ

THE UNIVERSITY LIBRARY                                        P.O. BOX 5900, RIVERSIDE, CALIFORNIA 92507

Gentlemen,

The University of California, Riverside, Library is interested in receiving as a gift your publication.

Would it be possible for the Library to be placed on your mailing list. If there is a charge for this subscription, or if you would prefer an exchange, please notify us before sending issues and we will place an order through our regular procedures.

Thank you for your kind attention to this matter. Your reply will be very much appreciated.

Sincerely,

Serials Department
University Library
P.O. Box 5900
University of California
Riverside, California 92507

# UNIVERSITY OF CALIFORNIA, RIVERSIDE

BERKELEY · DAVIS · IRVINE · LOS ANGELES · RIVERSIDE · SAN DIEGO · SAN FRANCISCO  SANTA BARBARA · SANTA CRUZ

THE UNIVERSITY LIBRARY                                   P.O. BOX 5900, RIVERSIDE, CALIFORNIA 92507

Dear Sir:

The University of California, Library, Riverside gratefully acknowledges receipt of your publication_____

_____

_____

_____

Will the continuation of the above title be available to us as a gift? We would appreciate your informing us of its availability at the bottom of this letter.

Thank you for your kind attention to this matter.

Sincerely,

Serials Department
University Library
P.O. Box 5900
University of California
Riverside, California  92507

University of California Librar
Riverside, California

GIFT REPORT FORM

DONOR'S NAME_____     DATE_____

    ADDRESS_____

_____

    TELEPHONE_____LIBRARY CONTACT_____

Examination or pick-up arrangements:  (Address, Date, Time)_____


Received in Library (Date):_____

Brief description of Total Gift:  Indicate the nature of the material and the
number of items.  Note those which are rare or of an unusual nature.


Total estimated value:_____
      (use predetermined scale)

Remarks:


Plating instructions:_____

Gift acknowledge:
    printed form_____
    carbon attached_____
    dated_____

Report of Gift Acceptance, Form 1507:  sent  Yes_____     No_____     Dated:___

Inventory value reported to donor:           Yes_____     No_____

Donor card (date made and/or added to)_____


Special remarks:

The Gift and Exchange Department should keep its own records concerning the original transaction of a title, but when it has been established, it should be turned over to be included in the Serial Record, to be checked in just as any purchased material.

**Preliminary Sorting**

The material may be screened before searching. Some items may be automatically sorted out immediately and discarded, or sent to a needy area or library, or maybe used in any of the Special Agency programs.
1. Outdated almanacs and college catalogs probably will be discarded.
2. Non-current serials will be based on library needs.
3. Reference materials such as Who's Who might be utilized in other departments of the library or branches.

When a title is offered to the library as a gift or exchange item, the Gift & Exchange Department determines any library holdings, then using the same criteria as for a paid subscription, and with the aid of library staff and faculty members, determine the value and the cost of processing and maintaining a "free" title.

1. If not wanted, the Gift & Exchange Department informs the source that the title is not wanted.
   a. Occasionally it seems impossible to have the titles stopped. These are entered in the Serials Record with a note to "discard on receipt."
   b. If the title is questionable, or dependability of receipt uncertain, put a note in the Serials Record to "Send to the Vertical File" of the proper Division until the decision is further determined.
2. If the title is wanted, the Gift & Exchange Department sends a letter of interest to the agency offering the title, verifying the fact that the title is actually free.
   a. If true, the title is forwarded on to the Catalog Division.
   b. Records are set up in the Serials Record as for any purchased title.
3. If the title is offered on an exchange basis, Gift & Exchange Department sends a list of the library's available items for exchange.
   a. If the agency withdraws the offer as not acceptable, it is closed by both parties.
   b. Acceptable offers are set up in the usual manner.
4. If a title has been coming for a period of time and no longer

available by gift or exchange, new decisions must be made to determine whether or not to purchase.

5. "Zeros" or "Snags"

Titles which come into the Serials Department but cannot be located in the Serials Record may be considered as "O's." These may not be true "O's," but must be searched more carefully for the entry. True "O's" are those titles which come into the Serials Department as gifts or as an offer for exchange, and which are not in the Serials Record. They must be turned over to the Gift and Exchange Department for sorting, verifying, evaluating, writing about, and establishing like any other titles being worked on in the Gift and Exchange Department.

6. "Gap" Records

Know your lacks. Make notations on cards or lists of the most important lacks. These could even be incorporated in the Serials Department's Want List File. Be sure to flag them down with a proper symbol to segregate them from the lacks to be purchased. Computers could be used here by running off a list occasionally.

7. Claiming

Claiming of titles is a joint procedure between the Serials Department and Gift and Exchanges.

a. Those titles that miss a number only now and then may be incorporated into the usual claiming procedure of the Serials Department.

b. Those titles that have broken down completely should be turned back to the Gift and Exchange Department for further investigation and special letters.

## Disposal of Duplicates

Many librarians consider the time spent on the disposal of unwanted duplicates, a waste of time. They do take time and space, especially if they are to be utilized in any large projects, because they must be held long enough to accumulate to allow for making sizable lists. It also takes time to list the titles with the needed accuracy. As usual, the old adage holds true, anything worth doing is worth doing well!

VARIOUS APPROACHES

1. They may be held to fill in missing numbers for binding.
2. They may be used to circulate.
3. They may be offered to local institutions or other libraries.

4. They may be utilized in special exchange programs.
5. They may be sent to USBE.
6. If the law allows, they may be sold. Most public libraries must turn over such money to the state. Private libraries may derive benefits.

## Special Programs

While some money is involved in the various special programs, still they are usually anchored in the Gift and Exchange Department. They coincide with the usual exchange lists and may fit into the records kept for these other programs. Also they usually take a different kind of claiming than the current journals. The claiming often takes a special letter and also a careful checking of the whole program, if it looks like exchange has broken down.

The U. S. Government-sponsored programs have done much good, and have expanded the acquiring of difficult-to-locate material. If it could be certain that the government will continue to fund these programs, it would be possible to discontinue less adequate programs. But since the funds could be cut off, or substantially decreased at any time, this could throw a heavy burden on book funds of the various libraries involved if they had to continue the titles by purchase.

### USBE (Universal Serial & Book Exchange)

The USBE is a private, non-profit organization which was formed in 1949. It was a successor to the American Book Center for War Devastated Libraries. Later it became the United States Book Exchange, and now is called the Universal Serial & Book Exchange. The original plan was that each library agreed to exchange for equal value, certain types of their own duplicates with the USBE.

It is now a "clearinghouse of publications from all coutries and covers all subject fields."[4] It has 40 sponsoring library associations and more than 1600 member libraries all of which assist in formulating policies. The stock now includes about four million periodical issues of 35,000 titles from the earliest to current copies and 100,000 books and documents (out-of-print and in-print) in research fields.

Those libraries that are members send in their duplicates. They receive no money credit, but they may receive the publications they request. Any library may become a member for $25.00 plus handling and shipping charges as well as a fee for each item ordered. The fees vary according to what is ordered.

USBE is one of the best ways of filling in back sets and issues. It

314

may take longer to get the more scarce and expensive items, but even these do become available.

A brochure is available free by writing to:
USBE Universal Serials & Book Exchange, Inc.
3335 V Street, N.E.,
Washington, D.C. 20018, U.S.A.

## SALALM (Seminars on the Acquisition of Latin American Materials)

Librarians interested in acquiring Latin American materials have combined efforts and formed discussion groups. In the early 1930's committees were meeting with some results. The Council on Library Resources, the Inter-American Cultural Council, the Organization of American States of the Pan American Union have all initiated active programs of inter-American development.

In 1956 a meeting was held by librarians and others interested in acquiring Latin American materials. This turned into the organization called SALALM (Seminar on the Acquisition of Latin American Library Materials). It has met annually since then, and has become the best organized area group in the United States and has served as model for other such groups.

Its purpose is to study ways of selection, acquisition and processing of library materials from the Latin American nations and dependent territories of the Caribbean. It "has published annually its *Final Report and Working Papers* from the seminar, and has sponsored the publication of other material related to the problem of Latin American acquisitions. One of the subcommittees of SALALM is called the Library-Publisher-Bookdealer Relations Subcommittee. Not only are U. S. librarians members of SALALM, but the membership includes librarians from Latin America, Europe and Asia, and includes also Latin American book dealers and publishers."[5]

A very enlightening pamphlet is available on request to:
Ms. Lou Wetherbee
SALALM Secretariat
Benson Latin American Collection
The University of Texas at Austin
Austin, Texas 78712

## LASA (Latin American Studies Association)

This program represents a cross section of Latin American specialists in various areas. It met first in November 1968. It publishes the *Latin American Research Review*. (LARR)

## NSDP (National Serials Data Program)

(See p. 230-233).

## DEU (Duplicate Exchange Union)

DEU has been run for many years by the Serials Section of the American Library Association. Its object is to facilitate exchange of materials among smaller libraries that are participating in the program.

## NPC (National Periodicals Center)

In the early part of 1978 the Council on Library Resources started a study to see what plans could be implemented and what would be needed for location, personnel and finances to make the National Periodicals Center a reality. A 272-page document resulted, which is available on request from the Library of Congress Information Office, Washington D.C. 20540.

The Center's aims are so ambitious and comprehensive that it is still being viewed with skepticism by some librarians. It would eventually, have any part of any journal on all subjects except clinical medicine, available to any library, within a 24-hour period, with even copyright problems settled. It is envisioned that the USBE (see p. 313) would take an important part with its 40,000 titles now available.

With a program such as this one, along with the better coordination of the networks, where will the challenge come for that special breed of people called serials librarians? To keep up with the most current happenings, it would be well to check the current library literature as the months go by.

## Center for Research Libraries

The Center for Research Libraries is a library serving libraries, which allows faculty and graduate students access to vast collections of research materials. It is a collection of over three million volumes pertaining to research. There are 100 member libraries which may borrow and use the material on the same basis as their own.

It is a non-profit organization, founded in 1949 by a group of ten libraries, aided by grants from the Carnegie Corporation and the Rockefeller Foundation. It has become an international organization and includes material covering world-wide interests. The types of material include newspapers, periodicals, archives, government documents, political ephemera, dissertations, censuses, all of which are acquired by purchase, exchange, or gift. Not only current but older works are included. If material is not on hand, the organization will attempt to acquire needed items, if sufficient funds are available. Because some material will have to be acquired on microfilm, it may take several months of waiting. One must be a member.

There is a Handbook available which gives detailed description of subject matter, and lists the libraries which are members. This handbook may be gotten by writing to:
Center for Research Libraries
5721 Cottage Grove Ave.,
Chicago, Ill., 60637


## ERIC (Educational Resources Information Center)

ERIC was started in the 1960's as a group of clearinghouses to help unify the previously scattered research reports and articles published by the numerous professional education organizations throughout the country. It is a part of the National Institute of Education. ERIC's designers opted for a network of organizations rather than a single monolithic information center located in Washington. ERIC was conceived, therefore, as a network of 'clearinghouses' located across the country in 'host' organizations that were already naturally strong in the field of education in which they would operate."[6]

The various networks have responsibiilities of cataloging, indexing and abstracting the information, then after it is screened for quality and legibility it is sent to the computerized center of ERIC Processing and Reference Facility.

The costs must be paid by the person wanting the material and it comes in either microfiche or hard copy. Both non-copyrighted and copyrighted (when permission is granted) are available.

"ERIC, therefore, emerges as a network with four levels. The first or Governmental level is represented by NIC and Central ERIC (the funder, policy setter, and monitor). The second or non-profit level is made up of 16 Clearinghouses located at universities or professional societies. The third or commercial level consists of the centralized facilities for managing the data base, putting out published products, making microfiche and reproducing documents. Fourth and last are the users who receive the benefits of these activities."[7] For the central address see under Reprography in the chapter on TOOLS. Bibliographic information is kept up-to-date in the monthly abstracting journal, *Resources in Education.*

# UNITED NATIONS PUBLICATIONS

Every United Nations publication, except those listed below, may be ordered by a sales number. this number includes the year of publication, the subject — category in roman numerals, and the individual title number. Those not listed by a sales number are the official records, which are listed by a document symbol, and periodicals, which are listed by volume and issue number.

## Standing Order Service

The standing order service makes it possible, by ordering once, to receive all titles in any category one chooses, or even single recurrent titles, just as soon as they are off the press. Prices vary from edition to edition and year to year.

CATEGORIES OF STANDING ORDERS

There are five different categories of standing orders for United Nations publications.
1. Over-all standing order includes United Nations publications in all subject-categories including UNICEF publications, and the official records. Not included are the publications of the International Court of Justice, mimeographed documents and periodicals available on annual subscription. This overall standing order will cost something over $900.00. The cost, of course, will rise with each year.
2. Standing orders may be placed for one or more subject-categories These include: category I - General information; category II -Economics; category III - not listed; category IV - Social questions including UNICEF; category V - International law.
3. Title and series publications standing orders may also be purchased separately. In many instances these are irregular publications.
4. Mimeographed documents. These are essentially for official and internal use. Many appear later in official documents.
5. International Court of Justice is divided into five series, each of which is available separately.

Prices of these various categories vary so much and change with each year, that it would be well to write for the pamphlet — United Nations Publications standing order service; a guide for librarians and booksellers. Use it in conjunction with the United Nations reference catalogues of sales publications.

Orders may be placed with booksellers or direct with the United Nations:
United Nations Publications
United Nations
New York, N.Y. 10017

For customers located in Europe, Africa and the Middle East the address is:
United Nations Office at Geneva
Distribution and Sales Section
Palais des Nations, Geneva,
Switzerland

DEPOSITORIES

A library may become officially designated as a depository, and is entitled to receive all generally distributed documents published after joining. These documents are published in various languages and the library may choose the language wanted. These depositories are no longer free.

INTERGOVERNMENTAL AGENCIES

Publications of the Intergovernmental agencies are available through separate sales organizations. Addresses for these may be located by writing to the United Nations Service.

MICROFICHE

It is now possible to purchase much United Nations material on microfiche. A detailed list of available microfiche may be received on request.

REPRINTS

Reprints of selected United Nations publications are available from:
Kraus Reprint Corporation
Route 100, Milwood, N.Y. 10546

## NOTES

1. Andrew D. Osborn, Serial Publications; Their Place and Treatment in Libraries. 2d ed., rev. (Chicago: American Library Association, 1973). p. 313.
2. Edward C. Wall, "A new Look at Free Magazines," American Libraries, 8 (February 1977): 85-89.
3. Raymond L. Hough, "Use the Exchange Services," American Libraries, 8 (April 1977): 182.
4. Your Guide to USBE Services. (Washington: Universal Serials & Book, Exchange, 1977).
5. Lee Williams, Curator, Latin American Collections, Yale University Library. (Personal correspondence, Nov. 3, 1976).
6. Albert James Diaz, Microforms in Libraries; a Reader Weston, Connecticutt: Microform Review, c1975), p. 311.
7. Ibid. p. 312.

### Additional References

Library Materials Available for Research. Chicago: The Center for Research Libraries.

Louisiana State University Library. A Manual on Serials. 1976.

"National Periodical Center: Planning Study Set," Library Journal, 103 (January 15, 1978): 122.

SALALM: Facts about the Seminar on the Acquisition of Latin American Library Materials. Austin, Texas: Benson Latin American Collections, University of Texas, 1976/77.

"Special Report: the National Periodicals Center; a Castle in the Air Gets a Blueprint," American Libraries. 9 (October 1978): 511-

United Nations. Standing Order Service: a Guide for Librarians and Booksellers. New York: United Nations Publications, 1977.

# CHAPTER XIV
# REPROGRAPHY

With a book like Diaz, A. J., *Microforms in Libraries: a Reader,* already published on microforms it seems almost redundant to discuss this topic. The book is a compilation of articles on the history, acquisition, cataloging, organization, equipment, maintenance, sources, standards and specification as well as user reaction. However, a quick resume including some of the most recent trends may help to give an overall idea which will prepare one for a deeper study if the necessity arises.

What is reprography? The term is relatively new. It encompasses many types of processes such as photography, microphotography, and photocopying, as well as multilith, multigraph, mimeograph and various forms of offset duplication. In some instances it may include video and audio taping and other sound reproduction. To summarize, it is a twenty-five dollar word for the ten-cent one of "making copies."

Serial librarians must learn all there is to know about the various kinds of microforms, in order to make a more intelligent selection of the proper ones for the needs of the library. They should read everything they can find regarding durability, space and equipment needed for the different types.

## Evolution of Microfilm

This quick survey will show how microfilm evolved as one branch of photography and in itself developed into many forms. Many men in different countries experimented and advanced the various techniques of photography from the daguerreotype to the "dry plate" and its silver halide gelatin emulsion to the more recent, improved archival film.

Cameras were improved and aided the expanded possibilities of microforms as we know them today. The Leica of the 1920's was one of the first to be used extensively, but it did not lend itself to the higher production requirements of a large-scale copying program because of its limited film capacity (5 feet of film) and the necessity to advance the film manually. The Recordak camera was being developed about the same time as the Leica and from these beginnings came the modern rotary camera being widely used today. Now film strips may be made up to 1000 feet, although the usual length for libraries is 100 feet.

True, acquisition and serial librarians will have small need of worrying with the technicalities of producing film, but it behooves them to be aware of past pitfalls and tragedies that have resulted from film produced with certain chemicals. This is especially true if they are filling in or own long runs of early film. Let it be known that the past mistakes have resulted in strict standards being followed by all manufacturing companies today. Ordering microfilm at present has become a safer and simpler procedure, due to all the heated discussions and controversies in the not-too-distant past.

A short account of the problems of early film might be in order. The old nitrocellulose base film emitted hydrochloric acid fumes. If there was poor ventilation these fumes caused deterioration of everything around except itself — including the boxes in which it was stored, as well as the silver film stored near it; even the metal equipment was corroded. As late as the years 1966 through 1970 the deterioration was plaguing the industry.

A further hazard of the old film was that because its content was almost that of gun cotton it was explosively flammable and dangerous in manufacture, in use, and in storage. This nitrate film was an open invitation to trouble.

The latest and biggest disaster in which nitrate film was involved was the millions of dollars worth of rare and irreplaceable early films and prints which were destroyed by fire May 29, 1978. They were housed in several buildings on the George Eastman estate, the founder of Eastman Kodak Company.

Although Kalvar film is a polyester, there was a while before 1970 that it was causing trouble. The Microfilming Corporation of America (MCA) which was a wholly owned subsidiary of the New York Times, distributed copies of back issues of the Times to libraries on Type 16 Kalvar. Since 1970 MCA is gradually straightening out the problems of the old film with libraries.

It is worth noting here that Peter R. Scott of M.I.T. has defended the durability and accompanying problems of the Kalvar film. The whole matter of ideal storage conditions is questioned by him. He contends that ideal storage facilities do not exist in any library for any film, in fact, he says they may not exist anywhere. "No serious photographic scientist could maintain that silver film is archival under the conditions normally encountered in libraries. This is not to say that such films as Kalvar film as well as other vesicular film and Diazo film may not outlast the books which exist in libraries."[1]

## Permanency Depends on Many Factors

One main factor threading through every step, from processing to storage and reader usage is that of dust-free areas.

1. TYPE OF FILM USED

Film most commonly used now is called "safety film" and meets the requirements of ANSI PH1.25, 1965 or any latest revisions (see "Standards" section for explanation). It consists of a "clear, pliant base, coated with a photosensitive emulsion of silver halides." Other photosensitive emulsions commonly being used are "diazo and vesicular materials produced by such manufacturing companies as Kalvar and Xidex. These films are developed by light, heat, or chemicals, depending on the type."[2]

2. PROCESSING

Processing is one of the most important factors to insure permanency. The base is coated with a light-sensitive emulsion which contains the silver salts.

a. Fixing bath.

The developed film is then put into the fixing bath, or hypo, which is largely sodium thiosulfate which extracts the undissolved silver. Thorough washing with water is then needed. Careless washing will leave residues that cause the film to deteriorate.

b. Drying.

Drying is the next step. It must be uniform. If overdried it will result in making the film brittle, and creating static electricity, which in turn picks up dust. It must be made dry enough to discourage fungi.

3. ENVIRONMENT OF THE STORAGE AREA

The level of humidity and temperature must be carefully monitored. Ideal humidity must be kept at a level (35% is a fair level) that will not encourage growth of fungi or molds and microscopic blemishes. Temperature should not go above 80° in storage areas or in the reading rooms. Taken into account in the reading rooms must be the number of people, the lights and the machines, all of which may very well raise the level. The high temperatures will buckle the film at the edges, which makes it difficult to run the film through the machines.

Much depends on the length of time the film is exposed to unfavorable situations. If corrected soon enough the film will be able to withstand the situation. Other hazards are fire and water. It goes without saying that the area should be fireproof. Steel cabinets also will protect the film. If the film is accidently subjected to great amounts of water, it must be rewashed immediately, otherwise it soon sticks together. Contact a microfilming company, such as University Microfilms or Bell and Howell for proper and safe procedures before attempting to move wet film!

4. THE AMOUNT OF USE AND QUALITY OF THE MACHINES

The fourth factor for permanency is the amount of use and the quality of the machines. "Scratches, abrasions, dust, and dirt impair the life of microforms, as well as reading equipment, their presence should be detected and ameliorative measures taken."[3] The glass flats of microfilm readers should open during film transport to keep most heavy scratching from taking place. All glass flats on all microform machines should be cleaned daily using lint free cloths.

## Standards

Since 1971 a special task force of the American National Standards Institute has been studying specifications regarding microfilm and has still not found all the answers. Through the years it has been found that the amount of use and proper storage facilities as well as the more technical factors of bases and emulsions used in producing the films are prime factors in determining the length of preservation. The task force group has agreed upon three film classifications:
1. Medium term film — will have a useful life of 10 years.
2. Long term film — will have a useful life of 100 years.
3. Archival film — will be as permanent as anything that can be made.

STANDARDS SOURCES

1. ANSI PH5 Series (American National Standards Institute). All other sources are based on ANSI PH5.
2. Library of Congress procedures.
3. National Micrographics Association.

ANSI (American National Standards Institute) is a non-government, volunteer institute. Users and manufacturers have joined together to set up a guide for standards for many products besides microfilm. Neither the government nor manufacturers can be compelled to follow them. They are revised periodically and it is advisable to check the latest revisions. These standards are divided into many subject categories, which are listed in the institute's annual catalog. This is free upon request from their headquarters.

The standards for photographic reproduction of documents are the PH 5 series. The standards are inexpensive. The other standards to use are:
1. PH 4.100 and higher numbers. They refer to photographic grades of chemicals.
2. PH 4.1 through PH 4.34 refer to photographic processes.
3. PH 1 refers to photographic materials.

The standards for film must cover the characteristics for archival records, which is silver gelatin type on cellulose ester base. There is a small, solid triangle imprinted at regular intervals along the edge of both positive and negative film, so that the user may readily assure himself that he is using the best certified film. Two triangles identify the positive film. This does not absolutely guarantee archival qualities, but it is as near as one can come.

IN SUMMARY

"The permanence of photographic records depends on the chemical stability of the film, how the film is processed, and the conditions under which the processed film records are stored. The stability of the film layers is determined in manufacture and processing, while storage is controlled by the user."[4]

The variables are legion. The chemicals vary, the strength of solutions, constancy of replacement of solutions at the proper time, sufficiency of washing to remove processing chemicals, the temperature of processing solutions, and development time. The film processes are as variable as the developing. For a good explanation of standards, Allen B. Veaner's article is most enlightening, also see Diaz (both references in the Bibliography).

**Formats**

Not only have techniques and cameras gone through many changes, but the various formats of microforms have expanded to great dimensions and each should be chosen with regard to the needs of the library, and of course the availability of titles offered. More and more titles both current and back files, are being offered simultaneously on various formats by reputable publishers.

## MICROFILM

Microfilm is photographic film, usually in black and white, which has a much-reduced image on it. When done for personal use it is of an esthetic nature, and when professionally produced for libraries the subject matter is of a scholarly or technical nature.

The various sizes of silver film strips are cut from the originally manufactured wide webs. The most common small strips measure 8mm (5/16 inch), 16mm (5/8 inch), and 35mm (1-3/8 inches). The 35mm is the commonest. This was set as the standard by Thomas A. Edison.

## MICROFICHES

Microfiches are sheets or cards 3" x 5" or 4" x 6" in size, usually with an arrangement in 7 rows and 14 columns which results in 98 pages to each fiche, depending, of course, on the size of the material to be filmed, and the reduction used. However, other arrangements and sizes may be found. They may be inserted film or strips of film.

A comparison of roll film and fiches.

1. They both save space over the hard copy, but fiches take even less than roll film.
2. They are both more durable than hard copy, but roll film is more durable than fiches, because the latter are susceptable to abrasions if not handled with extreme care. They must be picked up only at the very edges.
3. Many more titles are becoming available on both but the whole current year of a journal must be completed before getting on roll film, while a single issue may be reproduced on fiche.
4. Back files of a journal may include several years on one roll of film, making its use less available to many patrons needing it at one time, while fiches will serve more people.
5. Individual fiche may get lost between pages of hard copy, while rolls of film could not get lost in the same manner.
6. Fiches are easier to install in the reader, but once a roll of film is installed much more material is available, and successive pages may be easily brought into view.
7. Fiches may be re-arranged to fit a particular subject, while roll film

is more suited for material to be retained in sequence such as long runs of back files of journals. Fiche is more easily replaced.

## MICROPRINT

Microprint is put out by the Readex Microprint Corporation. According to their brochure they have made great efforts to search the country and libraries to make their editions as complete as possible.

The cards are 6" x 9", and each card contains 100 pages reduced 12 to 18 diameters. For newspapers there are less than 100 pages. They are contained in boxes 6½" x 10" and no special cabinets are needed for storage. They may be stored in the same environmental conditions as conventionally printed books. Special attention has been considered for the archival requirements.

For many years the criticism of microprint was that enlarged copy was unobtainable, but that has now been rectified.

## MICRO-OPAQUES

Micro-opaques include both microcards and microprint. "When a negative is printed to photographic paper rather than to film, the paper is called micro-opaque."[5] Because the enlarged images are formed by reflected instead of transmitted light, they require special viewers.

## CASSETTES AND CARTRIDGES

Cassettes with 16mm film are becoming increasingly popular, especially for scientific and technical journals. The cartridge gives a degree of protection to the film and is easy to place into the reader. "Roll film in cartridges manufactured by different producers may not fit the machines of competitors. Cartridges leave one end of the roll free, while cassettes contain the complete roll with supply and takeup capabilities in the same unit."[6] The 16mm size of film was in disfavor with librarians until recently when cassettes or cartridges have become available. Their advantages are that they protect and reduce the amount of rewind of the film. The disadvantage is that they will not fit in all machines.

## COLOR MICROFILM

Color microfilm is somewhat more expensive than black and white and therefore the pictorial matter must be important enough for its use. The print may not be legible and must get close inspection upon receipt. Also, at best, the colors in photographic images are only representations of the colors photographed. The hues of dyes used are very susceptible to sunlight, and the film should be stored from light as much as possible. The color fades rather rapidly under use. It should be noted that one may also get color in microfiche.

### Aperture Cards, Film Chips And Film Strips

The above listed formats are the least used in libraries. The film is cut apart into separate pieces and inserted into aperture cards, or transparent jackets.

## Equipment
### Selection

Equipment is more and more being oriented to library use. There are dozens of different makes and models available. Some will now accept either 16mm or 35mm film and some will accept standard size fiches but usually a special attachment will be needed for the different formats. Some allow for different reductions.

Keep in Mind the Following Points:

1. The quality of readers. Consider the life-span and keep in mind obsolescence for both parts and the need for changing machines.
2. Choose equipment that is not too complicated. Threading devices should be simple enough for all sorts of users.
3. Durability should be considered — the fewer the motordriven parts, the fewer places there are to break down.
4. Horizontal screens for roll film are more conducive to long periods of reading and note-taking.
5. Curved screens are good for people with glasses (especially bifocals) who may get seasick feelings with regular screens.
6. The types of microforms needing different types of readers. Microfiches usually need special readers, but they are less expensive than the ones for roll film. Filmed newspapers must have a machine that is able to rotate.
7. Quantity of readers needed. The more film and users the more readers, of course, will be needed.
8. Tables for equipment should be considered. U-shaped tables will provide space for both right- and left-handed users. Allow space for typewriters, books and other items.
9. Good lighting should be considered.
10. Consider portable machines that may be checked out or moved about.

11. Reader-printers will be needed by every library with readers. Reader-printers will allow for images to be shown on a screen and will also allow prints to be made from them. "They are made by several manufacturers to accept various formats and to print out on different kinds of photographic stock."[7] The price for these will vary depending on whether they accommodate film or fiche, the various reduction rates, and whether they use wet or dry printing processes.

## Maintenance of Equipment
TYPES OF MAINTENANCE NEEDED

1. Machines should be checked daily for:
    a. Light bulbs. They frequently need changing. Some last only a few hours, others last up to 500 hours. They should be the correct wattage, and they cost from $1.50 to $5.00 or more.
    b. Daily cleaning of all glass and metal parts touching the film. Camel-hair brushes, kept free of oil may be used. There are new film-cleaning devices now available.
2. Other repairs may be needed, either minor or major, depending on the quality of the equipment, quantity of readers and amount of use. All these may make costs for labor a variable item.

## Personnel

The daily maintenance should be kept up by personnel which need not necessarily be professional, but should be trained in the proper techniques, and staff should be available to help with problems at all hours that the equipment is available to users, so that preventive maintenance may be on hand at all times.

USER AWARENESS AND ACCEPTANCE

This leads us to the need of training, not only library personnel, but the patrons as well. They must be made aware of the various types of material available, and the proper handling of the machines. When library tours are held for either students, faculty or off-campus patrons, demonstrations should include the use of the readers and indoctrination of the particular advantages of such a library.

## Ordering of Microfilm

Ordering of microforms is much the same as for books, and the film must be spot-checked when received, for defects and proper titles and volumes. Cumulated indexes and special items such as supplements must be noted for catalogers and patrons.

PUBLISHERS VARY IN THEIR ORDERING PROCEDURES:

1. Some offer discounts for dual subscriptions.
2. Some allow discounts upon return of the hard copy.
3. Some charge the same for each.
4. Some charge more for the microform edition.

## Statistical Count

The statistical count of microforms, which at first appears to be a confusing problem, may be simplified by a separate count of both volumes and the number of reels or fiches. Of course, completed or partial volumes must be considered, as also several volumes to a reel or box. The Central State University at Edmond, Oklahoma, in their pamphlet, *Where Microfilm is a Working Reality*, has a page on "counting materials for statistical reporting" which gives a good summary of all aspects.

## Advantages of Reprography

According to Osborn, an original book is usually preferable to microfilm. However, there are those current librarians who are taking an entirely different point of view with regard to books versus microforms and would change library materials into almost complete microform collections, well nigh eliminating books (for further discussion see pp. 333-336).

This brings up an interesting comparison. There are still those people who prefer the physical book to all the microforms in the world. Their arguments are that they cannot face the continual glare of light for long periods of research, and less research by these people may result. Another argument is that no matter how carefully the machines are checked daily, some will go in and out of focus while the film is being turned, and some very few people will become seasick. Those people who are sold completely on microforms and electronics insist the patron can be educated to their use. If microforms are to be the only source for the future of information, let us hope the die-hards who prefer books will vanish along with books.

It is up to the librarian to balance between the two, using judicious judgment on the advantages and disadvantages. The library is a service institution and it exists only to facilitate the needs of its readers.

Some of the following advantages and disadvantages pertain to libraries that are producing film for various readers, as well as those who are just servicing it.

## Advantages

1. The saving of space is one reason for film.
2. One is able to obtain material not otherwise available, such as rare books and very expensive material unobtainable in the original.
3. It replaces material that is deteriorating.
4. It may be used instead of binding journals in some cases. The originals may be kept three or four years and discarded (see the discussion on this type of library pp. 334-336).
5. Bulky material such as newspapers, and massive scientific and technical reports are more easily reduced to better storage space. Also newspapers are printed on inferior paper and will not last long in the original.
6. For interlibrary loan microfilm is more easily sent through the mail, and eliminates travel and expense for the reader, as well as wear on the original.
7. Microfilm usually saves money on long runs of back files, and is sometimes easier to acquire.
8. It allows easier access to volumes when the bound volumes may be in remote storage.
9. When a library wants to keep certain information always on file for all patrons, one format, either the hard copy or microform may be loaned, while keeping the other on hand.
10. It is possible, now, to purchase some periodicals simultaneously in paper and microfiche editions. In many cases the microfiche copy arrives before the paper edition. Also, many times the microfiche subscription price is much less than the paper subscription.

## Disadvantages of Reprography

1. Correct temperature and humidity is needed at all times for preservation. (This should be considered for all types of material.)
2. Must be dust free in all processes and storage and reader environment.
3. There are many formats requiring various reading machines. This is not as much of a problem as formerly, because most film and fiche readers have multiple lens systems which will take not only the regularly filmed material but exceptions as well.
4. The material to be photographed comes in so many sizes.

5. In the process of filming, the original is apt to suffer, especially in the cases of fragile, rare, or tightly bound books.
6. The film must be spot checked for perfect copy and completeness. (This is less frequent now than in the past and, besides, all orders, be they paper or film, should take the same careful scrutiny when first received, as already mentioned.)
7. Catalogers need easy access to readers.
8. It is difficult to put ownership on the film.
9. It is difficult to determine the statistical count. This may be simplified (see p. 330).
10. It requires special reading machines. (This is becoming less and less a problem, except for micro-opaques.)
11. It is limited to space where reading machines are available. (Although more and more portable machines are becoming available. See pp. 335-6 for a different arrangement.)
12. Extra library personnel may be needed to monitor the machines depending on arrangement of the library.
13. The machines are subject to hard usage and regular preventive maintenance is required.
14. Patrons need special instruction on how to use and protect both the film and the machines. Signs will help.
15. Library security systems now in use have no provisions to include microforms as they do for books.
16. Maps and plans are distorted. Microforms should not be used for calibrations.
17. Cannot reproduce color microfilm and fiche in hardcopy yet.

## Costs

There are so many variables to consider, that it is difficult to arrive at an over-all conclusion of costs. However, a set of cost factors that are similar in all libraries may fit into a general pattern.
1. The need to purchase both hard copy and microforms must be considered (see p. 336). They do increase the total acquisition cost, but may reduce binding costs.
2. Replacement of microforms may be less than hard copy.
3. Subscription costs may vary from publisher to publisher, depending on the medium selected. Microfiche is less expensive than roll film.
4. All costs will depend on the amount of usage and the number of microreaders needed.
5. Type of microreaders vary. They may vary from $150.00 for a manually operated fiche reader to $3000.00 for a fully automated microfilm reader. Also the number of portable circulating and per-

sonal fiche readers that are available may make a difference.
6. Maintenance costs depend on the quality and quantity of micro-readers, and the amount of use to which they are put. Are the repairs minor or major? This will affect the labor costs.

For comments on expanding the sources of the budget, one revolutionary approach is suggested on p. 336.

### Past, Present and Future of Reprography

In the past as well as in the present, microform projects have been developed, only as someone had the vision to visualize the needs and the possibilities of meeting these needs. Let us hope that in the future more vision will create "more coordination of effort both by the various filming companies as well as scholars and librarians. Bibliographical control is needed, to know what has already been done. A national program is needed."[8]

There are small items of comparison to be made with the past and the present. In the past, it was necessary to be careful to use copying machines that give a permanent image when missing pages were being copied to complete a book for binding. It might be well to be on the alert, even today. The test for this is to make certain the print does not smudge. Most recent processes are electrostatic and do not have the smudging problem. Also in the past, there was the problem that photographs did not copy well, but came out as ghostly images. This is becoming less and less a problem. Until recently one could not get colored reproductions, so that art magazines had to be always purchased in the original. This technique must be considered with great care for library use.

## Two Philosophies Regarding The Use Of Microfilm

There are two philosophies or systems that libraries may follow in deciding on the use of microfilm. Both are equally good and it all depends on what is needed in the individual library.

### 1. The Conventional System

The first, and most conventional is usually taken by the libraries who have already spent thousands upon thousands of dollars filling in back files with original copies of journals. Microforms will undoubtedly take a lesser precedence than the book collection and the film will be housed in the more conventional manner in special fireproof cabinets and rooms that are dust-free, with proper humidity and temperature.

The large library may even have a microfilm department that reproduces master film of local newspapers, archives, and must meet the demand for long articles for research projects. Such a department is in the library of Louisiana State University. This type of library must still be aware of archival film, and attempt to utilize it in the strictest sense of the word.

## 2. Microform Libraries

The second system of microforms for libraries is one in which microforms take the place almost entirely of printed material. This system is slanted toward libraries that find themselves experiencing rapid growth with incomplete, limited collections, storage space, and budgets. It is a philosophy entirely foreign to the early established and conventional libraries. Perhaps it envisions all libraries of the future?

Special libraries are also good candidates for the microform libraries. They are often hampered for space, and demands for multiple copies of articles, and specialized uses of materials are usually considerable. Stephen Torok has taken a "wide-angle view" of the future of microforms. He says, "Without a question, the microform is one of the most important inventions to serve the requirements of almost unlimited access to every piece of information at a reasonable price and rapid retrieval."[9] He envisions uses in:

a. Color graphics
b. Unconventional library materials
c. Micropublishing of federal depository items
d. Nonprint materials
e. Producing catalogs
f. Holography — which is material wholly written by the person in whose name it appears. "Its potential is fantastic."

There are two factors that may hasten such libraries. One is the dilemma that has befallen paper in the last hundred or more years. Before 1850 paper was made from linen rags and coated with gelatin. It was very durable and was thought that it would last almost forever, given the proper environment. After that date the industry turned to wood pulp and coated it with alum-rosin compounds which was cheaper to produce. However, it gives off sulphuric acid which eats the paper. Also inks used in offset printing are less permanent than the inks used 150 years ago. Large libraries with many volumes are finding shelf after shelf of nothing but dust between the covers of books published in the more recent years. Poor environment, dust, cockroaches, silverfish, heat, humidity and mold have all taken their toll on these books. Much is being done to try to preserve them, but at present the methods being used are still too expensive and unproven to cover all current books.

The other factor which may hasten building up such libraries is the fact that more and more titles, both current and back files are being offered in microforms. Libraries are automatically purchasing the microform editions wherever available.

Advocates of microform libraries say they are not using microforms to replace worn out original volumes but are purchasing microforms in place of paper volumes. Envisioning libraries of the future one may even go so far as to say that the computer version of information will probably supplement or replace even microforms, although computer technology must make more advances, and become more nationally unified and even more economical than it is at present.

Some of the libraries that are using mass microform collections as working libraries are; Central State University Library at Edmond, Oklahoma, University of Wisconsin, Princeton University, the National Archives in Washington, and the University of Southern California. All have excellent microform facilities.

The first premise of this type of library is that knowledge is the same, regardless of the format in which it appears, be it paper, film, fiche or whatever media. All should then be integrated into one alphabetical sequence, on open shelves for constant use by all patrons. Nonarchival films with a reasonable working life will then be acceptable and the collection will be housed under normal library storage conditions. It should be kept in mind that both hard copy and microforms would benefit by optimum storage conditions.

Another premise is that by shelving all formats together, the patrons would learn to accept whatever type of format, just so the knowledge is available. The intimidation of having to enter a new environment for film would then be diminished.

Now that all formats are to be shelved together, different types of shelving are needed. These may be found in many of the library supply companies, and are designed in such a way that the film shelves will intermingle and interface with the regular metal shelves. They include a vertical insert four inches from the front, so that the boxes of film are aligned at the front to remain even with the hard copy shelving. It must be noted that microfiches should still be filed and serviced in closed stacks because they need special supervision due to the fact that they are so easily shuffled and misfiled. (Highsmith is now selling boxes for microfiche which allows the fiche to be interfiled with books on the shelves.)

Reshelving the boxes of microfilm is made easy by drawing a triangle across the whole shelf of film, which keeps the boxes in proper order by aligning them with the pencilled line. This makes film easier than hard copy to keep in order.

Funding for a library of this sort also takes a different aspect. Current paper issues are needed only for a certain length of time so why keep them when they are to be replaced with microforms? Sometime, some may be returned, and some may be sold. Because binding serials has now been eliminated, these funds may also be added to the serial budget, as well as the funds for replacements and back files or hard copy. Federal funds may be available, but be wary of depending on federal funds for continuing serials (see p. 99).

## Equipment

Reader equipment must also be included in over-all costs, and with an entire library made up essentially of microforms, many more readers will be needed. Maintenance of these readers will cost somewhat more. Replacement of equipment must also be considered.

## Environment

For this discussion see p. 323-324. Suffice it to say here, that all the factors needed to preserve an archival collection is of less importance to a mass microfilm library which is used merely as a working collection.

## Summary of Such a Library

1. Provides an economical method of completing and expanding a small periodical collection.
2. Research material in microforms are readily available.
3. With proper orientation, patron acceptance of microform use is quite possible.
4. One alphabetical arrangement of all library materials in whatever format, encourages expanded use of the library.
5. Makes information easy to locate.
6. Less personnel is needed because professional staff, already servicing reference material, is on hand to oversee all formats.
7. Non-professional staff may be used for the daily maintenance, provided proper training is given.

## DEFINITIONS

If very accurate, definitive definitions are needed, it is recommended that one check Spencer's book, *The Focal Dictionary of Photographic Technologies*. It is technical but concise and understandable (see the Bibliography).

ACETATE FILM is a film base that is a cellulose acetate and derivatives.

ARCHIVAL FILM should be on a polyester base with a silver halide emulsion.

BASE OR SUPPORT is a film composed of a thin plastic layer coated with a light-sensitive emulsion.

COPYFLO is a trade name of Xerox Corporation for Xerographic printers and materials. It is limited to reproduction from microfilm.

DTR (Diffusion Transfer Reversal). Substances added to the silver halide solvents allow a more rapid transfer to the receiving sheet. It is inexpensive, and is letter size. The negative image may be transferred to many weights and colors of paper.

DIAZO FILM has a dye emulsion (light sensitive diazonium compound).

ELECTROFAX processes single sheets and not books. "Electrofax process differs from Xerography in that a coated, rather than a plain paper is used. In Xerography, the photo-conductive element is a selenium plate or drum. The image is formed on the selenium coating and then transferred from it to the receiving sheet. In Electrofax, the photo conductive element is a coating of zinc oxide on the receiving sheet itself. Despite the fact that a coated paper is used the materials costs are still quite low, being in the neighborhood of $3\frac{1}{2}$ cents for letter size sheets."[10]

ELECTROSTATIC COPYING PROCESSES is one of the great departures from conventional silver halide photocopying which has had far-reaching significance. These machines utilize either plain or zinc-oxide coated papers. The plain paper process utilizes photoconductive substance capable of holding a static charge. On the second process the zinc-oxide is on the paper.

EMULSION is composed of silver halide crystals suspended in the gelatin mixture. This will not become visible until processed through a developer and fixer.

ENLARGEMENT PRINTS are paper prints made from microfilm. See

HIGH-SPEED STABILIZATION PROCESS below for a description of quick processing.

HARD COPY is an enlarged copy usually made on paper, as well as the original volume.

HIGH-SPEED STABILIZATION PROCESS is a recent process and becoming more and more popular. "In this process ordinary photographic materials are used but the processing of the exposed materials is radically different. In conventional processing, photocopies after development of the latent image, must be rinsed, fixed, washed, and dried before they can be used. The fixation step involves the actual removal of unwanted silver halides which would affect the stability of the image. In the stabilization process, the developed image is simply passed through a stabilizing solution and then through a set of rollers which squeezes out most of the moisture, yeilding copies which are as near to being dry as DTR copies. The function of the stabilizing bath is to convert the unexposed and underdeveloped silver halides remaining in the paper into substances which are relatively inert to the subsequent action of light, heat, or atmospheric gases."[11] Stabilized prints are not permanent or archival.

HYPO is a sodium thiosulfate solution used to dissolve the unexposed silver salts.

KALVAR PROCESS. A thermoplastic resin is used in place of gelatin, and heat softens the dry film to produce the image.

MICROFICHE (see p. 326).

MICROFILM (see p. 326).

MICROFORM relates to any form of microimages, either on film or on paper.

MICRO-OPAQUES (see p. 327).

MICROPRINT (see p. 327).

NITRATE FILM is a photographic film of cellulose nitrate which, because of its flammability has been discontinued.

PHOTOMICROGRAPHY is a photo, usually made through a microscope of any small image, and is a magnified image.

POLYESTER FILM has a polyester base known as Estar, has dimensional stability and is very strong and tough.

THERMOFAX is a process which uses heat rather than light to form the image.

1. This limits copying capabilities on the process.
2. Only printed texts or written manuscripts in ink which are capable of absorbing and dissipating heat will record.
3. Dye-based inks, which include most colored inks, and ball point pens do not record.
4. Fine details are lost.

THIOSULFATE is the chemical in the "fixing bath" or hypo. It is largely sodium thiosulfate and is used to "fix" the image. It dissolves the unexposed silver halide.

VERIFAX PROCESS is widely used.
1. A negative is first exposed and then "activated" in a solution.
2. Unlike DTR, the positive copies are made by physical transference of the negative image to a receiving sheet of plain paper instead of by chemical means of a gelatin coated stock.

Advantages
1. Many copies may be made from a single negative.
2. Costs of successive copies are very low.
3. It is possible to transfer the negative image to other kinds of positive stock.

VESICULAR FILM is a fairly recent film. It is a light sensitive diazo compound in a gelatin coating and when immersed in water allows the gelatin to soften and unexposed diazo compound to wash out leaving the image. If a thermostatic resin is used in place of gelatin the dry film is softened by heat.

XEROX is used in most libraries. The Xerox 914 machine is an optical copier and is most successful for books, which are placed face down and a print comes out in 35 seconds. It is a trade name for the xerographic process developed by the Xerox Corporation, and should not be used indiscriminately for any photocopy. It is an electrostatic process.

Advantages
1. Completely dry
2. Very fast
3. Inexpensive

## NOTES

1. Peter R. Scott, "Microproduction Laboratory M.I.T. Kalvar Defended." *Microfilm Review*. (October 1976): 256-257.
2. E. Stevens Rice, *Fiche and Reel*. 3rd. ed. rev. (Ann Arbor: University Microfilms International, 1977), pp. 1-2. This pamphlet gives a good explanation that a layman can understand of the various formats and processes of microforms.
3. Albert James Diaz, ed. *Microforms in Libraries/a Reader*. (Weston, Connecticutt: Microform Review, Inc., 1975) p. 140.
   There is no index in this book but it is well captioned. It covers almost everything a librarian should know about Microforms and it has copious bibliographies throughout the book.
4. Ibid., p. 234.
5. Rice, op. cit., p. 7.
6. Ibid., p. 13.
7. Ibid., p. 7.
8. Diaz, op. cit., p. 292.
9. Stephen Toruk, "Microforms at SLA/Pittsburgh." *Microform Review*, 2 (October 1973): 252-254.
10. Lowell H. Hattery and George P. Bush, eds. *Reprography and Coypright Law*. Washington: American Institute of Biological Sciences, c1964, p. 43.
11. Ibid., p. 44.

### Additional References

Adelstein, Dr. P. Z. "A Process Report: ANSI Activities on Stability of Processed Diazo and Vesicular Films." *The Journal of Micrographics*, 9 (January 1976): 99-101.

Central State University Library. *Whose Micro-Film is a Working Reality*. Edmond, Oklahoma: n.d.

Curtis, Ron. "The Central State University Story: The Microform Decision." *Microform Review*, 3 (January 1974): 23-24.

Gregory, Roma S. "Acquisitions in Microfilm." *Library Trends*, 18 (January 1970): 373-384.

LaHood, Charles G. Jr. and Robert C. Sullivan. "Reprographic Services in Libraries.' *(L.T.P. Publications* No. 19). Chicago: American Library Association, 1975: p. 74.

Reed, Jutta R. "Cost Comparison of Periodicals in Hard Copy and on Microform." *Microform Reveiw*, 5 (July 1976): 185-192.

Stephens, G. W. W. *Microphotography — Photography and Photofacrication at Extreme Resolution*. New York: John Wiley, 1968.

Stevens, Rolland E. "The Microform Revolution;" *Library Trends*, 19 (January 1971): 380.

Veaner, Allen B. "Microproduction and Micropublication Technical Standards: What They Mean To You, The User." *Microform Review*, 3 (April 1974): 80-4.

Verry, H. R. *Document copying and Reproduction Processes*. Fountain Press. 1958.

Webb, J. "Las Vegas, Microforms Were Hot at A.L.A." *Microform Review*, 2 (October 1973): 249-259.

## Books on Reprography that May Be of Use to Librarians

Diaz, Albert James. op. cit.

Gaddy, Dale, *A Microform Handbook*. Silver Spring, Maryland: National Microfilm Assoc., 1974.

Harrison, Helen P., *Film Library Techniques; Principles of Administration*. New York: Hastings House, 1973.

Hattery, Lowell H. ed., *Reprography and Copyright Law*. Lowell H. Hattery and George P. Bush eds., Washington: American Institute of Biological Sciences, 1964.

Spencer, D. A., *The Focal Dictionary of Photographic Technologies*. New York: Focal Press. 1973.

# CHAPTER XV
# COPYRIGHT LAW

In the early days of the copyright law no one could have possibly foreseen how far photocopying would go. By 1935, with all the new techniques being developed, photocopying was being used so much that new decisions and definitions had to be made. At that time the Joint Committee on Materials for Research and the Board of Directors of the National Association of Book Publishers formulated a "fair practice code" called "The Gentlemen's Agreement."

## The Gentlemen's Agreement of 1935

A library, archives office, museum, or similar institution owning books or periodical volumes in which copyright still subsists may make and deliver a single photographic reproduction or a part thereof to a scholar representing in writing that he desires such reproduction in lieu of loan of such publication or in place of manual transcription and solely for the purpose of research; provided:

1. That the person receiving it is given due notice in writing that he is not exempt from liability to the copyright proprietor for any infringement under the copyright law.
2. That such reproduction is made and furnished without profit to itself by the institution making it.

It allows one to quote from an author's writings, within limits, and to utilize his ideas, giving him due credit. But at that time it was still not realized to what extent photocopying was really going to go. Whole sections of books and articles were copied for each student in a class, or each worker in a laboratory, or each doctor in a hospital. This came about as new equipment and techniques were developed, making duplicating material more easily and inexpensively available. Authors became apprehensive about royalties. Publishers feared that fewer subscriptions would result. True, the number of subscriptions is balanced against profits, after the publishing and printing costs are subtracted. It was feared that photocopies and interlibrary loans would play havoc, and publishers intimated that libraries should pay more for their subscriptions, and pass the extra cost on to the users. This was received with less than enthusiasm by both librarians and the library patrons.

A wave of dissension was added to by the law suit of Williams & Wilkins against the government in 1968 for copyright infringements. The first decision was in favor of Williams & Wilkins but it was appealed by the government and Williams & Wilkins lost.

In 1976 Congress passed the first revision of the U.S. copyright law since it was originated. The original revision which was passed through congress was discussed and a compromised version culminated. It is still not satisfying authors, publishers, teachers and librarians. Some items are too general, some too specific. It is very complex, as are all laws, and there is a "Carefully calculated ambiguity of the law."[1] The guidelines at present are not meant to be definitive. Much evaluation and reevaluation will be needed.

It became affective January 1, 1978. The Copyright Office will go through a five year period of study and the results will be reported to Congress. CONTU (National Commission on Technological Uses of Copyright Works) was a temporary commission set up by Congress to tackle some of the issues Congress ducked in the new law. CONTU no longer exists. So much is being written and so many opinions are being expressed, so much is beginning to jell, so many new committees are forming, that it would be well to consult the current library literature for the latest happenings. It seems much can become out-dated before it can be published.

The parts of the first revision of the new law pertaining to scholars, teachers and librarians are well outlined in *The Chronicle of Higher Education*, Oct. 11, 1976.[2]

A teacher may not:
"Make multiple copies of a work for classroom use if it has already been copied for another class in the same institution; make multiple copies of a short poem, article, story, or essay from the same author more than once in a class term, or make multiple copies from the same collective work or periodical issue more than three times a term; make multiple copies of works more than nine times in the same class term; make a copy of works more than nine times in the same class term; make a copy of works to take the place of an anthology; make a copy of 'consumable' materials, such as workbooks."

A teacher may:

"Make a single copy, for use in scholarly research, or in teaching, or in preparation for teaching a class, of the following: A chapter from a book; An article from a periodical or newspaper; A short story, short essay, or short poem, whether or not from a collected work; A chart, graph, diagram, drawing, cartoon, or picture from a book, periodical, or newspaper."

"Make multiple copies for classroom use only, and not to exceed one per student in a class, of the following: A complete poem, if it is less than 250 words and printed on not more than two pages; An excerpt from a longer poem, if it is less than 250 words; A complete article, story, or essay, if it is less than 2,500 words; An excerpt from a prose work, if it is less than 1,000 words or 10 per cent of the work, whichever is less; One chart, graph, diagram, drawing, cartoon, or picture per book or periodical."

Teachers will be most interested in Section 107 which defines the educational guidelines for them and gives statutory recognition to the "Fair Use doctrine" for the first time.

A library may:

"For interlibrary-loan purposes: Make up to six copies a year of a periodical published within the last five years . . . (or) of small excerpts from longer works; Make copies of unpublished works for purposes of preservation and security; Make copies of published works for purposes of replacement of damaged copies; Make copies of out-of-print works that cannot be obtained at a fair price."

Librarians are the ones who have the most questions and fears, and rightly so, because they will have the closest contact with all interested parties, and feel they may be most liable to violations.

Section 108 "defines the conditions and limitations under which libraries may make copies for their internal use and for interlibrary loan. Nothing in Section 108 limits a library's right to fair use of copyrighted works; the new law reconfirms most of the rights librarians had before and even extends some. It prohibits 'systematic copying' but this is no problem since few academic or public libraries engage in systematic copying as defined in Section 108 (g) (2) and the CONTU guidelines."[3]

1. The Librarian versus Recordkeeping.

No specific form or rules have been set for librarians to follow. The only stipulation is that the records must be kept for three years.

This problem should not prove as difficult and time-consuming as it appears at first glance. There have already been several studies made, both at the University of Pennsylvania Library and Cornell and they have both come to the conclusion that the number of times in a year that the necessary statistics needed for those restricted five copy items is negligible. The only time the interlibrary loan problem is likely to arise is when one research project needs several articles from one journal, and the costs should be agreed upon by the parties in advance.

2. The Librarian versus the Responsibility of Enforcing the law.

Neither the librarian nor the Copyright Office is charged with the enforcement of the law. The only requirement of both parties is that a warning of copyright restrictions be placed at all copying counters or near copy machines.

Librarians are not even responsible for potentially illegal use of unsupervized copying at self-service machines provided the warning has been posted.

3. The Librarian versus Reporting

It has not yet been defined as to where or to whom reports of statistics are to be made. This is still one of the ambiguous parts of the law, nor has the question of what to do with the records after the three-year period has elapsed.

"Ben H. Weil has been appointed to serve as program director of the Association of American Publishers/Technical-Scientific-Medical Copy Payments Center Task Force, which is expected to design and implement a payments system by January 1, 1978. The center would periodically invoice the users and allocate the payment, less a processing charge, to the appropriate publisher. I wish the center luck, but my guess is that the processing charges will far exceed the royalty payments, making it a financially precarious service."[4]

4. The Librarian versus Teachers and Classrooms

This is a phase that is going to create some puzzles. "The basic question seems to be whether or not multiple reproduction of copyrighted works which may be barred under Section 108(g) are permissible when the requester is a teacher acting in conformity with the educational guidelines."[5] These educational guidelines in Section 107 may be at variance to the guidelines in Section 108 for librarians. Undoubtedly librarians will be serving teachers in photoduplication, and it is just possible that librarians may be violating their own guidelines.

5. Librarians versus Interlibrary Loan

This is one phase that has been causing much concern with librarians. It is certainly a section that will be watched closely by the publishers, since it has been causing them much concern for years. They will devise a way of keeping track of libraries who reprint more than the five copies a year of a periodical published within the last five years. So it is going to be vital that the statistical count be kept carefully. However, take heart; it isn't so bad as it might seem according to De Gennaro. It is suggested that interlibrary loan records already give sufficient detail so that an extra copy of these records might be kept when needed. It is also suggested that only a very small number of requests will qualify for the needed recordkeeping.

## 6. Publishers

As has already been stated, publishers have always been plagued with the idea that interlibrary loan, or resource-sharing is reducing the number of library subscriptions, and they consider it even more possible now, because libraries are having to meet such drastic inflationary prices and budget costs. "The troubles that publishers have are caused by rising costs and changing market conditions and not by library photocopying or deficiencies in the copyright law. These troubles will not be resolved by the collection of royalties on a few journal articles or the sale of a few more library subscriptions."[6]

Librarians should be aware and on the lookout for unscrupulous approaches by publishers. One has already taken advantage of the new law to bluff librarians into buying "copyright privileges" that librarians have always had both before and after the new law was passed.

## SUMMARY

Now that some time has elapsed, and various librarians have put their fears and questions into perspective, publishers and librarians are beginning to agree that the law may not be too bad after all, and that nothing has actually changed according to Richard De Gennaro. He says, [the] "guidelines are fair to authors, publishers and librarians. I do not believe they will significantly affect the way most libraries serve their readers. Most libraries in public and academic libraries need not try to master the legal intricacies of the new law or make elaborate preparations to implement it. The leaders of library associations and their legal counsel should and will continue to monitor and influence the implementation and administration of the new law; . . . "[7]

Still another consoling comment is, " . . . confronted with the need to legislate with respect to an 'evolving situation' Congress wisely chose a flexible course. That flexibility makes our lives a bit more complicated but it has the virture of leaving the shape of the future to our own imagination and good sense."[8]

With such knowledgeable lawyers and librarians assuring us, it looks as if we will be able to surmount the problems of the new law in due time.

There are other phases of the new law that are of interest to librarians and for thoses who wish to pursue it further might be well to read the full text of the article by De Gennaro, and the one by Flacks. Also recommended is the American Library Association's *Librarian's Guide to the New Copyright Law,* reprinted from the *Washington Newsletter,* V. 28, No. 13, Nov. 15, 1976. It is available from the Order Department, A.L.A. Huron St., Chicago, Il. 60611. It costs $2.00.

There is another phase of copyrighting that must be considered and that is the changes in the United Kingdom copyright agreements. So far this agreement has given British publishers control over publishing rights in the Commonwealth countries. This means that American firms will be able to sell publishing rights to their books directly to Australia or to Nigeria, or to publish books in the overseas markets themselves.

### NOTES

1. Lewis I. Flacks, "Living in the Gap of Ambiguity; an Attorney's Advice to Librarians on the Copyright Law," *American Libraries.* 8 (May 1977): 252-257.
2. *Chronicle of Higher Education* 1966-    . Lancaster, Pa. etc. Educational Projects for Education, Inc. Oct. 1976.
3. Richard De Gennaro, "Copyright, Resource Sharing, and Hard Times: A View from the Field," *American Libraries,* 8 (September 1977): 430-435.
4. Ibid., p. 432.
5. Flacks, op. cit., p. 256.
6. De Gennaro, op. cit., p. 434.
7. Ibid., p. 430.
8. Flacks, op. cit., p. 257.

# CHAPTER XVI
# MISCELLANEOUS TOPICS

## CIRCULATION OF JOURNALS

### General Comment

Because routines and policies for reading rooms and circulation of journals have undergone fewer changes in recent years than other techniques, the discussion here will be brief. These topics have already been adequately covered in other books and articles.

Since the 1920's, when photocopying became possible, the trend has been to use this method for articles needed from the journals. With new types of copying methods, this now takes the place of loaning out the journals if only an article is needed.

One thing to consider is the question of mutilation. Would more mutilation occur by strictly following a no-circulation policy? This might be obviated by providing the various microform possibilities. On the other hand, if volumes are allowed to circulate, there is possibility of wear on just transporting the volumes from one place to another. Journals are usually pretty heavy items to lug very far.

Another thing to consider is the fact that other patrons may be needing other articles in the same volume, and these patrons will be inconvenienced by having to wait for the return of the volume.

### Length of Time for Loans

Journals are usually circulated on special charges and time schedules. Most often they are charged out on a temporary basis for varying lengths of time. Because articles are usually shorter than books, they may be read more quickly. Also, because the most timely information is found in the current articles, all patrons should be given

equal opportunity to read them. The demand is seldom great.
1. Day loans or overnight are the most usual.
2. Three-day loans are sometimes granted.
3. Week loans are the least usual.

### Current Unbound Issues

1. Some libraries lend current numbers as soon as received.
2. Some, next to the last number, or older.
3. Some, three months old, or older.

### Bound Volumes

1. If the article is not more than ten pages it might be advisable to have it photocopied if equipment is available.
2. Journals in less demand might be more available for circulating.
3. Early volumes (although those volumes that are fragile would not go out).
4. Monographs and annuals might be allowed to circulate. Again, demand must be considered.

## Types of Material Usually Not Circulated

1. Reference works.
2. Often-used journals.

## Various Types of Libraries
### Academic

1. Faculty might get loans on a more liberal basis.
2. Grauate students usually have the privilege of working in carrels, so the journals are really available on short notice.
3. Undergraduates are seldom given this privilege.

### Small Libraries

1. Those libraries that do not bind their journals usually may loan back files.
2. There is opportunity to be more flexible on all counts.

### Special Libraries

Special libraries may also be more liberal in loaning their journals. They usually have a smaller clientele and have closer contact with all personnel. Even here the often-used journals should be available to everyone. This is done by a liberal use of photocopying.

### Routing Journals

This is usually an internal service to personnel within the library and special libraries. However, the constant drawback is that the issues may get filed in someone's desk instead of getting passed on promptly to the next person. An alternative to this is photocopying and circulating tables-of-contents.

### Interlibrary Loan

Now that so many new approaches are available through the various library networks, fewer physical volumes are actually loaned. It is costly to send them through the mail, not to speak of the damage done to the volumes, and here again, photocopying has become so easily available.

### Tattletape

While devices for checking out material belong mostly to the Circulation Department, it might not be amiss to mention one here, because it is becoming a part of more and more libraries. This is Tattletape which is a brand name for a device which the 3M Company manufactures. It is a magnetic tape which is inserted in the gutter edge of the pages of a book or periodical, or in the spine of a bound volume (some University of California libraries are having them bound into books sent to the bindery). The tape is deactivated when a volume is checked out and the patron can walk through the turnstile. However, if a patron tries to take out materials not checked out, the turnstile mechanism causes a buzzer to sound, indicating that a volume is being stolen. When a book that has been checked out is returned, the tape is re-activated.

## READING ROOMS

As with all library reading rooms the periodical reading room should, first of all, consider the needs of the readers. Those who are interested in study and research should have available a quiet area, with tables and writing space. Those browsing the more popular magazines should have comfortable lounging space with less need for quiet. Plan for future capacity if possible.

The journals are usually the current numbers and may include newspapers and government documents as well, depending on the library. The larger libraries will undoubtedly have separate service areas for these other types of material.

## Some Thoughts on Separating a Serial Reading Room from the Book Area

ADVANTAGES

1. Coordination of reader services.
2. Standardization of circulation procedures.
3. More control over unbound issues.

DISADVANTAGES

1. Most patrons have little interest in what format the material appears. Books and journals are all the same, and people do not like to have to go to various areas to get what they want on their subject.
2. More personnel is needed to cover two areas.

## Some Thoughts on Separating the Public Services of Journals from the Technical Serials Department

ADVANTAGES

1. Public Services are usually open more hours than Technical Services.
2. Processing department is left free for technical procedures.
3. The serials record should never be available to the general public. The unchecked numbers of journals are too easily taken away and lost before they are recorded in the record, causing claiming problems. But the record and reading room should be close enough to utilize the expertise of all personnel and the record.

DISADVANTAGES

1. Many phone calls are often needed between the two services.
2. Costly mistakes are created when only one phase is known to each worker.
3. More personnel is needed when two or more areas must be serviced.

### Treatment

Magazines are physically difficult to display and keep in order, because of their varying odd sizes, and binding problems.

SHELF ARRANGEMENT

1. They are sometimes arranged alphabetically.
   a. Main entry.
   b. Title.

2. Sometimes they are arranged by subject matter.
   a. Loosely by word designation.
   b. Loosely by first letter of call number.
   c. By call number.

PHYSICAL POSSIBILITIES

1. They may be laid on shelves or tables.
2. Placed in pigeon holes.
3. Shelved in special shelving.

All arrangements must provide for back issues of the current volume. This probably will mean providing both sloping or upright and flat shelves, unless back files are shelved separately and paged (which is a costly alternative in terms of staff time and space but which does preserve materials).

MEDIA FOR PROTECTION

1. Plastic, transparent covers.
2. Spiral back covers.
3. Manila folders.

## Summary

The ultimate object of all serials work is to provide journals to the patron. The reading room and/or the stacks are the respositories for these journals which should be on hand or traceable at the time the patron needs them. To this end close coordination and cooperation must be utilized every step of the way. Like an orchestra where every part — though important in itself — must blend harmoniously with all other parts to make a symphony, so it is with serials. The expertise of each person must combine and interweave with all other parts to bring this final service into being. Above all, the close cooperation between reference people and those working in serials will develop the special skills of reading the Serials Record and create an understanding of each other's problems and needs that is incalculable.

Those workers checking in the current issues must keep the flow up-to-date. Those claiming and ordering replacements must back up the checkers. Those ordering new subscriptions and paying invoices on new ones and renewals must back up all the previous routines. Those cataloging the material must make it possible for everyone to easily locate the titles. "Public service duties affect a cataloger's duties substantially, for an entirely different outlook is created. The cataloger will think of additional helps for the patron while cataloging. Added entries will be made that will help the particular clientele of a given library find something more easily. Subjects that are of special interest will receive emphasis. The kinds of cross-references that would be the most effective would be utilized. The cataloger would know whether to class broadly or narrowly, depending upon the use of the material." And so it goes; the reader and reading room must always be uppermost in everyone's mind as the work of serials progresses day by day. All this and so much more of this intertwining of the aspects of serials are so well covered in Lynn S. Smith's book, *A Practical Approach to Serials Cataloging*,[1] that it would be well worth anyone's time to read it.

## NOTES

1. Lynn S. Smith, *A Practical Approach to Serials Cataloging*. (Greenwich, Connecticut: J.A.I: Press, 1978).

# INDEX

AACR (Anglo—American Cataloging Rules 1967) **187-89**, 192-94, 197, 203, 206
AACR 2 (Anglo—American Cataloging Rules 1978) 187-89, **192**, 197, 204, 206, 234
ACRPP (Association pour la Conservation et la Reproduction
    Photographique de la Press) 249
ALA Cataloging Rules for Author and Title Entries 186, 226
AMA 239
AMS Press Incorporated 249
ANSI (American National Standards Institute) **323-25**
Abbreviations 187, 193, 197, 237, **239-40**, 283
Abrahams Magazine Service 242
Absorbed publication notes 201
Abstracting and indexing services 81-82, 86, 91-92, **238-39**, 251, 307
Acetate film 337
Acme visible files 30
Acquiring foreign journals **129-37**
Acquisition policy 81
Acronyms, Initialisms and Abbreviations 240
Added copies 175
Added entries 187, **192-93**
Adding cross-references 69
Additional charges **92-93**, 110, 122
Address 34, 130, 174
Address labels 35, 64, **155**, 261, 275
Address stencil 265, 273
Addresses, 240-41
    AMS Press 249
    American Binder 283
    American Library Association—Order Department 348
    Association pour la Conservation et la Reproduction
        Photographique de la Press 249
    Bliss, P and H. 242
    Canner, J.S. and Co. 249
    Carrolton Press Inc. 249
    Center for Research Libraries 316
    China Book Import Corp. 135
    China Books and Periodicals, Inc. 135
    Consumer Advocate Office 260
    Coordinating Council of Literary Magazines (CCLM) 248
    ERIC Document Reproduction Service 249
    Gonzalez, Sr. Jesus Cruz 136
    Guozi Shudiam 134
    Inter Documentation Co. 249
    Johnson, Walter, J. Inc. 242
    Kraus Periodical Co. 242
    Kraus Reprint Corp. 318
    Library of Congress Information Office 315
    Mezhdunarodnaya Kniga 132
    PBS Prebound Periodicals 283
    Readex Microprint Corp. 249
    Seminar on the Acquisition of Latin American Library Materials
        (SALALM) 135, **314**
    Special Libraries Association 307
    USBE 314

United Nations Educational, Scientific and Cultural
        Organizations (UNESCO) 318
United Nations 318
United States Postal Service, Consumer Advocate Office 260
Universal Serials & Book Exchange (USBE) 314
University Microfilm International 250
Wetherbee, Lou 314
Zeitlin Periodicals Co., Inc. 242
Addresses, back issues 241-42
Addresses, Cuban publications 136
Addresses, gifts and exchanges 50
Addresses, libraries, librarians, societies, institutions 240
Addresses, microforms and reprints 249
Advance payment 106, 110, 111, 140
Advantages of,
        agents 121
        arrangement of holdings in the Serial Record 28
        blanket orders 141
        chain ownership of newspapers 12
        classifying periodicals 208
        more than one agent 123
        multiple order forms 163
        one fund for a serial budget 90
        ordering directly from the publisher 117
        placing foreign orders with one agent in each country 128
        provided through agents' service charges 123
        publishers 117-18
        reading rooms, various approaches 352
        reprography 330-31
        using an agent 121
        using more than one agent 123
Advertisements 6, 82, 293
Agent—librarian—publisher relations 125-26
Agents 92, 108-11, **120-29,** 132, 135, 143, 148-49, 151-56, 176, 179-81
        advantages 121
        antiquarian 120
        cards 151
        changing 124, 138, 148
        check-in service 123
        consolidated lists 139
        disadvantages 122
        discounts 92, 118, 120, 122, 138
        domestic 93, 123, 128, 138-39
        field 125
        foreign 128-29, 138
        fulfillment 125
        international 93, **125,** 241
        large 92, 120, **124,** 139, 148
        legal responsibility of the agent 121
        lists 122
        local 129
        medium 92, **124**
        one agent versus many 123
        placing foreign 128-29
        placing foreign orders with one agent in each country 128
        quotations 122, 139

    reasons for reduced number of agents 121
    secondhand 120
    selecting 122
    service charges 92, 118, **122-23,** 137
    small 92, 120, **124**
    specialized 120, 125, 138
    "sole distributor" 107
    standing orders 64, 141, 317
    trends in publishing and subscription agencies 8-9, 11-13
    types 124-25
    want list 51, 153
Agents' catalogs 241
"Agitators" notebooks 132
*Agricultural Index* 239
Aids to check for serial selection 82, **242-44**
Aims of a serials record 20
"Air-taxis" 6, 253
Airmail 110, 128, **253,** 256, 259
Alkire, Leland G. 239
All-union government 133
Allen, Charles Geoffrey 240
Allen, Robert V. 133
Allen, Walter C. 244
*Allende years. A Union List of Chilean Imprints, 1970-1973 . . .* G.K. Hall. 137
Allerton Park Institute 244
"Alphabet Soup" 76
Alternative treatment of microforms **334-36**
Alum-rosin 334
American Binder 283
*American Book Trade Directory* 240
American Courier Corp. 263
American Express, current exchange rates 113
*American Libraries* 115
American Library Association 238
American Library Association. Duplicate Exchange Union of the Resources
    and Technical Division (DEU) 315
*American Library Directory* 240
*American Library Directory,* Up-dating-service 240
*American Magazine* 5
American Management Association (AMS) 239
American Medical Association (AMS) 192, 239
*American Mercury* 82
American Methodist Association (AMS) 239
American National Standards Institute (ANSI) **323-25**
American Publishers/Technical—Scientific—Medical Copy Payments
    Center Task Force 346
Analytics 37, 51, 173, 201
*Anglo—American Cataloging Rules* (1967) (AACR) **187-89,** 192-94, 197, 203, 206
Anglo—American Cataloging Rules (1978) (AACR 2) 187-89,
    **192,** 197, 204, 206, 227, 234
Annals (see Analytics)
Announcements 20, 82, 106, 119, 127, 140-41, 172, 238
*Annuaire de la Presse et de la Publicite* 243
*Annuaire european* 244-45
Annual budget, fluctuation 89
Annual budget, formula 91

358

Annual export catalogs 133
Annual indexes 47, 108, 176
Annual reports 281
Annuals 32, 121, 226, **247**
Anti-Christ 132
Antiquarian agents 120
*Anuario Espanol de la Publicidad* 244
Aperture cards 328
*Applied Science and Technology Index* 239
Archival film 321, **323-24**, 327, 334, 337
Archive tape 76
Area managers 122
*Art Index* 239
Assigning of serial funds 89-90
Associated Press 13-14
Associated pour la Conservation et la Reproduction Photographique
    de la Press (ACRPP) 249
*Atlantic Monthly* 5
Atti 142
Authority file **37**, 40-42, 71, 159
Authorship 187, 192
Automated cataloging operations **212-22**
Automated serials checking **76-78**
Automated systems 100, 190, 206, 209, 218, 237
Automatic claiming 150, **272**
Automation 8, 18, 28, 90, 124, 206
Automation of cataloging data 212
Auxiliary sheets (see, Cards—current checking-in)
*Avisa, Ralation oder Zeitung* 10
*Ayer Directory of Publications, Newspapers and Magazines* 242-48
Back files 20, 35, 51, 86, 90-91, 120, 140, 157, 175-76 **180-81**, 204, 265, 326, 331
Back issues 130, 173, **241-42**
Bans and embargos 130, 134
Bantam 9
Barter exchange 83, 133, 139
Base or support—film 337
Basic journals 80, 85
Basic questions of organization 20
"Batch" 76, 213
Bell and Howell 324
Bibliographic information 27, 29, 38, 51, 76, 125, 127, 133, 137, 142, 185, 191,
    194, 202, 205-06, 210, 212, 218, 226
*Bibliographie de la France* 245
Bibliographies 155, 185
Bidding 137
Bids 137-39
Biennials 32
Binding, 21, 24, 38, 51, 86, 92, 144, 173, 179, 186, **277-303**
    abbreviations 283
    advertising 281, 293
    binding notice 295
    binding notification slip—hold for missing numbers 297
    book pockets 173
    brittle pages 176
    buckram 284, 292
    calendar year 299

canvas 292
catalog department 277, 297
changes of title 285-86, 288, 303
collation 197, 285
color 283
computerized 300-03
consolidated orders 143
contract 283
cumulated indexes 288-89
dates on spines 299
decisions **277-82**
department 21
development of performance standards for binding 284
duck binders 292
duplicate subscriptions 84, 282
ephemeral titles 281
experiment station publications 282, 294
features that may need notification of changes throughout the library 285-86
fiscal biennial volume 299
fiscal volume 299
flexible glue 284
flow chart 298
general comment 277
gold lettering 283-84
headbands 284
history of each title 277
incomplete volumes 281, 290
indexes 23, 285, 288-89, 293-94, 296
information 18
lamination 175
leather 284, 292
lettering 283, 290
location 277
maps 285, 288, 293
microforms 280-81
mint condition issues 283
missing numbers 277, 290
monographs 293
mutilation 84, 280, 282-83, 285, 292
newspapers 292-93
norbinding 291
notices 67
notification slip 295
numbering and internumbering 196
pamphlets 291
permabinding 292
photographs 300
plastic adhesive 291
prebound 84, 280
priority usage 281
quality of cloth 283
reasons for substitute binding 290
reference material 282
requests for binding notification slip 296
review 299-300
routines 294-300
routing 296-97

rubbings 284, 290
serials that may require notification of changes throughout the library 285
series and sub-series 293-94
sewing 284, 288
special collections 293
special problems 292
specifications 283
spines 281-82, 284, 288-90, 292
spiral 292
split volume 288
standards 284
stapling 291
string binding 291
stubbing 281-82, 291
substitutes for complete binding **290-92**
supplements 284-86, 289
TP 294
TPC 294
TPIC (title page, index and contents) 294
thickness of physical volumes 288
title pages and indexes 288
togic 292
university studies 293-94
vellum 284
vinyl material 284
ways to economize 283-84
Binding—computerized, **300-03**
current volume record 300
description and diagrams 301
Hertzberg computer customer list 302
Louisiana State University library (LSU) 300-03
print-out 302-03
sample page 302
title changes 303
Binding—decisions **277-82**
all titles 281
what to bind 280-81
what not to bind 281
when to bind 282
*Biological Abstracts* 118
Bis 275
Blanket orders 33, 83, 120, 131, **141-42**
Bliss, P. and H. 242
Book budget 89, 90
Book committees 83
*Book Publishers' Directory* 240
*Booklist* 251
Books and serials about serials **244-45**
Books on Reprography that may be of use to librarians 341
*Boston American* 11
*Boston Newsletter* 11
Bowker, R. R. 191, 220, 238
Bradford, Alexander 5
Branch libraries 83
Breakdowns,
agents 126

librarians 126
postal services 127
publishers 126
technical processes and outside influences 127
British Commonwealth 9, 114
British Museum rules 186
British trade market 9
*British Union-catalogue of Periodicals* 244
Brown, Clara D. 244
Budget—annual formula 91
Budgetary problems 142
Budgeting and accounting 89-104
Budgeting—cutting costs 99
Budgets 80, 84-85, **89-100,** 121-209, 219, 305
Buff cards 31
Buff liquid paper 29
*Building Library Collections* 81
Bulk mail 257-58
Bulk ordering 83, 141
"Bullet" symbol 147
*Bulletin of Bibliography* 64, 245
*Bulletin of Reprints* 249
*Bulletin* of the Public Affairs Information Service 246
"Business rate" mail 254
Business relations between library and agent 125-26
Buttress, F. A. 240
CC4 109
CCE (catalog of copyright entries) 230
CLNO (call number) 76
COD (collect on delivery) 259
CONSER (conversion of serials) 215, **220-22,** 228
CONTU (National Commission on Technical Uses of Copyright Works) 344
COPICS (Copyright Office Publication and Interactive Cataloging System) 230
Cpl 108
CRHD (current holdings) 77
Cabinets 30-31, 157-58, 324
Call number 18, 46, 51
Call number (CLNO) 76
Campbell, Gladys 5
Canadian dollar 113, 136
*Canadian Serials Directory* 244
Cancelled titles 69, 80, 117
Cancelling titles **85-86,** 90, 100, 107, 118, 121, 141
Cancellation 69, 86, **110,** 130, 137, 175
"Captive market" 85
Cards, **45-63**
     agents' 151
     aperture 328
     buff 31
     build-up 30
     cross-references 64
     deep build-up 30
     discards 64
     duplicates 36
     financial 30, **62,** 101
     gift acknowledgement 46

    lined 47
    memberships 63
    minor titles coming because of a more important title 45
    posting holdings 196, 199
    "rider" cards 34
    saving space 34
    size 30, 38
    special directives 64-66
    specifications 30
    temporary records 36
    title varies 29, 53-54
    UCR cards 71-75
    white 31, 38
Cards—back file or holdings cards 45, **51-61**
    annuals 60
    biennials 61
    blank 51
    holdings 27, 30, 35, 51-61
    incomplete 52
    inside of holdings card 54
    irregulars 51-53
    lined holdings 51
    membership 63
    numbered, (1-200) 56, (1-300) 51, 57, (1-400) 58, (1-600) 51, 59
    split year 51
Cards—current 27, 31, **45-51**
    back of 45, 51
    bi-monthlies 49
    blank 45
    dailies and weeklies 45, 48, 141
    duplicates 36
    "flimsies" **30, 36, 45-51**
    "half auxiliaries" 45-51
    irregulars 47
    monthlies—semi-bi- 31, 45, 48-49, 141
    quarterlies 45, 50, 141
    weeklies 45, 48, 141
Carrolton Press, Inc. 249
Cartridges 327
Cassettes 204, 327
Catalog Division 20-21, 28, 33, 37, 42, 66-67, 101
Catalog of copyright entries (CCE) 230
*Catalog of National Archives; Microfilm Publications* 250
*Catalog of Reprints in Series* 249
Catalogers 40
Cataloging—automated **212-22**
Cataloging Distribution Service (CDS) 211
Cataloging routines 185-222, 228-30
Ceased and delayed information 238
Ceased titles 20-21, 34, 45, 106, 117, 123, 150, 197, 201, 204, 241, 245
Cellulose ester base 325
Censorship 84, 130, 132
Center for Research Libraries 315-16
Central Agency Guozi Shudian 134
Central Serials Record 17-18, 21
Central sorting centers 253

Central State University, Oklahoma 330, 335
Changes of titles 28-29, 64, **69**, 108, 241, 285-86, 303
Changing agents 124
Changing from purchase to gifts and exchanges and vice versa 69
Charges, unexplained 92, 110
Chase Manhatten Bank, current exchange rates 113
Check-in service 123
Checkers 30, 71
Checking in, 24, 70 (see also, Cards)
    automated serials checking-in 76-78
    back volumes 52
    bound volumes vs. unbound volumes 52
    cards (see, Cards)
    current issues 35, **46-51**, 70
    gift acknowledgement cards 46
    holdings 29, 35, **51-61**
    indexes 36
    loose material 36
    mail procedures 35
    microforms 52
    minor titles 45
    new titles 40, 42, **67-68**
    newspapers 33
    procedures 31-78
    reprints 46
    sample copies 64
    serials 76-78
    special directives 64-65
    UCR cards **71-75**
    unbound volumes 32, 52
*Chemical Abstracts* 91, 118
Chi Wang 134
*Chicago Daily News* 11
*Chicago Today* 11
Chile 136-37
China 130, **134-35**, 261
China Book Import Corp. 135
China Books and Periodicals, Inc. 135
Chinese 3, 9
*Choice; Books for College Libraries* 251
*Christian Science Monitor* 143, 156
    ordering 143
    indexes 143
*Chronicle of Higher Education* 344
Circulation of journals 86, 173, **349**
    academic 350
    general comment 349
    government publications 203
    interlibrary loans 351
    length of time for loans 349
    routing 351
    small libraries 350
    special libraries 350
    tattle tape 351
    types of material that may be circulated 350
    types of material usually not circulated 350

      unbound volumes 350
      various types of libraries 350
"Citizen rate"—mail 254
City presses 14
Claiming 18, 20, 22, 24, 28, 32, 34-35, 37-38, 45-46, 51, 69, 93, 108, 118, 120-26,
      128, 137, 143, 149-50, 157, 172, 174, 179, 181, 247, **265-73**
      automatic **272**
      systematic **272**
*Classified List of Periodicals for the College Library* 251
Clearinghouse for Federal Scientific and Technical Information. U.S. Department of
      Commerce, Springfield, Virginia. (see, National Technical Information Service.
      (NTIS)) 147
*Cleveland News* 11
Code, zip 252, 258
Codes, reading subscription labels 112
Coffee houses 5, 10
Collapsed titles 106, 312
Collation, 197, **285**, 296
Collect on delivery (COD) 259
Collection analysis 122
Collection development 101
*College and Research Libraries* 251
College and university libraries 81
*College Blue Book* 240
Color 36, 51, 284
Color codings 20, 31-32, 36, 157
Color microfilm 327
Colored plates 180
Colored tabs 31, 149, 153, 271
Colored pencils 32
Commerce Clearinghouse 118
*Commerical and Financial Chronicle* 113
Communication channels 209
Comparison of,
      costs of back files 153
      costs of subscriptions 91, 123, 175
      how to post holdings 28
      roll film and fiches 326
Competitive bidding 137
Comptes rendus 142
*Computer Abstracts* 239
Computer version of information 186, 335
Computerized 13, 29, 125
      based indexes 239
      binding 300-03
      form 157
      lists 123, 186
      records 100, 277
Computers 76, 99, 110-12, 148-50, 154, 209
Conglomerates 8-9, 11, 14, 262, 271
*Consolidated Index of Translations into English* 252
Consolidated orders 143
*Consumers' Advocate* 260
*Consumer's Guide to Postal Service* 253, 260
Contents notes 201
Continuations, definition 17

"Continued by" 29, 196, 199
"Continues" 29, 196, 199
Continuing subscriptions versus temporary funds 99
Contract,
    agents' 138
    binding 283
Conversion of foreign money 110, **112-13,** 125, 128
Conversion of Serials Project (CONSER) 215, **220-22,** 228
Coordinating Council of Literary Magazines (CCLM) 248
Cooperative sharing 83, 85, 100, 219, 347
Copyflo 337
Copying machines 329
Copyright 316
Copyright laws 179, **343-48**
Copyright Office Publication and Interactive Cataoging System (COPICS) 230
"Corantos" 10
Core journals 81, 99, 251
Corporate authorship 188, 192
Corporate entry 186-87
Costs 80, 91, 123, 153, 175, 332, 336
Coupons,
    deposit accounts 147
    UNESCO 105
*Courant* 11
"Cover-to-cover" translations 140
Credit memos 107, **111**
Criteria 80, 84-85, 187, 238
Cross-references 28, 31, 51, 67, 69, 186, 188-89
"Crossed" checks 114
Crowley, Ellen T. 240
Cuba 130, **135-37**
*Cuban Acquisition and Bibliography* 137
Cultural Revolution 134
Cumulated indexes 51, 91-92, 172, 288-89, 330
Cumulations 106
Current holdings (CRHD) 77
Current mail 21, 31
Customs regulations 128, 130, 260
Cutting costs in budgeting 99
Czarist regime 131
DEFN (Definition) 76
DEU (Duplicate Exchange Union) 247, 306, **315**
DM (West German mark) 113
DMO (East German mark) 113
DTR (diffusion-transfer-reversal) 337
Daguerreotype 321
Dating of invoices 112, 114
Davinson, Donald E. 244
Deacquisition (see, Deselection)
Dealers (see, Agents)
Deep build-up of cards 30
Definitions, (DEFN) 76
    bulletins 17
    continuations 17
    magazines 17
    microfiche 326

    microfilm 326
    monographs 18
    periodicals 17
    proceedings 17
    reprography 321 (see also, pp. 337-39 for various terms concerning reprography)
    serials 17
    sets 18
    transactions 17
De Gennaro, Richard 84-85, 345-47
Deletion sheets 110
Departmental book funds 90
Departmental libraries 28
Deposit account 148
Depositories 83, 145, 318
Descriptive cataloging 194-95
Descriptive cataloging division (LC) 226-27
Deselection **84-86,** 209, 219, 307-08
Designated depository libraries 145
Desuperimposition 193
*Detroit Times* 11
Developing countries 305-06
Diagrams 301 (see also, Cards, Forms, Letters)
    computerized binding information 300
    dimensional standards for letter-sized mail 255
    Library of Congress record organization charts 231-32
Diaz, Albert James 321, 324-25, 327, 329, 333
Diazo 323, 337
Dictionaries **239-40**
*Dictionarium Bibliothecarii Practicum in XXII Lenguis* 240
Diffusion-transfer-reversal (DTR) 337
Dimensional standards for letter-size mail 255
Direct ordering **117-20**
Direct "renewal cards" 149, 174
Direct renewal file 31, **149,** 174
Directives 35-36
Directories 186, 211, 238
*Directory of Dealers in Secondhand and Antiquarian Books in the British Isles* 242
*Directory of Institutional Photocopying Services* 250
*Directory of Library Reprographic Services* 250
*Directory of Periodicals Publishing Articles on English and
    American Literature and Languages* 244
*Directory of Special Libraries and Information Centers* 241
Disadvantages of,
    agents 122
    arrangement of holdings in the Serial Record 29
    blanket orders 142
    chain ownership of newspapers 12
    more than one agent 123
    multiple order forms 163
    one fund for a serial budget 90
    opening current mail within the department 21
    ordering directly from a publisher 120
    placing all orders for foreign material with one domestic agent 128
    placing foreign orders with one agent in each country 129
    publishers 120
    reading rooms—various approaches 352
    reprography 331-32

Discard 31, 66-67, 86, 146
"Discard on receipt" 33, 64, 272, 311
Discarding issues 68
Discount titles 122-23
Discounts 92, 107, 118, 121-2, 125
Discounts versus service charges 92, **137**
"Display" 36, 173, 294
Distinctive address label 155
Divided holding 28-29, 188-89
Divisions of a Serials Department 24
"Doc Ex" (Documents Expediting Project) 147
Documents 32, **144-48**, 226, 245
    checking in 144
    deposit account 148
    depositories 83, 145
    foreign 144
    state 120
    United Nations 317-18
    United States 144-48
Domestic agents 93, 123, 128, 138-39
"Dot" 147
Drop shipping 112
Drum-like files 30
"Dry plate" 321
Drying of film 323
Duplicate Exchange Union (DEU) 247, 306, **315**
Duplicate subscriptions 84, 90, 172, 282
Duplicates 36, 47, 68-69, 109, 124, 142, 152, 312-13
Duplicating volumes 140
Duplication 27, 117, 138, 155, 200, 273, 275
Duration notes 198
Dust factor 86
Dutch florin 114
Dutton 9
EBSCO 124, 241
*EBSCO Bulletin of Serial Changes* 241, 245
EBSCO *Librarians' Handbook* 241
EBSCO Subscription Services 241
ERIC (Educational Resources Information Center) 316
East German mark (DMO) 113
Eastman Kodak Company 322
Edison, Thomas A. 326
*Editor and Publisher—International Yearbook Number* 248
Editor notes 200, 212
*Education Index* 239
Educational Resources Information Center (ERIC) 316
Electrofax 337
Electrostatic copying processes 337
Elsevier 9
Embargos 130, 136
Emulsion 337
*Encyclopedia of Associations* 240
Enlargement prints 337
Environment for storing film 323
Ephemeral duplicates 275
Ephemeral material **67**, 175, 208, 237, 293, 305

Equipment 19, 27-31
*Europa Yearbook* 244-45
European Common Market 114
European Yearbook (see, *Annuaire european*) 244-45
Evolution of Microfilm 321-32
Exchanges (see, Gifts and Exchanges)
Exchange basis, 133, 139
Exchange lists 152
Exchange programs 131
Exchanges with China 134
Exchanges with Cuba 136
Exchanges with Soviet Union 133
Exchanges (see Gifts and Exchanges)
Exclusive Want List 153
Experiment station publications, binding 282, 294
Expiration dates 69, 123
Export catalogs 133
Export license 136
Express mail 259
Extra files 20
Eye-finding devices in the files 30
FTC (Federal Trade Commissions) 9, 11
FUND (fund) 76
Faculty members 20, 46, 82-86, 90, 118, 142, 180-81, 219, 315
Farber, Evans Ira 251
Faxon 124, 241
*Faxon, Librarians' Guide to Periodicals* 241
*Faxon, Serials Updating Service* 241
*Feature Writer, Photographer and Syndicate Directory (Working
    Press of the Nation, V.4)* 243
Features of serials that may require routing to the Catalog Division **285-86**, 209-10
Federal Trade Commission (FTC) 9, 11, 14
*Fiche and Reele* 323
Field agents 125
Files,
        Acme 30
        agents' cards 151
        authority 37, 40-42
        building up of cards 30
        current 27, 31
        direct renewal 149, 174
        exchange list 152
        exclusive list 153
        extra 37, 148-53
        holdings 27-28
        new serials title 150, 155
        outstanding special orders 151
        publishers' and agents' lists 148
        "tickler" 140, 149, 238
        vertical 32
        want list 152
Filling in long runs of lacks 181
Filling in missing material **179-82**
Film chips 328
Film sizes 326
Film standards 324

Film strips 328
Final review and placing of a subscription 172
Financial clerk 68, 162
Financial records 30, **62-63**, 67, 106-09, 154, 161, 164
Finger-finding devices in the files 30
Firm order 156
First class mail 253-54, **257**, 263
First issue cataloging 228
Fixing bath 323
Flacks, Lewis I. 344, 346, 348
Flexibility 19, 31, 296
"Flimsies" 30, 36, **45-52**, 71, 279
Flow charts,
    binding routines 298
    checking in all serials other than a new subscription 70
    organization charts—Serial Record Division—LC 231-32
    receipt of first piece of a new subscription—unbound 177
    receipt of a new subscription—bound 178
    routing for a new subscription 177
Focal point for making the Serial Record accurate 68
Follow-up procedures (see chapter on Claiming)
Foreign agents 128, 176
Foreign documents 144
Foreign exchange of material (see, USSR, Cuba, Latin America, Special
    Programs, Gifts and Exchange chapter)
Foreign exchange of money **112-13,** 128
Foreign exchange traders 113
Foreign journals 176, 285
Foreign languages 22, 130, 142, 265
Foreign programs 141
Foreign publications 129-37
Form card cataloging (LC) 226-27
Formats of films 38, 325-28
Forms, 156 (see also Cards, Diagrams, Letters)
    agents 265
    authority slip 38
    binding—computerized current volume record 300
    binding decisions 278-80
    binding information—computerized 301
    binding notification slip 295
    binding notification slip—hold for missing numbers 297
    binding—Hertzberg Customer list 302
    change of bibliographical information slip 286-87
    claims 266-70
    collected development profile 101-04
    dimensional standards for letter-size mail 255
    direct renewal card 149
    financial records (UCR) 102-04
    L.S. numbers 154
    minor titles coming because of some more important title 45
    multiple binding 300
    multiple order 157-71
    new serial title slip 37, 150
    OCLC serials check-in record 76-78
    print-out from the binder 302
    projected forms (UWL) 167-68

    request for a replacement 182, 297
    routing slip with binding notification slip to Catalog Division 286
    serial review form 38-39
    serials catalog record screen display 217-18
    serials decision (binding) 278-80
    special directives 65
    statistical count of claims at the UCR library **93-98**
    statistical forms (UCR) 93-98
    subscription slip 37-38, 40-42
    temporary records 67
    work slip (subscription request) 37-38, 40-42
Formula, annual budget 91
Fourth class mail 254, **258-59**
Franklin, Benjamin 5, 262
Fraser, John 134
Free documents 144
Free government publications 147
Free magazines 246-47, 307
Free material 123, 144, 147, 241, **246,** 307
Freezing the Library of Congress catalog 234
French franc 114
Frequency 46, 172-73
Frequency notes 198
Frequency signals 31, 51
*From Radical Left to Extreme Right* 248
Fugitive and irregular titles 118
Fulfillment agents 125
Fundamentals of serials 17-25
Fundamentals of serial selection 81
Funds **89-93,** 100, 142
Funds, temporary 99
Fungi 323
Future of newspapers 13
GPO (government printing office) 144
Gable, J. Harris 244
Gaddy, Dale 341
Gale Research Co. 238
"Gang of four" 134
"Gap" records 312
"Gazetta" 10
"Gazette" 10
*Gebbie House Magazine Directory (Working Press of the Nation V.5)* 243
Gellatly, Peter 86, 182
*Gentleman's Magazine* 5
Gentlemen's Agreement 343
George Allen & Unwin 9
German mark 113
"Ghost title" 117, 127
Gift acknowledgement cards 46
Gifts and exchanges 31, 33, 40, 45, 64, 69, 70, 83, 85, 147, 157, 172, **305-13**
    claiming 272, 305, 312
    deacquisition 308
    discard 308, 311
    "discard on receipt" 33
    disposal of extra duplicates 312
    "Gap" records 312

gift acknowledgement cards 46
philosophy 307
preliminary 311
reference material 311
routines 311-12
sources 152, 306-07
tools 247
"zeros" 312
Gleason's 5
Global subscriptions 33, 63
Gonzales, Sr. Jesus Cruz 136
Government documents 99, 120, **144-48**
Government invoices 144, 147-48
Government Printing Office (GPO) 144
Government publications 121, 135, 142, 203
Government Publications; A guide to Bibliographic Tools 246
Great Britain 114
Grenfell, David 244
Guide to Magazines and Serial Agents 80, 120-21, 124, 126, 241
Guide to Microforms in Print 249-50
Guide to Reference Books 182, 239, 242
Guide to Reprints 249
Gun cotton 322
Guozi Shudian 134
Gutenberg bible 3
Gutenberg press 9
"Half auxiliaries" 30, 36, **45-51**
Half a Century of Russian Serials 244
Hall, G. K. 137
Handbooks 32
Hard copy 338
Harrassowitz 143, 276
Hartford Times 11
Hattery, Lowell H. 337-38
Hearst 14
Hertzberg 300
Hidden costs 92
High-speed stabilization process 338
History of serial processing 225-26
Holdings 21, 28-29, 35, 51, 196
Holdings cards (see, Cards)
Holography 334
"Hors serie" 110, 275
House organ publications 67, 246
Hough, Raymond L. 307-08
How multiple forms may be used internally 158
Huff, William 149
"Hybrid titles" 8
Hydrochloric acid 322
Hypo 323, 338
IFLA (International Federation of Library Associations and Institutions) 205
ISBD (g) (International Standard Bibliographic Description—general) 205
ISBD (S) (International Standard Bibliographic Description for Serials) 204-06
ISDS (International Serials Data System) 189-91, 205
ISSN (International Standard Serial Number) 76, 155, **190-91**, 204, 216, 220
Import and export licensing requirements 130, 260

Imprint 197
Incomplete volumes 27-28, 52, 54, 176
Incunabula 3
Independent Postal Service of America 263
*Index to Free Periodicals* 246
Indexes 23, 36, 81, 156, 172, 176, 185, 207-08, 216, 285, **288-89**
    annual 47, 108, 176
    cumulated 51, 53, 92, 172
    individual 156
    newspapers 143
    payments 156
Indexing information 123
Indexing services 81, 86, 91, 185, **238,** 251, 307
India 114
Initialisms 192
Inserts, binding 36
Instituto del Libro Cubano 136
Insurance, mail 260
Interdocumentation Co., A.G. 249
Interdisciplinary journals 84
Intergovernmental agencies, U.N. 318
Interlibrary loan 85, 100, 146, 180, 219, 331, 345, 346, 347
*Internal Publications Directory (Working Press of the Nation V.5)* 243, 246
International agents 125, 241
International aspect of publishing 9
*International Bibliography of Reprints* 249
International centre 190
International congresses 24, 32, 107, **142**
International Court of Justice 317
International currency 105
*International Directory of Little Magazines and Small Presses* 248
International Federation of Library Associations and Institutions (IFLA) 205
International mail 259
International money orders 260
International Serials Data System (ISDS) **189-91,** 205
International Standard Bibliographic Description—General (ISBD) (g) 205
International Standard Bibliographic Description for Serials (ISBD) (s) 204-5
International Standard Serial Number (ISSN) 76, 155, **190-91,** 204, 216, 220
*International Subscription Agents* 240
*International Yearbook and Statesman's Who's Who* 246
*International Bibliographie der Reprints* 249
*Introduction to U.S. Public Documents* 183, 246
Invoices, 24, 36, 62-63, 65-6, 69, 120, 139, 154, 174
    added charges 92, 110
    cancellations 110
    checks 111-12, 114
    code numbers 112
    commercial 256
    computers 110-12
    conversion rates 112-13
    credit memos 107, 111
    "crossed checks" 114
    dating 111, 113-14
    deletions 107, 110
    discounts 92, 107, 118, **137**
    foreign exchange 112-13
    government documents 144, 147-48

"hors series" 110
international congresses 107
irregular titles 38, 107-08, **117**, 138
items to keep in mind when paying invoices 108
L.S. numbers 115, 154
Latin American 112, 135
memberships 107, 127
payment in advance 106, 110-11, 140
payments in small amounts 105
pro-forma 110, 114, 139
renewals 89-93, 107
serial renewals 107
service charges 118
small amounts outside the United States 105
sources 108
statements 110-11
UNESCO coupons 105
when to pay 107
Irregular publications 117, 132, 173, 199, 247, 296, 317
*Irregular Serials and Annuals; an International Directory* 105, 191, 247
Issuing body notes 200
Items to keep in mind when paying invoices 108
Jacobs, R. M. 19, 78
Japan 133
Johnson, Walter J. Inc. 242
*Journal des Savants* 4
*Journal des Scavans* 4
Junk 86
Kalvar 322-23, 338
Kardex files 30, 71, 101, 168
Katz, William A. 7, 8, 11, 80-84, 119-21, 126, 143, 181-84, 239, 241-42, 245-46, 248
Key title 190-91, 205
Keypunched 76
Knight-Ridder 11
Kraus Periodical Co. 242
Kraus Reprints and Back Issues 318
Kraus, *Reprints of Selected United Nations Recurrent Publications* 249
LASA (Latin American Studies Association) 314
LC catalog, freezing the 234
LC (Library of Congress) (see under, Library of Congress)
LC, Serials processing at 225-35
LOCN (location) 76
L.S. numbers 111, 154
LSU (Louisiana State University) V, 29, 38, 158-64
Labels on packages 35, 155, 175
Lacks, 20, 153
Lamination 176
Lancour, Harold 15
*Language of the Foreign Book Trade* 240
Large agents 124
Latin America 135
Latin American collection 135
*Latin American Research Review* 314
Latin American Studies Association (LASA) 314
*Ledger* 5

Legal responsibility of the agent 121
Leica 321
*Der Leitfaden durch Presse und Werbung 248*
Lettering 283, 290
Letters for,
    claiming 266-70
    gifts and exchange (UCR) 308-10
    irregular titles 117
    missing pages and numbers 179-80
    new serial title 156-57
    ordering a new subscription 37, **156-59**
    "price and availability" missing pages 52
    subscription request 156-57
*Librarians' Guide to Periodicals 241*
*Librarian's Guide to the New Copyright Law 348*
*Librarians' Handbook: A Guide to Periodicals 241*
*Librarian's Practical Dictionary in 22 Languages 240*
*Library Journal* 91, 251
Library networks 8, 40, 173, 316
Library of Congress 146, 189, 190, 193, 202, 221, **225-35**
Library of Congress cards 173
Library of Congress, Exchange and Gift Division 241
Library of Congress Information Office 315
Library of Congress, standards for film 324
Library rate, mail 258-59
Library tools 155-56
*Life* 22
Linadex 67, 68
Linda Hall 21
Liquid paper 29
Lira 114
Lists, exclusive 153
Lists, subscription 122
Lit 114
"Little magazines" **7-8**, 11, **119**, 125, 248
Local agents 129
Location (LOCN) 76
Location of a Serials Department 21
Location within the Department 21
*London Gazette* 4
Long runs of holdings (see, Cards)
Long term film 324
Loose material 36, 154
Loose-leaf format 172
Loose-leaf services 91, 118
Lost volumes 68
Louisiana State University (LSU) V, 29, 38, 294
Louisiana State University library—computerized binding routines 300-03
Louisiana State University library—multiple orders 158-63
Louisiana State University library, *Serials Manual* 87, 244
*McClure's Magazine* 14
MARC—S (machine-readable cataloging for serials) **211-15**, 220-22, 230
MCA (Microfilming Corporation of America) 322
*MIMC; Microforms Annual 250*
MN (moneda nacional) 114
*MTLA; the Micropublishers Trade List Annual 250*

MULS (Minnesota Union List of Serials) 215, 220
Machine-readable cataloging for serials (MARC—S) **211-15,** 220-02, 230
*Magazine Directory (Working Press of the Nation, V.2)* 243
*Magazine Selection; How to Build a community-oriented Collection* 11, 18, 82-84, 119
Magazines, definition17
*Magazines for Libraries* 81, 239, 242, 245-46, 248
Mail, 70, 127-28, 136, 138, 153, 175, **253-63**
    "air-taxis" 6, 253
    airmail 110, 128, 256, 259
    American Courier Corporation 263
    bulk mail **257-58,** 262
    COD (collect on delivery) 259
    catalog cards 254
    checking in 35
    "citizen rate" 254
    dimensional standards for letter-size 255
    electronic systems 254
    express 259
    first class 253-54, **257,** 263
    foreign 253
    fourth class 254, **258-59**
    ISSN **190,** 256
    Independent Postal Service of America 263
    information 256
    insurance 260
    international 259
    international money orders 260
    library rate **258-59**
    mechanization 262-63
    money orders 260
    newspapers 254, 256-57
    non-local first class 253
    opening 21, 35
    other postal agencies 263
    parcel post 258
    past, present and future 262-63
    postal service 155, 191, 254, **256-60,** 262
    postal union 260
    postmaster general 253
    priority 258
    registered 259
    rush 259
    second class 119, 155, 254, **257**
    size 254-55
    sorting 262
    special delivery 259
    surface 110
    third class 119, 254, **257-58**
    types of 256-60
    UPS (United Parcel Service) 263
    United States Postal Service 254, **256-60,** 262-63
    what may happen to 261
    zip code 253, 258
Mailing labels 175
Mailing privileges 6, 130
Mailing rates 155

Main entry 186
Mainland China 134
Maintaining the Serials Record 24, 67
Maintenance of microform equipment 329
Manual file 17, 38, 71
*Manual for Foreign Languages for the Use of Librarians, Bibliographers, Research Workers, Editors, Translators and Printers* 240
*A Manual of European Languages for Librarians* 240
*Manual of Serials Work* 244
Maps 36, 197, 285, 288, 293
Master list 152
Material that may be included in the Serials Record 27-28, 32
Material that may be kept short periods of time 66, 281
Mechanization—mail 262
Medium-sized agents 124
Medium term film 324
Membership list 118
Memberships 33, **63-64,** 66, 107, 118, 138, 172, 314
Memo to Mailers 254
Mencken, Henry Louis 82
Merged titles 108, 119, 199, 201
Mergers 8-9, 11, 20, 22, 69
Metal tabs 30-31
Mexico 114
Mezdunarodnaya Kniga 132
Microfiche 38, 52, 219, 283, 285, 316, 318, **326,** 331
Microfilm 33, 38, 52, 76, 84, 143, 153, 219, 259, 283, 316, **326**
    checking in 52
    costs 332-33, 336
    definition 326
Microfilm printer 329
Microfilm readers 324, 328-29, 336
Microfilming Corporation of America (MCA) 322
*Microform Handbook* 341
Microform libraries 334-36
*Microform Review* 250
Microforms 81, 83, 121, 145, 182, 204, 239, 281, 325, 335, 338
*Microforms in Libraries; a Reader* 321
Micro-opaques 327
Microprint 327
*Micropublishers' Trade List Annual* 250
Minnesota Union List of Serials (MULS) 215, 220
Minor titles coming because of some more important title 45
Minor variations in titles 200
"Mint condition" issues 283
Miscellaneous financial topics 105-14
Missing and mutilated pages **179-81**
Missing numbers 52, 77, 121, 149
"Mixed" lists 92, 122, 124
Modern national popular magazines 5-8
Money orders 260
Money symbols 105
Monographic series 32, 121, 141-42, 172-73, 226, **247**
Monographs 18, 24, 38, 43, 46, 85, 167, 186, 194, 197, 201, 203, 206-07, 209, 212, 293, 350
Monographs, definition 18

Monthlies (see, Cards)
*Monthly Checklist of State Publications* 246
Morehead, Joe 183, 246
Most important points in the Serials Record 33
Movable type 3, 9
Mora, Irmre, ed. 240
Muller, Robert H. 248
Multmedia 204
Multiple order forms 41, **157-71**
Mutch, David 262
Mutilated pages 179-81
Mutilated or lost copies 179-81
Mutilation 84, 282-83, 349
NFAIS (National Federation of Abstracting and Indexing Services) 221
NPC (National Periodicals Center) 315
NSDP (National Serials Data Program) 190-91, **230-33**
NST *(New Serial Titles)* 190-91, 211
NTIS (National Technical Information Service) 146-47
NUC *(National Union Catalog)* 106, 242, 245
*Nachdruckverzeichnis von Einzelwerken, Serien und Zeitschriften aus
    allen Wissensgieten (Reprints)* 249
Names, forms of 192-93
National bibliographies 130, 211
National Commission for UNESCO 105
National Commission of Technical Uses of Copyright Works (CONTU) 344
National Federation of Abstracting and Indexing Services (NFAIS) 221
National lending library for science and technology 306
National library of China 134
National Library of Medicine 221
National Library of Peking 134
National Micrographics Association 324
National Periodicals Center (NPC) 315
*National Register of Microform Masters* 251
National Serials Data Program (NSDP) 190-91, **230-33**
National Technical Information Service (NTIS) 146-47
National Translation Center 252
*National Union Catalog* (NUC) 106, 242, 245
Networks (see, Library networks)
Nemeyer, Carol A. 249
New personnel working with claiming—philosophy 271-272
New serial title file 148, 150, 158, 163
New serial title slip 66
*New Serial Titles* (NST) 40, 64, 68, 106, 190-91, 209, 211, 219, 238, 242
*New Serial Titles—Classed Subject Arrangement* 209
New subscription letter (LSU) 156
New subscription order (UCR) 43-44
New titles 67, 80
*New York Herald* 14
*New York Times* 113, 143, 322
*New York Times Index* 207
*Newspaper Directory (Working Press of the Nation, V.1)* 243
Newspaper mergers 8, 11
Newspaper room 351
Newspapers **9-13**, 33, 81, 107, 112, 248, 292, 351
    binding 292-93
    checking-in 33, 281

    future of 12
    history 9-13
    indexes 143
    mail 107, 254
    mergers 11-13
    microfilmed 292
    ordering 143, 156
    paid in advance 107
    reasons for demise 12
*Newspapers in Microform: Foreign Countries* 248, 250
*Newspapers in Microform: United States* 248, 250
News-stands 83
*Newsweek* 22
*Newark Evening News* 11
Nijhoff 143
*Nijhoff Serials* 245
Nitrate film 322, 338
Nitrocellulose base film 322
"No more published?" notes 201
Non-depository publications 146-47
Non-GPO publications 146
Non-local first class mail 253
Non-subscriptions 33
Nonarchival film 324, 335
Norbinding 291
Notes (in cataloging) 198-204
*Notizie Scritte* 10
"Nouvellistes" 10
Numbered monographic series 85
Numbering and internumbering—binding 293-94
Numbering notes 197, 199
Nunn, G. Raymond 132
OCLC 135, 211-12, **215-18**, 220-22, 230
OCLC (automated cataloging) 76
Official title 40, 68, 155, 172
On-line system 76
One agent versus many 123
Order card 43-44
Order number 154
Order slip 37
Ordering, 24, **117-82**
    address label 35, 64
    agents 120-25
    blanket orders 120, **141**
    bulk ordering 141
    consolidated orders 143
    current missing issues 108
    don'ts 176
    directly from a publisher 117-20
    discounts 92, 107, 118
    expensive items 118
    Federal Trade Commission 9, 11, 14
    final review and placing the subscription **172-75**
    foreign countries 128-37
    foreign documents 144
    foreign publications 129-37

    government documents 120, 146, 147
    how to order 156, 172-73
    indexes and missing pages 155, 172
    indexes (newspapers) 143
    international congresses **142**
    iregular titles 118
    little magazines 119
    long runs of lacks 181
    loose-leaf services 118
    memberships 63, 107, 118, 127, 138
    microforms 329-30
    missing numbers, sources 179
    multiple order forms **157-71**
    new subscriptions 156
    new title slips 150
    newspapers 143
    periodicals in reprint 140
    philosophy of setting up subscriptions 155
    photoduplication 329-30
    procedures 156-57, 172-74
    publishers 117-20
    renewals 124, 181
    replacements 181-82, 297
    selecting an agent 122
    service charges 92, 118
    services 118
    small items 179
    societies and institutions 119
    sources 241
    special problems of 141
    state documents 120
    translations 140
    unusual arrangements 139
    university publications 119
    verification of title and price 155
    where to begin the subscription 156
Organ notes 200
Organization Chart—Serial Record Division, LC 231-32
Organization within the Serial Department 20
Organization within the library 20-21
Orne, Jerrold 240
Osborn, Andrew D. 3, 17, 21, 30, 78, 100, 137, 144, 163, 183, 239, 241, 245, 284, 306, 330
Ostwald, R. 249
Outdated collections 86, 336
Outstanding special orders file 151
"Over-riders" 45
*Oxford Gazette* 4
PBS Prebound Periodicals (formerly Periodical Binding Service of the American Binder) 283
PRC (payment record card) 101
PRC (People's Republic of China) 130, 134
Paid in advance 91
Palic, Vladimir M. 246
Pamphlets—binding 291
Papers (see, Newspapers)

Parcel post **258**
Pariseau, Earl J. 137
Past, present and future of mail 262-63
Past, present and futue of reprography 333
*Patterson's American Educational Directory* 240
Payment record card (PRC) 101
Payments 20, 22, 38, 62-63, 89-90, 106, 108, 121, 126
Payments in advance 106-07, 110-11, 121, 136, 140, 144, 149, 172, 174
Payments in small amounts outside the United States 105
Payments of new subscriptions and renewals 89
Peking Library 134
Pencil notes 32, 36, 51, 64, 68, 277
Penguin 9
People's Republic of China (PRC) 130, **134-35,** 261
Pergamon 276
Periodical Binding Service of the American Binder (PBS) 283
Periodical room 155 (see also, Reading rooms)
*Periodical Title Abbreviations* 239
*Periodicals and Serials; Their Treatment in Special Libraries* 244
Periodicals, definition 17
*Periodicals: a Manual of Practice for Librarians* 244
*Periodicals for School Media Programs* 251
Periodicals in reprint 140
Permabinding 292
Permanent funds 99
Permuterm index 92
Personnel 21-22, 29, 69, 123, 131, 253, 270, 277, 329
Phiebig 276
*Philosophical Transactions* 4
Philosophy of checking in duplicates 275-76
Philosophy of Gifts and Exchange Department 307-08
Philosophy of reviewing payments 106
Philosophy of setting up serial orders 155
Philosophy of the serials routines 19
Philosophy regarding the use of microforms 333-36
Photocopying 85, 179-80, 321, 349
Photomicrography 338
Pipics, Zaltan 240
Plastic protector 30, 31, 71
Plates and maps 36, 285
Pockets 36, 285
Points to consider when cancelling titles 85
Points to remember in claiming 272
*Political Handbook of the World, Parliaments, Parties and Press* 240
*Political Handbook and Atlas of the World* 246
Polk Directories 119
Polyester 322, 338
*Poole's Index to Periodical Literature* 242
Popular titles 5, 7, 92, 122, 124-25, 282
Postage 93, 137
Postal regulations 130 (see also, Mail)
Postal Service 155, 191, **254, 256-60,** 262
Postal Union Mail 260
Posting holdings (see, Cards)
Postmaster General 253
"Potential criminal" 19, 188

*A Practical Approach to Serials Cataloging* 245, 353-54
Prebound volumes 84, 121
Preceding publication notes 199
Prentice Hall 118
Preparations Department 295-99
Press Associations 13-14
"Prestige value" 118
Price and availability 52
Price indexes 91, 100-01
Print-out of automated binding 302-03
Print-out of serials cataloging record screen display 217-18
Priority binding 281
Priority mail 258
Problems and policies in setting up a new Serials Record 19
Problems of acquisition of Cuban library materials 136-37
Procedures for ephemeral material 67
Procedure for handling all material in the Serials Record 35-37
Proceedings, definition 17
Processing of film 323-24
Professional serials personnel 22, 70
Pro-forma invoices 110, 114, 139, 174
Protective edges 31, 51
Public 17, 19-21, 28
*Public Affairs Information Service Bulletin* 239, 246
Public catalog 21, 27-28, 68, 69, 155, 157, 168, 196
Public libraries 100
*Publick Occurences* 11
"Publish or perish" 82, 85
Publishers, (see also under Ordering) 85, 108, 110-11, **117-20,** 129-31,
        137-38, 141-42, 144, 148, 154-55, 173-74, 176, 179, 181, 191, 199-200, 347
Publishers, advantages of 117
Publishers' and agents' lists 148
Publishers' catalogs 108, 208, 238, **241**
Publishers, disadvantages of 120
Publishers, foreign countries 128
Publishers' lists 176
*Publisher's Practical Dictionary in 20 Languages* 240
Publishers' series 247, 289
*Publishers' Trade List Annual* 240, 242, 247, 251
*Publisher's Weekly* 251
Publishers, what to order directly from 117-20
Publishing, international aspect of 9
Purchase order 156
Purchased titles 31
Quality of a journal 82
Quality of microfilm machines 324
Quarterlies (see, Cards)
Quotes 122, **139**
RLIN (Research Libraries Information Network) 218
RMKS (remarks) 76
RSFSR (Russian Soviet Federated Socialist Republic) 131
RTHD (retrospective holdings) 77
*Radio and Television Directory (Working Press of the Nation, V.3)* 243
Reader-printers 329, 332
*Reader's Digest*, editors 263
*Readers' Guide to Periodical Literature* 251

Readex Microprint Corp. 327
Reading rooms, 323, **351-53**
    media for protecting journals 353
    physical arrangement 353
    separating Public Services from Technical Serials Department 352
    separating Serials Reading Room from book area 352
    shelf list arrangement 352-53
    treatment of journals 352-53
Reading subscription dates 112
Reasons for less funds 100
Reasons for demise of newspapers 12
Reasons for reduced numbers of agents 121
Reasons for substitute binding 290
Receipt of the first piece of new subscription—bound 178
Receipt of the first piece of new subscription—unbound 177
Receiving the first piece of an order 175
Recent development in journals and readers 84
Recent trends in publishing and subscription agencies 8
Recordak 322
Records for keeping track of payments 62, 101-04
Reference 21, 146, 173
*Reference Guide and Comprehensive Catalog of International Serials* 250
Reference material 282, 311
Refunds 121, 181
Regional depositories 145
Registered mail 259
Relations—agent, library, publisher 125-26
Remington Rand Corp. 30, 71
Renewal billing 89-93, 107
Renewal notices **105-06,** 110
Renewal of subscriptions 124
Renewals, 22, 107, 148
    claiming 137
    how to bring to mind 149
Replacements 22, 86, 120, 136, 175, 179, 282
*Reprint Bulletin* 249
Reprint editions 46, 153, 204, 318
Reprint from *Washington Newsletter* on copyright laws 348
Reprint periodicals 140
Reprint publishers 5
Reprints 46, 140, 176, 203, 211, **249**
*Reprints of Selected United Nations Recurrent Publications* 249, 318
Reprography 8, 86, 250-51, **321-36**
    addresses of Microforms and Reprints 249
    advantages 330-31
    archival versus non-archival film 324
    books on reprography that may be of use to librarians 341
    costs 329, 332-33, 336
    definitions 321
    disadvantages 331-32
    environment 323-24, 336
    equipment 328-29, 336
    evolution 321-22
    film classifications 324
    formats 325-28
    maintenance of equipment 329

    ordering microforms 329-30
    past, present and future 333
    permanency 323-24
    philosophies regarding the use of microforms—conventional
        versus—microform libraries 334-36
    processing 323
    reader-printers 329
    standards 323-25
    statistical count 330
    user awareness 329
Research items 91
Research Libraries Information Network (RLIN) 218
Reserves 86
Resource-sharing 85, 100, 219, 347
*Resources in Education* 316
Retain current issue only 66
Retrieval program 80
Retrospective holdings (RTHD) 21, 77
Reuters 14
Reviewing back file orders 175
Reviewing new subscriptions 175
Reviewing subscription costs 91, 175
Revising back file orders when received 175-76
Revising new subscriptions 175, 177-78
Rice, E. Stevens 323
Richardson, Selma K. 251
"Rider" cards 34
Roll film 322, 326-27
Rotary files 30
"Route to Vertical File" 32, 64
Routines for gifts and exchanges 311-12
Routines for binding 294-300
Routing for a new subscription—bound and unbound volumes 177-78
Rubbings 284, 290
Rush 137
"Rush" material 36
Rush slip 36
Russia 131-33
Russian republics 131
Russian Soviet Federated Socialist Republic (RSFSR) 131
SALALM (Seminar on the Acquisition of Latin American Library Materials) 135, **314**
SDI (Selective Dissemination of Information) 239
Safety films 323
Sample copies 64, 82
Samples (see Cards, Diagrams, Forms, Letters)
*Saturday Evening Post* 22
Saving space on the cards 34
"Scare-head" 10
Schatoff, Michael 244
Schellhardt, Timothy D. 263
Schmidt, C. James 89, 100
*Scholarly Reprint Publishing in the United States* 249
*Science Abstracts* 92
Science Book and Serial Exchange 307
*Science Citation* 92, 118
Scientific journals 4-5, 92, 122

Scott, Peter R. 322-23
Search Department 151
Searching titles 123
Second class mail 119, 155
Secondhand agents 120, 176, 265
Secondhand catalogs 134, 152, 180
Secondhand market 107-08, 130, 176
*Selected United States Government Serials* 246
Selecting an agent 122
Selection, **79-84,** 141-42, 226
 aids 82-83, 238
 balanced collection 81
 balancing budgets 80
 basic journals 80, 85
 book committees 83
 college, university and school libraries 81
 core journals 81
 cost of journals 80
 criteria 80, 84-85
 duplicate subscriptions 84
 factors 81-82
 fundamentals 81
 interdisciplinary journals 84
 public libraries 81
 recent developments 84
 sources for acquiring serials 83
 sources for requests 83
 special disciplines 81
 university and college libraries 81, 119-20
 vagaries of serials 19-21, 23, 188
Selective depository system 146
Selective Dissemination of Information (SDI) 239
Semi-annuals (see, Cards)
Semi-popular titles 125
Seminar on the Acquisition of Latin American Library Materials (SALALM) 135, **314**
Separates 65
Serial budget, annual formula 91
Serial financial card 30, **62,** 101
Serial fund 90
*Serial Publications; Their Place and Treatment in Libraries* 3, 21, 30, 78
 100, 183, 239, 244-45
Serial Record (LC) 225
Serial review form 38, 39
Serial selection 89, 251, (see also, selection)
Serials about serials 244-45
*Serials: Acquisition and Maintenance* 244
Serials check-in, automated 76-78
Serials control sub-system: Users Manual 78
Serials, decision forms 39, 40, 278-80
Serials, definition 17
*Serials in Transition* 245
*Serials Librarian* 244
*Serials Manual* 87, 244
Serials Mysteries 22
Serials Record, description 17-18, 20-21, 38
*Serials Review* 247, 251

Serials Updating Service 241
Serials want list 66
Serials, yearly estimate 91
Serien und Zeitschriften aus allen Wissensgieten (Reprints) 249
Series and subseries 293-94
Series statement 198
Service charges 92, 118, **122,** 137, 150
Service window 19-20, 29
Services 33, 63, 118, 173
Sets 32, 38, 226
Sets, definition 18
Sheehy, Eugene P. 239, 242
Shelf list 21
Shelving of microfilm 323, **335-36**
Shipping documents 130
Silver film 322-23
Silver gelatin 325
Silver halides 323
Simplification 20
Slavic countries 133
Sliding tabs 31
Small agents 124
Small libraries 147, 281
Small Press Review 248
Small publishers 127
Smart Set 82
Smith, Lynn S. 76, 245, 353-54
Snags 312
Sodium thiosulfate 323
Sodom and Gomorrah 3
"Sole distributor" 109
Sources from which to order 172, 241
Sources for,
        acquiring serials 83
        current exchange rates 113
        gift and exchange material 306-07
        locating long runs of lacks 152, 181
        locating missing and mutilated pages 179-81
        money symbols of the various countries 105
        sources of subscription 155, 173
Sources of Serials 241
Soviet Export Organization 132
Soviet Republics 131
Soviet serials 132-33
Soviet Union 131-33
Special collections 281, 293, 308
Special delivery, mail 259
Special directives 32, 36, 63, 65
Special files 148-55
Special libraries 21, 334
Special Libraries Association 307
Special orders and odd gifts 52
Special problems of binding 292-94
Special problems of ordering 141-43
Special programs 313-17
Special ratchet 34

Special services 118
Special slip orders 33, 66, **108,** 151, 175
Specialized agents 120, 125
Specifications
    binding 283
    cards 30
    reprography 323-25
*Spectator* 5
Spencer, D.A. 337, 341
Spiller, David 79
Spiral binders 292
Split titles 20, 69, 108, 235
Splitting titles 22, 85
Stamp 151, 196
*Standard Periodical Directory* 242
Standards,
    binding 284
    dimensions for letter-size mail 255
    reprography 324-25
Standing orders 64, 141, 317
Stapling-binding 291
State documents 120
Statements 110, **111,** 148
Static growth 86
Stationary tabs 31
Statistical analysis 68, 93, 209, 274, 296-97, 330
Statistical forms (UCR) 93-98
Statistics 25, 151, 158, 346
Steel cabinets 324
Steele, Richard 5
Stevens, Rolland E. 245
Storage 140, 142, 265
Streamlining routines 19, 261
String binding 291
Stub 291
Stubbing, definition 281-82
Subject cataloging 207
*Subject Guide to Microforms in Print* 251
Subject indexes 82, **239**
Subscription agents (see, Agents)
Subscription forms (see, Forms)
Subscriptions 33, 85, 132, 134
    Assigning of funds 89-90
    comparison of costs 139
    continuing subscriptions vs. temporary funds 99
    current 21
    duplicate 84, 90, 172, 282
    film 329-30
    final placing 174
    foreign 129-37
    global 33, 63
    new 40, 67-68, 80, 89-90, 100, 107, 109, 137, 150, 155-56, 172-74
    payments 85, 89-90
    reading dates 112
    receipt of a new—bound 178
    receipt of a new—unbound 177

refunds 121
renewals 91, 107, 138, **174-75**
reviewing costs 191, 175
revising new 177-78
selecting sources from which to order 172-73
where to begin 174
Substitute binding **290-92**
"Sucker lists" 33
Suggestion box 83
Sulphuric acid 334
Superimposition 193
Superintendent of documents 144-47, 172
Supplements 23, 32, 37, 38, 51, 106, 203, 206-07, 284, 289
Surface mail 110
Swets 143
Swiss franc 114
Symbols 34, 105, 109
Syndicates 14
Systematic claiming **272**
"T.F." ('til forbidden or until forbidden) 139
TPC (title page and contents) 294
TPI (title page and index) 294
TPIC (Title page, index and contents) 294
TRIP (titles requiring incessant processing) 101, 102
*TV and Radio Directory (Working Press of the Nation*, V.3) 243
Tabs,
    metal 31
    plastic protectors 31
    sliding 31
    stationary 31
Tariffs 130
*Tatler* 5
Tattletape 351
"Tear sheets" 179
Technical titles 92, 122, 203
Template 255
"Temporarily suspended" 69
Temporary binding (see, Substitute binding)
Temporary funds 99
Temporary notes 36-37, 69
Temporary records 67
Thermofax 338
Thickness of binding 288
Thiosulfate 339
Third class mail 119
*Ti Pao* 9
"Tickler" file 140, 149, 238
'Til Forbidden (until forbidden) 139
Title changes 29, 121, 128, 188-89, 210, 288, 303
Title entry 62, 108, 188
Title mergers 69
Title page and index information 123, 186, 195, 210, 288-89, 294
Title recording 192
Title splits 69
Title varies 29, 53-54, 69, 189, 199, 201
*Title Varies* 245, 251

Titles varies notes 201
*Title in Series; a Handbook for Librarians and Students* 247
Titles requiring incessant processing (TRIP) 101-02
Togic binding 292
Tombs of Egypt 3
Tools 20, 155, **237-52**
*Top of the News* 251
Torok, Stephens 334
"Trace slip" 37, 68
Tracing, a final review and placing a new subscription 37
Tracing lost volumes 68
Tracings 37
Transactions, definition 17
Translations 118, **140**, 202, 252
Translations, cover-to-cover 140
*Translations Register-index* 252
Transliterations 36, 203
Treasury Department 136
Trends in publishing and subscription agencies 8-9, 11-13
Types of agents 124-25
Types of mail 256-60
Types of tools 238
Types of Soviet serials 132
Typewriter ratchet 34
UCR (University of California, Riverside) 31, 37-39, 43-44, 71-75, 101-04, 168-71
UK (United Kingdom) 9
UN (United Nations) 317
UNESCO (United Nations Educational, Scientific and Cultural
    Organization) 105, 190, **317-18**
UNESCO coupons 105
UNICEF (United Nations Children's Fund) Publications 317
UPS (United Parcel Service) 263
USBE (Universal Serials & Book Exchange, Inc.) 181, 306, **313-14**
USGPO (United States Government Printing Office) 144
USSR (Union of the Soviet Socialist Republics) 131-33
UWL (University of Washington library)—multiple order forms 164-68
*Ulrich's International Periodical Directory* 105, 191, 243, 245
*Ulrich's Quarterly* 243, 245, 247
Underground presses 11
*Union List of Serials* and other automated projects **218-20**
*Union List of Serials in Libraries of the United States and Canada* 211, 225,
    238, 243, 245
Union Lists 211, 218-19, 238, 251
Union of the Soviet Socialist Republics (USSR) 131-33
United Kingdom open market 9, 348
United Nations Children's Fund (UNICEF) publications 317
United Nations depositories 318
United Nations documents 32
United Nations Educational, Scientific and Cultural Organization coupons 105
United Nations Educational, Scientific and Cultural Organization. *UNESCO Handbook
    of International Exchanges* 306
United Nations Educational, Scientific and Cultural Organization. *UNESCO Bulletin.*
    (Superseded by *UNESCO Chronicle* July 1955) 247, 306
United Nations intergovernmental agencies 318
United Nations microfiche 318
United Nations. Reference Catalogs of Sales publications 317

United Nations standing order service 317-18
United Parcel Service (UPS) 263
United Press 13-14, 120
United States documents 144-48
United States Government documents 144-48
United States Government Printing Office. (USGPO) 144
United States Government Printing Office. USGPO Style Manual
United States Government Printing Office. Subject Bibliographies 246, 251
United States Justice Department 9, 11
United States. Library of Congress. Library of Congress Catalog—Books: Subjects;
    a cumulative list of works represented by Library of Congress
    printed cards 251
United States Library of Congress. Library of Congress Catalog: National Register
    of Microform Masters 251
United States. Library of Congress. Library of Congress Catalogs.
    Monographic Series. 247
United States. Library of Congress. Library of Congress Exchange and Gift
    Division. Monthly Checklist of State Publications 246
United States Library of Congress. Processing Department. Monthly List of State
    Publications 246
United States Postal Services 191, 254, 256-60, 262
United States Superintendent of Documents. Monthly Catalog of United States
    Government Publications 147, 246
United States Superintendent of Documents. Selected United States Government
    Publications 246
Universal Serials & Book Exchange (USBE) 181, 247, 306, **313-14**
University Microfilm 324
University of Microfilms International 324
University of California, Riverside (UCR) 31, 37-39, 43-44, 71-75, 101-04, 168-71
University of Washington Library (UWL) 164-68
University Press 141
University publications 119-20, 140, 293-94
"Until forbidden" 99, **139**, 156
Unusual arrangements in purchasing journals 139
Uses of a Serials Record 21
Vagaries of serials 20-21, 23, 117-18, 188
Van Zant, Nancy Patton 246
Veaner, Allen B. 325
Verhandlungen 142
Verifax 339
Verification 40, 155, 241, 247
Verification list 106
Vesicular film 323, 339
Viking 9
Visible file 30, 226
Von Osterman, George Frederick 240
WLN (Washington Library Network) 167, 218
Wall, Edward C. 307, 314
Wall Street Journal 113
Wang Chi 134
Want list 51, 153
Want list file **152**, 159, 312
Washington Library Network (WLN) 167, 218
Washington Newsletter 348
Ways of recording financial records 100-04
Ways of reviewing subscription costs 91

Ways of saving on the budget 99
Weil, Ben 346
West German mark (DM) 113
Wetherbee, Lou 314
What may be included in a Serial Record 27-28, 32
What may happen in the cards 71
What may happen to mail 261
What may happen to a title 23
Wheel-type cabinets 30
When to pay invoices 107
*Where Microfilm is a Working Reality* 330
Why catalog serials 185
Williams and Wilkins 344
Williams, Lee 135, 137, 314
*Willing's Press Guide* 244, 248
Wilson, H. W. 238, 251
Winchell, Constance Mabel 143, 242-43
Wire rods 30
Withdrawals 68
Withdrawing lost volumes from the Serial Record 68
*Worterbuch des Verlagswesen in 20 Sprachen* 240
Work slip 40-42, 66-68
*Working Press of the Nation* 243, 249
*World* 14
*World Guide to Abbreviations, Organizations* 240
*World Index to Scientific Translations and List of Translations*
        *Notified to ETC* 252
*World List of Scientific Periodicals* (see, *British Union Catalogue of Periodicals*) 244
*World of Learning* 241, 246
*World Transindex* 252
Xerography 337
Xerox 339
Xerox Corp. 337, 339
Xidex 323
YYMMDD 76
Yale 135
*Yearbook of International Organizations* 241
Yearbooks 32
Yearly estimate formula for annual serial budget 91
Young, Margaret Labash 241
Zeitlin Periodicals & Co. 242
"Zero" material 33, 70, **312**
Zip code 253, 258

# DATE DUE